CAREER DEVELOPMENT
INTERVENTIONS

CAREER DEVELOPMENT INTERVENTIONS

Edited by

HARMAN D. BURCK, Ph.D.

Professor
Florida State University
Tallahassee, Florida

and

ROBERT C. REARDON, Ph.D.

Professor and Director
Curricular-Career Information Service
Florida State University
Tallahassee, Florida

CHARLES C THOMAS • PUBLISHER
Springfield • Illinois • U.S.A.

Published and Distributed Throughout the World by
CHARLES C THOMAS • PUBLISHER
2600 South First Street
Springfield, Illinois 62717

This book is protected by copyright. No part of it
may be reproduced in any manner without written
permission from the publisher.

© *1984 by* CHARLES C THOMAS • PUBLISHER
ISBN 0-398-04929-7
Library of Congress Catalog Card Number: 83-17872

With THOMAS BOOKS *careful attention is given to all details of manufacturing and design. It is the Publisher's desire to present books that are satisfactory as to their physical qualities and artistic possibilities and appropriate for their particular use.* THOMAS BOOKS *will be true to those laws of quality that assure a good name and good will.*

Printed in the United States of America
Q-R-3

Library of Congress Cataloging in Publication Data
Main entry under title:
Career development interventions.

   Includes bibliographies and indexes.
   1. Vocational guidance--Addresses, essays, lectures.
I. Burck, Harman D. II. Reardon, Robert C.
HF5381.C2654 1984   331.7'02   83-17872
ISBN 0-398-04929-7

**Dedicated to
Professor Harold F. Cottingham
(1913-1981)**

"I want to give students not only an awareness of the challenges they face, but also help them build their own resources to become professionals and to provide organizations with leadership or community agencies with services."

CONTRIBUTORS

ELLEN S. AMATEA, Ph.D.
Assistant Professor
University of Florida
Gainesville, Florida

HARMAN D. BURCK, Ph.D.
Professor
Florida State University
Tallahassee, Florida

E. JANE BURKHEAD, Ph.D.
Assistant Professor
Florida State University
Tallahassee, Florida

DONALD J. COCHRAN, Ph.D.
Staff Psychologist & Associate Professor
Illinois State University
Normal, Illinois

DOROTHY DOMKOWSKI, M.S.
Career Development Specialist
Curricular-Career Information Service
Florida State University
Tallahassee, Florida

MICHAEL J. GIMMESTAD, Ph.D.
Professor
University of Northern Colorado
Greeley, Colorado

LAWRENCE K. JONES, Ph.D.
Associate Professor
North Carolina State University
Raleigh, North Carolina

JENNIFER BORETZ KAHNWEILER, Ph.D.
Associate Professor
University of Cincinnati
Cincinnati, Ohio

JANET G. LENZ, M.S.
Assistant Director
Career Planning and Placement Center
University of North Carolina at Greensboro
Greensboro, North Carolina

ROBERT MACALEESE, Ph.D.
Associate Professor
Spring Hill College
Mobile, Alabama

CAROLE W. MINOR, Ph.D.
Assistant Professor
Northern Illinois University
DeKalb, Illinois

DANIEL J. MONTGOMERY, Ph.D.
Counseling Psychologist
Florida State University
Tallahassee, Florida

GARY W. PETERSON, Ph.D.
Associate Professor and Research Associate
Florida State University
Tallahassee, Florida

ROBERT C. REARDON, Ph.D.
Professor and Director
Curricular-Career Information Service
Florida State University
Tallahassee, Florida

JAMES P. SAMPSON, JR., Ph.D.
Assistant Professor
Florida State University
Tallahassee, Florida

WINIFRED O. STONE, Ph.D.
Associate Dean
Graduate Admissions
Bowling Green State University
Bowling Green, Ohio

PREFACE

THIS book, like its ancestor, *Facilitating Career Development*, is about the practice of career development. It differs from most current books in psychology and counseling because it attempts to emphasize growth and development in the vocational sphere of a person's life, especially the practical application of theories and concepts. It is our view that the practice of career development is certainly one of the most fundamental and challenging areas of professional activity for persons in the helping professions. Career choice and development, as a process, cuts across all helping professions and across almost all theoretical notions about human growth and development.

In this book, career is viewed as time-extended development of a purposeful life pattern through work undertaken by a person. Career development refers to the total constellation of psychological, sociological, educational, physical, economic, and chance factors that combine to shape the career of any individual. Work is a basic component of one's life-style and the manner in which one attempts to satisfy basic psychological needs. Work is defined as effort expended to create something of value to self or others, including leisure or other nonpaid activity.

We have intentionally avoided extensive reference to career education, although some of the strategies described in these chapters could be so labeled. This is not meant as any negation of the career education movement, which has had a dramatic impact in many sections of this country. It is, however, based on our belief that career development is a broader concept than career education, which is often viewed primarily as a school-based educational delivery system; that counselors have a legacy and mandate to promote individual career development, which precedes the present emphasis on career education; and that counselors can facilitate individual career development either in spite of, or in concert with, career education.

This book emphasizes practice. Practice is defined as those activities, strategies, interventions, and programs that persons in helping professions implement to help a variety of clientele to become more effective, adaptive, and maneuverable in their careers. Many books in this area have addressed theories of career development, collating scattered and segmented readings in the general area of vocational development, reporting techniques for the acquisition and dissemination of occupational information, and describing *either* counseling *or* programmatic ways of intervening in career guidance. The primary aim of this book is to present to practitioners those media, techniques, interventions, strategies, and delivery stystems that will be of immediate assistance when they are confronted by the person who is struggling with the question, "What will I do with my life?" or the school/organization wanting to improve the quality of the career progression of their students/ employees.

Chapter authors were selected because of their academic interest and professional commitment and involvement to career development interventions. We view them as practitioners — scholars of the career development field. These authors present extended descriptions of practical techniques for intervening with individuals, groups, or larger social systems to promote career development. Each of the chapters has been carefully edited to reflect the central purpose of the book, and the chapters have been written using a common format. It is suggested that the reader begin by reading Chapters 1 and 2 and the brief introductions to Parts II and III. In this way, an overview of the scope, content, format, and the unique contributions of each chapter can be quickly grasped.

We have endeavored to prepare this book for practitioners in the helping professions, especially vocational counselors, counseling psychologists, secondary level counselors, counselors in post-secondary settings (e.g. vocational technical and community colleges, colleges, and universities), employment counselors, academic advisors, placement officers, cooperative education directors, and other professionals working in a wide variety of settings. Similarly, the book would be of use for students enrolled in undergraduate and graduate programs such as psychology, counselor education, student personnel work, vocational rehabilitation, social work, or where there is an emphasis on career development interventions.

It should be noted that each chapter of this book has been written to reflect current and future trends in our society, to draw upon the results of validation studies and demonstration projects of career interventions, and to catalog the present state-of-the-art in this area. Several chapters, such as those having to do with the use of computers, services for disabled persons, programs in organizations, and professional and ethical issues involved in career development interventions, assemble new information on the cutting edge of the field.

We acknowledge the contributions of colleagues, former and present students, and the professionals at Charles C Thomas, Publisher. Specifically, we thank Trudie Hines Cross and our Word Processing Center crew for the excellent clerical skills in the preparation of the final manuscript.

H.D.B.
R.C.R.

CONTENTS

Page

Contributors vii
Preface xi

Chapter

Part I: Background and Assumptions

1. FACILITATING CAREER DEVELOPMENT:
   PAST EVENTS, CURRENT SCENES, AND THE FUTURE 5
   HARMAN D. BURCK
2. CONTRIBUTIONS FROM THEORIES 25
   ELLEN S. AMATEA

Part II: Counseling Strategies

3. USE OF INFORMATION IN CAREER COUNSELING 53
   ROBERT C. REARDON
4. USE OF TESTS 69
   ROBERT MACALEESE
5. SELF-ASSESSMENT 89
   LAWRENCE K. JONES
6. CONTRACTUAL ARRANGEMENTS 108
   DANIEL J. MONTGOMERY
7. GROUP APPROACHES 124
   DONALD J. COCHRAN
8. USE OF COMPUTERS 141
   JAMES P. SAMPSON, JR.

Chapter	Page

Part III: Program Strategies

9. DEVELOPING A CAREER RESOURCE CENTER 169
   CAROL W. MINOR
10. USING COMMUNITY RESOURCES 191
    JANET G. LENZ
11. CAREER PLANNING THROUGH INSTRUCTION 212
    MICHAEL J. GIMMESTAD
12. CAREER DEVELOPMENT OF WOMEN 233
    JENNIFER BORETZ KAHNWEILER
13. SERVICES FOR DISABLED PERSONS 251
    E. JANE BURKHEAD
14. SERVING ETHNIC MINORITIES........................... 267
    WINIFRED O. STONE
15. PROGRAMS IN ORGANIZATIONS 292
    DOROTHY DOMKOWSKI
16. ACCOUNTABILITY: A PRACTICAL MODEL 309
    GARY W. PETERSON
17. PROFESSIONAL AND ETHICAL ISSUES...................... 321
    DANIEL J. MONTGOMERY AND JAMES P. SAMPSON, JR.

Name Index 337
Subject Index 345

CAREER DEVELOPMENT
INTERVENTIONS

Part I
BACKGROUND AND ASSUMPTIONS

CHAPTER 1

FACILITATING CAREER DEVELOPMENT
Past Events, Current Scenes, and the Future

HARMAN D. BURCK

I have all my life marveled at Sam. Born the son of a farmer in 1866, he lived the history of which I can only read. Within his 90 years of life, he witnessed dramatic change in every sphere of his culture — social, sexual, religious, vocational, economic, and political. He lived through four cycles of revolutions of peace and wartime, times of poverty, and times of comfort. He saw the coming of technology and the myriads of inventions that it spawned, such as refrigeration, radio, television and the telephone.

He saw the mule replaced by the tractor, the horse replaced by the car, train, and even the plane. He was witness to the introduction of the computer, commercial jet travel, the birth-control pill and many other high-impact technologies. Born in a time and place where virtual slavery was the norm, he died in a time of equal rights and struggles for equality. He was continually intrigued by those "new fangled" ideas that piqued his imagination and often his temperament, too. I used to think no other time either before or after would or could see so much change. I now think I was wrong. (Wilson, 1982)

THE preceding vignette best exemplifies the tenor of this chapter: that work and career development in contemporary America is a process that is profoundly affected by inevitable rapid and extensive change. In this chapter the following definition of career development as proposed by the National Vocational Guidance Association and American Vocational Association (Joint Position Paper, 1975) will be followed: "career development refers to the total constellation of psychological, sociological, educational, physical, economic, and chance factors that combine to shape the career of any given individual." To go a bit further, career development is equated with human development. Career development considers the importance of feelings, attitudes, prejudices, opinions, and values of individuals, *as well as* measured aptitudes, achievements, interests, intelligence, and other personality traits in order either to explain their career progression or to help them in career development life-stages. These stages might include such events as entering elementary school, anticipated graduation from high school, entry into the labor force, career mobility and change, dissatisfaction with present employment, midlife crises including separation or divorce, boredom and depression, and remarriage, discrimination, preretirement anxiety, or the retirement doldrums.

The facilitation of career development is an extremely complicated, intricate, confusing, speculative, and uncertain enterprise whether professionals are providing occupational information, referring clients to job placement services, or doing counseling with bewildered people who were just "pink slipped" from positions held for many years; career development activities also might include thousands of combinations, variations, and permutations of the above.

The purposes of this chapter are to (1) point out some of the past and current events and attitudes affecting career development theory and practice, (2) indicate the complexity of the task of facilitating career development by looking at contemporary people, (3) present a preview of possible future psychological environments and physical environs, and (4) plead for innovative career development interventions.

THE PAST AND CURRENT SCENE

Whereas the writings of great pioneers in the field such as Frank Parsons, John Brewer, Jesse Davis, and others (who were, incidentally, social reformers rather than counselors) have always reflected complex and comprehensive theoretical notions about the task of vocational choice, history indicates an emphasis on the imparting of occupational information and the use of testing as primary tools.

This trait-and-factor approach, revolutionary and imaginative in its time, seems to have persisted as the most popular approach. As it has often mistakenly been interpreted, it consists of giving the client a battery of aptitude tests and interest inventories, then interpreting the results by matching the individual profile with particular sets of job requirements. Such an approach has met with little success today, largely because it is limited in helping with immediate specific decisions, is more descriptive than explanatory, and is unable to incorporate rapidly changing facts and trends in the labor market. Yet, many counselors still continue to operate exclusively from this model — the test profile in one hand and the occupational brief in the other.

In the early 1950s, as if to leave behind all that had been accomplished from theory and research, a sharp trend developed in which the major emphasis was to explore the dynamics and motivations of clients with an eye toward exploring and enhancing their self-concept. This resulted in the application of psychodynamic therapeutic theories and practices (psychoanalytic, client-centered, etc.) to vocational concerns. Testing became a no-no, and occupational information was banished to the basement. Theoretically and practically, this trend made an important contribution; yet, attempts to help youths with their career planning exclusively from these theoretical points of view have not been particularly productive because they (a) are too far removed from the career confusion the client may be experiencing, (b) usually have singular goals for all clients, and (c) lack important elements such as occupational information, labor forecasts and trends, decision-making competencies, and the relevance of cognitive processes.

So, the use of misinterpreted and outmoded theoretical models and the frequent and overzealous adaptation of inappropriate psychotherapy and personality change theories are partly responsible for the current state of affairs. At least three other factors also have contributed to the present situation of disinterest in career guidance: (1) the notion that vocational counseling is routine and simple, resulting in a low prestige factor, (2) the lack of academic excitement about the topic and lack of vocational guidance practice in most counselor education/counseling psychology programs, and (3) a singularity of approach in dealing with clients presenting vocational concerns.

First, helping clients with vocational concerns is viewed by many professionals as uninteresting, routine, simple, lower-level, and a service anyone with a little training (particularly if they have work experience!) can perform. Because of professional pettiness and narrowness, coupled with a lack of knowledge and skill, career counseling is seen as routine in practice, but that does not make it easy. Helping confused persons to start thinking about what they will do in life is as difficult, intricate, and challenging a task as is working with a sexually deviant client or a drug addict. In fact, looking at the complexity of the task, it is found that it is more intricate and difficult than much of so-called personal-social counseling. Could it be that a wider knowledge base and a greater diversity of skills and competencies are needed?

Applied psychology (especially clinical and counseling) has for years been struggling with the problem of professional identity, especially identifying what it is that makes them different. A clinical psychologist forcefully makes this distinction: "With a modicum of training and adequate interpersonal skills, many persons can do psychotherapy with some effectiveness; but few professionals have the breadth and depth of training in vocational assessment and counseling to which the counseling psychologist can lay claim" (Nathan, 1977). Further, he states that, "The counseling psychologist is, however, sanctioned by the community to render vocational counseling and guidance services for which no other professional has equal sanction. Ironically, this activity, for which the counseling psychologist has highest sanction, seems to be viewed by many . . . . as a lower level function . . . . (having) a second-order attractiveness."

Historically, counseling and guidance professionals have been charged with the vocational and occupational guidance of youth. Yet, ample evidence suggests that the profession has not delivered well in this area. For example, Ginzberg (1971) concluded that the "60-year-old school guidance movement has failed to reach its goals" and that counselors generally do not play "a decisive role in the career plans" of students. However, the need for services exists. Based on a study sample of 32,000 eighth, ninth, and eleventh graders at two hundred public and parochial schools, the American College Testing Program (Prediger et al., 1974) reports that 56 percent of the eleventh graders reported they "had received little or no help with career planning via discussions with counselors." Consider also, the results of a national profile report prepared by the College Board (1974), which involved over one million high school seniors: "though the . . . profile of college-bound students indicates that large numbers are, by their own account, seasoned and successful at academic work and ambitious for advanced placement and advanced degrees, approximately 70 percent also indicate a strong need for college counseling about educational and vocational plans and opportunities."

Today, counselors are involved in a myriad of other activities that they feel should consume their time: drug abuse, human relations, affective education, sexuality, parent effectiveness training, crisis intervention, outreach programs, and routine administrative duties. No doubt these interests and activities are very important and worthwhile endeavors, but it leaves precious little time in the life of the professional who has a concern for assisting people with their career development.

The above situation has helped shape a set of professional attitudes that have to do with the prestige and status afforded career counseling. Within the counseling profession there is low prestige for the counselor whose main interest and activity is facilitating career development. This is best exemplified in a article by Putsell (1965; also see Burck, 1966), in which the organization and structure of a unified counseling center is described. Putsell states that "His (vocational counselor) concentration on the vocational counseling frees the clinical psychologist to spend more time with students having emotional problems," and concludes ". . . a clinical or counseling psychologist trained at the doctoral level is apt to become dissatisfied if circumstances require him to spend most of his time doing routine vocational counseling which is uncomplicated by psychological difficulties" (1965).

All too often, vocational clients are referred to beginning practica students and interns and other junior staff members in order that senior staff may work with the so-called "real" counseling cases. Professionals constantly attempt to clearly separate vocational concerns from personal-emotional ones, although this is impossible to do, which the following example demonstrates. A first-year female student at a large university who had studied piano since age three and who had set her sights on becoming a concert pianist was suddenly but bluntly informed by her piano professor that she would never make it and that she ought to think of entering another vocational field. She was reported to be a vocational client by a beginning clinician. Obviously, she had a vocational problem, but a counselor would not get far until he/she thoroughly explored the emotional aspects of the situation.

Career counseling and programs must be reinstated into counselors' work priorities, and they must be afforded greater status and prestige.

Second, an event that has occurred in the academic preparation of counselors has been most distressing and contributory to the present situation; namely, the deemphasis of vocational counseling and the rather unconcerned fashion in which students have been introduced to it. A survey of most master's counseling programs would reveal that only one course is usually offered in this area, and it is often referred to as occupational information, although it might occasionally encompass a superficial introduction to several career development theories. Frequently, these courses are dull, being taught by junior faculty who have little interest, limited knowledge, and even less skill in the area. Consequently, many students complete counselor education programs in which they have acquired few skills or competencies that would assist them on their jobs and in which they have been exposed to little excitement about career counseling as a professional activity.

Schneider and Gelso (1972) state that "it is still possible to view counseling psychology as consisting of at least two related but different emphases: the 'personal' and the 'vocational'." Yet, there seems to be great concern by many professionals that counseling programs are not devoting enough time and effort in training their students in the vocational area. In fact, an empirical study by these two authors found that educational-vocational counseling "is viewed as less complex and interesting than personal counseling." From this study it is deduced that beginning counselors cut their teeth doing vocational counseling, but as they become more skillful, they then can focus energies on clients with personal problems.

Third, in practice it is noted that most counselors, whatever their theoretical counseling point of view, generally approach the task of career counseling in a singular procedural fashion. They commence the vocational counseling process in a rigid, standardized way; yet, when dealing with clients' concerns of a more delineated personal/

emotional nature, they usually try to start the counseling process where the clients are in their emotional development. Seldom does it seem that the vocational maturity level of the student is taken seriously into consideration. For example, clients whose immediate concerns are difficulty with authority (manifested by trouble with fathers, teachers, and others) somehow are treated in similar sorts of ways as students who are much more vocationally mature and who are trying to decide whether to major in music or biophysics.

In an attempt to validate the notion that career development for any one individual is a very complicated, intricate, and bewildering process, it is now necessary to point out how human behavior is conceptualized today, how people think about themselves, and the implications of this for facilitating career development.

AMERICANS TODAY

Today Americans are living in one of the most complex, affluent, technocratic, and turbulent societies ever known; a society that is undergoing rapid change among all of its institutions, e.g. work, religion, marriage/mate/family, economic, etc.

As a result, more than ever before, people find the problems of choosing and maintaining themselves in a career as confusing and intricate. They are confronted with a seemingly ever-increasing array of opportunities from which they might choose, yet many find themselves with little reliable and valid information and knowledge about the general nature of the work world, much less with comprehensive knowledge of specific job areas or the career planning process. Sorely lacking for most people are up-to-date specific and accurate labor forecasts and predictions, which they should be scanning.

In addition to the above confusion, people today seem to know little about themselves as people, their feelings and fears, their prejudices or preferences, their strengths and weaknesses, and they do not have an accurate understanding of their behavior. They desperately want to understand and become aware of these personal characteristics and attributes, sort them out in meaningful ways, and relate them to their career progression. To substantiate this statement, witness the soaring sales of psychological and educational self-help books.

Career planning and choosing has not always been this complicated. In bygone times, the son took over his father's farm and had a firm idea of what his job would consist — indeed, he had been involved in his future occupation for many years. Probably, he had been able to establish a fairly accurate assessment of how well he might perform such a job. Also, he lived in a rural society whose values and behavioral preferences were clearly spelled out and static. Similarly, in a predominately agricultural society, girls were taught and had modeled for them how to be a good wife and mother. Conversely, today's young people are far more distant from the eventual locus of work — in fact most of them could render only a few facts about their parents' jobs — where and what kinds of work they do. In fact, most of them have never visited their parents' work sites.

The ways in which theorists have conceptualized explanations of human behaviors and change in relation to career development have become extremely complex and diverse in recent years. There has been an explosive number of personality theories, all of which deviate radically from the traditional Freudian and behavioral explanations of human behavior, e.g. client-centered, reality therapy, Skinnerian, transactional analysis, existential-humanistic, neuropsycholiguistic, etc. Following these, theorists in career development such as Holland, Roe, Super, Tiedeman, Harren, Krumboltz, Crites, Osipow, and others have provided rich theoretical explanations of the crucial importance of certain personality constructs and attributes as organizers, influences, and energizers of career behavior. Such constructs include self-concept, self-understanding, self-awareness, attitudes, values, perceptual processes, life stages, developmental tasks, identity formation, problem solving, decision making, cognitive styles, career maturity, etc. These considerations must be taken into account, along with more traditional notions of career determinants such as interests, aptitudes, abilities, limitations, and work experiences. The reconceptualizations of who people are, how they got where they are, how they behave, and how professionals should go about assisting them have dramatic implications for changing the ways in which facilitation of career development is attempted.

The ways in which career theorists have conceptualized the life career stages also have become increasingly more complex. For example, the simple notion of career stages proposed by Super (1957) (i.e. growth, exploration, establishment, maintenance, and decline) was broadened by Murphy and Burck (1976); they inserted another stage, *renewal,* between establishment and maintenance to depict the tremendous importance of midlife crises and recovery. More recently McCoy (1977), theorizing about how educational programs should respond to life-cycle tasks faced by adults, proposed a scheme that looks partially like this:

Age	Developmental Stage	Career Tasks
18-22	Leaving Home	Choose career/enter work
23-28	Becoming Adult	Settle in work; begin career ladder
29-34	Catch-30	Progress in career
35-43	Mid-life Reexamination	Reexamine work
44-55	Restabilization	Adjust to realities of work
56-64	Preparation for retirement	Prepare for retirement
65 +	Retirement	Disengage from paid work

From the above examples, it is easy to see how differentiated and convoluted our thinking and concepts about the career development process has become.

Finally, Career Development Specialists must realize that people have as much, if not more, capacity to create problems for themselves (and others) than to solve problems, that they can very effectively sabotage huge business ventures or massive social programs in innocent and sometimes unintentional ways, and that they can become very different kinds of people if only they desire it. As observers of human behavior, it is interesting to note how frequently parents psychologically harm their children; how employees sabotage their supervisors' pet projects and in a burst of activity reduce production; and how some committee members, under the guise of cooperation, divert the group's tasks, and hopelessly stymie progress. People are not static — they can modify old traits and acquire new ones. Their potential for change is virtually unlimited. The implication of all this is that extensive knowledge and deep understanding of human behavior are needed by counselors as they work with their clientele and their career motivations, aspirations, and planning.

Now that thinking about human behavior and how it is constantly changing into more complicated and diffused ways has been pointed out, it is necessary to look at the psychological and physical context in which people live, work, and attempt to satisfy their life desires and ambitions.

FUTURE PSYCHOLOGICAL ENVIRONMENTS AND PHYSICAL ENVIRONS

In this section discussion will center on the psychological and physical environments people live in today and their possible future environments, with a special emphasis on the implications for the facilitation of their career progression.

Today, Americans find a vast array of inconsistencies and ironies in their environment, living in a society that, in terms of sex habits, is one of the most liberated in the world, yet where there is less intimacy and sensitivity in interpersonal relations than in many other countries. They will not give much thought to the fact that they will probably see their next door neighbors more frequently at the local shopping mall than from their own homes. Even though the unemployment rate may seem high, they will be able to read fifteen pages of want-ads in the Sunday edition of a large city newspaper. They may not be aware that society has changed drastically since the Second World War, but they might notice that present change is so pervasive and occurs at such a rapid rate that it taxes the coping behavior of the most healthy functioning persons. These changes affect every facet of their life: education, government, law, family, religion, peer groups, unions, professional organizations, and business and industry to name a few. All of this change, and its dynamics and implications, has serious implications for counselors as they approach the task of attempting to facilitate career development.

People will find that they will spend more of their lives in formal and informal educational settings. This will occur at both the preschool and at the post-secondary level. In most situations, after twelve to sixteen years of formal schooling, they will be in apprentice and/or training programs, whether in business, industry, military, or in the home. Not only in the amount of time but also in content and methods of delivery are vast changes taking place in education, e.g.

individualized and computer-assisted instruction, relating academic content to the work world, affective education, sex education, modular scheduling. People in educational settings today witness, and are part of, a swiftly changing educational process.

In their dealing with government at all levels, they will find that their life becomes more and more shaped by decisions made by governmental agencies. They will learn that local governments have all the problems, the states have all the rights, and the federal government has all the money. People are coming to depend more and more on government for the satisfaction of various needs, and they realize that the federal government can make wise or devastating decisions in dealing with other nations, as nations become more and more interdependent on each other to satisfy basic human needs. The world economic situation, at any one period of time, has impact on all other countries, i.e. inflation and recession of the early 1980s. Indeed, they may begin to wonder if a representative type of government has the flexibility, adaptability, and speed to deal adequately with the social problems they see around them.

All persons will see vast changes taking place in their family. In their lifetime, they may have witnessed the decline of the extended family, and they have seen the family unit relying more on emotional closeness (or lacking it) rather than living together for economic reasons. They certainly will become aware of the obscuring of fixed sex roles between parents, siblings, and relatives. In all probability, their mothers will be actively pursuing a career of their own that will be quite different from the father's but no less rewarding, intense, demanding, or personally important. In terms of their own career confusions and planning, youth will find few resources, skills, or knowledge from the family to assist them, although there may be real parental pressures for them to pursue one career choice over another.

Within their own religious sphere they will be a part of a dynamic philosophical questioning and searching, if indeed they are participants or observers of organized religion at all. Their religious leaders and others will be attempting to inculcate certain moral values or challenging them to explore their own sense of morality, which may seem to conflict with their own feelings and behavior or that which they observe in the everyday world.

As youths grow older, there will be one group with whom they will identify more, and by whom they will be most influenced — their peers. Many of their values will be challenged by this group, and peers will be most influential in shaping certain behaviors — from hair styles, clothes, and automobile preferences to work values and vocational and educational plans. The older youths become, the more this peer group will be the satisfiers of their psychological, social, and physical needs and the shapers of their career aspirations.

Females will have some special developmental tasks to master. Because of a legal mandate, and hopefully a growing recognition that women should have the same career opportunities as men, the female will need to consider carefully how she would like to fuse her desires for motherhood with her career aspirations, or whether she even wants to marry. Occupational information and working role-models will be incomplete or nonexistent in many job areas. If she is interested in vigorously pursuing an active and demanding career, her mate (if she chooses to have one) must be carefully selected in order for her to have an understanding and cooperative spouse rather than one who might be old-fashioned in views and expectations about women and motherhood.

As people learn about business and industry, they will find that this segment becomes more complex organizationally and ever changing. They will find that, more and more, a worker's sophistication at interpersonal skills is equally important as specific job-related skills and competencies.

People today are aware that something seems to be wrong with their quality of life. In one way or another, discontent seems to surface and be expressed in the nature of complaints and dissatisfaction with work. Most people seem confused about this and realize that the problem is large, obscure, and complex. The following facts will help conceptualize this problem:

1. Many workers see their jobs as dull, repetitive, meaningless, and offering little challenge or autonomy.
2. Productivity of the worker is low — as measured by absenteeism, turnover rates, wildcat strikes, sabotage, poor-quality products, and a reluctance by workers to commit themselves to their work tasks.
3. Blue-collar blues are manifested as a result of blocked mobility and occupational rigidity.

4. Most young workers view the work place as authoritarian.
5. Dull and demeaning work over which the worker has little or no control, as well as other poor features of work, contribute to an assortment of mental health problems.
6. As work problems increase, there may be a consequent decline in physical and mental health, family stability, community participation and cohesiveness, and balanced socio-political attitudes, while there is an increase in drug and substance abuse, addiction, aggression, and deliquency.
7. Whereas most Americans have received great increments in pay and fringe benefits, dissatisfaction and discontent with work continues to spread across the country like a disease (*Work in America*, 1973).

One of the most important tasks of a contemporary Career Development Specialist is to assist people today to prepare themselves for the future. A look at American society reveals one glaring theme: *rapid, pervasive, and extensive change*. The following facts, trends, predictions, and directions affecting all aspects of our life are gleaned from futuristic writers (Toffler, 1980; Yankelovich, 1981; Harris, 1981; Ferguson, 1980; and others).

First, some facts:

1. From 1980 to 1990 we will have a larger population, but the composition will be different. The biggest increase will be among the elderly; the biggest decrease will be among those under twenty. Projected increases for the total population will be about 10 percent.
2. The labor force has changed drastically. The total number of blue collar jobs decreased while women and blacks have increased dramatically relative to men and whites. More people are employed in part-time, evening, and weekend work. In the information sector of the labor force there has been a sharp increase, a slight decline in the service section, reduction in industry, and a continued sharp decline in agriculture.
3. In education, there will be an increase in the number of elementary students, but a decrease at the high school level. Colleges and universities will press hard to find new students (e.g. retired, military, international students) as enrollments drop significantly from the 1970s. The 1980 census showed that in

1960 only 41 percent of the population had finished high school, in 1970, 52.2 percent had, but in 1980, 66.3 percent of the population were high school graduates.
4. In the home vast changes have taken place. Both marriage and divorces are on the rise. Interracial marriages, legal abortions, and the number of unmarried women giving birth have increased. Single parent households become more and more common in every neighborhood, such that now one in five children lives in a one parent family.

A look at the literature of futurists reveals vast and accelerated trends, directions, and predictions such as the following:

1. *Telecommunications and microelectronics* are advancing so rapidly (think what a hand computer cost five years ago) that very soon many people will be able to work at home and perform hundreds of tasks that now require expensive travel and time. People also will have access to tremendously wide variations of information and communication resources. The marriage of data processing and telecommunications will allow the slow and gradual elimination of written records, mail, and similar communication and record keeping functions. Just think, no paper work but rather computer work.
2. Parallel to the above are profound *technological advances*. Essentially, these are the delivery components of science and engineering. They tend to be very specific. Whereas, these sectors of the labor market tend to put some people out of work, they create more jobs than they eliminate. Unfortunately, technological jobs do abolish unskilled jobs and create either semi-skilled or skilled positions, resulting in the need for employees with more advanced education and training (for example, in the areas of management, marketing and advertisement, and service technicians). Light amplification by stimulated emission of radiation (lasers) and optic fibers are two good examples of advances in this area that are making profound changes in such areas as medicine, industry, defense, and even checking out at the local supermarket.
3. There will be drastic changes in the *demographic composition of the labor force*. Whereas this has been discussed above, the age theme is the same: shortage of young employees, a middle-

aged bubble, and a large percentage of older persons. The Census Bureau predicts that by 1990, 53 percent of the labor force will be twenty-five to forty-four years old. Older workers will increase by 7.6 percent per year.

4. Nothing should be written today about helping people progress more comfortably through their career progression without having an ample section about the *surge of women in the work force*. Women now represent about 50 percent of those working. There is no doubt that women still are underpaid, overworked, and discriminated against; these conditions are, indeed, changing particularly for those females who choose not to tolerate such situations.

5. *Competition for jobs,* especially those in higher income ranges, will become fierce. As the work force becomes overeducated and more aware and mobile, there could even be a backlash against affirmative action programs. We may well expect social and generational conflict if the unemployment rate among high school males (particularly blacks and Hispanics) continues to be so disproportional.

6. There will be a *slowdown in real economic growth*, particularly in the more industrialized countries of the world. The result of this could be a severe recession and perhaps a depression. This will cause a lowering of the level of affluence and standard of living. As more aggressive countries enter the world competition in business and for resources, international tensions and geopolitics will change, perhaps leading to more limited wars.

7. The world has witnessed the profound economic effect of the crude oil crisis of the early 1970s. The formation of this cartel has been a strong contributing factor to international inflation and shifting of priorities both military and political in countries around the world. Such combinations of agreements between certain countries to limit competition will lead to *fierce competition for natural resources,* including everything from coffee beans to copper and uranium. The implications of this for the size and composition of the work force are tremendous, if not alarming.

8. *Immigration from underdevelopment and Third World nations* can possibly lead to racial polarization and conflict and can lead to and increase people's perception and demand for entitlements.

These people certainly will increase their percentage in the work force. There are serious implications here for all social and human services from food stamps to education in general.

9. All levels of *government will continue to be big,* and we can expect increased revolts against taxation. This will affect greatly those who rely on social programs of all kinds (remember, the aged is the fastest growing group in this country). Social Security as we know it now will have to be greatly changed, both as to financing and distribution of benefits. Our national government, which is now large and so pervasive, may become unable to respond to national crises for fear of offending the many special interest groups it represents. At least two alternatives in this situation may be that (1) this could result in a stronger, politically conservative, authoritarian type or (2) a loosely defined confederation of sovereign collectives who would demand to control their own destinies.

10. As our society becomes more populated with groups with their own rights, our *identification and suggested solutions to social problems will have to change.* We will need less simplistic and linear solutions to multicausal, complex, and entangled social problems. This will require great minds and problem solvers who are understanding, tolerant, and humane.

11. There will continue to be a *great shift in human values.* This shift will be from the traditional work ethic as we know it today to a focus centered more on the worker as an equal. Greater emphasis will be on the quality of the work and nonwork (leisure) life, resulting in greater participation in making decisions and solving problems. Different kinds of incentives that provide workers with more control over their work environments (i.e. pay, raises, promotions, strategies, etc.) are desperately needed now. Flex-time, job-sharing, cottage industries, and other imaginative and innovative schemes will come about in order to reduce workers' feelings of alienation and increase their feelings of inclusion.

12. *A continuing awareness and demand for individual rights.* A greater degree of mobility (both geographical and social, as well as career) will create constantly changing temporary groups of people banding together for everything from leisure activity to social rights and political activism. This "unity for a purpose"

phenomenon will force all kinds of changes, not only in laws per se but in social mores and folkways.
13. A *greater health awareness*, as well as increased medical knowledge, will bring about more emphases on nutrition, exercise, stress reduction, the alleviation of psychological problems, health philosophies, and treatment interventions that will be more holistic and preventive.
14. *Robotics*. The U.S. Labor Department is still producing brochures advising high school vocational students of the likelihood of finding jobs as welders, spray painters, and machinists. These tasks can already be performed by robots. One prediction is that by 1990 half of the United States factory workers will be specialists trained to service and repair robots. "Seeing" robots, which have cameras that send signals to a computer that in turn can adjust the robot's position, are already available. Whether robots will be the job snatchers as predicted is only speculative. However, in Japan, a country far advanced in robotics, unemployment is on the increase, and it is a country where employees think in terms of lifetime employment; that is, where they stay with a company reaping high income and benefits when times are good and taking pay losses when things are not so good.
15. Finally, two trends described by Toffler (1980) that will have entrenching implications are *demassification and acceleration*. He mentions how quickly our society is becoming demassed; that is, the individualization of everything from magazines to custom built cars. Concerning accelerations, he refers to how much more rapidly we will live our lives, will have to make decisions, and how much more quickly historical change will take place.

The above facts about life now and the trends and predictions about the future should boggle, amaze, overwhelm, and perhaps raise the apprehensions of people who think about the future seriously. They might even frighten some people. The implication is that we need to prepare, equip, and possibly cajole people today (especially the younger ones) to think in terms of the future. The future is coming at us faster and faster. Preparation for change is not only mandatory but necessary for survival. In the next section, some of the justifications of need for more efficient and effective career development programs and interventions and some strategies for meeting them will be discussed.

CAREER DEVELOPMENT INTERVENTIONS: NEED FOR INNOVATION

People of all ages need career development services, but all of them do not need psychotherapy. As John Holland once noted: most clients want help, not love (1974). Previous apathetic attitudes about the importance of career counseling must give way to more broadminded conceptualizations about the tremendous importance of work in a person's life. This will demand totally new approaches to intervening in peoples' career lives. For example, in some recent studies about unemployment and its effect on individuals, the "pink-slip syndrome" appears. Being without work not only affects individuals personally but also their families, friends, co-workers, and neighbors. This mental health syndrome is contagious. With high unemployment, mental health clinics report sharp rises in the number of people seeking help for family disturbances or emotional problems, e.g. child and spouse abuse, alcoholism, parents-children problems, crime, suicide, heart disease, and other stress-related chronic ailments. Whereas these studies report only statistical correlations, there appear to be some multicausative factors embedded in the statistics.

WHAT'S NEEDED?

The task at hand seems obvious but not simple or clear. If only 25 percent of the trends predicted earlier in this chapter come true, industry and the labor force are in for some severe jolts. This nation cannot simply borrow present technological practices from countries such as Japan and Germany to produce goods to compete in supplying the world's needs and demands. As a nation we must devise innovative, creative, and competitive, need-fulfilling services and products, and we need to do this faster, and more efficiently than other countries. This demands a very different kind of work force —

one that is flexible, assertive, and creative.

The bottom lines regarding what we need to do in career development follow:

1. Our conceptualization of career development and the academic disciplines encompassed therein must drastically change. From a simple notion of matching people and jobs to a "test and tell them" approach, career development today broadly encompasses counseling, clinical and social psychology, philosophy, anthropology, history, learning theory, economics, engineering and technology, computers, and more.
2. We must focus our interventions on helping clients cope with vast and far-reaching changes in the labor market — information gathering and processing, problem solving, labor trends forecasting, and decision making. We must deal with value changes and value diversity among people. Our career interventions must be geared for people of all ages, not just the adolescent. All mental health facilities (public and private) need to assume responsibility for career development interventions as part of staff development.
3. The skills, attitudes, and knowledge that we must impart to all people are adaptation, self-directiveness, self-motivation, responsibility, resourcefulness, creativity, and maneuverability. Finally, people must become more tolerant of change, ambiguity, and the unknown as we rapidly and turbulently move from a society that is primarily industrial/labor based to one that is robotic/laser/knowledge/information based.

BIBLIOGRAPHY

Burck, H.D. Putsell's unified college counseling center: A reply. *Journal of College Student Personnel,* 1966, *7,* 3-4.

The College Board News. New York: College Board, Vol. 2, No. 2, January, 1974.

Ferguson, M. *The Acquarian conspiracy: Personal and social transformation in the 1980s.* Los Angeles: J.P. Tarcher, 1980.

Ginzberg, E. *Career guidance: Who needs it, who provides it, who can improve it?* New York: McGraw-Hill, 1971.

Harris, M. Why it's not the same old America. *Psychology Today.* August, 1981, pp. 23-51.

Holland, J. Some practical remedies for providing vocational guidance for everyone. *Educational Researcher,* 1974 *3*, 9-15.

McCoy, L.S. *Americans in transition.* New York: College Entrance Examination Board, 1977, pp. 36-61.

Murphy, P., and Burck, H.D. Career development of men at mid-life. *Journal of Vocational Behavior,* 1976, *9*, 337-343.

Nathan, P.E. A clinical psychologist views counseling psychology. *The Counseling Psychologist,* 1977, *7*(2), 36-37.

National Vocational Guidance Association and American Vocational Association, Joint Position Paper: Career Development and Career Guidance. *Journal of Employment Counseling,* 1975, 12, 73-85.

Prediger, D., Roth, J., and Noeth, R. Career development of youth: A nationwide study. *Personnel and Guidance Journal,* 1974, *53*, 97-104.

Putsell, T.E. A unified college counseling center. *The Journal of College Student Personnel,* 1965, *6*, 171-174.

Schneider, L.J., and Gelso, C.J. Vocational versus 'personal' emphasis in counseling psychology training programs. *The Counseling Psychologist,* Part I, Vol. 3, No. 3, 1972.

Super, D.E. *The psychology of careers.* New York: Harper & Row, 1957.

Toffler, A. *The third wave.* New York: William Morrow, 1980.

Wilson, N.H. School counseling: A look into the future. *The Personnel and Guidance Journal,* 1982, *60*, 353-357

Work in America. Report of a Special Task Force of the Secretary of Health, Education, and Welfare. Cambridge, Massachusetts: M.I.T. Press, 1973.

Yankelovich, D. New rules in American life: Searching for self-fulfillment in a world turned upside down. *Psychology Today,* April, 1981, pp. 35-91.

CHAPTER 2

CONTRIBUTIONS FROM THEORIES

Ellen S. Amatea

WHY do people select the careers they do? How do people make career choices? Why do people change their careers? Is there such a thing as a good vocational choice or a preferred way of making such a choice? To function effectively, career counseling professionals need to develop an explicit theory of career choice and development. Such a personal theory can be useful to the practitioner in several ways. First, it can provide the practitioner with a structure or conceptual map by which to organize data about an individual career client. Relationships between the client, the world of work, and/or the external environment can be highlighted given the specific assumptions of one's personal theory. Second, one's career choice theory can provide a focus for the development of specific counseling goals and objectives. Specific behaviors that one might hypothesize as necessary outcomes for one type of career problem or population might differ markedly from that set of outcomes expected from another type of clientele. Formulating one's ideas about career choice making and/or development can guide one's decision making regarding which set of outcomes should be the appropriate focus for career guidance interventions. Finally, a counselor's theory can suggest a method or set of methods for working with clients. Specific tools and resources needed to implement such methods can be located and/or developed, and a general sequence of counseling activities can be formulated.

How do counselors go about formulating their career choice

theory? Counselors need more than commonsense notions about career behavior and personal experience to develop their theory. A major resource useful in this process is the current body of knowledge called *career development theory*. During the past fifty years a significant number of theories have been formulated that attempt to describe or explain the career choice process. Many of these theories have not withstood the rigors of formal validation. Others have failed to provide much useful direction to the practitioner. Such theories have tended to fall into disuse.

A limited number of theories, however, have provided a rich source of ideas about career behavior and have spurred the development of a number of useful counseling resources and tools. This chapter will examine four such theories. These are the theories of John Holland, Donald Super, David Tiedeman, and John Krumboltz, which appear to have utility to the practitioner interested in formulating his/her ideas about career choice behavior.

So that the practitioner is able to evaluate the relative merits and contributions of each theory to the general body of knowledge of career behavior, each theory will be presented in a similar fashion. Information will be presented on (1) the philosophical origins or context for the development of the theory, (2) the basic concepts of the theory, (3) the model for career guidance intervention implied by the theory, (4) the conceptual tools and counseling resources emanating from the theory, and (5) the qualitative evidence for judging the validity of theory. Obviously, in one short chapter it is not possible to thoroughly acquaint the reader with even a limited number of theories in great depth. Thus, the reader will be referred to original source materials for further exploration.

Following the presentation of each of the four theories, a comparison of the strengths and weaknesses of these theories will be presented. In addition, implications for the development of one's own personal theory of career behavior will be discussed.

HOLLAND'S THEORY OF OCCUPATIONAL TYPES AND ENVIRONMENTS

John Holland's theory of occupational types and environments represents an extension of the tradition of the differential psychology

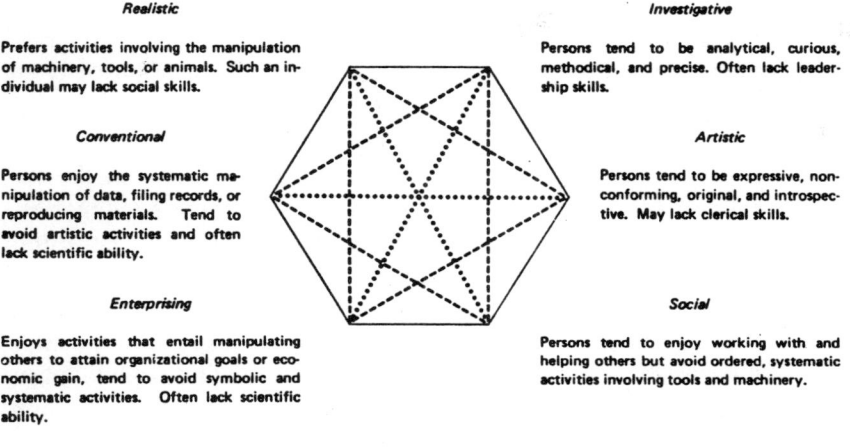

Figure 2-1. Holland's Hexagonal Model. Adapted from J.L. Holland, *Making Vocational Choices: A Theory of Careers.* Englewood Cliffs, N.J.: Prentice-Hall, 1973. This figure originally appeared in *ACT Research Report No. 29,* by J.L. Holland, D.R. Whitney, N.S. Cole, and J.M. Richards, Jr., 1969.

first expressed by trait-and-factor theorists and, later, by the theory of Anne Roe. Holland considers personality style to be the major determinant of vocational choice. He contends that an individual resembles one of six basic personality types: Realistic, Investigative, Artistic, Social, Enterprising, or Conventional. The more closely one resembles any given type, the more likely one is to manifest the behaviors, competencies, interests, and personality traits which characterize that type.

From Holland's perspective, people choose a work environment that allows them to express and exercise their particular personal style. Since work environments can be characterized in terms of the persons who occupy them, the best way to choose a career is to choose a job that provides the best fit between personal style and the profile of personal traits characterizing people in that occupation. Although a complete description and explanation of these types can be found in Holland's *Making Vocational Choices: A Theory of Careers* (1973), a brief description of each type with illustrative personality traits, competencies, and interests is presented in Figure 2-1.

Holland originally theorized that people could be characterized as belonging to one distinctive personality type. In later revisions of his theory (Holland, 1973, 1975), Holland modified his ideas and suggested that some individuals may use a wide range of different traits, behaviors, and competencies for coping with the environment and thus may fall into two or even more type categories. The combination of such type category memberships and its implications for the consistency of vocational preferences and congruence between person and job was the basis for his formulations of a series of relationships among the occupational types. These relationships are represented in Figure 2-1 by means of the solid and broken lines. As noted in Figure 2-1, Holland depicted these relationships among the six types as forming the corners of a hexagon. According to Holland, types adjacent on the hexagon are thought to be consistent with one another in terms of personal characteristics and competencies, whereas those hexagonally opposite are deemed to be mutually inconsistent with one another. To illustrate, a person would find it somewhat easier to reconcile interests in the Investigative career domain (e.g. botanical research) with a Realistic career preference (e.g. engineering) than with an Enterprising career preference (e.g. Salesperson).

Resources and Tools for the Practitioner

Holland's theory has been a rich source of tools for the career guidance practitioner. To assess vocational style or type, Holland developed two different psychometric instruments, the *Vocational Preference Inventory* (VIP) (1965) and the *Self-Directed Search* (SDS) (Holland, 1972). Each of these instruments has been extensively validated and used during the past ten to fifteen years. While differing in focus, both of these instruments are designed to yield a profile of interests organized in terms of Holland's personality typology. In the *Vocational Preference Inventory,* individuals indicate their vocational interests by selecting job titles that appeal to them. In the *Self-Directed Search,* first published in 1972 and revised in 1977, individuals provide information regarding their occupational daydreams, competencies, attitudes toward specific occupations, and self-estimates of their abilities. Raw scores on both the VPI and SDS are converted into a three-letter summary code reflecting a composite of three occupational types/environments. Information regarding the level of differentiation of interests across the types, the consistency of those interests, and the congruence between personal estimates and preferences for work environments are also available in an organized way for each individual.

In addition to assessing personal style, Holland has developed an occupational classification system that organizes occupations in terms of his schema of occupational types and environments. This classification system is illustrated in Holland's *Occupations Finder* (1977), a booklet containing some 500 common occupations, organized around the Holland coding system. Holland recently has developed a system for melding the *Dictionary of Occupational Titles* classification scheme with his own system, thus increasing the range of available jobs keyed to his occupational types (Gottfredson, Holland, & Ogawa, 1982).

Implications for the Career Counseling Process

Using Holland's theory of career choice or his assessment and occupational classification tools requires that the career counselor assume an enduring trait conception of personality. That is, an individual's profile of interests and traits as assessed by the VPI or SDS are illustrative of an underlying set of personal traits that presumably do not vary greatly over time or across situations.

In discussing the merits of this theory, Holland (1978) states that the strengths of his formulations lie in the fact that (1) predictions emanating from the theory provide useful forecasts of achievement and job satisfaction, (2) the theory provides a practical structure for understanding occupational and personal data, and (3) it suggests a practical structure for organizing occupational and personal data. Research conducted by Holland, Gottfredson, and Nafziger (1975), validating the diagnostic signs provided by the SDS with the degree of a person's self- and occupational knowledge and their decision-making ability, demonstrated that the SDS could have some utility in predicting client problem areas and suggesting potential remedies.

Holland contends that the role of the career counselor should be largely an informational one — providing clients with an organizational framework for understanding the way the work world is organized and how they can locate themselves in that work world. Such an informational role can be implemented in a variety of ways

— by printed materials, group activities, structured workshops — and only infrequently requires the labor intensive mode of one-to-one counseling. The Self-Directed Career Program (SDC) (Holland, Nafziger, & Helms, 1972) illustrates how vocational guidance services can be provided to groups of individuals with only a minimum of professional intervention.

According to Holland and Gottfredson (1978), organizing occupational information according to the typology makes the use of occupational materials easier and reduces counselor work. At the same time, the typological organization of occupational materials increases people's independence and competency for dealing with their own vocational questions and problems. Thus, Holland and Gottfredson contend that the typology and its tools can give more understanding and power to the client/user than is usually the outcome in other career choice models. The informational links between people and the work world can equalize the career guidance process, make it less mystical, and put more of the control for understanding information into the hands of clients.

Evaluating the Theory

Probably no theory of career development or choice has been researched as extensively as has Holland's. Large scale validations and applications of the typology and the various assessment tools (SDS, VPI) have resulted in almost 400 investigations to date (Holland, personal communication, 1982). In addition, since 1959 when Holland first published his theory, it has undergone substantial revision, refinement, and rethinking. Which concepts have been validated and which have not withstood the test of empirical investigation? What criticisms have been leveled against the theory itself?

Research attempting to validate the relationships between vocational type and job choice and thus establish the predictive validity of the typology have demonstrated that in large student samples the relationships between type and college major or initial job choice have been supported (Holland, 1973). Some investigators, however, have failed to verify this association (Hauselman, 1971; Hughes, 1972). In these cases, both the size of the sample and differences in aptitude and/or socio-economic status appeared to influence vocational preference more strongly than did personal type.

A major criticism leveled at Holland's original theory was that it did not sufficiently explain how people became the types they were. Critics contended that the theory did not provide any explanatory formulations regarding how skills or preferences were developed or how they changed. In recent years, Holland (Holland & Gottfredson, 1978) has attempted to extend the theory to include a more developmental frame of reference and to focus on life span issues and special groups.

Discussing his theory, Holland (1978) cites the following areas of weakness: (1) the hypotheses linking vocational environments to actual jobs are only partially tested and require much more exploration, (2) the hypotheses dealing with the relationships between people and jobs, though having substantial support, require more testing, and (3) the recent formulations about personal development and change, while receiving some support, require more thorough examination. In addition, Holland contends that there are many important personal and environmental contingencies, such as social class, intelligence, and special aptitudes, which are incorporated only indirectly or incompletely into his typology (Holland, 1978).

A basic criticism that also can be leveled at the theory is the deceptive ease assumed in assessing type. The process of assessing personal type appears quite easy. In reality, a skilled counselor is frequently required to assist those clients who have inconsistent or undifferentiated personal type profiles. Since such clients represent a substantial number of the persons seeking professional intervention, more significant counseling resources may frequently be needed.

SUPER'S DEVELOPMENTAL SELF-CONCEPT THEORY

Building upon the work of Buehler (1933) and the Ginzberg group (1951), Super and his associates attempted to weave together developmental, differential, and phenomenological perspectives in conceptualizing career behavior. Combining many diverse concepts from this broad range of academic areas and research traditions — such as the concepts of individual differences, occupational ability patterns, identification with role models, and multipotentiality — Super formulated a theory to "explain the process through which interest, capacities, values, and opportunities are compromised. . . " (1953).

Within a structure of stages and periods, Super and his associates specified the kinds of behaviors that contribute to career development. According to Super, each career stage has broad, distinctive tasks whose implementation depends upon the acquisition of specific skills and attitudes and whose accomplishment is necessary to both succeed in that stage and move on to the next stage. Super coined the term *vocational maturity* to epitomize the changing yardstick of unique career related behaviors that make up career development at different life stages (see Figure 2-2). Vocational maturity is used to denote the degree of development, the place reached on the continuum of vocational development from exploration to decline. Vocational maturity may be thought of as a vocational age, conceptually similar to mental age (Super, 1955).

Borrowing from the phenomenological tradition, Super conceptualized the career choice process as a process of compromise within

Stage	Age	Task
Growth	0-14	Try multiple experiences — Form self-concept — Develops an understanding of the meaning and purpose of work.
Exploration	14-24	Recognize and accept need to make career decisions and obtain relevant information — Becomes aware of interests and abilities and how they relate to work opportunities — Identify possible fields and levels of work consistent with these abilities and interests — Secure training to develop skills and advance occupational entry and/or enter occupations fulfilling interests and abilities.
Establishment	25-44	Achieve full competence in occupation through experience/training — Consolidate and improve status in the occupation — Advance vertically or horizontally.
Maintenance	45-65	Preserve skills through in-service/continual training — Develop retirement resources/plans.
Decline	65+	Adapt work to physical capacity — Manage resources to sustain independence.

Figure 2-2. Super's Career Development Stages and Selected Tasks. Adapted from D.E. Super, *The Psychology of Careers.* New York: Harper and Row, 1957.

which the development and implementation of the self-concept operates. Individuals choose occupations whose characteristics allow them to function in roles that are consistent with their self-concept. This self-concept, in turn, is a function of the person's developmental history.

To validate his theory of vocational development and the concepts of vocational maturity and adjustment, Super conducted a longitudinal research study, the Career Pattern Study. He initiated this study in 1951 by assessing specific attitudes of a sample of eighth and ninth grade boys. Super examined these same students again at their twelfth grade and again at age twenty-five. Differences in the evolution of five specific behavioral dimensions were examined both for individual subjects across time and for the group as a whole across time. Those five behavioral dimensions were (1) orientation to vocational choice, (2) information and planning about preferred occupations, (3) consistency of vocational preferences, (4) the crystallization of traits, and (5) wisdom of vocational preference.

Recently, Super (1980) expanded his theory by positing that there are a combination and sequence of various life roles that individuals hold over their lifetime. Such roles include that of worker as well as parent, mate, citizen, leisurite, and student. Super conceptualizes the relative sequence of involvement in these roles by means of a "life-career rainbow" and contends that self-actualization may take place in various roles (not just a formal work role).

Resources and Tools for the Practitioner

The concept of career development stages and concomitant skills is an appealing framework to many counselors and educators interested in organizing career guidance and/or education strategies for a particular age clientele. The assumption that people at a particular life stage by definition share common past accomplishments and present challenges simplifies decisions regarding appropriate career guidance goals and strategies. Following this line of thinking, Super and his associates have formulated a series of assessment tools designed to describe an individual's level of career maturity (i.e. the degree of their acquisition of particular career-related skills and attitudes). Both the *Career Development Inventory* (CDI) developed by Super and his associates (1972) and Crites' *Career Maturity Inventory* (1961) are designed to assess the relative level of vocational problem-solving and planning skill and attitudes of high school students. In addition, Super and his associates (1970) devised the *Work Values Inventory* to assess the relative degree of importance an individual attaches to certain work values.

With such assessment tools, the career counselor can assess a client's vocational maturity and identify appropriate vocationally relevant tasks to be accomplished. If clients are vocationally immature, that is, not at the level of career planning skill of their agemates, Super views the counselor's task as that of designing or suggesting appropriate ways for them to acquire these deficit skills and behaviors. An example of this approach might be the following: if it was determined that a ninth grade student was operating at a vocationally immature level demonstrating little awareness of the need to eventually make a career decision, the client would not be in a position to make informed choices clearly regarding his/her current educational planning and course work. The goal of counseling in this case might be to assist the client to develop more of a sense of the need for careful planning rather than to emphasize the development of a specific career or educational plan.

Implications for Career Counseling / Guidance Practice

Counselors operating from Super's theoretical viewpoint would find themselves much more in the role of designing educational experiences in which information-giving would be but one facet of their role. The distinctive demands of various life stages would require the facilitation of different attitudes and skills at different ages and stages; thus, information-giving, though common to the late adolescent period, would be but one function they would perform.

Evaluating the Theory

A sizeable portion of career-decision research activity has been devoted to validating the tenets of Super's theory. One type of research activity, discussed in an earlier portion of this chapter, focused on validating both the nature and sequence of career related behaviors at various life stages. A second type of research activity has focused on relating self-concept, as elicited by means of self-descriptive instruments, to predicted and actual job choice.

Although self-concept researchers have shown that there is often a significant association between the way that people view themselves and the work they are currently performing (Greenhaus, 1971; Hunt, 1967; Ziegler, 1970), many criticisms have been leveled against such research. One such criticism is that even if self- and occupational concepts are significantly related such a relationship does not demonstrate that self-concepts determine occupational choice (Hunt, 1967). Thoresen and Ewart (1978) speculate that "self-descriptions may be as much the consequence of occupational choices or achievements as their antecendent or cause; what people do in their work may determine how they view themselves."

Although Super's research and the research efforts of others (Gribbons & Lohnes, 1968; Crites, 1965) support Super's general theory of distinctive developmental stages, the specific dimensions of vocational maturity have not been confirmed clearly. Gribbons and Lohnes (1968), for example, contend that while vocational maturity is a most meaningful developmental concept and that career choice behaviors clearly emerge and persist over time, the differentiation of, several distinctive career development dimensions has not been substantiated. In a recent study, Westbrook and his colleagues (Westbrook, Cutts, Madison, & Arcia, 1980) attempted to substantiate the independence of career maturity attitudes and competencies in ninth grade and technical college students. Their findings led them to conclude that the multidimensional structure of career development behaviors could not be supported. Thus, at the present time, the core career development trait underlying most attitudinal and behavioral dimensions is that of informed planfulness (Gribbons & Lohnes, 1968).

Validation efforts related to Super's stage and task model of career development have been subjected to a different kind of criticism. Although the logic of the stage approach has achieved widespread acceptance, some researchers and writers, who openly challenge the idea that life inherently cycles in some progressive fashion, posit that certain contextual factors have a greater impact on the formation of attitudes, perspectives, and skills than differences in chronological age. Adult development theorists (Brim, 1966; Neugarten, 1968; Lowentha, 1975), along with researchers specifically concerned with women's psychological development (Gilligan, 1982), assert that common sociocultural expectations, as well as factors such as race, sex, and social class membership, exert an inexorable influence over the life-course and may blunt or even alter the way in which developmental stages occur. Thus, how an individual meets the world at any period of life cannot be anticipated or normed without attention being given to the social, cultural, and historical factors that define his or her life alternatives. Super's research and career development model of ages and stages can thus be criticized in that it represents only a narrow range of contextual and cohort differences, yet it seeks to generalize to entire age populations.

An additional criticism frequently leveled at Super's age and stage model is that there is limited documentation of the idea that tasks and behaviors performed at one stage are necessary for the successful execution of tasks at later stages of the career development process.

TIEDEMAN AND O'HARA VOCATIONAL DECISION-MAKING MODEL

Tiedeman and O'Hara (1959; 1963) view career development as part of a larger continuing process of differentiating an ego identity. Just how a person's ego identity evolves is, according to these theorists, dependent upon several factors: (1) the person's early childhood experiences with the family unit, (2) the resolution of certain psychosocial crises at distinctive developmental stages, (3) the consistency between society's meaning systems and that of the individual, and (4) the emotional dimensions of each of the above three factors. Career development, as a facet of the larger process of identity development and differentiation, is thus seen as evolving in a sequence of developmental life stages or events. Of particular interest to these theorists was the specification of the process of career decision making. Tiedeman and O'Hara view the decision process as comprised of distinctive stages. They believe that each of these stages can best be described in terms of the individual's conceptualization of him/herself, of the choice task, and of oneself in the choice process. Borrowing from Piaget's formulations of cognitive development, Tiedeman and O'Hara formulated a two-stage process of career choice differentiation and career choice integration. These two stages were labeled anticipation and implementation. Each of these stages consisted of a series of distinctive steps or phases. The anticipation stage was comprised of the exploration, crystallization, choice, and clarification phases; the implementation stage was comprised of the social induction, reformation, and integration phases.

Such formulations of career choice clearly illustrate the heavy influence of both psychodynamic and developmental theory. The thinking of both Erikson and Piaget structured many of Tiedeman and O'Hara's formulations about the career decision process. Tiedeman and O'Hara not only hypothesized about career decision making, but they also spelled out general postulates about the career development process. They contend that "life confronts the individual with discontinuties in his experience of himself at different life stages. Such discontinuities (similar to Neugarten's concept of 'social clocks') are presented by the environment and caused by the nature of societal expectations" (1963). These discontinuities, according to Tiedeman and O'Hara, present the individual with problems to be resolved, in which success results in the individual gaining an increased sense of self-competence and control over his/her behavior and environment. Such changes in one's view of self lead to a greater "sense of agency" — the owning of responsibility for one's behavior — and, in turn, to further purposeful action as new discontinuities and their attendant tasks are confronted.

Resources and Tools for the Practitioner

A major contribution to the practitioner of Tiedeman and O'Hara's work has been the conceptualization of the career decision-making process and the specification of critical changes in an individual's concepts of self and the career decision-making task (Dudley & Tiedeman, 1977). Vincent Harren (1966; 1978), in particular, has translated the seven-phase psychological process described by the theory into an intriguing diagnostic tool useful for locating which phase of career decision-making an individual is in at a given time. Harren's *Vocational Decision-Making Checklist* (VDC) (1965; 1966) and his more recent *Assessment of Career Decision-Making* (ACDM) (1978) were constructed to test empirically Tiedeman and O'Hara's vocational decision-making paradigm. Research to date demonstrates considerable construct validity for the instrument and the theory upon which it was based (Harren, 1978). An interesting extension of these early conceptualizations of decision making has been the search for independent variables such as cognitive style, sex role socialization, and age, which appear to significantly impact upon the staging of the career decision-making process (Tiedeman, Katz, Miller-Tiedeman, & Osipow, 1978).

Implications for the Career Counseling Process

The theoretical formulations of Tiedeman and his associates have done much to shape the thinking of career development researchers and practitioners along psychodynamic and structural cognitive lines (Kroll, Dinklage, & Lee et al., 1970). Linking the theoretical heritage of psychodynamic theorists with developmental psychologists, Tiedeman and his associates have strongly shaped a view of career choice-making as a *planful* process that can be facilitated by the acquisition of both generic cognitive processes and specific career related kinds of knowledge and experience. In that context, career guidance and counseling practice is largely a process of linking significant educational experiences with appropriately appearing developmental discontinuities.

Evaluating the Theory

In an evaluation of various theories of career choice, Carkhuff and his associates (Carkhuff, Alexik, & Anderson, 1967) endorsed the efforts of Tiedeman and his associates in attempting to integrate a wide range of different theoretical formulations into a choherent theory. In that same article, however, they faulted these theorists for their "esoteric" and overextensive efforts at theory building and for the limited way in which these extensive theoretical links were tested out empirically.

Truly, the theory spells out several different levels of needed empirical investigation. Whatever might be said for the esoteric qualities of the theory overall, the career decision process described in the theory received substantial support. Heller (1976), Perry (1968), and Hilton (1962) are but a few of the theorists who have substantiated that the career decision-making process is not an explicit, logical, "open-and-shut" process. Instead, as Heller (1976) noted, it is rather a "muddling through" process involving the acquisition of greater and greater clarity regarding both what needs to be done in decision making and what are the outcomes of such decision making.

KRUMBOLTZ'S SOCIAL LEARNING THEORY OF CAREER SELECTION

Krumboltz's social-learning model of career selection, the only new theory of career choice to be formulated in the last decade, suggests a rationale for career selection based upon a social learning model of human behavior. The theory suggests that career preferences, occupational skills, and an individual's selection of educational experiences, occupations, and fields of work are both the composite and consequence of many past and present experiences and the cause of anticipation of future experiences. These experiences may be classified into four sets of factors: (1) genetic endowment and special abilities, (2) environmental conditions and events, (3) specific learning experiences, and (4) a set of "task approach" skills (see Figure 2-3 for a listing of the characteristics comprising

I. "ENVIRONMENTAL" FACTORS
(These factors influence the individual but are generally beyond his or her control, at least in any immediate sense. They are not amenable to change through counseling.)
  A. Genetic Endowment and Special Abilities
     (1) Race, (2) Sex, (3) Physical Characteristics, (5) Intelligence, (6) Music and Art Abilities, and (7) Muscular Coordination
  B. Environmental Conditions and Events
     (1) Number and Nature of Job Opportunities, (2) Number and Nature of Training Opportunities, (3) Social Policies and Procedures for Selecting Trainees and Workers, (4) Rate of Return for Various Occupations, (5) Labor, (6) Natural, (7) Technological, (8) Social, (9) Educational, and (10) Family and Neighborhood Structures

II. "PSYCHOLOGICAL" FACTORS
(These processes and skills determine a person's thoughts, feelings and actions. Counselors try to help clients understand and change these "inner influencers.")
  A. Past Learning Experiences
  B. Task Approach Skills (Abilities and predispositions for coping with and interpreting the environment in relation to self and predicting future events.)
     (1) Value Clarifying Skills, (2) Goal Setting Skills, (3) Skills in Predicting Future Views, (4) Alternative Generating Skills, (5) Information Seeking Skill, (6) Estimating Skills, (7) Skills in Reinterpreting Past Events, (8) Skills in Eliminating and Selecting Alternatives, (9) Planning Skills, and (10) Generalizing Skills

Figure 2-3. Social Learning Analysis: Factors Influencing Career Decision. Adapted from J.D. Krumboltz et al. A social learning theory of career selection. *The Counseling Psychologist,* 1976, *6,* 71-73.

each of these four sets of factors). These sets of factors influence each other in reciprocal ways (Krumboltz, Mitchell, & Jones, 1976; Mitchell, Jones, & Krumboltz, 1979).

Krumboltz and his associates posit that there are three distinctive types of outcomes of the interactions of these four sets of influencing factors: (1) self-observation generalizations, (2) task approach skills, and (3) actions. As a result of learning experiences, an individual can observe his/her performance in relation to the performance of others and can make generalizations and evaluations of that performance. ". . . Because the human being is capable of speech, she/he is able to utter statements which report these observations and conclusions. Comparison with others is usually part of the process, but idealized standards can be learned against which one's behavior is compared" (Krumboltz, Mitchell, & Jones, 1976). Self-observation generalizations, defined as overt or covert self-statements evaluating one's own actual or vicarious performance in relation to learned standards, result. Such self-observation generalizations and conclusions may, according to the theory, not be accurate, or rather they may be a function of the setting or the persons with whom one is associating; the result, however, is such psychological attributes as self-descriptions of traits and interests.

Task-approach skills are a second theorized outcome of the interaction of environmental and personal factors. Krumboltz and his associates contend that "human beings are capable of relating their observations of themselves and alter their environment in such way as to make possible projections into the future as well as inferences about the past. . ." (1967). Task approach skills, defined as cognitive and performance abilities and emotional predispositions for coping with the environment, are used by an individual to interpret one's experience in light of self-observation generalizations and to make covert and overt predictions about future events. Such task approach skills may include work habits, mental sets, perceptual and thought process, performance standards and values, problem orienting, and emotional responses (Krumboltz et al., 1976). Krumboltz and Baker (1973) have related the concept of task approach skills more specifically to career development with the specification of a number of "career development management" skills. These skills include value clarifying, goal setting, predicting future events, alternatives generating, information seeking, estimating, reinterpreting past events, eliminating and selecting alternatives, planning, and generalizing.

Outcome behaviors are the ultimate result of the above-mentioned processes, with each behavior generating consequences that affect the relative frequency of similar behaviors in the future.

Resources and Tools for the Practitioner

Krumboltz and his associates' formulations about the career selection process are relatively new and untested. They provide, however, several advantages to the practitioner. First, the theory suggests a means by which client self-attitudes and behaviors might be acquired, maintained, and/or changed. Thoresen and Ewart (1978) contend that understanding how career attitudes and choices are formed permits the counselor to help clients take a more active role in changing the direction of their lives. Secondly, utilizing a cognitive-social-learning perspective permits the application of generic behavior change strategies designed for other contexts and life problems. Such generic strategies, commonly referred to as behavioral self-control strategies, are defined as learnable cognitive processes that a person uses to develop controlling actions, which in turn function to alter factors influencing behavior (Thoresen, 1976; Thoresen & Coates, 1976). Thoresen and Ewart (1978), in a provocative article entitled "Behavioral Self-Control and Career Development," propose a model for understanding the process involved in acquiring relevant career task approach skills, Krumboltz's CDM's, as well as a suggested method for getting the client to perform the different task approach skills.

Implications for the Career Counseling Process

This social-learning-model of career selection suggests a role for the career counselor as a behavioral engineer developing multicomponent educational programs to teach a variety of different skills in career decision making, both for a specific setting or for specific client groups. To paraphase Thoresen and Ewart (1978), advocates of Krumboltz's theoretical approach, the career counselor's role embraces the task of teaching people how "to become better architects of their own lives."

Evaluating the Theory

There are no published studies to date attempting to document or validate various aspects of Krumboltz's theory. Clearly there is a need for such research. Behaviorists contend that such research should be longitudinal in nature and should be intensive descriptions of individuals. Children, adolescents, or adult career changes should be studied intensively by carefully choosing and systematically varying certain critical cognitive and social variables.

COMPARING CAREER CHOICE THEORIES

In reading about each of these career choice theories, one is struck by the diversity of ideas regarding both why people make the choices they do and how they make such choices. Some theorists, such as John Holland, conceptualize the career choice process largely as an *event* that occurs sometime during late adolescence. Such theorists are concerned with specifying the factors and/or processes at work in career choice and predicting the direction of such choices. In contrast, theorists such as Donald Super, David Tiedeman, and John Krumboltz view career choice as but one event in a long-term *sequence* of events that are influenced by an array of factors operating over the lifetime of the individual. These theorists focus upon describing the career choice process rather than predicting the content or structure of such choices. Who is right? Are the concepts of Super, for instance, correct, or not? Or are Holland's formulations closer to the truth? If so, which set of ideas should guide the practitioners in developing their own ideas about career choice behavior?

A major dichotomy in thinking exists among these four career theorists regarding the most critical aspects of career behavior and of how career counseling professionals can facilitate such behavior. Figure 2-4 illustrates the dimensions along which these theorists vary. These dimensions are their views on the nature of career choice, the purpose of their theory building, the philosophical/research tradition of the theory, the major explanatory concepts, the role of the counselor, the conceptual tools and counseling resources emanating from the theory, and the qualitative/empirical support for the theory.

As one looks at these differing views on the nature of career choice, the purpose of the theory, and the philosophical/research tra-

COMMON CRITERIA	HOLLAND	SUPER	TIEDEMAN	KRUMBOLTZ
Nature of career choice	Point-in-time event	Evolutionary process	Evolutionary process	Evolutionary process
Purpose of the theory	To provide a link between persons and job world and to explain/predict a specific job choice	To describe the process of which self and reality are comprised — specify skills and tasks	To describe the process of career identity development and differentiation	Specify those antecedent and consequent events affecting career choice process
Philosophical/research tradition of theorist	Differential	Phenomenological Developmental	Cognitive Developmental	Behavioral — learning theory
Major explanatory concepts	Jobs as people Environments Differentiation of interests	Vocational maturity Vocational self-concept	Career choice Integration and differentiation Decision-making stages	Self-observation Generalizations Task approach Skills
Role of the counselor	Informational	Educational and corrective	Design of educational experiences	Behavioral engineer
Conceptual tools and counseling resources	Tests: SDS and VPI Occupations Finder Coding system	Assessment of career maturity (CMI & CDI) Career development stage model	Assessment of stages of decision making and interactional variables	Concept of generic self-management skills
Qualitative evidence regarding theory's validity	Relationships among jobs and types tested partially	Self and occupation concepts related; Stage and task model limited applicability	Validation of increasingly complex formulations of decision-making task	Limited attempts at validation

Figure 2-4. Comparing Career Choice and Development Theories.

dition of the theory, one is reminded of the old tale of the three blind men attempting to identify an elephant for the first time. In attempting to discern what kind of beast it was, each blind man utilized only the data immediately available to him by touch. Since each blind man touched a different part of the elephant, the three men formed different conclusions as to the nature of the beast. Similarly, each of the four career theorists presented here was influenced by the philosophical lens through which he viewed the nature of the beast. Holland, in the differential tradition, examined individual's choices through the use of large scale correlational sampling and examined the relationship among specific predictor variables. In contrast, Super, influenced by the developmental tradition, was involved in more longitudinal intensive small sample research designs, which allowed him to examine career behavior over time. Tiedeman, in acknowledging his debt to the cognitive developmentalists, verified the cognitive framework of career decision making through sampling of special clientele at specific ages and stages and utilized age-stratified sampling techniques. Krumboltz, in following the social learning tradition, translated many general learning principles into the specific context of career selection.

The role of the career counseling professional is also viewed quite differently within each of these theoretical perspectives. Holland views the actual role of the career professional more as an information organizer. In contrast, Super, Tiedeman, and Krumboltz view the career professional as a designer of educational experiences anticipating needed skills and competencies at certain key life points.

While at first glance these theorists may appear to hold competing explanations of the same phenomena, a closer look reveals that each has chosen to examine and explain a different facet of career behavior. Rather than reject competing explanations of career behavior in favor of one such theory, each of these theories provide a rich source of ideas for understanding a different part of the "beast." Examining the relative focus and contributions of each of these theories can be a first step in developing a more comprehensive personal theory of career choice.

SUMMARY

The career choice theories presented in this chapter have not been described in exhaustive detail, nor have all of the significant theories been presented. The theories discussed, however, have been selected to illustrate the broad array of different perspectives on the career choice process from which the career counselor can draw in formulating his/her ideas about this phenomena.

BIBLIOGRAPHY

Brim, O. Socialization through the life cycle. In O. Brim and H. Wheeler (Eds), *Socialization after childhood: Two essays.* Boston: Wiley, 1966.

Buehler, C. *Der menschliche lebenslauf als psycholoisches problem.* Leipzig: Hirzel, 1933.

Carkhuff, R., Alexik, M., and Anderson, S. Do we have a theory of vocational. choice? *Personnel and Guidance Journal,* 1967, *45,* 335-345.

Crites, J. A model for the measurement of vocational maturity, *Journal of Counseling Psychology,* 1961, *9,* 255-260.

Crites, J. Measurement of vocational maturity in adolescence: I. Attitude test of the vocational maturity inventory. *Psychological Monographs,* 1965, *72,* (No. 595).

Crites, J. The Career Maturity Inventory. In D. E. Super (Ed.), *Measuring vocational maturity for counseling and evaluation.* Falls Church, Va.: American Personnel and Guidance Association Press, 1974.

Dudley, E., and Tiedeman, D. *Career development: Exploration and commitment.* Muncie, Indiana: Accelerated Development, 1977.

Edwards, K., Nafziger, D., and Holland, J. Differentiation of occupational perceptions among different age groups. *Journal of Vocational Behavior,* 1974, *4,* 311-318.

Gilligan, C. *In a different voice: Psychological theory and women's development.* Cambridge, Mass: Harvard University Press, 1982.

Ginzberg, E., Ginsburg, S., Axelrand, S., and Herman, J. *Occupational choice: An approach to a general theory.* New York: Columbia University Press, 1951.

Gottfredson, G., Holland, J., and Owaga, D. *Dictionary of Holland occupations codes.* Palo Alto, Calif.: Consulting Psychologists Press, 1982.

Grandy, T., and Stahmann, R. Family influence on college students' vocational educational choice: Predicting from Holland's personality types. *Journal of College Student Personnel,* 1974, *15,* 404-409.

Greenhaus, J. An investigation of the role of career salience in vocational behavior. *Journal of Vocational Behavior,* 1971, *1,* 209-216.

Gribbons, W., and Lohnes, P. Shift in adolescent vocational values. *Personnel and Guidance Journal,* 1965, *44,* 248-252.

Harren, V. A study of the vocational decision-making process among college males. (Doctoral dissertation, University of Texas, 1964). *Dissertation Abstracts International,* 1965, *25,* 5114.

Harren, V. *Assessment of career decision-making: Preliminry research and user's manual.*

(Unpublished manuscript), 1978.

Hauselman, A. Personality and the choice of an undergraduate major: A test of Holland's theory. (Unpublished doctoral dissertation, University of Kentucky, 1971) *Dissertation Abstracts International,* 1972, *33,* 9397.

Heller, F. Decision processes: An analysis of power sharing of senior organizational levels. In R. Dubin (ed.) *Handbook of work, organization, and society.* Chicago: Rand McNally and Company, 1976.

Hilton, T. E. *Cognitive processes in career decision making.* Pittsburgh, Pa: Carnegie Institute of Technology, 1962.

Holland, J. *The psychology of vocational choice.* Waltham, Mass.: Blaisdell, 1966.

Holland, J. *Making vocational choices: A theory of careers.* Englewood Cliffs, N.J.: Prentice Hall, 1973.

Holland, J. Some practical remedies for providing vocational guidance for everyone. *Educational Researcher,* 1974, *3,* 9-15.

Holland, J. *Manual for the vocational preference inventory.* Palo Alto, Calif.: Consulting Psychologists Press, 1975.

Holland, J. *The occupations finder.* Palo Alto, Calif.: Consulting Psychologists Press, 1977.

Holland, J. *The self-directed search.* Palo Alto, Calif.: Consulting Psychologists Press, 1977.

Holland, J., Gottfredson, G., and Nafziger, D. Testing the validity of some theoretical signs of vocational decision-making ability. *Journal of Counseling Psychology,* 1975, *22,* 411-422.

Holland, J., and Gottfredson, G. Using a typology of persons and environments to explain careers: Some extensions and clarifications. In J. Whiteley and A. Resnikoff (Eds.), *Career counseling.* Monterey, Calif.: Brooks/Cole, 1978, pp. 146-170.

Holland, J., Hollifield, J., Nafziger, D., and Helms, S. *A guide to the self-directed career program: A practical and inexpensive vocational guidance system.* Center for Social Organization of Schools, Report No. 126. Baltimore: John Hopkins University, 1972 (ERIC Document Reproduction Service No. 064-516).

Hughes, H. Vocational choice, level and consistency: An investigation of Holland's theory on an employed sample. *Journal of Vocational Behavior,* 1972, *2,* 377-388.

Hunt, R. Self and other semantic concepts in relation to choice of a vocation. *Journal of Applied Psychology,* 1967, *51,* 242-246.

Kroll, A., Dinklage, L., Lee, J., Morley, E., and Wilson, E. *Career development: Growth in crisis.* New York: John Wiley, 1970.

Krumboltz, J., and Baker, R. Behavioral counseling for vocational decision. In H. Borow (Ed.), *Career guidance for a new age.* Boston: Houghton-Mifflin, 1973.

Krumboltz, J., Mitchell, A., and Jones, G. A social learning theory of career selection. *The Counseling Psychologist,* 1976, *6,* 71-73.

Lowentha, M. Psychological variation across the adult life course: Frontiers for research and policy. *Gerontologist,* 1975, *15,* 6-12.

Mitchell, A., Jones, G., and Krumboltz, J. *Social learning and career decision-making.* Cranston, R. I.: Carroll Press, 1979.

Neugarten, B. *Middle age and aging.* Chicago: Chicago University Press, 1968.
Osherson, S. *Holding on or letting go: Men and career change at mid-life.* New York: Free Press, 1980.
Perry, W. *Forms of intellectual and ethical development.* Cambridge, Mass.: Harvard University, Bureau of Student Counsel, 1968.
Super, D. A theory of vocational development. *American Psychologist,* 1953, *8,* 185-190.
Super, D. *The psychology of careers.* New York: Harper and Row, 1957.
Super, D. *Work values inventory manual.* Boston: Houghton-Mifflin, 1970.
Super, D. A life-span, life-space approach to career development. *Journal of Vocational Behavior,* 1980, *16,* 282-298.
Thompson, A., Linderman, R., Super, D., Jordan, J., and Myers, R. *Career development inventory.* Palo Alto: Consulting Psychologists Press, 1980.
Thoresen, C. *Self-control: Learning how to C.A.R.E. for yourself.* Madison, Wisconsin, Counseling Films, Box 1047, 1976 (Film).
Thoresen, C., and Coates, T. Behavioral self-control: Some clinical concerns. In M. Hersen, R. Eisler, and R. Miller (Eds), *Progress in behavior modification.* (Vol. 2) New York: Academic Press, 1976, pp. 301-352.
Thoresen, C., and Ewart, C., Behavioral self-control and career development. In J. Whiteley and A. Resnikoff (Eds.), *Career counseling.* Monterey, Calif.: Brooks/Cole, 1978, pp. 171-206.
Tiedeman, D., Katz, M., Miller-Tiedeman, A., and Osipow, S. *The cross-sectional story of early career development.* Washington, D.C.: American Personnel and Guidance Association Press, 1978.
Tiedeman, D., and O'Hara, R. Vocational self-concept in adolescence. *Journal of Counseling Psychology,* 1959, *6,* 292-301.
Tiedeman, D. and O'Hara, R. *Career development: Choice and adjustment.* New York: College Entrance Examination Board, 1963.
Westbrook, B., Cutts, C., Madison, S., and Arcia, M. The validity of the Crites model of career maturity. *Journal of Vocational Behavior,* 1980, *16,* 249-281.
Ziegler, J. Self concept, occupational member concept, and occupational interest area relationships in male college students, *Journal of Counseling Psychology,* 1970, *17,* 133-136.

Part II
COUNSELING STRATEGIES

INTRODUCTION

Chapters 3 through 8 present something old and something new for professionals concerned with vocational guidance and career counseling.

Chapter 3 presents an old, familiar friend and tool in guidance: the information services. Most professional writing about information and its use in vocational counseling discusses almost exclusively the different kinds of information and how it should be presented to counselees. Reardon, in this chapter, takes a more complex and aggressive stance in discussing the use of information in counseling. He presents not only the problems and purposes but also the acquisition and actual use of information in the decision-making process. Finally, he ends with some very practical comments and suggestions for the counselor using information in facilitating career development.

Assessment, in one form or another, has been identified and discussed as an indispensible process in vocational guidance since the days of Frank Parsons. In Chapter 4, MacAleese takes a refreshing and critical look at the broad area of assessment as it applies to minorities, women, employed persons, and other groups, and then he discusses at length the assessment of aptitudes, achievement, interests, vocational maturity, and values. Specific inventories and tests are briefly analyzed. In Chapter 5, Jones draws upon history, research, and contemporary practice to forcefully argue for the legitimacy and use of self-assessment in career interventions. He reviews recent developments in this area, including new instruments and techniques that are available to practitioners, and notes some cautions for practitioners. Together, these two chapters bring new information to bear on a topic of critical importance to career specialists.

The contents of Chapters 6, 7, and 8 generally are not found in books dealing with career development, and in this sense, represent something of a departure. Montgomery's chapter, "Contractual Arrangements," takes a straightforward, no-nonsense behavioral approach to the advantages and characteristics of this technique, along with a step-by-step description of how the counselor should negotiate and execute various types of agreements and contracts. He includes sample contracts and statements that might be used in such career counseling arrangements.

In Chapter 7, Cochran has analyzed literature and reflected on the proper use of groups in the facilitation of career development. He presents a clear rationale and then quickly moves to the presentation of three validated career development groups: Vocational Exploration Group, Job Club, and Life Planning Workshop. For each, Cochran carefully explains the procedures and offers a brief critique.

Finally, Sampson presents a comprehensive review of the use of computers in career development in Chapter 8. He focuses on the systems presently being used to support career counseling practice for youth and adults. Sampson also reviews topics that practitioners might best consider in adopting one computer-based system rather than another. He closes with thoughtful sections on the evaluation of these systems and where the emerging technology may lead those working in career development.

Counseling, the most familiar method of direct client service, has been the primary means of helping people with career development problems from the earliest days of the Vocational Guidance Movement. The six chapters in Part II are designed to provide the practitioner with both some old and some new innovative techniques and ideas that can be translated into improved professional career counseling practice.

CHAPTER 3

USE OF INFORMATION IN CAREER COUNSELING

Robert C. Reardon

WHILE the lack of information is generally viewed as one of the basic problems in career decision making, and Frank Parsons more than seventy years ago identified information as the second essential step in vocational counseling, surveys continue to report counselor problems in how to locate and use information in career counseling (McDaniels & Nelson, 1977). Sinick (1956) observed that although the ability to use occupational information is one of the professional competencies identified as needing professional preparation there is scant knowledge about the topic, and it may remain "one of the weakest links in the counseling process" (Brammer & Shostrum, 1959).

The purpose of this chapter is to provide counselors with some ideas that will make this counseling competency a stronger link in professional practice. The chapter begins with an analysis of some of the problems of using information in career counseling. It continues with discussion of the various purposes for using information, information as a part of the decision-making process, the classification of information methods, and an analysis of client needs for information. Finally, the chapter focuses on specific suggestions for the counselor, with respect to personal attitudes and the acquisition of new skills.

PROBLEMS

There are several problems the counselor will encounter in using occupational information. One difficulty involves the poor quality of the materials, although improvements have been made in recent years. Some materials, for example, fail to describe the psychosocial aspects of work, such as the exercise of personal values and attitudes in the job, the status/position of the worker, the authority relationships involved, the patterns of social interactions among workers or the public, the contribution of the job to a larger social good, and the life-style of the worker away from the job. Chapman and Katz (1982), in an extensive study of the use of career information by high school students, noted that poor quality of the material is compounded by the lack of a suitable career decision-making context for using the material. They noted that client career goals and an explicit decision-making process must accompany the effective use of career information.

Other difficult problems have to do with the counselees themselves. Regardless of their good intentions, many have trouble getting motivated to search for and use information (Chapman & Katz, 1982). This may be especially true of clients with low social and interpersonal skills (Miller, 1982). The "law of least effort" suggests that persons first use their peer-kin network to meet problem-solving information needs (Hudson & Danish, 1980). This may be especially true of persons not having extensive educational backgrounds or experience using professional resources. Unfortunately, verbal ability and academic success appear to be important factors associated with the effective use of career information in career planning (Chapman & Katz, 1982). Other counselees may be unable to choose among competing alternatives that each have similar advantages/ disadvantages, or they may have poor job stereotypes based on limited personal work experience, biased information from friends, parents, and television, or poor social attitudes. However, the most difficult kind of counseling problem probably relates to the counselee whose job goals are inappropriate or who is being pressured into a choice by parents or peers. In this instance, the use of information is an especially delicate matter requiring expert professional counseling skills.

In addition to inadequate information materials and unmotivated or confused counselees, both counselors and clients may be very unfamiliar with the *sources* for and *use* of occupational information in counseling. Although experienced counselors know that many counselees come to counseling with specific requests for information, some of these counselors have failed to develop and maintain their professional expertise in this area. Thus, both counselors and clients have experienced a "learned helplessness" (Hudson & Danish, 1980) because of an inability to overcome barriers to the effective location and use of information needed for career planning.

Goldman (1967) has analyzed this problem as a dilemma that counselors must face squarely if they are to use information successfully in counseling. Some counselors feel that using objective facts and data disturbs the subjective nature of the counseling relationship. The use of information interferes with the counselor's ability to focus on the client's feelings and attitudes. Moreover, in using information counselors are likely to play an authoritative role, not unlike physicians. The counselor prescribes the appropriate information as an antidote for the counselee's decision-making ills. Of course, if counselors are unsure about the prescription, e.g. the reliability and validity of the information materials, they are in a precarious position to be helpful. As Goldman (1967) stated:

> . . . If counselors don't use the most complete and up-to-date appraisal and environmental information possible, they are neglecting to provide their clients with one of the important elements of a good plan or decision. . . . On the other hand, bringing assessment and environmental information into the counseling room seems to disturb the counseling process, by shifting from feelings/values/goals to facts, and by evoking from the counselor persuasiveness and defensiveness, rather than acceptance, clarification, interpretation.

In short, problems in the use of occupational information center around the nature and quality of the information materials, the needs of the counselee, and the counselor's perception of the helping role. The following sections of this chapter focus on ways to overcome these problems.

PURPOSES

The purposes for the use of information in counseling are quite varied. Some purposes, for example, are quite unrealistic given the limitations of the materials, the counselee's readiness, and so forth.

Samler (1964) observed that information should be used for self-exploration, vicarious role assumption, and self-understanding. Patterson (1964) has noted that occupational information should be used in counseling to help clients clarify the goals they want to reach and move in the direction they want to go, assuming the means to the goal are not illegal or injurious to self or others. However, what if the client's goals are poorly planned; what if the client is unmotivated?

Rusalem (1954) identified two purposes for using information in counseling. The exploratory role of information would help counselees come to view themselves as adults — to test reality as they read or listen to information. One may think of students who are adrift in their decision making and then find reassurance in being able to reaffirm their vague perceptions of what they thought a physical therapist did with what being a physical therapist actually involves. The information is thus used as a stimuli to help counselees elicit, explore, and clarify their needs, values, attitudes, aspirations, and expectations of their work role and self-concept. They can project themselves into various occupations and learn more about how and why their perceptions and cognitions function as they do. The verification role of information involves the continuous reality test over a period of time. The counselee examines conflicts and inconsistencies between the job and self-concept. The purpose of information here is to help clarify and understand feelings subsequent to a choice.

Isaacson (1971) has surveyed the literature and identified four purposes for the use of information in counseling:

Motivational. — Information may be used to stimulate the counselee to identify alternatives or confirm tentative choices. This can sometimes be an exhilarating experience for the counselee, because it is a step in the direction of autonomy and the beginning of career planning.

Instructional. — The use of information here involves a more careful, systematic assessment of the counselee's needs in order to design appropriate learning experiences. The focus, unlike *adjustive*, which follows, is on cognitive understanding of a particular occupation or, more broadly, the process of career development. The purpose of information may involve attitude change, increased understanding of the career decision-making process, or other goals. It must be assumed, of course, that the counselor is sufficiently informed and can help the counselee locate, use, and evaluate the appropriate materials.

Adjustive. — Information can help the client refocus and accommodate discrepancies between plans and success in a field. The purpose is to help correct perceptual distortions of self or the environment. As noted earlier, a typical problem involves over- and underestimates of potential self-achievement. Printed or canned information is probably most appropriate here because it enables the counselor to limit the presentation of information and focus instead on the couselee's perceptions of the information.

Distributive. — The purpose of information in this instance primarily involves placement in, rather than selection of, an occupation. The counselor is primarily involved in helping the counselee locate and use appropriate job information before entering a specific job position.

Thus, the purposes of using information in career counseling are varied. The role of the counselor in using information depends on the situation, e.g. the location of the counseling agency, and the needs of the counselee. In the case of most career counselors, it seems that all four purposes identified by Isaacson would be appropriate. The implications for counselor practice are significant and will be amplified in later sections of this chapter.

DECISION MAKING

A bit of reflection suggests that a focal point of most counseling involves planning and decision-making activities. Whether the counselee is concerned about running away from home, marriage, coming out of the closet, or suicide, the matter of choice is a central part in counseling.

Virtually all models of decision making, of which choice may be seen as a part, stress the importance of information. Figure 3-1 graphically depicts the process (Dunphy, 1969).

Step No. 2, Stating Alternatives, basically involves an environmental assessment and information search of the options available for the solution to the problem or the answer to the question identified in Step No. 1. It is apparent that Step No. 2 is especially critical in career counseling and also one of the key problem areas noted earlier. For example, it was suggested that there are basic

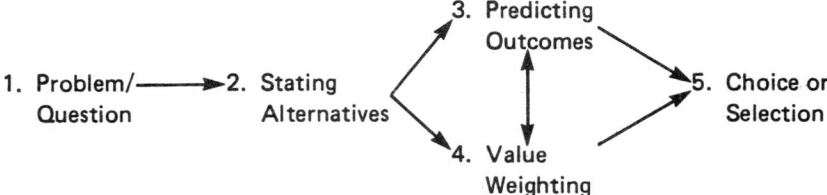

Figure 3-1.

weaknesses in the quality of the information available: counselees are either unmotivated to locate the needed information or they are looking for inappropriate information; counselors are ignorant and/or conflicted over their role in helping the counselee locate and use information. Thus, it is somewhat meaningless for counselors to focus on Steps 1, 3, and 4, where they are probably most comfortable, because the quality of the choice as an outcome of decision making (Step 5) can be dramatically determined by what happens in Step No. 2, the information-alternative search.

If counselors are committed to focusing on the client's desired outcomes, the use of information in counseling fits into the decision-making process by helping the counselee to clearly specify the nature of the problem and/or questions to be answered, to identify and locate all relevant information about the alternatives, and to clarify those alternatives and examine the likelihood for desirable outcomes. From this vantage point, counselors fail to perform satisfactorily if they are not helpful at Step No. 2, and from the counselee's point of view, this is likely the area of greatest need.

ACQUIRING INFORMATION

One possible reason for the lack of counselor helpfulness in the use of information involves the typically passive approach the counselor utilizes. The strategy or method used in helping the counselee locate information can be quite varied, and must be tailored to suit the person, time, and place.

Albert Thompson (Hollis & Hollis, 1969) has classified the methods by which counselees might obtain information. They range

Classification	Examples
1. Prestructured or fixed	a. Publications. b. Audio-visual materials. c. Planned programs, such as visiting speakers, career days, etc.
2. Input controlled by counselee	a. Programmed instruction, such as SRA Job Experience kits. b. Computer-based Systems, e.g. SIGI, DISCOVER, CHOICES, GIS c. Interviews with a worker.
3. Simulation of the situation	a. Role playing or career games. b. Synthetic work environment, such as a hospital room recreated for nurses training.
4. Real situation	a. Direct observation, such as "shadowing" a worker or a field visit. b. Direct exploration, such as volunteer work or participation in cooperative education. c. Actual job experience.

Figure 3-2.

from those in which the counselee or counselor have minimum involvement (passive role) to those in which they have maximum involvement (active role).

This classification scheme has some special implications for the counselor. At level No. 1 the counselor can simply open a file or flip a switch to provide information for the client. At level No. 4, however, the counselor would have to be more actively involved with the client in using the information. The counselor would have to have firsthand knowledge of the referral resources and maybe even be able to create such information resources especially for the counselee. It is also important to note that as counselees move towards information sources where they have maximum control, the impact of the information on feelings, values, and attitudes probably increases. While the counselee may not be able to get in touch with feelings about nursing from reading a printed brochure, it will probably be easier following a role play exercise or volunteer work experience. All of this, of course, creates another bind for the counselor who wants to passively focus primarily on Steps 3 and 4 of the decision-making model. Unless the counselor actively helps the counselee locate and use career information in which the counselee has maximum involvement, the counselor is not really being fully helpful in the decision-making process.

The study by Chapman and Katz (1982) showed that a wide variety of career information resources are being used in secondary schools. Of the thirteen categories of resources identified, the most frequently used category was bound references (98%), followed by school arranged experiences (95%), occupational briefs and kits (91%), educational directories for occupations (86%), and personal contact with school staff (86%). Least common were simulations (18%), computerized systems (24%), and noncomputerized sorting materials (keysorts and needlesorts — 34%). The most common single resource was the *Occupational Outlook Handbook* (92%), followed by the *Dictionary of Occupational Titles* and conferences with counselors (both 83%).

Besides school-based resources, Chapman and Katz identified twenty-three commonly used external occupational information resources: they include classes of people outside of school (relatives, friends, someone in the line of work of interest, employment service representatives, former students, employers, college admissions officers, armed forces recruiters, someone else outside of school), seven places to get information outside of school (public library, district or regional career center, state employment service, a local college, a private employment agency, an armed forces recruiting office), and seven kinds of nonschool activities (work, watching people at work, watching TV, watching movies, clubs, general reading, or reading for fun).

McDaniels (1982) has observed several events during 1950 to 1980 that have brought more sophistication to career information activities, including expanded roles of (1) the Department of Labor, (2) commercial publishers, (3) media, (4) technology, (5) personal information, and (6) career information. McDaniels also noted the accomplishments of the National Occupational Information Coordinating Committee (NOICC) in establishing policies and coordinating federal and state activities. State Occupational Information Coordinating Committees (SOICCs) have developed Occupational Information Systems (OIS) and Career Information Delivery Systems (CIDS), in addition to coordinating various state agency efforts.

COUNSELEE NEEDS

Before describing the ways in which the counselor can improve the use of information in career counseling, it is important to discuss briefly some of the important needs of counselees.

As noted earlier, most counselees probably want help in decision-making and planning. They frequently come for vocational counseling with some fairly well defined information needs. However, in addition to the need for information, some authorities have raised the question as to whether or not counselees actually use the information or if they use it appropriately (Biggers, 1971).

For some clients it is especially important that the information be easily accessible and comprehensible. Some other counselees are in special need of encouragement and motivation to move ahead in the planning activities. Others have special needs for reality-based experiences in this age of rapid economic change.

The most difficult counselee problems involve those instances where an inadequate self-concept is influencing the perception of occupational information (Step No. 1 in decision making). Fear of change, lack of interpersonal skills, fear of failure, perceived barriers to growth, parental aspirations, and other psychological influences can cause perceptual distortions of information, which then significantly complicate the decision-making process. Rusalem (1954) observed that "it is not what exists in 'reality' in a vocation which enters into occupational thinking, but what comprises the individual's personal perceptions of it." Self-concept, then, is central to the counselee's perception of information, and the counselor must exercise professional skills in determining whether or not the counselee's self-image is sufficiently adequate to engage productively and effectively in career decision-making activities. Miller (1982) suggests that self-esteem is important in information acquisition and reality testing because it influences exploratory behavior.

SUGGESTIONS FOR THE COUNSELOR

While the quality of the materials and the sophistication of counselees may increase, counselors themselves must assume a major responsibility for improving the use of information in career counseling. Unfortunately, there do not seem to be any shortcuts or panaceas for improved practice in this area. Thus, a basic assumption must be that counselors are no longer content to put the use of occupational information in counseling at the bottom of the prestige of practice list — but rather, they view it as an essential function in career counseling worthy of renewed professional attention.

Counselors must learn both content and process of career information. This first step is absolutely essential to the effective use of information in counseling. The counselor must know what information is available, where it is located, and how it can be best used by the counselee. Indeed, the counselors must know the formal, standard information resources so well that they can use them without fumbling or stumbling. *The Occupational Outlook Handbook, The Dictionary of Occupational Titles (DOT)*, and one or more commercially produced filing systems are minimum resources the counselor should know. The *DOT*, for example, can be useful in showing counselees the scope and depth of various occupational areas, the data-people-things concept, the worker traits notion as it relates to the level of occupation and idea of field or occupational groups. When counselors model the use of information as an important treatment resource, the counselee too will realize the importance and value of the information materials.

Ideally, the counselor would also have available the "covert information" described by Overs (1967). This information is not recorded or filed and usually erratically communicated among counselors. It often modifies, amends, corrects, or contradicts the overt (formalized) information. Sources for covert information include present and former clients, informal meetings with administrators, professional contacts, newspapers, observations gathered in field visits, etc. It excludes gossip. The identification and creation of such information requires maximum involvement and participation on the part of the counselor.

Moreover, counselors should stop being defensive and timid about the use of information — they should use everything they know if it will help counselees in their decision making. The appropriate safeguard is to inform the counselee of the nature and source of all information transmitted by the counselor. It seems that counselors have copped out of learning and using career information for two bad reasons: the belief that rapid socioeconomic change will make much occupational information obsolete in a few years and the fear that developing and sharing personal bits of information will limit the counselee's freedom of choice. Both reasons offer little help to the counselee caught up in the confusion of a choice that must be made in the next few days or weeks.

While counselors must be willing to immerse themselves in information, they must also attend to the counselee's perceptions. Counselors must help counselees evaluate the information available — they must facilitate the use of information in the decision-making process. Counselors must know the client well enough to be able to hypothesize how they will react to or use the information presented to focus on the counselee's feelings and attitudes. When it becomes apparent that the client is unprepared to use information, either because of lack of motivation or a perceived threat in the decision-making outcome, counselors must be sufficiently flexible to back off from the information per se and attend to the emotional state of the client.

Some authorities (Goldman, 1967; Hudson & Danish, 1980) have observed that it might be necessary for an information specialist, perhaps a paraprofessional, to dispense information and for the counselor to attend to the client's emotional assimilation of the information. This author suggests that information mastery is still the responsibility of the counselor. However, the professional use of such information involves the exercise of expert, discriminating judgment on the counselor's part. Counselors must be aware of their biases, so that they will not allow the presentation of information to prejudice the counselee towards or away from certain choices. One of the most powerful criticisms of contemporary career counseling practice concerns the counselor's alleged biased direction of the career choices of women and blacks into traditional, stereotyped occupations. It is clear that the professional use of information in career counseling demands the most professional counseling skills and counselor attitudes.

Miller (1982) urges counselors to intervene with unmotivated, anxious clients by reducing the threat posed by the use of exploratory behavior in the social or interpersonal area. Such clients may need to begin information acquisition within a supportive group setting where there is an atmosphere of acceptance, trust, and psychological safety. Some computer-based systems may also provide such a safe, protected setting for career exploration. Unless career counselors first treat the anxiety associated with low self-esteem, clients may be completely unable to venture forth to ask questions of career resource persons, read information materials, shadow persons in occupations, or engage in other reality testing behaviors intended to make them more autonomous or independent.

Other clients experiencing career decision-making problems might need to develop skills in information seeking and acquisition. The counselor can help by providing instruction on the development of such skills, including those in the interpersonal area. Hudson and Danish (1980) noted that counselors might teach clients (1) how to identify information sources, (2) identify the specific behaviors needed to acquire information (personal interviewing skills, library skills, operating a computer terminal, etc.), (3) assessing one's initial competence of the behavior, and (4) developing evaluation criteria for knowing whether or not information needs are met.

The use of modeling procedures in career counseling has been reported by Stewart (1969) and Thoresen, Krumboltz, and Varenhorst (1967). Basically, the procedure involves creating an audio or video tape where a model counselor reinforces the model client's expressions of a high need for information or questions asked. Information-seeking statements can include the following: "I suppose I ought to find out; Can I take a test to find out; What are the requirements for; Maybe I could talk with; Last month I wrote to. . . ." The model counselor uses appropriate verbal and nonverbal reinforcements such as these: "Yes, that would be a good thing to know; I'm glad you're wondering about that because such information is certainly important in your decision; Very good; Mmhmmmm;" nodding, smiling, etc. The model counselor also asks leading questions and helps the client develop a contract as to appropriate next steps.

Research reports suggest that the use of model tapes in conjunction with personal or small group counseling can have a significant effect on the rate of information-seeking behaviors with some counselees (Krumboltz & Schroeder, 1965; Thoresen & Krumboltz, 1967). The use of such modeling procedures is especially important for some unmotivated clients.

Principles for using information in career counseling have been identified by several authorities (Patterson, 1964; Isaacson, 1971; Sinick, 1956). These principles are summarized as follows:

a. There is a recognizable client need, sometimes inferred by the counselor, for information. In some cases, the client's request for information may be premature or the client may not share a perceived need for more information. In either case, the counselor attends to the immediate client needs for learning or decision making and times the presentation of information accordingly.
b. Information is not generally used in an evaluative way to praise or condemn the client, and it is not usually used to manipulate a client to make a certain choice. Of course, it is not appropriate to be absolute in either case, because there are certain exceptional circumstances where information could be used in just these ways.
c. The counselor should seek to maximize clients' location and use of information materials in order to develop their problem-solving skills. The problem here is that too little counselor help can be interpreted as a lack of interest, which is especially important to avoid. To determine just how much help to provide, the counselor must rely on prior experience with the client, assessment of the client's immediate situation, the amount of motivation the client has for solving the problem, etc. A set approach such as reading the material aloud with the client during the counseling hour is sterile and likely to fail in most cases. When in doubt, it is probably best to err in the direction of too little help after a sound relationship has been established. After all, the final responsibility rests with the client, even if that means failure in decision-making activities.
d. The counselor must help the client evaluate and explore the personal meaning of information materials. This is especially true if the purpose for using the information is adjustive or instructive.
e. The selection of the proper means of acquiring the informa-

tion, maximum versus minimum client control, is especially crucial, and requires expert judgment from the counselor. Such factors as the stage in the decision-making process, the amount of time available, the variety of resources available, and the client's reading level would all combine to help determine the selection. Poor readers, for example, might prefer sound-filmstrips or audiotapes, while many college students prefer printed materials, which they can skim rapidly. Ideally, the counselor would have a large resource center available and a wide range of materials from which to choose. Stewart (1969) has identified the acquisition of information in terms of six client behaviors: write, observe, read, listen, visit, and talk. It may be helpful for the counselor to discuss the ranges of these behaviors in detail with the client before selecting the means of acquiring information. Anxious clients with few social skills may need special help before they can visit or talk as a means of securing information.

f. The counselor can maximize client readiness for using information materials by reinforcing the client's needs for information and by generally helping to develop good questions for which answers can be sought.

g. The counselor must make sure that all relevant information (both positive and negative aspects) about an occupation is considered by the counselee. This can be done during the clarification phase after the counselee has gathered some information and is in the process of evaluating it.

h. It is especially important for counselors to help clients focus on the appropriate next step rather than some distant goal. While clients must view each choice as a step in the career development process, they also must view job and educational alternatives from an entry as well as terminal vantage point.

SUMMARY

The use of information in career counseling has been plagued by nagging, difficult problems, but this area of professional activity must assume a new, higher priority in counseling practice. This chapter identified some of the purposes for using information and the diverse means for acquiring information materials. It was suggested that information be viewed in terms of the decision-making process.

Although client needs were identified as an important factor in the improved use of information in counseling, the practicing counselor was identified as the target for primary attention. It was suggested that counselors will have to change their attitude toward the use of information in counseling, and generally become more active in developing their expertise and assuming their responsibility in this area. Some of the counselor binds and hang-ups were identified and solutions were proposed. Traditional principles and new strategies for using information were described.

BIBLIOGRAPHY

Biggers, J. The use of information in vocational decision-making. *Vocational Guidance Quarterly*, 1971, *19*, 177-182.
Brammer, L., and Shostrom, E. *Therapeutic counseling*. Englewood Cliffs, N.J.: Prentice-Hall, 1959.
Chapman, W., and Katz, M. *Summary of a survey of career information systems in secondary schools and assessment of alternative types*. Princeton, N.J.: ETS, 1982.
Dunphy, P. W. (Ed.). *Career development for the college student*. Cranston, R.I.: Carroll Press, 1969.
Goldman, L. Information in counseling: A dilemma. *Personnel and Guidance Journal*, 1967, *46*, 42-46.
Hollis, J., and Hollis, L. *Personalizing information processes: Educational, occupational, and personal-social*. New York: Macmillan, 1969.
Hudson, J. and Danish, S. The acquisition of information: An important life skill. *Personnel and Guidance Journal*, 1980, *59*, 164-167.
Isaacson, L. *Career information in counseling and teaching*. (2nd Ed.) Boston: Allyn & Bacon, 1971.
Krumboltz, J., and Schroeder, W. Promoting career planning through reinforcement and models. *Personnel and Guidance Journal*, 1965, *44*, 19-26.
McDaniels, C. Comprehensive career information systems for the 1980s. *Vocational Guidance Quarterly*, 1982, *30*, 344-350.
McDaniels, C., and Nelson, L. Counselors speak out on occupational information. *Occupation Outlook Quarterly*, 1977, *21*, (3), 14-15.
Miller, M. Interest pattern structure and personality characteristics of clients who seek career information. *Vocational Guidance Quarterly*, 1982, *31*, 28-35.
Overs, R. Covert occupational information. *Vocational Guidance Quarterly*, 1967, *16*, 7-12.
Patterson, C. H. Counseling: Self-clarification — the helping relationship. In H.

Borow, (Ed.), *Man in a world at work.* Boston: Houghton-Mifflin, 1964. pp. 434-459.

Rusalem, H. New insights on the role of occupational information in counseling. *Journal of Counseling Psychology,* 1954, *1,* 84-88.

Samler, J. Psycho-social aspects of work. *Personnel Guidance Journal,* 1961, *39,* 458-465.

Sinick, D. Occupational information in the counseling interview. *Vocational Guidance Quarterly,* 1956, *4,* 145-149.

Stewart, N. Exploring and processing information about educational and vocational opportunities in groups. In J. Krumboltz and C. Thoresen, (Eds), *Behavioral counseling.* New York: Holt, Rinehart, and Winston, 1969. pp. 211-234.

Thoresen, C., and Krumboltz, J. Relationship of counselor reinforcement of selected responses to external behavior. *Journal of Counseling Psychology,* 1967, *14,* 140-144.

Thoresen, C., Krumboltz, J., and Varenhorst, B. Sex of counselors and models: Effect on client career exploration. *Journal of Counseling Psychology,* 1967, *14,* 503-508.

CHAPTER 4

USE OF TESTS

Robert MacAleese

HISTORICALLY, the measurement of vocational interests has been the responsibility of the vocational counselor (Srebalus, Marinelli, & Messing, 1982), and this work, at least in the public's eye, has been exemplified by the trait-and-factory theory of assessment. The counselor's job was simply to match the characteristics of an occupation with the individual's characteristics to indicate the relative suitability of that profession for the person. Once a person found a suitable vocation, they then should remain in it.

Although perhaps never as simple as indicated above, vocational counseling has become an increasingly complex field in the last decade. Social influences such as affirmative-action programs, technological advance, increased individual geographic mobility, and breakdown of traditional male-female occupational roles have led to the concept of "career development" as a dynamic, ever changing process in an individual's life span (Herr, 1977).

What, then, is the proper use of assessment in the entire career-decision process? Zunker (1981) states that, ". . . career decision-making is seen as a continuous counseling process within which all aspects of individuality receive consideration. . . . Thus, assessment results constitute counseling information which can provide the individual with an awareness of increased options and alternatives."

Prediger (1974a) suggests that the role of testing in career guidance is threefold: (1) to stimulate, broaden, and provide focus to career explorations, (2) to stimulate exploration of self in relation to career, and (3) to provide "what if" information with respect to various career choice options.

While much emphasis has been placed on the use of more informal self-assessment techniques because of the controversy surrounding the use of some standardized tests (Bolles, 1978; Kotter, Faux, & McArthur, 1978) to identify career development skills, this chapter will focus on the role of normed, standardized instruments as used in career assessment.

The focus of this chapter will be on the practical uses of various assessment techniques for practicing career counselors. Reasons for using assessment techniques will be given and several types of assessment techniques will be discussed. Finally, two categories of assessment techniques will be mentioned whose use has been given a great deal of professional attention. First, assessment techniques used as selection tools for admission into colleges or professional programs and, second, assessment techniques used in organizations.

USE OF ASSESSMENT RESULTS

Given the nature of assessment — as a mechanism to aid in decision making — those in vocational, educational, or personal counseling, whether performing in academic settings or in community service programs, should have access to assessment devices that will aid their clientele in proper planning.

The two most frequently cited criteria in selecting assessment instruments are essentially (a) validity — does the instrument measure what it is intended to measure? — and (b) reliability — regardless of what the instrument measures, does it do so consistently? Test reliability will frequently exceed validity, but both are very important.

How assessment tools are used also depends on the testing objectives the counselor has in mind. Zunker (1982) states the following three ways assessment results may be used to provide essential information.

1. *Diagnostic uses of information.* This refers to assessment instruments used for either or both of the following purposes: (a) the identification of specific skills or strengths in content areas preparatory to training or beginning work, which would usually be accomplished by the use of achievement and/or aptitude tests, and (b) to increase a

client's self-awareness, which typically would be accomplished through the use of personality tests, career inventories, or interest inventories. The search is basically for the cause or reason behind the client's behavior.

2. *Predictive uses of assessment.* Assessment results here serve a predictive function in that they yield information regarding probable courses of action that the client *might* undertake, such as job training. The focus here is on how successful the various options open to clients may be. Diagnostic uses of assessment instruments frequently lead the counselor to make accurate predictions regarding his client's future capabilities.

3. *Comparative uses of assessment.* Here, the individual's interests, abilities, or values are compared with a criterion group, as is done with the Strong-Campbell Interest Inventory. A key point for counselors to remember is that their client's dissimilarities when compared to a specific occupational group are every bit as important as their similarities.

METHODS OF ASSESSMENT

The major types of assessment techniques used in career counseling are those that measure the factors of aptitude, achievement, interests, vocational maturity, and work values. The purpose of this chapter is to describe several instruments that measure these factors, with the emphasis on how they may provide information of practical value to the counselor.

The assessment techniques that were selected for inclusion in this chapter meet the following criterion: they demonstrate promising and innovative ways of delivering test data that the counselor can use as information. They may be either relatively new instruments or widely-used ones that have been revised in response to new technical knowledge.

ASSESSMENT OF APTITUDES

Aptitude tests are designed to measure specific skills or the chance of a person being able to acquire certain skills through occupational or educational programs (Super & Crites, 1962). For adult clients, they mainly are used as selection devices for occupational training. For younger clients, these tests are often useful in helping them select fields or subjects in which they have the best possibility of success. They can be given whenever pupils in specific fields are having difficulties that appear to be due to lack of specific ability or aptitude. Since the time in a student's career when they might be most concerned over educational or vocational planning would probably be during the eleventh or twelfth grade, these likely are to be the most strategic points for group testing or multiple-aptitude testing.

There are two types of aptitudes: simple and general. Simple aptitudes may be thought of as specific aptitudes, such as finger dexterity, musical ability, or clerical skill, and have a relatively direct relationship to many different kinds of work. General aptitudes are more complex and may in fact be extremely difficult to measure as the occupation requires more advanced levels of specialized training or education. In an increasingly complex technological world, there will be many new professions for which there will initially be no normative data. This occurred in the not-so-distant past, for example, with the first group of space astronauts. Generally, however, counselors should compare their client's aptitude test scores only with groups that have had standardized data collected and should be aware that aptitude scores are correlated more highly with success in job-training programs than with actual success in the field itself.

There are a number of specific aptitude tests that are popular. However, both in terms of cost and time, the administration of multiple-aptitude batteries may be preferable, especially if the client's past career experiences have been varied. Several of the more popular general aptitude tests will be briefly described. For a more detailed discussion of specific aptitude tests, the reader is encouraged to consult Aiken (1979).

General Aptitude Test Battery (GATB)

This is a multiple-aptitude test battery, marketed by the U.S. Department of Labor, and used primarily by state employment counselors. It is composed of twelve tests: eight are paper-and-pencil and four are apparatus tests. They measure nine aptitudes: intelligence (an advantage of many multiple-aptitude tests is that they include an intelligence test), verbal, numerical, spatial, form perception, clerical perception, motor coordination, finger dexterity, and manual dexterity. It is designed for use from the ninth grade through adulthood and the data generated are correlated with over 500 occupations listed in the *Dictionary of Occupational Titles* (DOT). *Occupational Ability Patterns* (OAP's), consisting of minimum scores on the tests, were originally established, but as Srebalus, Marinelli, and Messing (1982) mention, these are now infrequently used by career counselors.

Differential Aptitude Tests (DAT)

The DAT basically consists of six tests: V, verbal reasoning; N, numerical ability; A, abstract reasoning; S, spatial relations; M, mechanical reasoning; and C, clerical speed and accuracy. In addition, there are two achievement tests (spelling and grammar).

Validity data on the DAT have been collected from some 60,000 students in forty-three states and predict high school achievement as well as (to a more limited extent) college achievement. Two follow-up studies have been completed with large samples of high school students, but the predictive validity of the DAT regarding occupational criteria is questionable, as is the case with most other aptitude tests. The general advantages of the DAT are that extensive data collection supports its educational norms and that the test has been developed in a highly competent and technical manner. Its main disadvantages are the amount of time required for administration and its relative lack of occupational norms.

In keeping with the purpose of this chapter, however, the primary concern is not with reviewing the test but rather to point out the innovations that have been developed and how they can be used. The Psychological Corporation has introduced the DAT *Career Planning Program* (CPP), consisting of the following: two forms of the DAT (S or T), The Career Planning Questionnaire (CPQ) and answer sheet, and the Career Planning Report. On the Career Planning Questionnaire, students are asked to list their preferences from among ninety-two school subjects, activities, and sports. They are also asked to list their preferences among one hundred occupations. The time of administration is approximately forty minutes, and it may be either group or individually administered.

Computerized scoring of the answer sheets is also offered, comparing the students patterns of DAT choices with their occupational preferences and most valued activities. Two copies of the report, including a profile of the client's DAT scores and narrative report, are returned to the counselor. This report includes descriptions of the aptitudes measured by the DAT, and informs students whether their choice of career goals seems appropriate considering their aptitudes. It also suggests alternative occupational groups for the student to review.

The accompanying counselor's manual was written by Donald Super in collaboration with the staff of The Psychological Corporation. It presents background information with suggestions for interpretation and use of the report.

How will these additions to the DAT help the practicing counselor? First, the interpretation of the test results is computerized, meaning that the counselor does not have to do an extensive amount of calculations to be certain the raw data accurately match the correct norms. Second, specific suggestions are available in the manual as an aid in communicating the results to the student. As the interpretation of the results is couched in easily understood terms, the counselor may consequently find it easier to involve the parents in a discussion of the report's implications for the student's career development. Normative data based on a nationwide restandardization are also included.

The test gives students more information upon which to make decisions about their career choices at a time when it becomes necessary for them to begin identifying options. It also clearly points out the areas in which probability of the student's further success is greater. One of its biggest advantages is that it takes into account students' future educational plans and choice of school subjects in indicating whether these appear to be congruent with their career goals.

Flanagan Aptitude Classification Tests (FACT)

The FACT consists of sixteen subtests, each corresponding to a specific job behavior, such as Inspection, Coding, Mechanical Ability, Patterns, Comprehension, etc. Little specific information is given regarding the test's validity, and if all subtests are administered, it would take over three hours. However, since the test booklet lists specific test patterns of scores for general occupations, if clients have expressed vocational interests, those specific tests can be given.

Other aptitude tests that are frequently used but that will not be mentioned in detail are (1) The *SRA Primary Mental Abilities-Revised* by Science Research Associates (259 East Erie Street, Chicago, Illinois 60611) and (2) *The Armed Services Vocational Aptitude Tests Battery* (ASVATB), published by the U.S. Department of Defense. Cronbach (1979) mentions that this test may be the most frequently used test of all, exceeding even the GATB.

ASSESSMENT OF ACHIEVEMENT

Achievement tests are designed to test the level of ability that exists at present from what are generally standardized experiences. Seligman (1980) gives four possible reasons for their use:

1. They provide an objective measure of how much a person has learned.
2. They can indicate the relative standing of that person's level of learning in a group (class, school, nationwide sample).
3. They can indicated whether and in what educational areas a person is in need of remediation.
4. They can indicate in what areas the person seems to have marked academic strength.

Achievement tests are numerous. They can be either criterion referenced, which assess achievement relative to a predetermined level of proficiency, or norm referenced, which compare the individual to others who are similar with respect to educational level, age, or other significant variables.

It is often difficult to differentiate aptitude tests from achievement tests. Seligman (1980) suggests that the difference is primarily in the norms: achievement tests are normed on persons who, by and large, have undergone virtually the same types of educational experiences. Aptitude tests cover a much broader range of learning experiences and are more concerned with how assessment data will be predictive of future success.

Achievement assessment, as the assessment of aptitude, can be accomplished by using a battery of general survey tests, a more diagnostically-oriented battery, or a specific test. All can be effective, but again, as with aptitude tests, if cost and time elements are not a major consideration, using a battery of tests to aid in career counseling is often preferable.

California Achievement Tests (CAT)

The California Achievement Test is a multi-aptitude test battery designed to measure reading, mathematics, and language skills on the elementary through high school level. Zunker (1982) mentions that the test has an impressive history of development, with adequate validity and reliability. Scores for each content area are broken down into specific skill scores and compared with national norms.

Stanford Achievement Test

This test measures skills similar to those on the CAT, with the addition of science and social studies skills from Grade 4; normative data is nationwide. Extensive research has been done on this test, which has been revised several times. It is especially useful in helping individuals in making plans for college because of the high levels of skills that are assessed (Zunker, 1982).

Wide Range Achievement Test (WRAT)

The WRAT is a widely used assessment instrument, especially by vocational counselors in rehabilitation settings. It measures the person's separate spelling, reading, and arithmetic levels. It can be used with children or adults, but usually it is used to test persons of relatively low educational levels for vocational placement. The subtests are similar to the Wechsler Intelligence tests in that each question becomes progressively more difficult. Its brevity and specific diagnostic characteristics make it a useful test.

ASSESSMENT OF INTERESTS

Interest inventories are mainly used for three reasons: (1) to identify the client's unknown interests, (2) to confirm stated interests, and (3) to identify discrepancies between aptitudes and interests. Two techniques in this area, the *Strong Campbell Interest Inventory* (SCII) and the *Kuder Preference Record*, have been used for long periods of time as the mainstays of the career counselor.

Strong Campbell Interest Inventory (SCII)

The Strong Vocational Interest Blank (Stanford University Press) was the old standby of interest inventories, familiar to almost every counselor. In 1974, several changes were made in the SVIB, and it was merged into the SCII (Form T 325 for computer scoring).

Since in the past, men and women usually entered different occupations, the SVIB provided separate norms, scales, and profiles for each sex. Now, even though men and women do show substantial differences in the strengths of their interests in some areas, the SCII uses only one booklet and profile (separate normative data are retained for each sex). Men now respond to items formerly only included in the women's booklet and vice versa.

This edition of the SCII provides a profile that arranges the person's scores according to six occupational themes, twenty-three basic interest scales (based on Holland's six occupational personalities) and 124 occupational scales ordered according to Holland's (1973) classification system. This profile provides the counselor with more information, and that information is clearly presented, probably more so than in earlier forms. Helpful suggestions are also given in the Inventory for interpreting the data, and computerized scoring is available.

Kuder Preference Record

Along with the SCII, the Kuder (Science Research Associates) is probably the interest inventory with which counselors are the most familiar. There are actually four Kuder inventories, but the Kuder Occupational Interest Survey (KOIS, Form DD) is the most recently developed.

The KOIS is especially effective for counseling students who may be considering nonprofessional occupations. This form has over one hundred occupational scales and forty-eight college majors are listed. A V score is indicative of validity of each profile. Interpretation of the data is based on the degree of relationship existing between the client's pattern of interests and the interest pattern of the occupational group in question. These occupational groups are specific, as compared to the more general occupational groupings used in the SCII. Thus, it is possible for the counselor to use this instru-

in the SCII. Thus, it is possible for the counselor to use this instrument in a very precise fashion. Another advantage in terms of time savings to the counselor is that the form DD can be machine-scored.

As Anastasi (1961) has stated, many of the scores for women are obtained with scales developed using male criterion groups in fields where men predominate but that do offer some vocational opportunities for women.

ACT Interest Inventory

The American College Testing Program publishes the ACT Interest Inventory as part of their Assessment of Career Development Program. It consists of ninety items that measure student interest in six major areas: social service, business contact, business detail, trades, scientific, and artistic. These correspond to Holland's six types of personal orientations. The time of administration is approximately fifteen minutes, and the students respond to the items on a five-point scale that indicates the degree to which they would enjoy an activity.

The counselor receives a Student Profile Report, which indicates how much student's scores compare to other entering college students and how their scores relate to those college seniors in twenty-four educational majors. This is termed the Educational Major Score and is plotted on the ACT Map of College Majors. This map is divided into two dimensions. The horizontal consists of a people-related/things-related continuum, while the vertical dimension consists of ideas-related majors plotted in terms of creative arts and social services, and higher scores fall in the area of data-related activities (Zunker, 1981).

The ACT has also introduced the World of Work Map for Job Families (1972), used in conjunction with ACT's national testing program, which classifies *occupations* into two bipolar dimensions: the Data and Ideas and the People and Things. The CPP Student Report locates on which of the regions on the map the student falls. Prediger (1974b) views the map as analogous to a traveler's map, in that the students are given a start towards finding their way, but must look further for the necessary details. First, students receive an exploring booklet, which leads them to the realization that they are "on the map." They are then encouraged to ponder the implication of their preferences for data, people, or things. The goal is to provide them with a broader focus for occupational exploration and to try to place the test results in a larger context.

The interest map visually demonstrates the students' areas of major interest and allows them to explore new alternatives they may not have previously considered. Prediger (1974b) also suggests that if the field in which students have scored highest does not seem to attract them the counselor can suggest that "those fields are good possibilities, but . . . there are others which are also possibilities." Again, this helps keep as many options open to the students as possible and provides them with information upon which to make decisions. The counselor also may consider directing them towards extracurricular guidance materials, such as providing them with DOT codes corresponding to their preferences.

The Vocational Preference Inventory

Another interest inventory that has gained acceptance is Holland's Vocational Preference Inventory (Consulting Psychologists Press). Holland designed this instrument primarily as a personality inventory rather than a vocational inventory. It is composed of 160 occupational titles, and the clients indicate their amount of interest by responding "yes" or "no" to each occupation. A profile is then compiled (Holland, 1965) consisting of eleven scales, such as Intellectual (a high score on this scale would be indicative of a person who thinks through problems more than acting them out), Social (those who score high have social interests and tend to be relatively more insightful in interpersonal relationships), and Artistic (those who tend to be imaginative, original, and somewhat unconventional).

There appear to be several advantages to this instrument. First, it provides a very broad range of information concerning the client's life-style, coping mechanism, vocational interests, and self-concept in a short period of time. Second, it has several time-saving advantages in that it is self-administering, scoring is quickly accomplished, and the time of administration is from fifteen to thirty minutes. Third, Holland (1965) states that the occupational content of the VPI reduces the need of the clients to fake their answers, since the VPI is not usually perceived as a threatening test of personality. Last, this is an instrument that can be used to complement and provide a further check on data obtained by other instruments in a test battery to provide counselors with a multifaceted view of their clients. Holland suggests it may be very helpful as a screening inventory to gather information that will help the counselor determine what path to take regarding their clients' career planning in future sessions.

One possible disadvantage of this instrument is that it lacks adequate empirical evidence to permit anything other than a subjective, clinical interpretation of the profile data (for a comprehensive discussion of the merits of the actuarial versus the clinical interpretation of tests, see Goldman, 1961).

Inherent in the above is the implication that interpretation of the information is best left to the counselor with a sound clinical background in testing and personality theory. This is, as was previously mentioned, a personality inventory as well as an instrument to assess vocational interests, and the counselor should be aware of this.

ASSESSMENT OF CAREER MATURITY

Career maturity is a term that implies that the choice of a career progresses or develops over time. This development then may be broken down into characteristic stages through which a person passes. As Erikson (1963) has shown, personality development is an ever changing, dynamic process as people attempt to meet their needs, and career development is an integral part of that process.

Career Maturity Inventory (CMI)

Crites (1973) developed the Attitude Scale of the Career Maturity Inventory (formerly the Vocational Development Inventory) as a way of assessing peoples' vocational maturity through determining their attitudes toward various occupations in terms of empirical behaviors. This instrument, which has primarily been used in research, consists of fifty true-false statements regarding the attitudes students take toward work, which may determine their later vocational choices after finishing their schooling, such as "A person can do any kind of work as long as he tries hard," or "It is probably just as easy to be successful in one occupation as it is in another." The data is summarized and presented as the Attitude Scale (AS). Herr and Cramer (1972) suggest that it certainly may help counselors in terms of planning if they know their clients stage of career development. The rationale behind this assumption is that if the counselors assume clients are proceeding in a series of steps toward maturity, then they can keep them up-to-date with changes and help them personalize the information. For instance, should a college student indicate that he has little or no idea what work will be like upon graduation, or that he is having difficulty preparing himself for a vocation, he needs to be given very basic information on vocational possibilities, in addition to working on improving his decision-making skills. It probably would also be helpful to help him explore the possibility of taking a summer job in order to familiarize himself with the world of work. However, if another client who is a high school senior indicates she feels there is only one occupation that is right for her and thinks that by the time she graduates she should make that decision, the counselor might want to discuss whether she has been exploring other possibilities. She may have narrowed her alternative plans for the future too much should her present outlook change. This instrument helps counselors validate their personal impressions of how their clients development is progressing, as well as checking clients feelings about decisions they must make about their future careers. The CMI also consists of the Competence Test (CMI-CT), in which the client makes judgments about descriptions of vignettes that allegedly reveal the client's own competencies in the career area.

Westbrook, Cutts, Madison, and Arcia (1980) criticize Crite's claim that the CMI is a multidimensional inventory, instead claiming there is a high degree of relationship between the Career Choice Competencies.

Vocational Identity Scales

Two instruments in particular have been designed in order to help clients understand why they are unable to make adequate career or educational decisions.

The first, Osipow's (1976) Career Decision Scale, consists of sixteen reasons persons often give that they feel explain their career indecision. The clients are then asked to identify which applies to them. Thus it primarily serves as a stimulus to further exploration of career or educational issues; it can be used with high school students through adults.

The other test, Holland's *My Vocational Situation Test*, is marketed by Consulting Psychologists Press, Inc., 577 College Avenue, Palo Alto, California, 94306. It consists of eighteen True-False Items, which constitute the Vocational Identity Scale. Two other items are related to either specific barriers the person feels with respect to occupational decisions or lack of vocational information. The test is used in a diagnostic fashion in that it quickly pinpoints problem areas and can differentiate clients who need intensive career counseling from those who only lack information. In addition, it functions as a projective technique in that there are opportunities for clients to subjectively elaborate on their answers with emotionally significant material.

ASSESSMENT OF VALUES

The values held by people, the importance they place on certain activities, are closely related to the individual's interests and attitudes (Aiken, 1979). As such, they are inevitably closely linked with career goals. Since values tend to remain relatively stable over time (Gordon, 1975), their identification may help in determining the progress of a person's career development.

The Work-Values Inventory

One of the more useful instruments is Super's *Work-Values Inventory* (Super, 1970). It is designed for grades seven through adult and takes only fifteen minutes to administer. It attempts to measure fifteen values that are associated with vocational success, such as intellectual stimulation, altruism, creativity, and esthetics. These fifteen factors are then further subdivided into four more inclusive categories, termed by Super (1970) as material, goodness of life, self-expression, and behavior control. Although predictive validity data has yet to be established and long-term reliability has been questioned, this approach may have practical implications for the counselor in that it attempts to measure a number of values related to work that previously have not been tapped. Specific examples are also provided in the manual as to how the work values are related to occupations.

ASSESSMENT TECHNIQUES USED FOR THE PURPOSE OF SELECTION FOR THE PROFESSIONS

These tests, such as the Medical College Admissions Tests (MCAT), the Law School Aptitude Tests (LSAT), the Scholastic Aptitude Test (SAT), and others, have been the backbone behind admissions staff decisions at institutions both large and small for over two decades. It is highly probable that almost every counselor reading this has taken one or more of them before they entered a post-secondary institution.

Criticisms of these tests and their administration has been considerable in recent years. It basically has been twofold. First, these persons who take the tests should have access to the results. Citing the Family Rights and Privacy Act of 1974, which provides, at least in part, that educational institutions receiving funding from the Department of Education must allow parents (and eligible students) to have access to their records, critics claimed that disclosure of the questions and answers of the above examinations was essential so that the applicants would know the basis upon which they were judged. New York's Truth-in-Testing Law (1980) required the disclosure of questions and answers determining examinees scores on post-secondary and professional school admissions test within thirty days of the release of tests scores (Haney, 1981).

Although, at least as far as the MCAT is concerned, the law has not yet been enforced (nor in California, which also has its' own law); the Educational Testing Service strongly objected to it, claiming principally that it would be prohibitive to try to devise an unlimited pool of questions that would be applicable and that such a practice could seriously compromise test security.

The second criticism has been that the testing agencies should give the individual examinees information on the intended use of the tests and also make public the limitations, such as possible limited predictive validity with regard to job or school performance.

This last criticism frequently has been leveled at standardized tests in general, aptitude tests in particular, and especially the Scholastic Aptitude Test (SAT), administered by the College Entrance Examination Board. The SAT has come under fire during the last few years when at least two students discovered scoring errors. However, a four-year study done by a panel formed by the prestigious

National Academy of Science (APA *Monitor*, April 1982) drew different conclusions: " . . . college admissions tests predict first year college grade performance 'reasonably well' and ability tests predict 'equally well for all groups of test takers'. . . ."

However, the same committee also concluded that the tests could have serious limitations, such as not being able to *guarantee* that distributions of scores would not differ for racial or ethnic groups, and suggested that such tests should not be made as critical to selection decisions at undergraduate colleges and universities as they are at present. This may already be happening; admissions directors at such selective private schools as Harvard and Stanford say that achievement tests are probably better predictors and that they rely more and more on what high school has to say about the student's work than on aptitude test scores (Williams, 1982).

ASSESSMENT TECHNIQUES IN BUSINESS AND INDUSTRY

This category of assessment ironically has burgeoned in response to numerous criticisms of the ways in which organizations have proceeded in selecting and promoting employees.

The use of assessment techniques in business and industry begins with employee selection. For numerous reasons, the majority of college graduates hired for their first job will quit that job within five years. The first job is a very important one; however, Super and Hall (1978) found a high degree of relationship between the level of initial job challenge and later success demonstrated in a variety of organizations. Typical selection techniques in use such as letter of recommendation and interviews have run afoul of the requirements of the Equal Employment Opportunity Commission (EEOC), which has alleged that those selection procedures discriminate against educationally and culturally deprived individuals. Not only is such discrimination unethical, it is illegal as it violates the EEOC's (1972) guidelines as well as the Civil Rights Act of 1964.

The Assessment Center

Briefly, the assessment center has become a popular method of selection that places applicants in a realistic but simulated job situation. This approach was initially used by the Office of Secret Services during WW II and has since been refined by American Telephone and Telegraph Company, among others.

Assessment centers usually involve several candidates at a time who are evaluated as they work through a series of exercises, such as the "in-basket case." The in-basket typically contains problems, questions, or directives that managers would find in the mail when they returned to work from a vacation. They have a limited amount of time to process such material and may later be required to justify their decisions in an interview with the assessors. Leaderless group discussions may also be used as part of the assessment process to evaluate each person's leadership and persuasive skills. Advantages of this approach to assessment have been cited by Alexander (1979) and Cascio and Silbey (1979), the most prominent one being that persons selected for managerial jobs by means of assessment center perform better and are promoted faster than those selected by means of more "traditional" techniques. Another advantage is that in training the assessors, the assessors themselves become more skilled at making decisions. Disadvantages have typically been (1) the cost, which averages around 600 dollars per candidate, (2) the questioned emphasis on glibness and quantity of verbal production as criteria for selection and/or promotion rather than quality, and (3) the problem of having to train the assessors unless consultants are hired.

It is suggested that assessment centers are a useful supplementary technique when used with other methods of employee selection. Indeed, their use is not limited to business and industry, as almost any organization could benefit from more closely defining acceptable job performance. When used in performance evaluations, however, it must be kept in mind that actual job behavior is not being assessed.

Evaluation of Job Performance

Performance evaluations have always been vital, both to the organization and to the individual employee. In everyone's career, performance evaluation is practiced in one form or another. Whether or not an employee is being considered for a pay raise or promotion has a direct bearing on self-esteem, emotional security, and satisfaction with career development.

Fair employment legislation has made performance evaluation increasingly difficult. Most evaluations are still based on supervisor's ratings, which are subjective by their very nature since most supervisors and managers come from the ranks of the workers. Court decisions have found them often to be discriminatory (Schneier, 1978).

A new assessment technique, the Behaviorally Anchored Rating Scale (BARS), has been developed in an attempt to evaluate performance in terms of behaviors called "critical incidents," or in other words, incidents that supervisors and employees alike agree are absolutely essential to the performance of a job. The incidents that deal with the same behaviors are then grouped together and items for the BARS are constructed. The employee is then evaluated on a Likert-type, five-point scale. The biggest disadvantage of the BARS is that it has had only mixed success in reducing rating errors. Apparently, at least in some cases, poor test construction has kept it from being more successful. Its biggest advantage is that it meets the EEOC guidelines for fair employment practices.

SUMMARY

This chapter has discussed the use of assessment procedures in five different areas of career development; aptitude, achievement, interests, vocational maturity, and work values. Several criticisms of assessment procedures were presented, and selected assessment procedures were discussed with descriptions and suggestions for employing them in career counseling situations. It has been shown that there are new assessment procedures that may be employed, such as the Assessment Center and the BARS Rating scale, and that counselors are limited only by their innovativeness, imagination, and flexibility within the framework of their training in attempting different ways to interpret and personalize the data obtained from those instruments.

BIBLIOGRAPHY

Aiken, L. R. *Psychological testing and assessment.* Boston: Allyn and Bacon, 1979.
Alexander, L. D. An exploratory study of the utilization of assessment center results. *Academy of Management Journal*, 1979, *22*, 152-57.
The American College Testing Program. *Handbook for the ACT Career Planning Program.* (1972 ed.) Iowa City, Iowa: Author, 1969.

Antastasi, A. *Psychological testing.* (3rd ed.) New York: MacMillan, 1961.

Bolles, R. N. *A practical manual for job-hunters and career-changers What color is your parachute?* Berkeley, California: Ten Speed Press, 1978.

Campbell, D. P. *Manual for the Strong-Campbell Interest Inventory.* Stanford, California: Stanford University Press, 1974.

Cascio, W. F. and Silbey, V. Utility of the assessment center as a selection device. *Journal of Applied Psychology,* 1979, *64,* 107-118.

Crites, J. O. *Career Maturity Inventory.* Monterey, California: McGraw-Hill, 1973.

Cronbach, L. J. The Armed Services Vocational Aptitude Test Battery — A test battery in transition. *Personnel and Guidance Journal,* 1979, *57,* 232-237.

Erikson, E. *Childhood and society.* New York: Norton, 1963.

Goldman, L. *Using tests in counseling.* New York: Appleton-Century, 1961.

Gordon, L. V. *The measurement of interpersonal values.* Chicago: Science Research Associates, 1975.

Haney. W. Validity, vaudeville and values: A short history of social concerns over standardized testing. *American Psychologist,* 1981, *9,* 1027.

Herr, E. L. The roots of career education. *The College Board Review,* 1977, *105,* 6-17, 32-33.

Holland, J. L. *Manual for the Vocational Preference Inventory.* Palo Alto, California: Consulting Psychologists Press, 1965.

Holland, J. L. *Making vocational choices: A theory of careers.* Englewood Cliffs, N.J.: Prentice-Hall, 1973.

Kotter, J. P., Faux, V. A., and McArthur, C. C. *Self-assessment and career development.* Englewood Cliffs, N.J.: Prentice-Hall, 1978.

Osipow, S. H., Clarke, G. C., and Barak, A. A scale of educational-vocational undecidedness: A typological approach. *Journal of Vocational Behavior,* 1976, *9,* 233-43.

Prediger, D. J. The role of assessment in career guidance. In Herr, E. L. (Ed.), *Vocational guidance and human development.* Boston: Houghton-Mifflin, 1974a.

Prediger, D. J. Innovations in test interpretation. A symposium presented at the national convention of the American Personnel and Guidance Association, New Orleans, April 1974(b).

Schneier, D. B. The impact of EEO legislation on performance appraisals. *Personnel,* 1978, *55,* (4) 24-34.

Seligman, L. *Assessment in developmental career counseling.* Cranston, R. I.: The Carroll Press, 1980.

Srebalus, D. J., Marinelli, R. P., and Messing, J. K. *Career development: Concepts and procedures.* Belmont, California: Wadsworth, 1982.

Super, D. E., and Crites, J. O. *Appraising vocational fitness by means of psychological tests.* (Rev. Ed.) New York: Harper and Row, 1962.

Super, D. E. *Work values inventory manual.* Boston: Houghton-Mifflin Co., 1970.

Super, D. E. and Hall, O. T. Career development: Exploration and planning. *Annual Review of Psychology,* 1978, *29,* 333-372.

Westbrook, B. W., Cutts, C. C., and Madison, S. S. The validity of the Crites model of career maturity. *Journal of Vocational Behavior,* 1980, *16,* 249-281.

Williams, D. A. Is the SAT a dirty word? *Newsweek,* July 19, 1982, p. 68.

Zunker, V. G. *Career counseling: Applied concepts of life planning.* Belmont, California: Wadsworth, 1981.

Zunker, V. G. *Using assessment results in career counseling.* Belmont, California: Wadsworth, 1982.

CHAPTER 5

SELF-ASSESSMENT

Lawrence K. Jones

SELF-ASSESSMENT refers to a variety of techniques that are used to help individuals gain a clearer self-picture, simplify their career exploration, and facilitate career decision making. The methods used in self-assessment include success factor analysis, paper-pencil instruments, occupational card sorts, self-interviews, guided fantasy, and self-rating scales. They all stimulate individuals to consider different aspects of themselves and evaluate their presence or strength. These factors may include abilities, temperaments, values, skills, interests, or competencies.

This chapter will begin with a brief history of the use of self-assessment in the past eighty years of career guidance. This is followed by an examination of the major factors that account for the renaissance of self-assessment in career counseling and the role of self-assessment in career decision making. The different self-assessment techniques are then considered, followed by cautions in their use.

HISTORICAL PERSPECTIVE

Self-assessment was an integral part of career counseling in the early days. Frank Parsons, often referred to as the father of vocational guidance, considered self-analysis an essential step of vocational counseling: "To *Know Thyself* is the fundamental requisite"

(1909). He recommended that there be "A self-examination, *on paper*, done in private, under instructions of the counselor, developing specially every tendency and interest that should affect the choice of a life work." Individuals wrote their answers to a comprehensive list of more than 100 questions covering such areas as physical health, ideals, habits, favorite amusements, ambitions, reputation, appearance, temperament, and character. Another well known writer of that period, Edwin Brewster (1917), viewed self-assessment with some ambivalence ("Much of this adolescent introspection is more or less unwholesome.") but recommended that ". . . one may as well utilize the instinctive impulse to aid his vocational impulse." In fact, he entitled his chapter *The Duty of Self-Analysis*.

In the 1920s and '30s, the role of self-assessment began to diminish and paper-and-pencil tests began to play an increasingly important role in career counseling. The publication of tests such as the *Strong Vocational Interest Blank* and the *Kuder Preference Record* were followed by many other standardized tests, and together they largely supplanted the use of self-assessment techniques in career counseling. Standardized tests offered the promise of accurately matching individual's characteristics with the demands of an occupation; the tests also provided a scientific aura to a field that was striving for recognition as a profession. Self-assessment at this time came to be viewed as unreliable and unscientific.

In the past ten or fifteen years, attitudes toward self-assessment have gradually evolved to the point that self-assessment today plays a prominent role in career counseling. This resurgence is reflected in popular self-help books like Bolles's (1972) *What Color Is Your Parachute?*, career education texts and workbooks, computer software, and self-administered, paper-pencil treatments such as Holland's (1977) *Self-Directed Search*.

What has accounted for this dramatic turnaround? There are many factors that have played a role. An understanding of some of these is necessary for the counselor to put standardized testing and self-assessment in perspective.

WHY A REBIRTH OF SELF-ASSESSMENT

Recognition of the Limits of Standardized Tests

In 1972, Leo Goldman shocked the career guidance field with his article "Tests and Counseling: The Marriage that Failed" (Goldman, 1972b), in which he argued that nearly all tests were designed for selection purposes, not counseling and, therefore, were of limited usefulness to counselors and their clients. He demonstrated that the validity of aptitude tests in predicting job success for an individual is so low that they are practically meaningless in a counseling situation. What was so surprising was that this was written by the author of *Using Tests in Counseling* (Goldman, 1971), the standard, classic text used in counselor education programs at the time. To illustrate Goldman's point, consider Ghiselli's (1966) review of studies prior to 1965; they show that the average validity correlation between aptitude tests and training criteria was 0.30 and 0.19 for proficiency in occupation — not the stuff from which individual predictions are made.

Disagreement still abounds over the issues raised by Goldman. A subsequent issue of *Measurement and Guidance* (October, 1972) was devoted to the controversy, and the reader is urged to study the arguments presented. Most counselors are not ready to discard aptitude tests, but they are now more cautious in their use and more open to self-assessment approaches.

Interest inventories also have come under scrutiny. One of the false assumptions among vocational counselors according to Dolliver and Nelson (1975) has been that "vocational interest test results are more accurate than the expression of vocational interests" in predicting future occupation. In his exhaustive review of research done comparing the predictive validity of the *Strong Vocational Interest Blank* (SVIB), Dolliver (1969) concluded that "The predictive validity of expressed interests is at least as great as the predictive validity of the SVIB." Dolliver laments the failure of counselors to use available techniques that elicit from clients expression of vocational interests such as a vocational incomplete sentences blank or a vocational card sort. "The inattention to these methods has probably stemmed from the view that expressions of interests are not worthwhile. The studies reviewed indicate that even simple, direct questions elicit expressions of vocational interests which have predictive validity that is equal to or surpasses the predictive validity of the SVIB." Dolliver's conclusions have been strongly supported by numerous other studies and reviews (e.g. Borgen & Seling, 1978; Whitney, 1969), yet, these studies are not cited in the manual of the successor to the SVIB, the

Strong-Campbell Interest Inventory (SCII) (Campbell & Hansen, 1981). Nevertheless, counselors are increasingly paying greater attention to their clients expressed vocational interests.

Concerns also have been raised about sex bias in tests, particularly in vocational interest inventories. According to the AMEG Commission on Sex Bias in Measurement (AMEG, 1973) sex bias is "that condition or provision which influences a person to limit his or her consideration of career opportunities solely on the basis of that person's sex." According to the Commission's report, one sex could be limited in its occupational options because of the way the inventory is constructed or the results reported. For example, career interest inventories typically suggest artistic and social occupations to many women as opposed to scientific or leading/sales occupations. This has been viewed by some as evidence of sex bias; others have argued that it is evidence of a pervasive socialization process and not the fault of the tests (Diamond, 1975; Tittle & Zytowski, 1978). This debate has prompted counselors to look for alternatives in the realm of self-assessment, such as the occupational card sort technique where, for example, Cooper (1976) found that a card sort was more effective than the SCII in broadening the career options of women.

Potential Negative Effects of Tests in Counseling

The search for alternatives to testing has also been stimulated by concerns over potential negative effects of test use in counseling; these effects fall in three areas: (a) actions and attitudes, (b) perceptions of clients, and (c) counselor/client relationship. With regard to counselor actions and attitudes, a number of prominent writers (e.g. Goldman, 1972a) have called for more extensive training of counselors, as they feel that counselors lack the technical sophistication required to understand and interpret tests effectively. Another frequent criticism is that counselors are too test- and score-oriented in their career counseling. Their approach to counseling has been characterized as "test'em and tell'em" or "three interviews and a cloud of dust." Another related concern is that tests may obscure the client's individuality. By their attention to group averages on selected factors, counselors can easily lose sight of the individual and his or her unique characteristics and potentials. Those who choose science, for example, may resemble each other in several ways, but they differ from one another in many more. In her recent book, *In-*

dividuality, Leona Tyler (1978) has called for the increasing use of ideographic along with nomothetic techniques and offers suggestions and a theoretical foundation for our advance in this area.

The perceptions of clients is another concern. Do they understand the results? Interpreting test results effectively can be a challenging endeavor, even for the most advanced counselor. For example, it is not uncommon for counselors to express difficulty in understanding and interpreting the results of the popular and sophisticated SCII. To illustrate, how does one explain to a client that like-named occupational scales do not measure the same thing (e.g. female versus male engineers)? Another problem is that tests can foster client dependency. Tests create the impression among some clients that good career decision making requires help *outside* themselves: tests to "tell me what to do" and counselors to administer and interpret them. This is further aggravated by client ignorance of tests resulting in an exaggerated belief in their precision and predictive power.

The use of tests may also inhibit the counselor/client relationship. Carl Rogers (1946), for example, views their use as ". . . a hindrance to the counseling process whose purpose is to release growth forces. They tend to increase defensiveness on the part of the client, to lessen his acceptance of self, to decrease his sense of responsibility, to create an attitude of dependence upon the expert." His client-centered counseling approach does not necessarily exclude testing, but tests should be used only if it is a real desire of the client and its purpose is to help the client understand him or herself (Patterson, 1964). To avoid these potential relationship problems created by testing, self-assessment approaches are attractive because their results are immediate (no delay for scoring) and open to understanding, they do not ordinarily create defensiveness, and the process is a mutual, shared counselor/client activity.

Move from Vocational Choice to Career Development

Today we refer to our work as career counseling and career development rather than vocational counseling. With the individual's first occupational choice, our work extends *beyond* a simple matching of a person with a job. Consideration is given to such things as the different life roles one may play and how these are integrated with a person's values and preferred life-style. We are also interested in this person's subsequent career decisions and try to lay a framework and develop skills that can be used later with them. Our work also includes influencing the factors and decisions that have led up to this first occupational decision through career education in the schools.

Consequently the role of assessment in counseling has changed. Today there is greater emphasis on using assessment to stimulate exploration of self in relation to career and to provide a framework for career exploration (Prediger, 1972). In adult career counseling we see a growing emphasis on skills assessment, sometimes referred to as "success factor analysis" or "motivation skills assessment" (Bolles, 1972; Haldane, 1960). The popular press encourages individuals to engage in their own self-assessment. Self-empowerment is the objective of the popular self-help books, and they are replete with colorful scales, maps, graphs, and tests to accomplish this. Thus, the role of self-assessment has broadened and become more evident.

Cost-Effectiveness Comparisons

With the increasing emphasis on accountability and the scarcity of funds to support human services, there has been a growing interest in self-directed career interventions that do not require costly counselor time. A recent study by Krivatsy and Magoon (1976) provides support for this new direction. In comparing the effects of the SDS, an adaptation of the SDS, and traditional vocational counseling, they found the treatments about equally effective *and* that traditional counseling cost six times more per subject than the SDS.

SELF-ASSESSMENT AND CAREER DECISION MAKING

Our attitudes and beliefs about ourselves play a preeminent role in our career decision making. We each have a dynamic, idiosyncratic collection of words, phrases, and sentences that we use in thinking about and describing ourselves and the world. These linguistic constructions are referred to as *cognitive constructs* or, more simply, *constructs*. According to Kelly (1955), "Man looks at his world through transparent patterns or templates which he creates and then attempts to fit over the realities of which the world is composed. The fit is not always very good. Yet without such patterns the world appears to be such an undifferentiated homogeneity that man is unable to make any sense out of it. Even a poor fit is more helpful to him than nothing at all." Kroll and his colleagues (Kroll, Dinklage, Lee, Morley, & Wilson, 1970) describe how the constructs of self, the self-concept, develop through a process of differentiation and integration; we develop a language and an ability to distinguish how we are different from and similar to other persons and things. This self-organization and self-evaluation process is a persistent process throughout life. It is these self-constructs, or self-statements, that we use in thinking and decide on a course of action, such as deciding on a career.

Assessment in career counseling usually involves measuring the strength of a particular trait in an individual. The trait is a construct created by a career counselor or vocational psychologist to represent reality. Thus, interest inventories are frequently given to measure "vocational interests," such as "social interest." These constructs are of great usefulness to us, as they permit communication and thinking about the complexities of the work world. For example, a knowledge of the basics of Holland's (1973) hexagon with its six types (Realistic, Investigative, Artistic, Social, Enterprising, and Conventional) provides a useful framework for clients to (a) examine their own characteristics and how they relate to the work world, (b) explore occupations, and (c) discuss their career decisions with a counselor. These constructs can create problems, however; they can narrow our vision so as to blind us to the unique characteristics and potentials of the individual. We are not only interested in using the constructs we have learned from our professional training but also in the unique constructs of each individual's self-view.

Most self-assessment techniques do require to judge the strength of a specified trait, but the way in which they are asked to respond often provides considerable freedom for the expression of individuality. For example, in the evaluation of abilities in Figler's (1975) *PATH* workbook, the person is first asked to name and describe any abilities he or she has. Then, the individual rates the strength of a wide range of abilities listed under such headings as "numerical" and "managerial," and finally, the person records the "best you ever did" with respect to twenty different activities (e.g. "Decision I ever made," "Performance I ever gave") and identify the abilities needed to accomplish them. It is the combination of these three assessments that comprise the individual's self-evaluation of abilities.

Some self-assessment techniques are even more open-ended and require the person to use his or her own idiosyncratic constructs. A good example is the occupational card sort, where in one step, for example, individuals must group occupations according to their reasons for their interest in them (e.g. "I am an outdoors person and like to work with concrete things.") In discussing this technique, Tyler (1978) makes several cogent remarks: ". . . individuals show very different strategies or patterns of behavior as they carry out the assigned task. Some rule out many things [occupations] as possibilities. Some organize them into broad categories; others make fine distinctions; still others produce one large group and a lot of singles. Some use familiar concepts about kinds of work to be sought or avoided; others are highly idiosyncratic." She concludes, "It makes no sense to try to scale these choices and rejections along some standard dimensions of values or needs. Shall we attempt to reduce this multiplicity to an order that makes statistical analysis possible but loses sight of salient aspects of individuality, or shall we accept and attempt to deal with it even if it does not fit our established assumptions about the nature of science? And if so, how?"

To summarize, career decision making involves our use of various constructs for representing ourselves and the world about us in considering a course of action. Self-assessment techniques provide constructs that individuals can use in organizing their thinking and evaluating their options. They also may elicit constructs unique to the individual that assist them further in clarifying their self-picture and relating themselves to the world of work.

SELF-ASSESSMENT TECHNIQUES

The variety of self-assessment techniques developed by career counselors is a testimony to their creativity and resourcefulness. The different techniques are discussed here according to the methodology they use.

Success Factor Analysis

This is the term used for the basic concept developed by Bernard Haldane (1960) for use in career counseling with business executives. Very simply, it is a method for identifying the skills one possesses and enjoys using. This idea, sometimes referred to as "skills identification" or "motivation skills assessment," has been popularized by Bolles (1972) in *What Color is Your Parachute?* and Figler's (1979) *The Complete Job-Search Handbook*. To simplify Haldane's (1960) approach, he had his clients identify the two achievements that most pleased them for each five-year period of their life. The top ten were written across the top of a chart and a comprehensive list of skills was printed down the side. Using this grid clients then checked off the skills required by these achievements. Thus, the skills and their frequency of use were determined.

The Quick Job-Hunting Map of Bolles (1975) adopts a similar approach. Individuals begin by identifying their "seven most enjoyed or satisfying accomplishments"; these may be the seven *"most satisfying accomplishments or achievements," "jobs* you have held," or *"roles* you have (or have had)." They describe each of these on a separate sheet of paper and then write the names of the seven experiences across the top of a chart. Along the left-hand margin, for eleven pages, hundreds of skills are listed in fifteen skill families. Using the grid formed by the experiences and skills, squares are colored in with one color if the skill was used in the experience; another color is used if the skill was used *and* the person enjoyed using it. In this way individuals can graphically identify "skill families" they enjoy using.

This approach has been modified for college use by Richard Gummere, Jr., (1972) at Columbia University. Success Factor Analysis is the basis of the DIG program, "Deeper Investigation of Growth." It embodies the philosophy found in the approaches using this technique: individuals should identify what they *enjoy* doing and the skills inherent in these activities. They should take pride in these skills and look for jobs (or create jobs) where these skills can be transferred and enjoyed. Thus, the question becomes "Does this job offer me the opportunity to use the skill I enjoy performing?" rather than "Do I have what they (the employer) are looking for?"

Several problems can arise with success factor analysis. Since skills are learned, they are influenced by time and opportunity. A person thirty years old has had more time to develop and hone skills than someone fifteen and, consequently, is more likely to benefit from the analysis. Similarly persons may have been unable to learn skills by virtue of their race, sex, or social circumstance. Another problem is difficulty in identifying skills. Most individuals lack the vocabulary and practice for doing this analysis.

This is further aggravated by our attitudes toward skills. We tend to trivialize our skills and put them down (Figler, 1979). A person may derogatorily refer to themselves as "compulsive," and yet, a fairer label may be "well organized" — a quality of great value in many jobs. For these reasons, the counselor may play an invaluable role in helping an individual perform his or her own factor analysis.

Paper-Pencil Instruments

There have been several instruments published in the past decade to assist individuals in their educational and career planning. Best known is Holland's (1977) *Self-Directed Search* (SDS), which is based on his six personality types: Realistic (R), Investigative (I), Artistic (A), Social (S), Enterprising (E), and Conventional (C). Using an assessment booklet, individuals indicate their occupational daydreams, preferred activities, competencies, and occupational preferences. They then assess their abilities in twelve different areas. These responses are self-scored and a three-letter occupation code is obtained — such as, RIE (Realistic, Investigative, Enterprising). They then turn to an occupational classification booklet, *The Occupations Finder*. The *Finder* contains several hundred occupations organized according to their three-letter codes. Under RIE, for example, such occupations as Heavy Equipment Operator and Machinist are listed. In this way, persons are able to relate their preferences and abilities to numerous related occupations, and since the DOT number for each occupation is provided, occupational information may be easily located in the numerous reference books and systems based on the DOT system.

A similar type of paper-pencil instrument is the Harrington and O'Shea (1981) *Career Decision-Making System* (CDM). In its self-scoring version, an eleven-page booklet directs a person in identifying their preferred job groupings (e.g. one of the eighteen listed is Customer Services), their most enjoyable school subjects, the level of education to which they aspire, their most important values, their strongest abilities, and the activities and occupations in which they are most interested. Based on their responses a "career code" is obtained in which two of six interest areas are represented, such as Business-Clerical (the Holland types have been renamed in the CDM). The career code is then associated with career clusters, in this case to Management, Sales Work, and Data Analysis. Individuals then turn the *Interpretive Folder* where the six interest areas and career clusters are described. For each of the eighteen career clusters, information is provided as to typical jobs, related school subjects, required training, job values, abilities, and related DOT worker trait groups.

Occupational Card Sort

This technique was developed by Leona Tyler (1961) as a research tool for understanding individuality. Her subjects were asked to sort 100 names of occupations, each printed separately on a small card, into three columns: those they "Would Not Choose," "Would Choose," or were unsure of — "No Opinion." Next, she asked them to take the Would Not Choose occupations and group them into smaller piles according to their reasons for rejecting them (e.g. "These jobs work with numbers and I dislike math.") Similarly, the Would Choose occupations are sorted into smaller groups for reasons that are important to the individual (e.g. "I like the prestige of these occupations, and you make good money, too.")

It was Tyler's (1961) belief that ". . . the core of individuality consists of a person's choices and the way he [or she] organizes them." She found great variation among the users with respect to their quickness, decisiveness, and satisfaction in doing the task. They also differed in how they used the three categories: positive, negative, and undecided. An unanticipated finding was that a significant number of her subjects mentioned spontaneously, "This kind of thing is good for you. It makes you think." This finding has provided a strong simulus for its subsequent use in career counseling.

Since Dolliver's (1967) article describing his adaptation of Tyler's card sort, interest in the occupational card sort as a career counseling tool has grown and a number of articles have appeared (e.g. Cooper, 1976; Dewey, 1974; Jones, 1980). Several published card sorts have recently been reviewed (Dolliver, 1982).

One published occupational card sort is the *Occ-U-Sort* (O-U-S) (Jones, 1981). Individuals use a deck of sixty cards, each about the size of a business card. On the front of the card is the occupational title with its DOT number, educational level, and two-letter Holland occupational code. On the back is a brief description of the occupation drawn from the DOT. The cards are sorted into "Might-Choose," "Would Not Choose," and "Uncertain" piles and then resorted into smaller groups of occupations, as previously described. In addition, following Dolliver's (1967) adaptation, the Might Choose cards are rank ordered according to "your preferences." This last step can be an important values-clarification activity, as it frequently brings the issues surrounding an individual's vocational indecision into focus.

Based on the occupations they put in the Might Choose pile, O-U-S users obtain a Holland three-letter code that helps them find many other similar occupations in a booklet, the *Guide to Occupations*. There are 555 occupations listed in the *Guide*, first, according to the Holland six types and then according to the worker trait groups of the U.S. Department of Labor's *Guide for Occupational Exploration* (GOE) (1979) and the *Worker Trait Group Guide* (Winefordner, 1978). For example, an individual having an "A" in his or her code would find a section labeled "Artistic" under which are eight worker trait groups (e.g. "Literary Arts" and "Visual Arts") that contain the names of numerous occupations. For easy access to occupational information resources, both the DOT and GOE numbers are given. The O-U-S may be self-administered and self-interpreted with the *Self-Guided Booklet* or it can be counselor administered.

The features of an occupational card sort are difficult to appreciate until a counselor has actually tried it out. Holding and sorting the cards establishes a unique relationship between the user and the process, adding significance to the results. The results are immediate, and it avoids the potential judgmental overtones of a test. It encourages the expression of individuality and self-reliance. In the hands of a perceptive counselor it can be a rich source of information: the counselee's self-perceptions, knowledge of occupations, and approach to decision making, and it can help clients articulate their self-view and factors that are important to them in making a career decision.

Guided Self-Interview

Included under this category are a variety of written exercises where individuals examine themselves and then make inferences about appropriate careers. Of course, this was the approach pioneered by Parsons (1909) with his 116 questions to which individuals were asked to respond. A more recent version is Gaymer's (1970) detailed self-assessment project where persons analyze their strengths and weaknesses and their feelings with respect to such topics as "working with people," "creativity," "location and mobility," and "tension and stress." As with Parsons, she stresses a written analysis: *"Thinking about it is not enough. Down on paper it must go!"*

The value of written exercises has been largely overlooked in career counseling until recent years when numerous books and program materials have included them. Writing demands organization and articulation. By specifying our self-view, the sentences we use in talking to ourselves about our ideas and feelings, we often arrive at greater self-understanding. "As is true of any writing that comes out of one's own existence," Lillian Smith has said, "the experiences themselves [are] transformed during the act of writing by awareness of new meanings which settled down on them . . . the writer transcends her material in the act of looking at it, and since that material is herself, a metamorphosis takes place: *something happens within*: a new chaos, and then slowly, a new being" (Silberman, 1970).

To illustrate the variety of self-interview exercises, several will be briefly described here from two workbooks. In *Self-Assessment & Career Development* (Kotter, Faux, & McArthur, 1978), users keep a twenty-four-hour diary of their activities and then make inferences about themselves. An analysis of their day may reveal, for example, that they jump from one activity to another or that they spend a significant portion of time interacting with friends and acquaintances. This information, along with an analysis of how it is recorded (e.g. Names of people given? Detailed or sketchy account?), may provide useful information. Another exercise included in the workbook is called a "life-style representation." Students are asked to describe either their past, current, or future life-style (or all three) in words and pictures. Students have approached this in a variety of ways: diagrams, collages, drawn pictures, and short essays. The activity requires individuals to focus on their way of life: use of time, relationships with others, possessions, geography, etc. The process of doing the activity and an analysis of the representation can assist in determining where and how an occupation fits into one's life.

Kirn and Kirn's (1978) *Life Work Planning* contains numerous self-assessment exercises done in groups of four or five persons. For example, "I am . . ." is written at the top of fifteen sheets of paper and participants write down "whatever comes to mind." The five least important "I am . . ." statements are discarded, the remaining ten are rank-ordered according to their importance, and the statements are read to the group and discussed. In another exercise the ten "most significant constraints in your life" are listed, analyzed as to whether they are imposed or chosen, and then discussed with group members. Here is one more example: two self-portraits. Using colored pens or crayons, two self-portraits are drawn on a large sheet of paper using one of the sets of themes given; for example, "Myself at work and myself away from work." The drawings are then shared and discussed with group members.

Guided Fantasy

Career counselors are finding that fantasy and daydreams can be valuable tools in career counseling; a recent article by Morgan and Skovholt (1977) provides a valuable review of the concepts and uses of this technique in career counseling. Typically, guided fantasy consists of three parts: (a) relaxing the person(s), (b) leading the person through the fantasy, and (c) helping the person examine and reflect on the experience. Fantasies described by the authors include

1. "The Award Ceremony" where individuals are asked to imagine that they are to receive a special award at a great banquet. This exercise can assist clients in clarifying their own personal goals and motivations.
2. "The Opposite Sex" where persons imagine working a typical day in a nontraditional occupation for their sex (e.g. males as nurses, secretaries, or elementary school teachers). In this way, related feelings and attitudes can be assessed and implications drawn.
3. "A Day in the Future" asks participants to imagine events during a typical work day, five, ten, or fifteen years in the future and can stimulate a rich variety of images that can be

beneficially analyzed later. For example, Does the person live alone, work alone? Where does the person live, work (i.e., city, suburb, rural)? Type of work?

Through the relaxation and imagery of guided fantasy, individuals can be stimulated to consider aspects of themselves that may be repressed or ignored. An altered self-view may emerge as they examine their innermost thoughts and feelings. The process can also provide valuable information to the career counselor.

Self-Rating Scales

Rating oneself on a numerical/word scale is a fairly common experience and is a simple, straightforward approach to self-assessment. An example is Figler's (1975) "Rating Satisfactions from Work" where participants rate thirty-three work values on a scale from one to four — from "Not important at all" to "Very important in my choice of career." Among the values rated are "Help Society," "Competition," and "Time Freedom." A one sentence description is provided for each value to clarify its meaning. Another example is Rosenberg's (1957) "Requirements for Ideal Job or Career" where ten values (e.g. "Give me an opportunity to be helpful to others") are rated on a four-point "importance" scale — from "Most Important" to "little or No Importance, Irrelevant, or Distasteful." Dolliver (1967) has discussed using this scale in conjunction with an occupational card sort to further clarify motives in choosing a career.

CAUTIONS

As with any techniques, self-assessment can be misused. There are a number of areas specific to self-assessment that counselors should consider. Among these is self-scorer reliability. If there is self-scoring, errors may be made in transposing numbers or in computations. To illustrate, in a study done with college students using the original (1970) SDS (Christensen, Gelso, Williams, & Sedlacek, 1975), 18 percent made errors that resulted in a mistaken high-point code and 54 percent had a mistaken summary code. A comparable study (Tracey & Sedlacek, 1980) done with the revised (1977) SDS found error rates of 12 percent and 26 percent, respectively. Thus, depending on the complexity of the scoring process and the computational abilities of the users, counselors need to take necessary precautions to ensure score accuracy.

The validity of self-estimates is another issue. How accurately can individuals estimate their own abilities, values, interests, and achievements? While the research is not conclusive (Goldman, 1971), there is general support for the notion that persons can predict their vocational choice and scholastic ability at least as well as standardized tests do. It should be noted, counselor predictions are generally less valid than these statistical predictions (Meehl, 1954). At least three points can be made safely: (a) individuals *do* vary in the validity of their self-estimates, (b) *under*estimating abilities (e.g. women reentering the workforce) can be as serious as overestimating, and (c) *reality testing* is of great value in testing the validity of self-estimates.

Self-estimate methods are frequently found in books and materials that depend upon self-direction. The self-motivation required to pursue these self-help approaches should not be underestimated. Such approaches often require a strong commitment. Consequently, provisions should be made for an adequate support system and counselor assistance when needed.

Finally, self-assessment should be used thoughtfully. The counselor should have a well developed career counseling theory. Any manuals or other relevant materials should be carefully studied. For example, Holland's (1973) book should be required reading for any approaches using his theory. Because self-assessment approaches are relatively easy (and sometimes fun) to use, they should not be used without the same thoughtful consideration given to the use of standardized tests or any other counseling precedure.

SUMMARY

Self-assessment has seen a rebirth in the past decade as counselors have become disillusioned with standardized tests and begun to see its merits. Assessment with standardized tests involves measuring a specific construct considered to be useful in considering a career decision, such as "mechanical ability." This information can sometimes be helpful, but we now realize that equally valuable information can be obtained by simply asking the person for this information. In addition, self-assessment does not limit us to the constructs measured by standardized tests. We can include other constructs such as "skills," as in success factor analysis. Furthermore, we can use the idiosyncratic constructs of the individual as in the occupational card sort. When properly used, self-assessment procedures provide a low-cost, effective method for helping clients articulate their self-concepts and the career-related issues in making a good decision. This is done in an open way that fosters active client participation and self-reliance. When used thoughtfully, self-assessment is a promising, new counselor tool for facilitating career development.

BIBLIOGRAPHY

AMEG Commission on Sex Bias in Measurement. AMEG Commission report on sex bias in interest measurement. *Measurement and Evaluation in Guidance,* 1973, *6,* 171-177.

Bolles, R. N. *What color is your parachute?* Berkeley, CA: Ten Speed Press, 1972.

Bolles, R. N. *The quick job-hunting map.* Berkeley, CA: Ten Speed Press, 1975.

Borgen, F. H., and Seling, M. J. Expressed and inventoried interests revisited: Perspicacity in the person. *Journal of Counseling Psychology,* 1978, *25,* 536-543.

Brewster, E. T. *Vocational guidance for the professions.* New York: Rand McNally, 1917.

Campbell, D. P., and Hansen, J. C. *Manual for the SVIB-SCII (Form T325).* Stanford, CA: Stanford University Press, 1981.

Christensen, K. C., Gelso, C. J., Williams, R. D., and Sedlacek, W. E. Variations in administration of the Self-Directed Search, scoring accuracy, and satisfaction with the results. *Journal of Counseling Psychology,* 1975, *22,* 12-16.

Cooper, J. F. Comparative impact of the SCII and the vocational card sort on career salience and career exploration of women. *Journal of Counseling Psychology,* 1976, *23,* 348-351.

Dewey, C. Exploring interests: A nonsexist method. *Personnel and Guidance Journal,* 1974, *52,* 311-315.

Diamond, E. E. (Ed.). *Issues of sex bias and sex fairness in career interest measurement.* (National Institute of Education Report). Washington, D. C.: U. S. Government Printing Office, 1975.

Dolliver, R. H. An adaptation of the Tyler Vocational Card Sort. *Personnel and Guidance Journal,* 1967, *45,* 916-920.

Dolliver, R. H. Strong Vocational Interest Blank versus expressed vocational interests: A review. *Psychological Bulletin,* 1969, *72,* 94-107.

Dolliver, R. H., and Nelson, R. E. Assumptions regarding vocational counseling. *Vocational Guidance Quarterly,* 1975, *24,* 12-19.

Dolliver, R. H. Card sorts: In Kapes, J. T. and Mastie, M. M. (Eds.), *A counselor's guide to vocational guidance instruments.* Falls Church, VA: American Personnel and Guidance Association, 1982.

Figler, H. E. *PATH: A career workbook for liberal arts students.* Cranston, R. I.: Carroll Press, 1975.

Figler, H. E. *The complete job-search handbook.* New York: Holt, Rinehart, and Winston, 1979.

Gaymer, R. *Career planning & job hunting.* Toronto: Maclean-Hunter Limited, 1970.

Ghiselli, E. *The validity of occupational aptitude tests.* New York: John Wiley & Sons, 1966.

Goldman, L. *Using tests in counseling.* 2nd ed. New York: Appleton-Century-Crofts, 1971.

Goldman, L. It's time to put up or shut up. *Measurement and Evaluation in Guidance,* 1972, *5,* 420-423. (a)

Goldman, L. Testing and counseling: The marriage that failed. *Measurement and Evaluation in Guidance,* 1972, *4,* 213-220. (b)

Gummere, Jr., R. M. DIG/Columbia University's program to help students find answers. *Journal of College Placement,* 1972, *32,* 38-45.

Haldane, B. *How to make a habit of success.* Lee's Summit, Missouri: Unity Books, 1960. Distributed by Hawthorn Books.

Harrington, T. F., and O'Shea, A. J. *Career Decision-Making System.* Circle Pines, Minn.: American Guidance Service, 1981.

Holland, J. L. *Professional Manual for the Self-Directed Search.* Palo Alto, CA: Consulting Psychologists Press, 1979.

Holland, J. L. *Making vocational choices.* Englewood Cliffs: N. J.: Prentice-Hall, 1973.

Holland, J. L. *Self-Directed Search.* Palo Alto, CA: Consulting Psychologists Press, 1974.

Jones, L. K. Issues in developing an occupational card sort. *Measurement and Evaluation in Guidance,* 1980, *2,* 206-215.

Jones, L. K. *Occ-U-Sort Professional Manual.* Monterey, CA: Publishers Test Service of CTB/McGraw-Hill, 1981.

Kelly, G. S. *The psychology of personal constructs.* New York: Norton, 1955.

Kirn, A. G., and Kirn, M. O. *Life work planning.* 4th Ed. New York: McGraw-Hill, 1978.

Kotter, J. P., Faux, V. A., and McArthur, C. C. *Self-assessment and career development.* Englewood Cliffs, N. J.: Prentice-Hall, 1978.

Krivatsy, S. E., and Magoon, T. M. Differential effects of three vocational counseling treatments. *Journal of Counseling Psychology,* 1976, *23,* 112-118.

Kroll, A. M., Dinklage, L. B., Lee, J., Morley, E. D., and Wilson, E. H. *Career development.* New York: Wiley & Sons, 1970.

Meehl, P. E. *Clinical versus statistical prediction.* Minneapolis, Minn.: University of Minnesota Press, 1954.

Morgan, J. I., and Skovholt, T. M. Using inner experience: Fantasy and day-

dreams in career counseling. *Journal of Counseling Psychology,* 1977, *5,* 391-397.
Parsons, F. *Choosing a vocation.* New York: Houghton-Mifflin, 1909.
Patterson, C. H. Counseling: Self-clarification and the helping relationship. In Borow, H. (Ed.), *Man in a world of work.* Boston: Houghton-Mifflin, 1964.
Prediger, D. Tests and developmental guidance: The untried relationship. *Measurement and Evaluation in Guidance,* 1972, *3,* 426-429.
Rogers, C. R. Psychometric tests and client-centered counseling. *Educational and Psychological Measurement,* 1946, *6,* 139-144.
Rosenberg, M. *Occupations and values.* Glencoe, Ill.: Free Press, 1957.
Silberman, C. E. *Crisis in the classroom.* New York: Random House, 1970.
Tittle, C. K., and Zytowski, D. G. (Eds.). *Sex-fair interest measurement: Research and implications.* (National Institute of Education Report). Washington, D. C.: U. S. Government Printing Office, 1978.
Tracey, T. J., and Sedlacek, W. E. Comparison of error rates on the original Self Directed Search and the 1977 version. *Journal of Counseling Psychology,* 1980, *27,* 299-301.
Tyler, L. E. Research explorations in the realm of choice. *Journal of Counseling Psychology,* 1961, *8,* 195-202.
Tyler, L. E. *Individuality.* San Franciso: Jossey-Bass, 1978.
U. S. Department of Labor. *Guide for occupational exploration.* Washington, D. C.: U. S. Government Printing Office, 1979.
Whitney, D. R. Predicting from expressed vocational choice: A review. *Personnel and Guidance Journal,* 1969, *48,* 279-286.
Winefordner, D. *Worker trait group guide.* Bloomington, Ill.: McKnight, 1978.

CHAPTER 6

CONTRACTUAL ARRANGEMENTS

Daniel J. Montgomery

IN recent years, counselors have used a variety of behavioral and cognitive behavioral techniques for treating career related problems. These include Rational Emotive Therapy (Weinrach, 1980), assertion training (Lange & Jakubowski, 1976), modeling and behavior rehearsal for interpersonal skills and job interview training (Babee & Keil, 1973), and a combination of behavioral procedures (Azrin, Flores, & Kaplan, 1975).

This chapter will discuss the application of treatment contracts, another behaviorally based procedure, to career counseling. Specifically, it will cover the nature and types of contracts, the advantages of contracts to the counselor and the client, the use of contracts to increase behavior change and to reduce undesirable and uncooperative behavior, and how to avoid ethical and legal problems. The chapter will also provide step-by-step instructions for negotiating workable contracts.

WHAT IS A CONTRACT?

From a legal standpoint, Friedman (1965) defines a contract as an agreement between two or more parties ". . . for the exchange of what the parties consider equivalents." In counseling, the term contract has been used in a variety of ways. These include (1) the "business contract," (Haimowitz & Haimowitz, 1976) or what McNamara

(1978) calls "A professional service agreement," which stipulates the fees, length and time of meeting, etc; (2) the "informed consent" agreement, which describes the type and risk of the treatment; and (3) the "therapeutic" or "treatment contracts," which are used as a therapeutic technique. The latter would include contracts used for goal setting and treatment evaluation (Montgomery & Montgomery, 1975), to reward or punish client performance, e.g. contingency contracts (Homme, 1971), or contracts designed to increase client compliance by way of public commitment such as "no suicide contract" (Goulding & Goulding, 1979).

In this chapter, the term "procedural agreement" will be used to refer to "business contracts" and "professional service agreements." "Informed consent" will refer to agreements informing clients of the general nature of counseling, benefits, and alternatives. The term "therapeutic contract" will refer to contracts used as a form of intervention, such as contingency contracts and contracts specifying goals, treatment plan, etc., and the term "contractual agreement" will refer to contracts in general whether they are business contracts, therapeutic contracts, or informed consent agreements.

WHY CONTRACT?

The need for contracts stems from society's growing concern for accountability and quality assurance. Courts, insurance companies, and consumer groups have held physicians accountable for their work and have required a variety of safeguards to protect patients. It is only recently, however, that similar expectations have been placed on counselors, psychologists, and other mental health professionals.

The move toward greater accountability and quality assurance has been prompted by a variety of developments that are necessitating a change in the way in which counselors and therapists conduct their practices. These changes include access to third party payments, consumer rights pressure, government regulations, and judicial concern for client rights.

As counselors gain access to third party payment, insurance companies will expect greater accountability (Motta, 1981). Some insurance companies have taken a significant step in this direction by requiring providers to practice peer review, set goals, and document procedures.

Government is also acting to insure that counselors are accountable for their actions. Everstein, Everstein, Heyman, True, Frey, Johnson, and Seidon (1980) predict that measures such as the professional standards review organization, established by Congress to develop peer review systems in health care, the Mental Health Center Act of 1976, and changes in Medicare and Medicaid regulations will force counselors to justify the type and quality of services they offer.

With insurance companies and government agencies requiring accountability and quality assurance, counselors need to account for what they are doing. It is naive to think that career counselors will not be affected by these pressures.

Although it is true that career counselors are sued less frequently than counselors and psychologists in general, this in no way excuses them from their responsibility to conduct their practices according to accepted ethical standards and to provide clients, insurance companies, and regulatory groups with assurances of quality services.

The use of therapeutic contracts, procedural agreements, and informed consent agreements is one way career counselors can respond to these concerns. Contractual agreements are a relatively simple, efficient, and economical first step toward meeting societal pressure to document the type and quality of services available.

ADVANTAGES OF CONTRACTS TO CLIENTS AND COUNSELORS

In addition to the increased accountability, the use of contractual agreements has other advantages. From the client's perspective, contracts provide protection. Procedural and informed consent agreements allow the client to know, in advance, not only the fees, length of treatment, and other parameters but also what procedures will be used, their benefits and risks, and the alternatives.

Because clients are informed in advance, the chance of client-counselor misunderstanding is greatly reduced. Conflicts over the amount charged, the length and frequency of sessions, and the like can be avoided. Also, because clients know the possible benefits and risks of the procedures being used, they are less likely to have unrealistic treatment expectations. Similarly, the therapeutic contract, when used in conjunction with a procedural and informed consent agreement, will help clients understand the treatment process. When the clients are involved in developing a contract, they assist in selecting treatment goals, setting target dates, and deciding on the responsibilities of both parties. As a result, clients have a clearer understanding of the career counseling process and how they are expected to behave. From Gambrill's (1977) perspective, contractual agreements are a means of socializing the client to the expectations and requirements of counseling. With greater knowledge of the counseling process, clients are in a better position to protect their rights.

Another advantage of contracts is that they provide clients with the information necessary to confront suspicious or unorthodox practices, question counselor or therapists' pronouncements, and when appropriate, terminate or select alternative treatment. Contracts not only help the buyer beware (caveat emptor) but also allow the buyer to choose (opet emptor) (Szasz, 1978).

Counselors also may benefit from the use of contractual arrangements. Although critics of contracting have argued that contracts create unnecessary paperwork, reduce the placebo effect, interfere with transference and drive potential clients away, there are decided benefits for career counselors. These include protection of counselor rights, avoidance of client manipulation, management of uncooperative client behavior, and enhanced treatment effect (Montgomery & Montgomery, 1975).

Both parties have specific responsibilities and privileges in contractual agreements. Clients have responsibilities and privileges, as do counselors. Examples of counselor responsibilities are punctuality, provision of quality services, and professional conduct. Examples of counselor privileges are the right to cancel the session if the client is late, terminate if the client fails to pay fees, and insist that treatment be limited to scheduled appointment times.

Because privileges and responsibilities are specified in the contract, the career counselor can confront contract infringements. These include client failure to keep appointments, pay fees, procedural issues, and unwillingness to do what is necessary for counseling to succeed. For instance, if the client contracts to review occupational literature or write a resume, the counselor can use the contract to confront the client or insist on renegotiation and, in extreme cases, referral or termination. Contractual agreements allow counselors to follow the dictum of never working harder than their client and foil client attempts to transfer responsibility for change to the counselor (Montgomery & Montgomery, 1975).

Contracts also shorten treatment and may improve outcome of career counseling. Studies show that time limits such as those used in contracts may expedite therapeutic gains rather than hinder treatment (Gambrill, 1977). Furthermore, the act of commiting oneself, verbally or in writing, may increase compliance (Levy, 1977, Levy, Yamashita, & Pow, 1979). This is especially true if the agreement is linked to a contingency, a reward, or a punishment (e.g. Harris & Brunner, 1971; Bouden, 1972).

In short, contractual agreements are a simple, economical, and efficient technique career counselors can use to justify their treatment techniques to outside agencies, protect themselves and their clients, and enhance treatment effectiveness.

CRITERIA FOR EVALUATING CONTRACTS

An effective contractual agreement, whether it is a procedural agreement, informed consent agreement, or a therapeutic contract, should meet several criteria. First, a valid contractual agreement should be moral, ethical, and legal. By moral and ethical, it is meant that the agreement should not infringe on the implicit or explicit standards of the helping professions. By legal, it is meant that the contract should not violate state or federal statutes. Second, both parties should be competent, i.e. legally of age and mentally capable. Third, an agreement should be voluntary. Both parties should enter the agreement of their own accord. Coercion invalidates a contract. (Contracting may be possible when one party is ordered to seek counseling. For a discussion see Goulding & Goulding, 1979, and Gambrill, 1977.) Fourth, contracts need to be clear and specific. Concrete and behavioral terminology should be used to specify goals, privileges, and responsibilities of both parties. Too often counselors accept general, vague, or poorly defined language when formulating contractual arrangements, with unfortunate consequences. Unless the terms of a contract are clear, concrete, and understood by both parties, misunderstandings and conflicts can develop.

Fees, length and duration of treatment, and other procedural arrangements are relatively easy to state concretely. However, this is not true with therapeutic goals. General, nonspecific treatment goals, e.g. "make the right career decision," "narrow my interests," or "understand how to make better decisions," are vague, confusing, and difficult to achieve. While these are legitimate requests, they are too broad to be meaningful. It is impossible to know if one has made "the right career decision," "narrowed one's interests," or "made better decisions."

Relying on client opinion is inadequate. Clients may conclude that a career choice is the right one by ignoring critical information; they may reduce their total interests from ten to four but feel they have not made substantial progress; or they erroneously conclude that because they feel better they can make better decisions.

Similarly, without concrete goals to evaluate progress, career counselors may distort what has occurred in counseling. The counselors' criterion for improvement may be too stringent or too lax; the counselors may place their standards on the client's behavior; or the counselors may confuse their needs for success with what actually transpired. Concrete contractual goals will help protect clients from counselors who promise help but provide inadequate services. Goals need to be stated in terms of concrete, observable client behaviors (e.g. collecting three pieces of information on careers in accounting, narrowing one's choice of careers from five to three, or filling out three job applications). By translating goals into observable behaviors, both parties will know when and if the contract has been fulfilled and whether or not additional help is necessary.

Finally, a valid contractual agreement should be one the client wants to carry out, is capable of carrying out, and is consistent with his or her values (Haimowitz & Haimowitz, 1976; Montgomery & Montgomery, 1975). If the client does not want to carry out the terms of the contract, cannot complete the contract, or feels it is wrong or immoral, the contract is inappropriate and counseling will fail.

EXAMPLES OF AGREEMENTS

There are four types of agreements that can be adopted for use in career counseling: (1) a statement of client's rights, (2) a procedural

Because individuals are unfamiliar with what goes on in counseling, this agency thinks it is important that you be informed of your rights before requesting assistance. As a recipient of our services, you have a right to:

(1) Know the qualifications and experience of the counselor you are seeing.
(2) Question any aspect of the counseling process, including the procedures being used, homework assignments, tests to be administered, or your counselor's actions.
(3) Refuse to engage in a counseling procedure without explanation.
(4) Terminate treatment at any time without explanation.
(5) Confidentiality. Your records, visits, and communications between you and your counselor will be kept in confidence and only will be discussed with our staff when and if your counselor feels such consultation is necessary. Otherwise, your communication will be kept confidential unless you sign a consent form to release the information to a qualified professional, a court subpoenas your file, your life or someone else's life is in danger, or evidence of a felony being committed is revealed in the session.

If you have any questions regarding the rights just discussed or your rights in general, please discuss them with one of our staff members or a person of your choosing before requesting counseling.

I have read, understand, and agree to the above conditions.

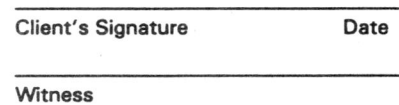

Client's Signature   Date

Witness

Figure 6-1. The Client's Rights Statement.

agreement explaining the business and administrative aspects of counseling, (3) an informed consent agreement that reviews the risks, benefits, and alternatives and explains the counseling process, and (4) the therapeutic contract that outlines the treatment plan.

1. *Statement of Client's Rights.* The statement of client's rights should be the first document a client sees when entering counseling. The statement can either take the form of an explanatory letter or a list of rights prescribed by ethical standards. Whichever format is selected, the statement should be brief and stated in language a layman can understand. (Hare-Mustin et al., 1981). In addition to specifying client's rights, the statement might explain the funding sources of the agency, the values or theoretical orientation of the counselor's agency (e.g. behavioral or Christian Counseling Services), or any other aspect of the agency that might lead to a conflict of interest. The client rights statement should have a place for the client to sign, signifying they have read and understood their rights. Figure 6-1 outlines some of the in-

formation that should be included in a client's rights statement. For other examples, see Hare-Mustin et al. (1981).

2. *Procedural Agreement.* After reviewing the client's rights statement, clients have the option of seeking or not seeking counseling. If the clients decide to begin counseling, a procedural agreement would be used to inform them of the administrative, financial, and other aspects of counseling. These include the counselor they will be seeing, for how long and how frequently, and at what expense. The procedural agreement might also include policies on cancellation, after hours calls, the limits of service, and any other general information that the agency feels is important for the client to know. As with the client's rights statement, it should have a place for the client to sign. See Figure 6-2 for an example.

The following information is provided so that you will have a better understanding of our services and our administrative procedures.

(1) Counseling in our Center is limited to 50-minute appointments once a week unless otherwise arranged by your counselor.
(2) The cost of service is pro-rated on the basis of your income. A schedule of fees is available from our receptionist.
(3) Cancellation is required 24 yours in advance of the appointment or you will be billed. Medical and other emergencies may be excused.
(4) Similarly, you will be entitled to a free session if your counselor fails to give you a 24-hour warning when cancelling the session.
(5) Telephone counseling is subject to the normal rates.
(6) Payment is due at the end of each session. We do not bill nor do we accept payments over time. Cash, check, or major credit cards are acceptable.
(7) You are free to terminate counseling at any time without charge even if you have contracted for additional sessions. Please give us 24-hour notice.

I have read, understand, and agree to the above conditions.

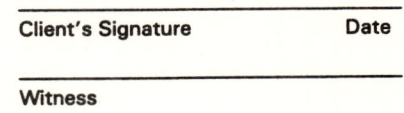

Client's Signature   Date

Witness

Figure 6-2. Procedural Agreement.

3. *Informed Consent Agreement.* Before clients can give consent, they need to be informed of the goals, procedures, benefits, risks, and alternatives to career counseling, the qualifications and orientation of the counselor, the limitations of confidentiality (if not already addressed in the client's rights statement), and other agency policy

pertaining directly to the counseling process.

The informed consent agreement differs from the client's rights statement by being more specific about the nature of the counseling process and in particular the procedures to be used by the counselor or agency. An example of an informed consent agreement is shown in Figure 6-3.

> Before beginning counseling in our agency, it is important that you know the qualifications of the staff you will be working with, the results you can expect, and the other alternatives available to you.
>
> Our Center is staffed by licensed professionals who meet the training standards set forth by the National Vocational Guidance Association. Depending on our caseload, you may be seen by a social worker, counselor, or psychologist, and you are encouraged to ask the professionals you are working with the exact nature of their qualifications and to determine to your satisfaction that they are capable of helping you. Please, if you have any questions in this regard, contact our Director or his/her representative and they will arrange an appointment with another staff member.
>
> As an individual seeking guidance from our Center, it is important that you understand what we can and cannot do for you. Follow-up studies of individuals who have sought our help show that 85 percent were very satisfied, 10 percent satisfied, and 2 percent dissatisfied, and the remaining 3 percent were unsure.
>
> Of the individuals seen for counseling, 60 percent went into fields they decided upon as a result of counseling and 40 percent did not.
>
> The Center, however, cannot place you in a chosen field, get you a job interview, nor in any way promise you employment. We can only help you plan a career goal. Moreover, because our tests and counseling show that you are qualified does not mean that there is a job available for you. Many jobs are acquired by word of mouth, friends, and other contacts. We can only help you decide what you want and what you may be qualified for.
>
> You may, during the course of counseling, be asked to take certain tests. Although these may help you in your decision, they will not provide you with a clear-cut answer. They will only suggest directions. Tests are not always accurate, and the results should only be used to help you explore alternatives or to learn something new about yourself.
>
> Information you share with your counselor will be stored in our computer, which can only be accessed by members of our staff. The only time the information you reveal to us will be made available to others would be in the event of a court order, a clear and present danger to yourself or others, or with your written consent.
>
> As the client's rights statement pointed out, you are free at any time to question any procedure, ask what alternatives are available, stop treatment, or ask for a different counselor. You do not have to give an explanation for your decision.
>
> If you would like to explore other options before starting counseling with our agency, we will provide you with names, addresses, and telephone numbers of other sources of help. The professionals staffing these agencies are also well qualified and licensed.
>
> If you have additional questions, we encourage you to ask your counselor or the Director.

Figure 6-3. Informed Consent Agreement.

I _____ agree to meet with Dr. Montgomery for ten 50-minute weekly sessions to work toward achieving the following goals:

1. Assess my ability to pursue graduate work in English.
2. Overcome my tendency to procrastinate when given a writing assignment.
3. Arrive at a decision of whether or not to attend graduate school in English and, if I do, complete the application forms by January 1, 1983.

To accomplish these goals, I agree to:

1. Take the Wechsler Adult Intelligence Scale (WAIS).
2. Submit 3 examples of my writing to the University Reading and Writing Lab for review and criticism.
3. Read Ellis and Knaus' *Overcoming Procrastination*.
4. Do rational homework assignments on a daily basis when assigned by Dr. Montgomery.
5. Attend all scheduled sessions and give 24-hour notice if I need to cancel.

And the end of ten sessions, Dr. Montgomery and I will renegotiate the contract. If at that time I have not accomplished the above goals, I can decide to terminate, seek referral, or negotiate a new contract.

Dr. Montgomery, in turn agrees to:

1. Attend all sessions.
2. Give 24-hour notice of cancellation.
3. Administer the WAIS.
4. Instruct me in the use of Rational Emotive counseling methods to help overcome my tendency to procrastinate.

I understand that Dr. Montgomery cannot promise that I will reach my stated goals, but that we agree that the steps outlined above are a reasonable way to approach the problem and we both agree to fulfill our respective responsibilities.

I further understand that all my records will be kept confidential unless Dr. Montgomery believes there is a clear and present danger to me or someone else or unless my records are subpoenaed or I give my written consent to release them.

In exchange for the ten sessions of counseling and the services listed above, I agree to pay $300.00 to Dr. Montgomery in ten $30.00 installments due at the time of the scheduled appointments.

If at anytime I feel uncomfortable with any aspect of counseling or have questions, I understand that I can terminate or question the procedure.

_____   _____
Client   Date

_____   _____
Witness   Date   Therapist   Date

Figure 6-4. Therapeutic Contract.

4. *Contract*. The contract can be viewed as a more detailed informed consent agreement. The informed consent agreement outlines the goals of career counseling, the potential benefits and risks, and the alternatives. The treatment contract should provide a de-

tailed explanation of the specific goals and the procedures to be used to achieve these goals. It is, in effect, a mutually agreed upon treatment plan that stipulates the client's objectives, the methods of intervention, the responsibilities of both client and counselor, and the means of evaluation outcome. See Figure 6-4 for an example.

As one can see from the examples, there is some overlap in the various forms. In fact, some professionals collapse the informed consent and treatment document, or alternatively, they make the agreement and rights statement a part of the therapeutic contract.

The difficulty with combining forms is that the counselor may want to employ them at different times in the counseling process. Clients need to know their rights when they first seek help, not on the fourth session when they sign a contract (although the counselor may want to review them at that time).

Moreover, the counselor will want to inform the client of agency policies on fees, appointments, etc, before starting counseling. If any of the procedural aspects of counseling are unsatisfactory to the client, the problems should be resolved in the first session. Also, the counselor needs to inform the client of the potential goals, benefits, risks, procedures to be used, and the alternatives as soon as possible. It is unwise to wait until a specific contract is worked out.

For these reasons, it is best to use all four forms. The client's rights statement should be given to the client before any other paperwork is completed. This will protect the anonymity of the client who decides against counseling after reading the rights statement. The procedural agreement and the informed consent agreement should be discussed and signed either during or after the first session. The treatment contract can be negotiated and signed whenever the counseling goals are identified, or if the client is having difficulty setting goals, the counselor can contract with the client to help him or her arrive at clearly defined goals for counseling.

NEGOTIATING A THERAPEUTIC CONTRACT

Negotiating a contract is an educational and therapeutic experience. It involves helping a client move from poorly defined goals to clearly defined behavioral objectives. Depending on the client and the skill of the counselor, a sound contract may be accomplished in a single session or may require a considerable expenditure of time and energy. To assist the counselor interested in using the contractual approach, the following guidelines have been set forth.

Step 1. The first step in contract negotiation is for the counselor to firmly but gently question the client's stated objectives. When a client states he or she wants to change a particular behavior, the counselor should ask two questions: (1) to define what the client wants to change in behavioral terms and (2) why the client wants to change stated behavior. For example, if the client wants to become more involved in work, the counselor would ask the client to define what is meant by "involved." To help the client translate a general goal into concrete, observable behavior, the counselor might ask the following questions: "What do you mean by involved?" "How would you behave or act if you were involved?" "If I were watching you, how would I know that you were involved?" If the client replies: "I would be more interested, happy, content, etc., the counselor needs to prod the client to state what is meant by "interested" or "happy."

Step 2. Once the client can define his or her objective, the counselor needs to assess the client's motive for wanting to change. To do this, the counselor needs to ask the question "why?" "Why," meaning what is the underlying purpose of the client wanting to change. If the client's response suggests that he or she entered treatment in order to please a boss, wife, family, or others, or because of some "should" or "ought" (e.g. "I should work harder," "I should stop procrastinating, stop drinking," etc.), the counselor needs to exercise caution. People seldom change because they should change or ought to change. Shoulds and oughts are the foundations for New Year's Eve resolutions but seldom result in new behavior patterns. Most of us know what we should do with our lives; the problem is doing it (Salter, 1951). Shoulds or oughts represent an ideal the client would like to achieve. The problem is that he or she often does not want to do what is necessary. For example, clients who should lose weight may want to lose weight but don't want to eat less.

To demonstrate how the counselor can use the "why" question to assess client motivation, an excerpt from an intake interview is shown below.

CLIENT: I need to take an interest test.
COUNSELOR: Why?

CLIENT:	(surprised) To find out what I'm interested in, of course.
COUNSELOR:	Yes, but why do you want to find out what you are interested in ?
CLIENT:	Because my wife said I should.
COUNSELOR:	Yes, but why do you want to find out?
CLIENT:	(pause) I guess I really don't. I mean I really don't care right now. I like what I'm doing.
COUNSELOR:	In other words, it's not you who wants the test, but your wife.
CLIENT:	Right.

In this exchange, the counselor used the "why" question to help the client see exactly what was motivating him and realize the interest test would be of little use. When the client admitted his motivation for entering counseling, he was in a better position to decide more readily for himself what he wanted. In this instance, the client wanted to discuss his marital relationship. If the counselor had not questioned the client's motives, it is unlikely that the client would have benefited from counseling. He would have taken the test to pacify his wife, ignored the results, and dropped out of treatment. However, by asking "why" and by focusing on what the client wanted, rather than what the client's wife might want, the counselor was able to let the client know that he was concerned and genuinely interested in the client's well-being.

Before accepting a treatment goal, the therapist needs to ask four questions: (1) Does the client want to engage in the proposed task (e.g. take a test, select a field of study, review occupational information, go to law school, etc.)? Or is the client acting on the basis of other significant people's expectations or values (parents, professors, peers, spouse, etc.)? (2) Does the client have the capability (intelligence, resources, opportunity) of achieving the desired goal? (3) Is the goal congruent with the client's values, beliefs, and attitudes? (4) Will the activity be reinforced by significant others in the client's environment? Affirmative responses to these questions will greatly increase the probability that the treatment goal will be achieved (Montgomery & Montgomery, 1975).

Step 3. The next step in contract negotiation might be labeled the problem-solving or confrontation phase. Having arrived at a behaviorally defined contract, which takes into account the client's values, capabilities, and desires, the counselor can begin to help the client move toward the therapeutic objective. How this is done will depend on the nature of the problem, the theoretical orientation of the counselor, and a number of other variables. However, for treatment to be successful, the therapist must place the responsibility on the client. The counselor can use his or her expertise to build a treatment program, but the client must be willing to do what is necessary to change.

The best way of dispelling the client's ill-founded hopes is to repeatedly challenge his or her efforts to avoid or transfer responsibility with key questions: What do you want to change? How do you want to behave differently? How are you stopping yourself? What do you plan to do to change things? These and similar questions place responsibility back on the client.

Step 4. Once goals are established, it is important to establish a set of subgoals or steps. Each step should help the client advance toward the objective. The treatment program should allow the client to work toward a goal through a series of successive approximations (Rimma & Masters, 1979).

Step 5. The counselor needs to be firm but supportive. Backsliding and game playing are inevitable. A competent professional should realize this and develop effective strategies for dealing with obstacles. Getting angry or irritated does not help. As Erickson (Haley, 1961) points out, a client's inability to engage in a particular behavior must be recognized as part of his problem and treated as such. There are a variety of ways of doing this, and the particular method one chooses will depend largely on the counselor's beliefs regarding the efficacy of certain approaches. They might include confrontation, paradoxical intention (Haley, 1961), or an examination of irrational beliefs (Ellis, 1977).

Step 6. Finally, if the contractual approach is to be used successfully, the counselor must continually reexamine and alter the original contract to correspond to new information. In the process of thinking through and carrying out a contract, the client and the therapist will receive continuous feedback. For a contract to be effective, the counselor must reassess his or her goals in light of the information and make the necessary changes. Initial contracts are not sacred and unchangeable.

SUMMARY

This chapter has shown how contractual agreements such as procedural agreements, informed consent, and treatment contracts can be used to provide accountability, quality assurance, protect clients and therapists, and enhance treatment outcome. The chapter has also set forth criteria and guidelines for career counselors wishing to use contractual agreements in their practices.

BIBLIOGRAPHY

Azrin, N.H., Flores, T., and Kaplan, S.J. Job finding club: A group assisted program for obtaining employment. *Behavior Research Therapy,* 1975, *13,* 17-27.

Barbee, J.R., and Keil, E.C. Behavior modification and training the disadvantaged job interviewee. *Vocational Guidance Quarterly,* 1973, *22,* 50-56.

Boudin, H.M. Contingency contracting as a therapeutic tool in the deceleration of amphetamine use. *Behavior Therapy,* 1972, *3,* 604-608.

Ellis, A., and Greiger, R. *Handbook of rational emotive therapy.* Berlin & New York: Springer-Verlag, 1977

Everstein, L., Everstein, D.S., Heymann, G.M., True, R.H., Frey, D.H., Johnson, H.G., and Seiden, R.H. Privacy and confidentiality in psychotherapy. *American Psychologist,* 1980, *35,* 828-840.

Friedman, L.M. *Contract law in America.* Milwaukee: University of Wisconsin Press, 1965.

Gambrill, E.D. *Behavior modification: Handbook of assessment, intervention and evaluation.* San Francisco: Jossey-Bass, 1977.

Goulding, M. M., and Goulding, R.L. *Changing lives through redecision therapy.* New York: Brunner Mazel, 1979.

Haimowitz, M.L. and Haimowitz, N.R. *Suffering is optional: The myth of the innocent bystander.* Evanston, IL: Haimowoods Press, 1976.

Haley, J. *Strategies of psychotherapy.* New York: Grune and Stratton, 1963.

Hare-Musten, R.J., Marecek Kaplan, A.G., and Liss-Levinson, N. Rights of clients responsibilities of therapists. *American Psychologist,* 1979, *34,* 3-16.

Harris, M.B., and Bruner, C.G. A comparison of self-control and a contract procedure for weight control. *Behavioral Research and Therapy,* 1971, *9,* 347-354.

Homme, L.E. *How to use contingency contracting in the classroom.* Champaign, IL: Research Press, 1971.

Lange, A.J., and Jakubowski, P. *Responsible assertive behavior.* Champaign, IL: Research Press, 1976.

Levy, R.L. Relationship of an overt commitment to task compliance in behavior therapy. *Journal of Behavior Therapy and Experimental Psychiatry,* 1977, *8,* 25-29.

Levy, R.L., Yamashita, D., and Pow, G. The relationship of an overt commitment to the frequency and speed of compliance with symptom reporting. *Medical Care,* 1979, *17,* 281-284.

McNamara, J.R. Socioethical considerations in behavior therapy research and practice. *Behavior Modification*, 1978, *2*, 3-24.

Montgomery, A.G., and Montgomery, D.J. Contractual psychotherapy: Guideline for change. *Psychotherapy: Theory, Research & Practice*, 1975, *12*, 348-352.

Motta, W. Use of contracts in psychotherapy. *Psychological Reports*, 1981, *49*, 319-325.

Szasz, T.X. A critical review of the moral dimensions of behavior modification. *Journal of Behavior Therapy and Experimental Psychiatry*, 1978, *9*, 199-203.

Weinrach, S.G. A rational emotive approach to occupational mental health. *Vocational Guidance Quarterly*, 1980, *28*, 208-218.

CHAPTER 7

GROUP APPROACHES

DONALD J. COCHRAN

GROUPS have become an integral part of career counseling for young adults. Numerous publications have emerged in recent years that are relevant to group work. These publications either make direct reference to the use of groups in their approaches (Borchard, Kelly, & Weaver, 1980; Harren, Daniels, & Buck, 1981; Shertzer, 1981) or contain materials that can be easily adapted to group formats (see appendix at chapter end for partial listing of adaptable materials). Many of these newly available approaches are contained in general self-help or career planning manuals; nonetheless they exist in abundance. This recent expansion and emphasis on materials for groups in career counseling is apparent in other than published materials. Unpublished and/or "in-house" materials are also available upon request from many practitioners.

With the recent upsurge of available materials, it is important that we as professionals rethink our reasons for using group formats in career counseling and sharpen our priorities in choosing appropriate materials and methods for our career counseling goals. Are we as professionals simply using groups for practical or economic reasons? Or are there other compelling reasons for the use of groups in career counseling based on knowledge of the decision-making

---

The author wishes to acknowledge the influence and contributions of Dr. David Hoffman, the coauthor of this chapter as it appeared in an earlier book edited by Reardon and Burck entitled *Facilitating Career Development*. Portions of this chapter contain revisions of his work.

processes of individuals? Hopefully, the latter is the case, although it is apparent that groups do save money and eliminate many practical problems for the practitioner.

Yalom (1970) has listed a number of "curative factors" that therapy groups provide. Many of these factors also exist in focused theme groups, e.g. career counseling groups. These factors can be considered as major contributors to the advantages of using group interventions as opposed to individual or non-face-to-face (self-help methods, media) interventions.

Yalom's list of positive factors that groups provide members includes the opportunity to (1) impart information, (2) appreciate the universality of their concerns, (3) be stimulated by group cohesiveness, (4) develop social skills through imitation and interpersonal learning, and (5) instill hope.

In career groups, imparting information has traditionally been a high priority. Information regarding the world of work and standardized information about the self, e.g. interest inventory results, continue to be the content of the discussions in many career group formats. Also, career groups are an opportunity for individuals to interact with others experiencing similar difficulties. The emotional relief and recharging that is experienced in a cohesive group can often help the individual direct more energy toward confronting life decisions and tasks. Groups also provide the setting for individuals to expand the social skills necessary, e.g. interviewing assertively, to achieve career objectives. By imitating others and receiving direct feedback, interpersonal learning is enhanced. Finally, the process of instilling hope is vital for individuals who are confronting difficult decisions. Although it is possible in a one-to-one setting for individuals to receive encouragement, the group can be an even stronger source of encouragement. Janis and Mann (1977) identify the lack of hope as a key factor in maladaptive decision-making strategies. Individuals in difficulty simply *do not believe* that there is a better alternative for them. The interpersonal power and diversity of viewpoints inherent in groups often can be instrumental in working through limited self-perceptions.

GROUP TYPES

Career group approaches in general and those described in this chapter have sprung from various historical roots. Some groups emerged from what has been called group guidance. These groups focus on specific content often related to occupational information and standardized test scores. Other group approaches draw their character from the human potential movement of the 1960s. Group process and personal style are the most important foci in these groups. Yet, others have mixed characteristics; they are used both to focus on general information about the self and the external world as well as the specific unique style of the decision maker. As a way to organize thinking about career groups, a hypothetical continuum will underlie the groups presented in this chapter. At one end of the continuum, groups are classified as primarily content oriented, while at the other extreme, groups are experiential and process oriented. The specific group examples presented in this chapter are organized according to this continuum. Beginning with the VEG group — the most didactic of the examples — to the Life Planning Workshop — the most experiential group example given — the groups are ordered from first to last. While this organizational scheme may seem arbitrary and problematic for some, hopefully it will serve more to clarify than to muddy the distinctions between the groups.

Table 7-1

Differentiating Groups

	Vocational Exploration	*Job Club*	*Life Planning*
Setting	Employment Service, Secondary, College, Adult.	Employment Service, General Adult Population.	Secondary, College, Adults.
Time	Varied, 3 sessions/2 hours, 6-hour workshop.	Daily 3-hour sessions for 2 weeks (10 days). Continued if necessary.	6- to 8-hour workshop or 3 sessions/2 hours.
Leadership	Teacher, Counselor, structuring and stimulating.	Counselor in a rotating reinforcer role.	Counselors co-lead in subgroups. Reflect, reinforce.
Procedures	Didactic discussion, feedback, planning.	Skill training with consistent reinforcement. "Buddy" system.	Self-exploration focused on past, present, and future.
Goals	To impart information related to person-job links.	To teach skills in job search and job placement. To use "networking" strategies in job search.	To formulate a specific, but flexible life-career plan. To increase self-awareness.

Assessment Implications

Before beginning the description of the group examples, assessment related to career issues requires mention. While Chapters 4 and 5 are focused on the assessment of the career development of individuals, a special type of assessment is implied by the continuum described previously. In the real world, it is often not possible to assess concerns and assign a client to a group offering that closely fits his/her needs. Lack of sophisticated assessment instruments or procedures, client complexity, and unavailability of multiple modes of career group counseling are among the chief reasons for a lack of "good fit" between the client and the delivery option. Nonetheless, in an ideal sense, it is possible to conceptualize client assessment and assignment according to the content/process continuum. The need for general standardized information supersedes the need for understanding specific personal decision-making style. In assigning clients to career groups, we must assume at least a minimum amount of general information and knowledge about the self and world of work before we can consider assigning clients to process-oriented experiential groups. Without this basic general information, it is unlikely that clients will find satisfaction in a less tangible group orientation. In short, a more complex level of decision-making skill is addressed in the process-oriented groups, while a more simplistic level of skill is the focus in content groups. Knefelkamp and Slepitza (1976) have applied a model of cognitive complexity to career decision making that elaborates this point. Cochran (1982) has combined stage and style models of career development that lead to the same theoretical conclusions related to content and process treatments. An inappropriate assignment in either direction along the continuum invites a group member's dissatisfaction and lack of progress. In the best of all worlds, a series of career group offerings would be available to individuals, along with adequate self-assessment and expert assessment processes leading to appropriate assignments.

GROUP EXAMPLES

Groups were chosen for inclusion as examples in this chapter for a number of reasons. Along with representation at various points along the hypothetical continuum mentioned above, there were practical reasons for selecting examples. The examples were chosen because (1) their descriptions were readily available in published form, (2) they have accessible and reasonably well designed evaluation studies, and (3) the procedures for members and leaders are relatively explicit. A number of other group approaches exist that might have served as useful examples, but limited space and reasons above precluded their use.

Vocational Exploration Group (VEG)

Rationale

The Vocational Exploration Group emphasizes man in the world of work and man-job links. It is a group approach using group dynamics and phenomena such as self-disclosure, peer acceptance, and sharing to enhance the process of learning about jobs in a new way, i.e. what can the job give the person? The process is concerned with thoughts about jobs and member acceptance of others' thoughts about jobs.

The rationale for the VEG (Daane, 1972) is the relationship between man and his work, and the goal of the VEG is the clarification for individuals of the man-job relationship. The originators of VEG present four basic dynamics that occur in the VEG: members gain in self-confidence, in sharing of job knowledge and resources, in understanding of man-job relationships, and in understanding job personalization (Daane, 1972).

VEG has five phases. Phase I is an inclusion phase that encourages exploration in the group setting and presents a twofold matrix through which participants view the world of work. The matrix consists of the job function and job preparation. Phase II is the sharing of previously gained job information and study of a prepared job information book. Phase III examines job demands and job satisfactions. Phase IV is expansion, relating one job to several others that are similar and a feedback chart that is used for members to give each other feedback regarding the jobs they see for each other. Phase V is a planning phase in which members look at the "next step" (Daane, 1972).

Procedures

The VEG begins by the members introducing each other with information gained from short interviews. This inclusive phase of the experience proceeds with a group exercise. As a way for the group members to get to know each other better, they tell a story about themselves. The theme is relating a fantasy about how each might spend a million tax free dollars if this were just given to them. In the final part of the inclusion phase, group members brainstorm and share their ideas about jobs via a job matrix chart. On one axis, job function (data, people, and things) is shown, and on the other, level of preparation (on the job training, HS graduation, college, professional certification, etc.) is shown. Members are asked to fill in the cells with jobs they have either done or have heard about. In this exercise there are no wrong answers. The leader supports and acknowledges *all* of the members' responses and works toward an inclusion and acceptance of *all* of the members and their ideas.

Members continue to share information and disclose more about themselves in the next phase of the experience. Members are asked to name their top and bottom job choice — the job they would most like to have and least like to have. Here the leader reinforces by repeating what members say and "pairs" similar responses. For example, the leader might say, "Sounds like both Joe and Phil are interested in jobs in the science field." These leader responses are meant to help members feel more comfortable in self-disclosure (repeating and reinforcing) and to help members identify with each other (pairing).

The next exercise relies heavily on the dynamics of the group. Members give feedback to each other based on their initial impressions of each other and the information that has been shared in previous exercises. Each member is asked to sit in the "cool seat" while the other group members assign a top and bottom job to him. After the leader models by accepting feedback from members, each member has an opportunity to occupy the cool seat and get the impressions of the other members regarding what jobs they think he/she would like or dislike. After this exercise the members respond to each others' feedback.

At this point, written exercises are used to summarize some of the information gathered. Members are asked to write three alternatives they are considering for themselves and to identify the data, people, and thing dimension of their alternatives as well as the level of preparation necessary. To familiarize members with these dimensions more fully, ambiguous photographs depicting people doing various work tasks are shown. Members are encouraged to project their views into the photos and to name job titles that apply to the photos. These titles are listed on large sheets (e.g. newsprint) according to their place on the data, people, things, and preparation matrix. As an additional stimulus to generate and share information about jobs, job information booklets are used to familiarize the members with different job titles. In these information sharing exercises there are no wrong responses. The leader acknowledges all of the contributions of group members. If one picture stimulates more than one job title, all of the titles are used for the matrix. For example, members might identify the same photo as a social worker, lawyer, salesperson, managerial supervisor, etc. Similarly, members might say that an insurance salesman fits in with "data" jobs *and* "people" jobs. The leader treats both of these as acceptable responses. The main objective of these exercises is to help members generate and share information about jobs and accept each other in the process.

The next phase of the group experience is designed to explore job demand and job satisfiers. The first exercise of this phase is introduced in the frame of reference that jobs do more than just supply money, they supply satisfactions of many varieties. A group of job satisfiers are presented (prestige, teamwork, service, craft work, etc.), discussed, and defined by the group. Each member is asked to identify his or her top and bottom job satisfier and share this with the group. Next, members look at interests and skills that they bring to the job setting and need to fill jobs. The leader and group discuss and define interests and skills (ability with members, design, relationships, selling, etc.) and assign a top and bottom skill to themselves. The final job demand focused upon is training. In this exercise members focus on four possible job situations:

1. Jobs they would like to have that they currently have enough skill and training to enter.
2. Jobs they would like to have but don't have enough skill and training to enter.

3. Jobs they would not like that they currently have enough skill and training to enter.
4. Jobs they would not like and that they do not have the skill and training to enter.

During this series of exercises the leader can pair responses to increase the identification of group members with each other. As a summary exercise to this section, a written exercise is introduced. Members list three alternatives again, either ones they listed before (see above) or new ones. This time they are asked to consider the dimensions of satisfiers and demands (interest and skill) along with training requirements and functions (data, people, and things). As members consider each of these alternatives they use a checklist to identify elements of the above four dimensions in their choices.

The next exercise is directed toward more expansion of the member's alternatives. Members are asked to review the training alternatives (jobs they either like or dislike and for which they may or may not have appropriate training) and to add as many alternatives to these areas as possible. They also are asked to consider their needs (satisfiers) and job demands they can meet in order to generate more alternatives for themselves. Job booklets may be used again at this point. Since the objective of the workshop is to help members learn how to make good choices rather than to make one final choice at the end of the group experience, this expansion exercise is included. Its objective is to give the members additional alternatives on which to practice their choice-making skills.

The final phase of the group experience is the planning phase. Again, a written exercise is used to summarize the thoughts and feelings of the members. Members record their current job goals and list their next step in moving toward the goals. A what, how, and when format is used to stimulate interaction. Each member shares his or her goals and plans with the group. For example, "I plan to get more information about apprenticeships (what) by writing to the State Labor Commission (how) as soon as I can find out where they are located (when)." At this point in the experience, it is important that the leader facilitates as much support as possible by the group for various group members and their plans. This is the point at which the group process can be most helpful. Here is a simple example of how this might be done: "Ann, you have mentioned some good ideas about what you want to do, but you seem a little confused about what your next step might be. Does anyone have some ideas that might be useful for Ann?"

As the group terminates, the goals and plans give the leader an idea of whether further counseling and/or information would be appropriate for various members. At this point, the leader can either ask to talk to some members individually or give information to all of the group on continued counseling/information options.

Critique

The VEG is an effective group model for those who need to make an immediate career decision, e.g. manpower training and employment service clients. It has also been used effectively with diverse populations. Powers (1978) reported significant differences between VEG users and controls on career maturity and clarity of vocational plan for a population of former drug abusers. Westover (1979) reported positive results for native Americans, Helbing (1976) for a population in the Netherlands, and Yates, Johnson, and Johnson (1979) for young American black students, which was substantiated by a six-month follow-up (Johnson, Johnson, & Yates, 1981). A new and expanded format for VEG is scheduled for publication in late 1982 that will include emphasis on satisfiers in leisure.

Job Club

The Job Club approach (Azrin & Besalel, 1980) to career counseling is unique in a number of ways. First, the group is open in that it does not have an exact ending point. Although Azrin and Besalel indicate that roughly 90 percent of the group participants achieve their goals within a relatively short time period, the format is designed to make it possible for members to continue after the initial period until their goals are reached. Unlike the other groups outlined in this chapter, the Job Club is focused on job placement as the prime objective for members. This objective is most timely considering that at this writing unemployment in the United States is higher than it has been in forty years. In this format, all members continue until they are placed on a job. Each activity of the group is focused on a specific subobjective (e.g. resume writing, interview rehearsal) leading toward the final objective of job placement. Overt behavioral change rather than process or attitudinal changes are stressed. Finally, members and group leaders roles are more highly prescribed than in the other groups described here.

Procedure

With a behavioral approach to placement counseling as the basis, the authors have used the concepts of reinforcement, self-recording of behavior, reducing response effort, and behavioral contracting to create this format. Each link in the chain of behaviors leading to job placement is specified for both the leader and participants.

Job Club is best described as a successful effort to provide a highly responsive environment in which group participants can improve their job search skills. The leader acts as a rotating reinforcer, while each member also has a "buddy" who consistently and immediately reinforces the participation. For instance, while one participant engages in job contact phone conversations, a buddy listens and uses a specified checklist to reinforce the conversation. The group is designed for up to twelve participants. Telephone, typewriters, and duplicating machines are required. The schedule includes three-hour meetings daily for two weeks — a total of ten meetings. The activities in the second week are similar for each day and can be continued beyond the two week period if needed.

Day One Activities. The highlights of day one include introductions and signatures of behavioral contracts, development of job leads, interview rehearsals. *Day Two*. Paired phone contacts, continued generation of job leads, completion of job application forms, and beginning preparation of resumes are the main activities in day two. *Day Three*. Day three includes continuing to fill in posted progress chart, more paired telephone contacts and interview rehearsals, and continued work on resume. *Day Four*. Day four's activities include continuation of progress charts, more telephone calls, writing letters, finishing resumes, and developing contacts for open letters of recommendation. *Day Five*. The final days activities of the first week include reviewing accomplishments, more calls, letters, rehearsals if needed, and filling in progress charts. *Day Six And All Other Days*. The activities for each day in the second week are identical. They include getting new job leads, reviewing checklists from actual job interviews, interview rehearsal if needed, and filling in the progress chart.

Critique

Published evaluative studies of Job Club have been quite positive. The first evaluation of Job Club (Azrin, Flores, & Kaplan, 1975) used clients from a representative general job-seeking population who were seeking jobs in a public employment service. In a careful experimental evaluation, the results indicated that individuals receiving the Job Club group treatment found jobs significantly faster and at a higher salary rate than did controls; the Job Club members found jobs at a significantly higher rate (90%) than did controls (55%). In another study (Azrin, Philip, Thiemes-Hontos, & Basalel, 1980) using welfare recipients, results showed that significantly more clients in Job Club obtained employment than did those in the control sample. This study essentially replicated the results in the 1975 study using a different population. Wesolowski (1981) in a study comparing six placement strategies found Job Club to be one of the two most effective methods.

Given the positive results in well designed studies, it is clear that Job Club is effective with the populations studied. These results are also highly objective and relatively less subject to measurement error. The most interesting question emerging from these studies relates to the generalizability of the approach. Can Job Club be used effectively with wider populations? With the apparent expertise of the designers of the program, it seems reasonable to speculate that a similar behavioral approach could be used to address the skills needed in other populations. While some may criticize the apparent rigidity in the format described in the *Job Club Counselors' Manual* (Azrin, 1980), the utility and power of the group to produce specified results is unquestionable. An additional manual for the Job Club participant entitled *Finding a Job* (Azrin & Besalel, 1982) is available to augment the current leader's manual.

Life-Planning Workshop (LPW)

As the title implies, the Life-Planning Workshop is aimed at experience and skill development broader than job selection and the use of occupational information. It represents movement toward a more effective growth experience. LPW was adapted for college students at Colorado State University in 1969 (Birney, Thomas, & Hinkle, 1970). The LPW format has been described as "a systematic program for helping college students take an active role in examining their present and future plans" (Johnson, 1977). Another recent adaptation by McIlroy (1978) uses a modification of this format to explore life-style. In this version of LPW, the process of consciousness, choice, and commitment are emphasized. The workshop is a one-day, six- or seven-hour experience, focusing on self-assessment in the present and projection of self into the future. The objective of the workshop is increased self-awareness and realization of the need for specific and flexible plans for the future.

Procedures

Workshops involve approximately eighteen to twenty participants who meet in small groups with facilitators. Members act as consultants, probers, and facilitators for each other, as the workshop moves through a series of structured exercises. The exercises described below are the primary activities of the workshop.

Life-Line: Participants draw a life-line on paper and divide it into two parts to emphasize the workshop's focus on the future. The members discuss how much living remains rather than focus on past failure or accomplishment.

Identification and Stripping of Roles: Participants identify significant roles in their lives and beginning with the least important strip themselves of each role. Discussion of feelings resulting from the loss of the role takes place after each role is stripped. Participants have time to fantasize about themselves without roles, followed by group discussion. Most of the remainder of the workshop is conducted while participants are free of the influence of roles.

Typical Day and Special Day of the Future: Participants, free of roles, are asked to imagine the future and to be whatever they want to be. Then, participants write a brief description of a typical day and a special day. Members help each other look for inconsistencies and realism of goals.

Life Inventory: Questions are posed for participant reaction (e.g. things I do badly and would like to stop doing, things I do well. . .). The exercise focuses on areas of potential change or areas of strength and may be thought of as a preliminary goal setting exercise.

News Release: Here, participants reflect on their lives from some point in the future, and write a news release that emphasizes role, accomplishment, pleasures, etc. Focus is on how a person is or is not moving in directions he or she wants. As in other exercise, discussion follows.

Reassume Roles: In this exercise, participants reassume their discarded roles or substitute other roles they now wish to assume in place of the original ones. Focus is on change and involvement in decision making about the present and future.

Goal Setting: Participants are asked to write specific behaviors that can be performed immediately and in the near future to direct themselves toward goals. Focus and importance of this exercise is on the individual's own involvement in change and planning toward desired goals.

The leader encourages members to participate as fully as they can in the exercises and facilitates interaction between members, which helps draw meaning and implications of the experience.

Critique

While the LPW does not contain any specific kinds of information about jobs, curricula, or the world of work, it provides an opportunity for information about the self of the participants that can be used to measure external kinds of information. The content of discussion following the fantasies and exercises often centers on the educational/career issues participants face.

Who is the LPW most appropriate for, or who seems to get the most out of this kind of program? Students at a crisis point in planning or students with very specific information needs are probably not going to get what they need from the LPW. This approach seems helpful for those who are aware of some difficulty with decision making generally or who are unclear about the extent of their own impact and power in choosing. Students struggling with the "Who am I?" questions inherent in career development and who value self-awareness and direct experience seem to get most involved and enjoy the Life-Planning Workshop.

Evaluations of LPW by Cochran (1972) and Menke and Cochran (1974) demonstrated positive changes as a result of the workshop. Using an experimental design, significant differences between experimental and control groups were found in information seeking, total number of alternatives considered, and congruence of alternatives with measured interests. Knickerbocker and Davidshofer (1978) reported significant gains in attitudes toward future planning and feeling reactivity using the LPW format. These controlled studies substantiate the conclusion that LPW's are effective in producing both overt behavioral changes and attitudinal changes related to career decision making.

SUMMARY AND CONCLUSIONS

Group counseling formats were presented in this chapter that serve the various career development needs of individuals. These groups were chosen primarily to represent the end- and midpoints of a hypothetical continuum for classifying career counseling groups. The continuum runs from content to process at its extremes with mixtures in the midrange. The Vocational Exploration Group (VEG) is primarily content oriented with a focus on job demands and satisfiers. The Life Planning Workshop (LPW) is process oriented with an emphasis on current personal life roles and the projection of a career plan into the future. Job Club represents the midrange with both a focus on content (e.g. resume writing, completion of job applications) and process (skills in job search based on networking).

It is clear that group usage in career counseling is on the increase. A current review of the literature as compared to ten years ago clearly substantiated the increasing emphasis on groups in career counseling. In general, this increased usage appears to be positive to clients and counselors alike. A word of caution is important, however, in light of the fact that more professionals are using group formats. While groups are potentially powerful and therapeutic, they can also be damaging in the hands of incompetent leaders. Hopefully, practitioners considering use of a group format will have ample training and experience in general group dynamics and small group leadership. Without knowledge and leadership skills, these groups may well fail to meet their objectives.

An additional comment related to the evaluation of groups is relevant. While usage of groups is on the increase, as is the availability of materials for use with career groups, evaluation research has not kept pace. The groups presented in this chapter have at least a minimum number of controlled experimental studies to substantiate their effects. This is not necessarily the case with well publicized and widely used career group formats. Optimistically, the likelihood of the availability of more credible research related to career groups seems great. Many of the conceptual problems related to specifying desirable outcomes, studying standardized career counseling methods, and assessing clients have been approached (Snodgrass & Healy, 1979; Healy, 1973, 1974) and partially clarified. Nonetheless, the impact of these types of studies on the mainstream of career counseling outcome research remains incomplete.

Considering the potential difficulties with group leadership along with the scarcity of credible outcome research, the state of the art is nonetheless quite positive. Apparently, many counselors are using these group approaches with generally productive results. Further, it is obvious to those who have seen effective career groups function that the potential remains great for this mode of delivery.

BIBLIOGRAPHY

Azrin, N. H., Flores, T., and Kaplan, S. J. Job-finding club: A group assisted program for obtaining employment. *Behavior Research and Therapy,* 1975, *13,* 17-27.

Azrin, N. H., and Besalel, V.A. *Finding a job.* Berkley, CA: Ten Speed Press, In Press, 1982.

Azrin, N. H., and Besalel, V.A. *Job club counselor's manual: A behavioral approach to vocational counseling.* Baltimore, MA: University Park Press, 1980.

Azrin, N. H., Philip, R. A., Themes-Hintos, P., and Basalel, V. A. Comparative evaluation of Job Club Programs with welfare recipients. *Journal of Vocational Behavior,* 1980, *16,* 133-145.

Birney, D., Thomas, L., and Hinkle, J. E. Life planning workshops: Discussion and evaluation. *Student Evaluation Report,* Vol. 8, No. 2, Colorado State University, Fort Collins, CO, 1970.

Cochran, D. Counseling theories: What really helps. Paper presented at International Round Table for the Advancement of Counseling. Cambridge, England, Dec. 15, 1982.

Cochran, D. *The effects of a developmental outreach program on vocational choice processes.* Unpublished doctoral dissertation, University of Arizona, 1972.

Daane, C. *Vocational exploration group: Theory and research.* Tempe, AZ: Studies for Urban Man, Inc., 1972.

Healy, C. C. Evaluation of a replicable group career counseling procedure. *Vocational Guidance Quarterly,* 1974, *23,* 34-40.

Healy, C. C. Toward a replicable method of group career counseling. *Vocational Guidance Quarterly,* 1973, *21,* 214-221.

Helbing, J. C. *De Beroepen Verkennig Groep.* Psychologisch Laboratorium Van de

Universitiet Van Amsterdam, Netherlands, 1976.

Janis, I., and Mann, L. *Decision making: A psychological analysis of conflict choice, and commitment.* New York: Free Press, 1977.

Johnson, R. Life planning and life planning workshops. *Personnel and Guidance Journal,* 1977, *55,* 546-549.

Johnson, N., Johnson, J., and Yates, C. A 6-month follow-up on the effects of the vocational exploration group on career maturity. *Journal of Counseling Psychology,* 1981, *28,* 70-71.

Knelfelkamp, L., and Slepitza, R. A cognitive-developmental model of career development — An adoption of the Perry scheme. *Counseling Pscyhologist,* 1976, *6,* 53-58.

Knickerbocker, B., and Davidshofer, C. Attitudinal outcomes of the life planning workshop. *Journal of Counseling Pscyhology,* 1978, *25,* 103-109.

McIlroy, J. Life-styling workshops: Some new developments. *Personnel and Guidance Journal,* 1979, *57,* 478-479.

Mencke, R., and Cochran, D. The impact of a counseling outreach workshop on vocational development. *Journal of Counseling Psychology,* 1974, *21,* 185-190.

Powers, R. J. Enhancement of former drug abusers' career development through structured group counseling. *Journal of Counseling Psychology,* 1978, 25, 585-587.

Snodgrass, G., and Healy, C. Developing a replicable career decision-making procedure. *Journal of Counseling Psychology,* 1979, *26,* 210-216.

Weselowski, M. D. Self-directed job placement in rehabilitation: A comparative review. *Rehabilitation Counseling Bulletin,* 1981, *28,* 80-89.

Westover, R. *The effects of vocational exploration training for native Americans.* Unpublished doctoral dissertation, Arizona State University, 1979.

Yalom, J. *The theory and practice of group psychotherapy.* New York: Basic Books, Inc., 1970.

Yates, C., Johnson, N., and Johnson, J. Effects of the use of the Vocational Exploration Group on career maturity. *Journal of Counseling Psychology,* 1979, *26,* 368-370.

APPENDIX

Aslanian, C. B., and Schmelter, H. B. *Adult access to education and new careers: A handbook for action.* Princeton, New Jersey: College Board Publications, 1980.

Bargo, M., Jr. *Choices and decisions: A guidebook for constructing values.* San Diego, CA: International Authors, B. V., 1980.

Bartsch, D., and Sandmeyer, L. *Skills, in life/career planning.* Monterey, CA: Brooks/Cole Publishing Company, 1979.

Bartsch, K., Most, E. B., and Girrell, K. W. *Effective personal and career decision making.* New York, NY: Westinghouse Learning

Corp., 1976.

Borchard, D. C., Kelly, J. J., and Weaver, N. P. K. *Your career: Choices, chances, changes.* Dubuque, IA: Kendall/Hunt Publishing Co., 1980.

Chapman, E. N. *Career search: A personal pursuit.* Chicago, IL: Science Research Associates, 1976.

Carney, C. G., Wells, C. F., and Streufert, D. *Career planning: Skills to build your future.* New York, NY: D. Van Nostrand Co., 1981.

Figler, H. E. *Path — A career workbook for liberal arts students.* Cranston, RI: The Carrol Press Publishers, 1975.

Kisiel, M. *Design for change: A guide to new careers.* New York, NY: New Viewpoints/Vision Books, 1980.

Kotter, J. P., Faux, V. A., and McArthur, C. C. *Self-assessment and career development.* Englewood Cliffs, New Jersey, 1978.

Harren, V., Daniels, M., and Buck, J. (Eds.). *Facilitating student's career development.* San Francisco: Jossey-Bass, Inc., 1981.

Harren, V. A. *The influence of sex roles and cognitive styles on the career decision-making of college men and women.* Carbondale, IL: Southern Illinois University, 1979.

Hollis, J. W., and Hollis, L. V. *Career and life planning.* Muncie, IN: Accelerated Development Company, 1976.

McCoy, V. R., Ryan, C., and Lichtenberg, J. W. *The adult life cycle.* Lawrence, KS: The University of Kansas, 1978.

Michelozzi, B. N. *Coming alive from nine to five: The career search handbook.* Palo Alto, CA: Mayfield Publishing Co., 1980.

Scholz, N. T., Prince, J. S., and Miller, P. M. *How to decide: A guide for women.* Princeton, NJ: College Entrance Examination Board, 1975.

Shertzer, B. *Career planning: Freedom to choose.* Boston, MA: Houghton-Mifflin Co., 1981.

Winefordner, D. W. *Career planning and decision-making for college.* Bloomington, IL: McKnight Publishing Co., 1980.

Zunker, V. G. *Using assessment results in career counseling.* Monterey, CA: Brooks/Cole Publishing Co., 1982.

CHAPTER 8

THE USE OF COMPUTERS

JAMES P. SAMPSON, JR.

COMPUTER applications in career development began in the mid-1960s. The systems emphasized (1) providing career information, (2) providing guidance functions, or (3) assisting with college selection. In some cases the student interacted directly with a computer (1 and 2 above), while in other cases the student interacted indirectly by filling out forms that were later processed by the computer (3 above). The computers in use were generally large mainframes operating at a remote location with computer terminals placed in a guidance office or counseling center. The Office of Education (1969) provided descriptions of these early systems. In the early 1970s smaller minicomputers began to compete with the large mainframes. Much cheaper than the large mainframes, their availability contributed to the spread of computer applications in career development.

In the late 1970s a major change in computer-assisted career guidance (CACG) began with the introduction of the microcomputer. This new resource provided several advantages over the larger and more expensive mainframe and minicomputers, including (1) lower equipment cost, (2) easier maintenance, (3) easier operating procedures, (4) elimination of telephone communication problems between a large computer and a remote terminal, and (5) independence from a computer center. These advantages plus the growing number of applications available on the microcomputer have been a major factor in the recent growth of CACG.

This chapter is designed to provide practitioners with an understanding of how computers can be used effectively in facilitating the career development of individuals. A rationale for computer use and a description of the various types of systems available will be presented. Emphasis is placed on providing criteria for evaluating computer applications and suggestions for effective implementation. Also, future trends will be discussed.

RATIONALE

Since the process of career development involves acquiring a broad knowledge of self and various occupational and life-style alternatives, the computer, with its extensive information processing capabilities, becomes a logical resource for career decision making. Not only can computers store and retrieve huge amounts of information but also they can organize it in an infinity of ways to meet the needs of different individuals. One objective of CACG systems has been to enhance the effectiveness of counselors by eliminating the repetitive and routine aspects of information dissemination, thus providing more time for interaction with students (Harris, 1972a). Counselors can spend more time assisting students in understanding the implications of information for future action (Super, 1970). As a result of this approach both the counselor/career development specialist and the computer are performing tasks that are best suited to their capabilities while avoiding tasks for which they are not as well prepared.

TYPES OF COMPUTER-ASSISTED CAREER GUIDANCE SYSTEMS

Six types of CACG systems are currently in use: (1) information systems, (2) guidance systems, (3) indirect access systems, (4) computer assisted testing systems, (5) placement systems, and (6) career library indexing systems.

Information Systems

Information systems are designed to provide individuals with a process for identifying appropriate occupations and for reviewing career information needed to narrow alternatives to a specific choice or choices. Information systems allow the users direct access to a microcomputer, minicomputer, or large mainframe computer via a teletype or cathode ray tube (CRT) terminal. As a result of interacting with the computer, the individual receives a printout that lists potentially appropriate occupations and describes various occupations and educational programs.

The most common pathway individuals take in completing an information system is as follows. (It should be noted that this is a generalization; some specific examples may vary.) The individual begins with a structured search for occupations. An exercise is completed prior to or during initial use of the computer that identifies desired occupational characteristics (e.g. some combination of preferences for work tasks, work settings, satisfaction of values, and use of specific abilities) that the individual believes to be personally appropriate. In addition to these self-ratings, test scores from interest and ability instruments, administered prior to or during computer use, also may be used as a focal point for exploring occupations. The computer then searches its data base and prints out a list of occupations that meets or exceeds the occupational characteristics identified by the user as appropriate. If the individuals do not receive on the list an occupation that they expected, they can access a "why not?" feature and view the factors that prevented a match. Users are then given the opportunity to modify their list of desired occupational characteristics and repeat the computer search for matching occupations to see how the new list of occupations differs from the previous one as a result of the modifications. This is a powerful feature of CACG systems in that it assists the user in understanding the cause and effect relationship between desired occupational characteristics and the likelihood of an occupation providing specific satisfactions.

The second major feature of an information system is the dissemination of occupational and educational information. The user has the option to skip the structured search for occupations and begin by directly accessing the available information. If an occupational file is selected the user identifies one or more occupations and then receives a general description or answers to specific questions. Information on job-seeking skills also may be provided. If an educational file is selected, the user receives some combination of information on preparation for entry into an occupation, programs of education and training at various institutions, available financial aid, military training options, and apprenticeship options. The occupational and educational information may be local, regional, state, or national. The information is collected from a variety of government and private sources. Updates of information range from continuous revision as new data are received to yearly revision. It should be noted that the quality and clarity of information presented varies from system to system.

Jacobson and Grabowski (1982) identify CHOICES, CIS, COIN, CVIS, EGES, GIS, and SCAD as information systems (their exact terminology is *online career information systems*). Katz and Shatkin (1980) specifically mention CIS and GIS information systems. A series of federal grants provided by the Department of Labor and the National Occupational Information Coordinating Committee have made possible the establishment of statewide career information systems. Jacobson and Grabowski (1982) state that these systems were "developed to meet the increasing need of youth and adults for relevant, reliable, and current information about education and occupations." CIS, GIS, CHOICES, or COIN have provided the basic structure for most of the twenty-five state systems that have been implemented or are in the process of implementation as of 1981. Jacobson and Grabowski provide a listing of statewide systems indicating the basic structure of the system and the source of federal grant funds. Figure 8-1 provides a glossary of acronyms for the CACG systems described in this chapter. Shatkin (1980) provides comparative descriptions of eighteen CACG systems including sources of further information. Moore et al. (1981) also provide a comparison of systems. Maze and Cummings (1982) describe and analyze CIS, GIS, SIGI, and DISCOVER and briefly compare most existing systems on several dimensions.

Guidance Systems

Guidance systems are broader in scope than information systems. In addition to the structured search and information dissemination functions described previously, guidance systems provide the user with (1) instruction in the career decision-making process, (2) assistance in prediction of future success, (3) assistance in developing future plans, and (4) monitoring of progress. It

ACSCI	Association of Computer-Based Systems for Career Information
CACG	Computer-Assisted Career Guidance
CALI	Computer-Assisted Library Index
CHOICES	Computerized Heuristic Occupational Information and Career Exploration System
CIS	Career information System
COIN	Coordinated Occupational Information Network
COIS	Corporate Occupational Information System
CVIS	Computerized Vocational Information System
DISCOVER	
ECES	Educational and Career Exploration System
ENCORE	
ESI-Hester	
EXPLORE	
GIS	Guidance Information System
GRAD II	
GUIDEPAK	
OCIPS	Officer Career Information and Planning System
SCAD	Student Career Assessment and Determination
SEARCH	System Exploration and Research for Career Help
SGIS	Student Guidance Information Service
SIGI	System of Interactive Guidance and Information
VIP	Vocational Information Program
VOCOMP	Vocational Computer-Assisted Matching Program

Figure 8-1. Glossary of Acronyms.

should be noted that all guidance systems do not provide each of the above functions. Also, a guidance system may or may not allow omission of a structured search for occupations. In discussing the monitoring function, Harris (1974) states that the computer is capable of (1) relating personal data to the individual's exploration, (2) recording the individual's path of decision making, (3) pointing out discrepancies, and (4) reviewing previous uses of the system. Guidance systems make greater use of the computer's data analysis and instructional capabilities as well as encompassing a greater portion of the total career counseling and guidance process.

Katz and Shatkin (1980) identify SIGI and DISCOVER as guidance systems (their exact terminology is *information and guidance systems*). Jacobson and Grabowski (1982) include EXPLORE along with SIGI and DISCOVER in this category. Harris and Tiedeman (1974) identify CVIS, ECES, SIGI, and DISCOVER as having guidance (monitoring) capabilities.

Differences Between Systems

Figure 8-2 provides a discussion of the differences between information and guidance systems. Since each CACG system varies to some degree, the generalizations presented in this figure are not equally valid for all systems.

Information Systems
  Shorter average system completion time
  Greater emphasis on local and state information
  Larger number of terminals and systems currently in use

Guidance Systems
  Interaction between the computer and the individual tends to be more conversational and personalized
  More time is generally spent on the assessment process prior to a structured search for occupations
  Greater emphasis on instruction and modeling of the career decision-making process
  Provision for monitoring of the individual's progress

Figure 8-2. Differences Between Systems.

Indirect Access Systems

Indirect access CACG systems are designed to assist individuals in identifying occupations, colleges, and sources of financial aid that meet their needs. This type of system is designated as "indirect" by Harris (1972a) because the user does not interact directly with the computer through a terminal. On a standardized questionnaire, clients indicate the factors that are important in their selection of an occupation and a college. Some indirect access systems also request that the user supply test score data. The questionnaire is then mailed to a central computer site where it is processed and the results are returned to the user. The printout, which may take several weeks to deliver, usually contains a list of occupations, colleges, and financial aid sources that match the factors identified on the questionnaire (Jacobson & Grabowski, 1982). Students tend to use this type of system only once (Harris, 1972a). The time delays and one-time use patterns that exist with these systems tend to reduce the exploratory behavior that is typically exhibited by individuals using the direct access systems described previously. The rapid computer response time and interactive nature of direct access systems encourage exploratory behavior in a way that is not possible with the indirect approach. Jacobson and Grabowski (1982) identify SEARCH, VIP, and VOCOMP as batch process (indirect access) systems. Sources of further information are also provided. A version of SGIS operates as an indirect access system in Canada (Cassie, Ragsdale, & Robinson, 1979).

Computer-Assisted Testing Systems

Most of the repetitive clerical and administrative tasks associated with testing can be effectively handled by a computer. This allows the counselor to concentrate more fully on helping an individual in determining appropriate tests, providing interpretative data, and integrating assessment data into the counseling process. The most common application of computer technology in testing involves optically scanning, scoring, profiling, and generating interpretative narrative reports for standardized paper-and-pencil instruments. A variety of interest, values, career maturity, and personality inventories as well as aptitude tests are available in this format. *A Counselor's Guide to Vocational Guidance Instruments* (Kapes & Mastie, 1982) identifies instruments that provide computer scoring and generation of interpretative narrative reports. Some computer applications combine the results of two or more instruments. GUIDEPAK combines the Strong-Campbell Interest Inventory with the California Psychological Inventory through the use of interpretive narrative reports and a user workbook (Pick, 1978).

The testing process is generally as follows: the individual begins by completing a paper-and-pencil instrument; the answer sheet is mailed to a central computer processing site where it is optically scanned, scored, and profiled (detailed narrative reports are sometimes produced); the results are returned to the original testing center where an interpretation is usually offered to the individual. One to two weeks will generally elapse from the completion of the test to the receipt of the results. One recent innovation uses a local microcomputer and printer as input and output devices to reduce the traditional time lag. The actual scoring process still occurs at a central computer site.

Another approach utilizes a microcomputer to administer the test in addition to the scoring, profiling, and report generation functions described earlier. The individual responds to items presented one at a time at the computer terminal. After the test is completed, the items are scored and profiled or stored for later processing. Clients evaluate their experience with computer-assisted testing as positive (Byers, 1981; Johnson & Johnson, 1981). Error rates for computer-assisted systems are lower in comparison with paper-and-pencil tests because items are presented one at a time (Byers, 1981). Space (1981) reports that professional staff spend less time engaged in clerically related assessment tasks and that the traditional turn-around time to complete the process is reduced from fourteen days to thirty minutes or less. Computer-assisted testing has also been shown to be cost effective when compared with traditional methods of assessment (Byrnes & Johnson, 1971; Space, 1981; Stout, 1981). Some computer applications provide for adaptive testing strategies where an instrument "is tailored to an individual during the testing process, such that those items that are most appropriate to the individual and most informative about the characteristic being measured are administered" (Vale, 1981). This approach generally results in further reductions in administration time.

One note of caution; most tests currently administered by computer were originally developed for a traditional paper-and-pencil approach. Differences in the administration process may make the original paper-and-pencil norms inappropriate for computer administered tests. New norms or evidence that existing norms are valid for use with computers is needed. Until this dilemma is resolved, test results using paper-and-pencil norms need to be interpreted with caution.

Placement Systems

A major factor in providing job placement services involves the collection, maintenance, and dissemination of employment information. The capabilities of the computer can be used to improve the effectiveness of placement personnel by increasing the quantity and speed of data processing. Comprehensive, current information is beneficial to clients in obtaining employment and to employers in hiring personnel. Computer-assisted instruction modules also can assist users in learning effective job search strategies. Mayberry (1978) describes a batch processing system, known as GRAD II, which provides students with a list of employers who have job openings that match their interests. A similar type of listing is provided employers that identifies appropriate applicant matches. The objective of the system is to "create a 'known' link between students and employers who are actively looking for each other, thereby cutting down the communications lagtime commonly found with most conventional methods" (Mayberry, 1978). A similar employer-student matching system is described by Barkhaus and Crandall (1976). Nagy (1978) describes a computerized scheduling system for on-campus employment interviews. Galloway (1978) describes a system that assists with record keeping, report generation, and text processing in a placement center. A microcomputer-based system being developed by the Florida Department of Education (Center for Career Development Services) entitled, *TIPS for Successful Employment and Living*, provides computer-assisted instruction modules on the job search, career progression, and selected life skills.

Career Library Indexing Systems

The focal point of a career resource center is the collection of career information materials. A comprehensive career resource center will contain as many as fifteen different types of print-based, audiovisual, human, and computer-based information. Individuals face a potentially overwhelming task in identifying and locating information relevant to their needs. A career library indexing system is designed to provide one comprehensive index of all materials. This approach has an advantage over professionally produced indexes of packaged career information, which fail to reference other types of material contained in the library. Indexes maintained manually in card files or notebooks consume considerable staff time for maintenance in comparison with computerized systems. One example of a computerized approach is the Computer-Assisted Library Index (CALI). "The ultimate goals of this system are to (1) make it easier to find appropriate information, thus increasing the amount of material that can be explored in a given time period; and (2) expand the role of the computer in completing clerical tasks, thus increasing the amount of time staff can spend assisting students in using appropriate information" (Sampson, 1982). Smith (1983) describes a microcomputer-based career library indexing system. With the increasing availability of microcomputer and data based management software packages, this type of computer application will eventually be a basic feature of career resource centers.

EVALUATION OF EXISTING SYSTEMS

Computer-assisted career guidance systems have been in operation long enough for some general conclusions to be reached about their use. The following evaluation focuses on information systems as well as guidance systems. Of the types of systems available today, these two are the most widely used.

Research and Evaluation Data

A number of studies have examined the effectiveness of CACG systems. Harris (1972b), Myers, Lindeman, Thompson, and Patrick (1975), and Pyle and Stripling (1976) found that use of CVIS, ECES, and SIGI resulted in career maturity gains for high school and college students. Counselors and CVIS were found by Price (1974) to be equally effective in facilitating high school students' course registration. Melhus, Hershenson, and Vermillion (1973) found CVIS and counselors to be equally effective in facilitating the vocational planning of high ability high school students. Low ability students made better progress in their vocational planning with intervention from a counselor. In a comparison between counselors and CVIS, Maola and Kane (1976) found the computer-assisted approach to be more effective in presenting occupational information. Chapman, Katz, and Norris (1977) found SIGI to be effective in facilitating college student's value clarification, career planning, and assimilation of occupational information. In a related study, Cochran, Hoffman, Strand, and Warren (1977) found SIGI to be effective in helping college students choose a major. Increased career awareness and information-gathering activities were the outcome of student use of GIS (Ryan, Drummond, & Shannon, 1980). Both Rayman, Bryson, and Bowlsbey (1978) and Savin (1979) report positive user evaluation of DISCOVER. The former study also found that DISCOVER helped students to be more specific about their career and educational plans. Cassie, Ragsdale, and Robinson (1979) and Reardon, Bonnell, and Huddleston (1982) report positive user evaluations of CHOICES. Extensive research reviews may be found in Clyde (1979), Parish, Rosenberg, and Wilkinson (1979), and Maze and Cummings (1982).

There appears to be consistent support for the contention that CACG systems can be an effective resource for helping individuals make career decisions. Many of the studies conducted up to this point have focused on user evaluations of systems (Clyde, 1979). A need exists to go beyond the emphasis of the previous studies, which was to establish the viability of CACG systems, and move to determining how this resource best can be used by individuals with widely varying characteristics and needs. Snipes and McDaniels (1981), Clyde (1979), and Parish et al. (1979) provide agendas for future CACG research. Additional areas needing investigation include (1) the interaction between various client characteristics and CACG effectiveness and (2) identification of situations where counselor intervention is most needed. Katz and Shatkin (1980) provide a framework for comparison and evaluation of CACG systems.

Counselor / Career Information Specialist Intervention Strategies

Most CACG system developers describe their programs as self-instructional, which is to say that the combination of available user workbooks, handbooks, and on-line prompts are sufficient to aid users in successfully completing the system. Evaluations of various systems do not always support this position. Cassie et al. (1979), Ryan and Drummond (1979), and Ryan et al. (1980) state that counselors are needed to help students understand CACG system operation. "Students knowledge of self is often so poor that they cannot make reasonable use of self determined aptitude levels" (Cassie et al., 1979). They further state that additional counselor assistance would result in increased system use by students. The North Carolina Occupational Information Coordinating Committee (1978) evaluated nine CACG systems and concluded that counselor intervention was required. In reviewing the Melhus et al. (1973) data, it seems especially important to provide counselor intervention for low ability students using CACG systems. Failure to provide for appropriate counselor intervention increases the likelihood of individuals failing to effectively use the system or failing to understand the outcome, e.g. "The computer told me that I should be an accountant." Public faith in computer generated data (Lister, 1970) further complicates this issue.

In a study comparing counselor intervention strategies, it was found that users preferred a structured intervention over a nonstructured approach while using SIGI (Sampson & Stripling, 1979). The structured approach included (1) orientation to the SIGI system, (2) introduction to each of the six subsystems, (3) discussion of the student's progress through the system, including problems encountered at the terminal, (4) referral to other appropriate career and academic resources, and (5) additional counseling initiated at the student's request. The nonstructured approach involved counselor intervention that was initiated when students felt the need for assistance. Students in the control group who received no counselor intervention wanted to talk with a counselor after completing SIGI. It appears that counselor intervention is an important aspect of an individual's use of both information and guidance systems. Sampson and Pyle (1983) provide guidelines for determining appropriate counselor intervention strategies.

Human Factors Design

Human factors design is concerned with the ways in which the user interacts with a computer. Systems that carefully incorporate human factors into their design are easy to use and understand. Failure to include human factors into the systems development process results in systems that can be confusing and frustrating to use. The potential benefits of a CACG system can be negated if the user is confused about its use or is frustrated with its operation. Important human factors for CACG systems include screen formatting, use of upper/lower case characters, appropriate reading level, user control of display advancement, a limited but powerful response set, step-by-step instructions, and summary displays. Guidelines for incorporating human factors into computer systems are provided by Johnson, Godin, and Bloomquist (1981). In evaluating present CACG systems, most evaluators agree that the guidance type has been most successful in making human factors an integral part of their design.

Theoretical Basis of Systems

Theories provide direction for the design of career development interventions. Theories indicate what needs to be done, for whom, how, and at what time. SIGI is an example of a system that is well grounded in a specific theoretical orientation. When a solid theoretical base for a CACG system does not exist, the implementation and evaluation process is more difficult.

CACG System Use With Various Populations

The initial emphasis in developing CACG systems was directed toward high school and college student populations. McDaniels, Snipes, and Peevy (1980) report that the twelve to twenty-two year old age group comprise the bulk of CACG users. As a result, other user populations have not been as well served by CACG systems. As awareness of the career development needs of adults, individuals with physical disabilities, women returning to the work force, disadvantaged students, and low ability students became more widely recognized, changes in CACG systems began to emerge. Support materials and intervention strategies for existing systems have been revised by counselors working with nontraditional populations. Such an approach was taken to assist deaf students (National Technical Institute for the Deaf, 1976) and women returning to the work force (Dickson, 1979) in using SIGI. CACG developers have revised some existing systems. A version of SIGI for adults with work experience is now in process. A version of DISCOVER appropriate for adults changing careers is currently available (Rayman, 1981). ENCORE is also available to assist adults with career planning. DISCOVER III is being designed for adults in business and industry. In some cases CACG developers are designing entirely new systems. COIS is designed for individuals in large business organizations (Amico, 1981). OCIPS is designed for Army Officers (Philips et al., 1980). VOCOMP and ESI-Hester are designed for rehabilitation clients (Kruger, 1980). A framework for CACG system development specific to the health professions has been proposed by Wright (1978). Research by James and Smith (1972) and Melhus et al. (1973) has provided useful information for counselors working with disadvantaged and low ability students.

CACG System Referral to Other Resources

Most CACG systems mention, in the text material presented on the terminal or in the supporting written materials, the advisability of reviewing additional career information and talking with a counselor if further assistance is needed. Some CACG systems suggest that counselor contacts are appropriate at several points during an individual's use of the program. These recommendations, however, tend to lack specific details as to how the counselor can provide assistance. The user, without an understanding of what is involved in counseling, may experience enough confusion and anxiety that he or she avoids contact with a counselor. Even though each individual's use of CACG system is different, a generalized description of a typical counselor intervention is possible, e.g. several approaches a counselor might take in assisting individuals in evaluating their abilities.

Cost Effectiveness

Developing comparative cost effectiveness data on existing CACG systems is a difficult task. The diversity of variables involved include hardware costs, lease costs, software development costs, local data base development costs, and data transmission costs (Clyde, 1979). These factors can result in considerable price variability at different institutions for the same CACG system. Katz and Shatkin (1980) estimate that most CACG systems cost 2 to 4 dollars for one hour of time spent by a student at a computer terminal. Even in today's time of limited financial resources, these cost figures seem acceptable in view of the positive effect CACG systems may have on an individual's career development.

Implementation of CACG Systems

The most important factor in ensuring successful operation of a CACG system involves the way in which implementation into the existing program takes place. The lack of an appropriate implementation process can lead to staff ineffectiveness and resistance, poor referral and financial support from the institution, and limited user awareness of the services available. Three factors discussed by Byrnes and Johnson (1981) that are important for successful implementation include (1) the readiness of an organization to change, (2) a planned strategy for change, and (3) an approach for overcoming possible staff resistance. Some CACG systems have been poorly implemented. Counselors and career development specialists were not involved in the needs assessment or decision-making process regarding system selection. The timetable for implementation was unrealistically short. No overall implementation plan was devised. Staff resistance was ignored or dealt with by administrative fiat. A critically important variable in effective implementation involves staff training. Clyde (1979) states that some CACG systems provide little if any staff training. Even when staff training is available, a lack of funding, which in some cases results from poor planning, prevents adequate staff development. Cassie et al. (1979) and Ryan et al. (1980) document CACG implementation problems. It is clear that considerable future efforts on the part of CACG system developers and local staff need to take place in order to improve the process of implementation.

FACTORS TO CONSIDER IN SELECTING A CACG SYSTEM

Figure 8-3 provides a summary of factors that counselors can use in evaluating information and guidance systems.

What research and evaluation data are available about the system?
What suggestions does the CAVG system developer make concerning counselor/career development staff intervention strategies?
What support materials in the form of workbooks, handbooks, and other off-line exercises are provided by the CACG system developer? Are the materials appropriate in terms of reading and age level for the populations being served? (Sample copies of support materials are usually available for review.)
How effectively are human factors incorporated into the CACG system design?
Does the CACG system developer identify the theoretical basis for their system? What suggestions are made for integrating the CACG system into the existing career development program?
How approapriate is the CACG system for the various populations being served in the existing career development program?
Does the CACG system provide the user with specific suggestions as to how a counselor can provide assistance?
What general cost effectiveness data is available? How will local variables (hardware, hardware maintenance, data base development, and data transmission) impact cost effectiveness?
Is the computer hardware capable of expansion if additional data processing needs are identified in the future? What additional software is compatable with the computer?
What suggestions does the CACG system developer make concerning implementation? What type of training services are available (both on-site and at remote locations)? Are implementation and staff training manuals/guides provided?
What sources are used in developing career information? How current is the information? How often is the information updated? How broad is the coverage of occupations included in the system? What combination of local, regional, state, and national information can the system support? What effort is required in developing a local data base?
What validity and reliability data are available on the assessment component of the system? What decision rules apply to the structured search for occupations?

Figure 8-3. Factors to Consider in Selecting a CACG System.

POINTS TO CONSIDER FOR EFFECTIVE USE OF CACG SYSTEMS

The following material provides an agenda of points for consideration *before* the arrival of a CACG system.

1. *Implementation Strategy.* The implementation strategy should begin with an assessment of present and future needs. Potential CAVG systems can then be evaluated in terms of these needs. Figure 8-3 can be used to assist in this process. After a decision is reached, a step-by-step plan for implementing the CACG system into the existing career development program needs to be formulated. Caution is necessary in developing a realistic timetable for implementation. Staff training and an opportunity to test the system with a limited number of users needs to be completed prior to full operation. A method for dealing with potential staff resistance needs to be devised. As the operations begin, potential referral sources can be introduced to the system. A target date for designing and initiating an evaluation process can also be agreed upon.

2. *Counselor/Career Development Specialist Intervention Strategies.* Intervention can be made on an individual, group, or classroom basis. Responsibilities can be divided on the basis of training and experience between counselors/career development specialists, clerical support staffs/paraprofessionals, and peer counselors.

3. *Ethical Considerations.* The use of computers in providing services creates some unique ethical problems. Some of the important issues include limiting storage of data to essential information, limiting the time information is maintained, ensuring the accuracy of information stored on the system, and restricting access to the information. Specific methods of ensuring confidentiality of student records is presented in Chapter 17. A discussion of ethical issues relating to confidentiality, use of computer-assisted testing, and the need for counselor intervention is presented by Sampson and Pyle (1983).

4. *Site Management.* Effective site management contributes to positive outcomes for CACG users. A method for scheduling and coordinating computer terminal and counseling appointments needs to be devised. It is advisable to make some type of ar-

rangement for maintenance of computer equipment. Responsibilities for providing assistance to individuals while at the computer terminal have to be determined. The timing and distribution method for support materials also needs to be determined. The potential settings for CACG systems are varied. McDaniels (1982) lists the following settings for CACG use: "Libraries, senior citizens' centers, CETA programs, employment agencies, correctional units, rehabilitative services offices, women's resource centers, and . . . large employers," in addition to traditional school and post-secondary locations. Cooperative arrangements have been used where one CACG system has been provided at several different settings.

FUTURE TRENDS

The decreasing cost and increasing availability of microcomputers will accelerate the use of CACG systems. Existing systems will be improved and new systems will be developed. Networking will allow individuals to access, via phone lines, occupational/education data bases and programs stored across the country. Hard copy teletype terminals will be used less often, while CRT (video display) terminals with attached page printers will become the norm. Indirect access systems will tend to be used less frequently. There will be increased integration of multimedia in CACG systems. For example, microcomputer controlled video discs will present career information (DISCOVER II presently has this capability). In the assessment area, adaptive testing will be more widely used. Standard paper-and-pencil tests will be used less frequently. Test results from different instruments will be analyzed by computer to produce an integrated report that addresses several aspects of career development at once. Generalized interpretations of test results will be presented on microcomputer controlled videotape or video disc. In placement and in large career library settings the computer will become an essential information resource. There will likely be increased efforts by national groups, e.g. the Association of Computer-Based Systems for Career Information (ACSCI), towards standardization of career information data bases contained in various statewide systems. National groups, such as ACSCI, will undoubtedly continue to work on refining standards for CACG system development, implementation, and operation. Finally, the unique ethical dilemmas that arise from using computers in the helping professions will continue to be examined by professionals and the general public.

In general, CACG systems will be available to a more diverse group of users in a greater variety of settings. These systems will emerge from being new and innovative approaches to providing services, as they have been viewed in the past, to being a standard component of a comprehensive career development program.

BIBLIOGRAPHY

Amico, A.M. Computerized career information. *Personnel Journal*, 1981, *60*, 632-633.

Barkhaus, R.S., and Crandall, R. Computer placement at a commuter campus. *Journal of College Placement*, 1976, *36*, 40-43.

Byers, A.P. Psychological evaluation by means of an on-line computer. *Behavior Research Methods and Instrumentation*, 1981, *13*, 585-587.

Byrnes, E., and Johnson, J.H. Change technology and the implementation of automation in mental health care settings. *Behavior Research Methods and Instrumentation*, 1981, *13*, 573-580.

Cassie, J.R.B., Ragsdale, R.G., and Robinson, M. *A comparative analysis of choices and S.G.I.S.* Toronto, Canada: Ontario Department of Education, 1979. (ERIC Document Reproduction Service No. ED 180 132).

Chapman, W., Katz, M.R., and Norris, L. *SIGI: Field test and evaluation of a computer-based system of interactive guidance and information.* Two volumes. Princeton, NJ: Educational Testing Service, 1977.

Clyde, J.S. *Computerized career information and guidance systems.* Columbus, OH: The Ohio State University, ERIC Clearinghouse on Adult, Career, and Vocational Education, 1979. (ERIC Document Reproduction Service No. ED 179 764).

Cochran, D.J., Hoffman, S.D., Strand, K.H., and Warren, P.M. Effects of client/computer interaction on career decision-making processes. *Journal of Counseling Psychology*, 1977, *24*, 308-312.

Dickson, J. *Enhancing a computer guidance system for women in transition.* Unpublished manuscript, Central Michigan University, 1979.

Galloway, J.L. A different approach to a familiar problem. *Journal of college placement*, 1978, *38*, 42-43.

Harris, J. (Ed.) *Tested practices: Computer assisted guidance systems.* Washington, D.C.: National Vocational Guidance Association, 1972a.

Harris, J. Analysis of the effects of a computer based vocational information system on selected aspects of vocational planning (Doctoral dissertation, Northern Illinois University 1972b) *Dissertation Abstracts International*, 1973,

33, 4089A-4090A. (University Microfilms No. 73-5045).

Harris, J. The computer: Guidance tool of the future. *Journal of Counseling Psychology*, 1974, *21*, 331-339.

Harris, J., and Tiedeman, D. *The computer and guidance in the United States: Past, present and a possible future*. Northern Illinois University, 1974. (ERIC Document Reproduction Service No. ED 095 372).

Jacobson, M.D., and Grabowski, B.T. Computerized systems of career information and guidance: A state-of-the-art. *Journal of Educational Technology Systems*, 1982, *10*, 235-255.

James, E.M., and Smith, J.D. *Traditional vs. computer-based vocational guidance and counseling systems: Implications for disadvantaged youth*, 1972. (ERIC Document Reproduction Service No. Ed 089 150).

Johnson, J.H., Godin, S.W., and Bloomquist, M.L. Human factors engineering in computerized mental health care delivery. *Behavior Research Methods and Instrumentation*, 1981, *13*, 425-429.

Johnson, J.H., and Johnson, K.N. Psychological considerations related to the development of computerized testing stations. *Behavior Research Methods and Instrumentation*, 1981, *13*, 421-424.

Kapes, J.T., and Mastie, M.M. *A counselor's guide to vocational guidance instruments*. Falls Church, VA: National Vocational Guidance Association, 1982.

Katz, M.R., and Shatkin, L. *Computer-assisted guidance: Concepts and practices* (ETS RR-80-1). Princeton, NJ: Educational Testing Service, 1980.

Kruger, R. *Occupational information systems and their use in rehabilitation — Revised)*. Fisherville, VA: Research Utilization Laboratory, Woodrow Wilson Rehabilitation Center, 1980. (ERIC Document Reproduction Service No. ED 179 823).

Lister, C. Privacy and large-scale personal data systems. *Personnel and Guidance Journal*, 1970, *49*, 207-211.

Maola, J.F., and Kane, G. Comparison of computer-based versus counselor-based occupational information systems with disadvantaged vocational students. *Journal of Counseling Psychology*, 1976, *23*, 163-165.

Mayberry, M.E. GRAD II — placement's answer to the hidden job market. *Journal of College Placement*, 1978, *38*, 36-41.

Maze, M., and Cummings, R. *How to select a computer-assisted career guidance system*. Madison, WI: Wisconsin Vocational Studies Center, University of Wisconsin, 1982.

McDaniels, C. Comprehensive career information systems for the 1980's. *Vocational Guidance Quarterly*, 1982, *30*, 344-350.

McDaniels, C., Snipes, J.K., and Peevy, E.S. *A feasibility study for a career information system for Virginia*. Prepared for the Virginia Occupational Information Coordinating Committee, 1980.

Melhus, G.E., Hershenson, D.B., and Vermillion, M.E. Computer-assisted versus traditional vocational counseling with high and low readiness clients. *Journal of Vocational Behavior*, 1973, *3*, 137-144.

Moore, R. et al. *Exploration of career information delivery systems via computerization*. Richlands, VA: Southwest Virginia Community College, 1981. (ERIC Doc-

ument Reproduction Service No. Ed 203 910).
Myers, R.A., Lindeman, R.H., Thompson, A.S., and Patrick, T.A. Effects of educational and career exploration systems on vocational maturity. *Journal of Vocational Behavior,* 1975, *6,* 245-254.
Nagy, D.R. A positive solution to campus interview scheduling. *Journal of College Placement,* 1978, *38,* 35.
National Technical Institute for the Deaf. *SIGI: System of Interactive Guidance and Information. A study of the use of a computer-based aid to career decision-making of the National Technical Institute for the Deaf.* Rochester, NY: Author, 1976. (ERIC Document Reproduction Service No. ED 142 797).
North Carolina Occupational Information Coordinating Committee. *North Carolina career information software delivery system study.* A report prepared by the Office of State Management Systems, 1978.
Office of Education. *Computer-based vocational guidance systems.* Washington, DC: U.S. Department of Health, Education and Welfare, 1969.
Parish, P.A., Rosenberg, H., and Wilkinson, L. *Career information resources, applications, and research 1950-1979.* Boulder, CO: University of Colorado, 1979.
Philips, S.D., Cairo, P.C., Myers, R.A., Ryan, T.G., Hoffer, G.L., and Cross-Silverman, M. *Career planning modules for the Officer Career Information and Planning System.* Alexandria, VA: U.S. Army Research Institute for the Behavioral and Social Sciences. Research Report 1257, 1980. (ERIC Document Reproduction Service No. ED 207 554).
Pick, D.J. *GUIDEPAK.* Palo Alto, California: Behaviordyne, Inc., 1978.
Price, G.E. Counselor and computer effectiveness in helping students select courses. *Journal of Counseling Psychology,* 1974, *21,* 351-354.
Pyle, K R., and Stripling, R.O. The counselor, the computer and career development. *The Vocational Guidance Quarterly,* 1976, *25,* 71-75.
Rayman, J.R. Computer-assisted career guidance for adults. *New Directions for Continuing Education,* 1981, *10,* 85-94.
Rayman, J.R., Bryson, D.L., and Bowlsbey, J.H. The field trial of DISCOVER: A new computerized interactive guidance system. *Vocational Guidance Quarterly,* 1978, *26,* 349-360.
Reardon, R.C., Bonnell, Jr., R.O., and Huddleston, M.R. Self-directed career exploration: A comparison of CHOICES and the Self-Directed Search. *Journal of Vocational Behavior,* 1982, *20,* 22-30.
Ryan, C.W., and Drummond, R.J. *Preliminary evaluation report MOICC: Guidance Information System.* University of Maine, 1979. (ERIC Document Reproduction Service No. ED 177 423).
Ryan, C.W., Drummond, R.J., and Shannon, M.D. Guidance Information System: An analysis of impact on school counseling. *School Counselor,* 1980, *28,* 93-97.
Sampson, Jr. J.P. A computer-assisted library index for career materials. *Journal of College Student Personnel,* 1982, *23,* 539-540.
Sampson, Jr., J.P., and Pyle, K. R. Ethical issues involved with the use of computer-assisted counseling, testing and guidance systems. *Personnel and Guidance Journal,* 1983, *61,* 283-287.

Sampson, Jr., J.P., and Stripling, R.O. Strategies for counselor intervention with a computer-assisted career guidance system. *The Vocational Guidance Quarterly,* 1979, *27,* 230-238.

Savin, G. *The DISCOVER program in Highland, Indiana, 1979.* Unpublished manuscript, School Town of Highland, IN (46322), 1979.

Shatkin, L. *Computer assisted guidance: Description of Systems* (ETS RR-80-23). Princeton, NJ: Educational Testing Service, 1980.

Smith, E. CAREER KEY: A career library management system. *The Vocational Guidance Quarterly,* 1983,*32,* 52-56.

Snipes, J.K., and McDaniels, C. Theoretical foundations for career information delivery systems. *Vocational Guidance Quarterly,* 1981, *29,* 307-314.

Space, L.G. The computer as psychometrician. *Behavior Research Methods and Instrumentations,* 1981, *13,* 595-606.

Stout, R.L. New approaches to the design of computerized interviewing and testing systems. *Behavior Research Methods and Instrumentation,* 1981, *13,* 436-442.

Super, D.E. *Computer-assisted counseling.* New York: Teachers College Press, Columbia University, 1970.

Vale, C.D. Design and implementation of a micro-computer-based adaptive testing system. *Behavior Research Methods and Instrumentation,* 1981, *13,* 399-406.

Wright, Jr. R.B. *An information system for career counseling and guidance in the health fields: Some considerations for planning.* Paper presented at the Annual Meeting of the Association for the Development of Computer-Based Instructional Systems, Dallas, Texas, March, 1978. (ERIC Document Reproduction Service No. ED 162 623).

Part III
PROGRAM STRATEGIES

INTRODUCTION

For several years now, many leaders in the counseling field have been arguing that counselors and counseling psychologists should disengage themselves from the total commitment to direct services, one-to-one, and small group approaches. For example, they have been describing "the Cube" (Morrill, Oetting, & Hurst, 1974), systems approaches (Hosford & Ryan, 1970), outreach (Morrill & Banning, 1973), subcultural needs of women and minorities (Lewis, 1972; Palomeras, 1971; Smith, 1970), political action (Solomon, 1982), and other ideas as alternatives to traditional practice. The concurrent theme has been concern about the survival of the profession. "I don't have much hope that a counselor, however good he or she may be, who can only deliver direct service to one client at a time will make enough impact on our society to continue to support that activity" (Parker, 1974).

Perhaps this very brief background serves to set the stage for the introduction to the chapters in Part III. The remainder of this introductory section (1) identifies some of the common themes in the following nine chapters and (2) briefly reviews salient points in them.

COMMON THEMES

There are four common themes in these chapters. First, each chapter offers or reviews practical programming ideas that a counselor could implement or modify. Wherever possible, the authors have limited their reports to validated prior efforts most appropriate for replication. The program descriptions or counseling techniques described are not inclusive but simply illustrative of best practice in the field. Second, a systems approach to program development is a common theme in these chapters. The authors refer to such topics as environmental assessments, writing goal and objective statements, using a wide variety of intervention techniques, pilot testing and feedback, product evaluation, and accountability. A third common theme is the use of instructional design principles. Students and other clients with career development needs can be instructed to solve problems, become assertive, get information, and make and implement choices if they are systematically exposed to planned learning experiences. Fourth, each chapter suggests that there is a need in the field for highly trained career specialists who can change organizations, be advocates for clients, endure and even thrive in spite of personal sacrifice, and are primarily judged by a commitment to help people effectively.

OVERVIEW

The foundation for virtually all career interventions are the material and human resources that career specialists can draw upon to support their work. Chapters 9, "Developing a Career Resource Center," and 10, "Using Community Resources," describe basic program goals and tested professional practice in these areas. Minor thoroughly reviews the most recent developments in career center operations, staffing, stocking, and evaluation. Lenz follows with a review of the benefits, issues, and strategies for fully utilizing community-based resources in career interventions.

In Chapter 11, "Career Planning Through Instruction," Gimmestad analyzes curriculum or course centered career interventions that have been carefully developed and tested in recent years. His analysis includes historical perspective on this oldest form of career intervention, as well as descriptions of some of the most noteworthy contemporary efforts in this area.

Chapters 12, 13, and 14 focus on the special career program needs of women, disabled persons, and ethnic minorities. In each chapter, Kahnweiler, Burkhead, and Stone have reviewed the literature on the special career related needs of these populations, conceptualized program goals and activities most likely to address these needs, and described exemplary prior efforts to remedy them. The authors have sought to direct the attention of other practitioners to the most important considerations involved in implementing comprehensive career interventions for members of these three groups.

In Chapter 15, "Programs in Organizations," Domkowksi provides a complete review of one of the fastest growing areas of career development activity. She has carefully studied and analyzed the issues most critical to successful program development in this area and follows with descriptions of some of the most significant work completed in recent years. The material in this chapter is drawn from literature sources presently unfamiliar to many career specialists, and her presentation provides previously untapped information for practitioners desiring to initiate programs in organizational settings.

Chapter 16, "Accountability in Program Development," by Peterson, and Chapter 17, "Professional and Ethical Issues," by Montgomery and Sampson, also break new ground for career specialists. Peterson argues for a reconceptualization of accountability in career interventions, suggesting that cognitive outputs rather than behavioral outcomes may better serve as indicators of program effectiveness. Montgomery and Sampson urge career specialists to become aware of unique ethical issues in the career area and to attend to the highest standards of professional practice.

Taken together, the nine chapters in Part III, *Program Strategies*, address a variety of professional issues, role relationships, program strategies, outreach activities, and priorities that career specialists are called to address in the development of comprehensive career interventions for youth and adults.

BIBLIOGRAPHY

Hosford, R. E., and Ryan, T. E. Systems design in the development of counseling and guidance programs. *Personnel and Guidance Journal,* 1970, *49,* 221-230.

Lewis, J. (Ed.). Women and counselors. (Special Issue) *Personnel and Guidance Journal,* 1972, *51,* 84-156.

Morrill, W. H., and Banning, J. H. *Counseling Outreach: A Survey of Practices.* Boulder, Colorado: Western Interstate Commission for Higher Education, 1973.

Morrill, W. H., Oetting, E. R., and Hurst, J. C. Dimensions of counselor functioning. *Personnel and Guidance Journal,* 1974, *52,* 355-359.

Palomares, V. H. (Ed.). Culture as a reason for being. (Special issue) *Personnel and Guidance Journal,* 1971, *50,* 83-147.

Parker, C. A. Epilogue: . . . The more they remain the same. *Personnel and Guidance Journal,* 1974, *52,* 439.

Smith, P. M. (Ed.). What guidance for blacks? (Special issue) *Personnel and Guidance Journal,* 1970, *48,* 707-789.

Solomon, C. (Ed.). Political action. (Special issue) *Personnel and Guidance Journal,* 1982, *60,* 577-640.

CHAPTER 9

DEVELOPING A CAREER RESOURCE CENTER

CAROLE W. MINOR

IN the years since Reardon and Burck's first book was published, there has been a virtual explosion in the number and types of materials available for career resource centers, in the functions career centers have undertaken, and in the number of centers actually operating across the country (Jacobsen, 1978). Career centers now exist in schools, libraries, business organizations, rehabilitation and employment offices, and other agencies. There are several reasons for the expansion of career centers, including the Career Education movement and its federal funding, the increase in midlife career changes (Heald, 1977; Schlossberg, 1977), women reentering the work force, and frequent recessionary cycles that make it difficult for many people to find a satisfactory job. These older people seeking employment, in addition to students preparing to enter the work force for the first time, are seeking information and other career planning services in larger numbers than ever before.

The career resource center can be the focal point of the entire career guidance program. It can provide the information, resources, and space for services such as career planning workshops, resume and interviewing workshops, and telephone career counseling (Roach, Reardon, Alexander, & Cloudman, 1982) as well as serving as a resource for career planning and other related courses. It can be located with or near counseling, placement, or cooperative education/work sampling programs. Its purpose is to provide information about educational and occupational options and experiences that enable individuals to analyze and synthesize these options in terms of their own interests, abilities, goals, and values.

This chapter focuses on important aspects in the development of a career center for those who recognize a need to develop one and who have access to potential resources. It outlines a model for the development of a career resource center and makes specific recommendations regarding materials, equipment, staffing, and organization. Topics addressed are (1) the goals of the center, (2) considerations in the development of a center, (3) establishing the center, (4) identifying sources of information, (5) operation and staffing, (6) evaluating the center, and (7) the expanding functions of career centers.

GOALS

The first and perhaps most important step in building a career resource center is to determine the goals to be met. Principal considerations at this point are the needs of the population to be served, the needs of the sponsoring institution, and how the center will function in the context of the institutions' total career guidance program.

There are important questions: What is the age level of the target population? What is their reading level? What is their level of career maturity? Will the center be used primarily for individual exploration (junior high), or will it be used for more specific information and decision making (senior high, college, agency)? Will it be a placement library also? Will it serve only individuals seeking career information on a voluntary or referral basis, or is there also a need for materials that can be used by teachers in the classroom or by counselors in groups or classes? What kinds of staff will be available? Will counseling be available in or near the resource center, or will clients have to be referred for counseling? Will the clients be motivated already, or will the center have to stimulate their interest in exploring careers?

There are three goals for most career resource centers:
1. Providing up-to-date information about careers on a level appropriate for the target population.

2. Providing up-to-date information about further education or training appropriate to the educational level of the target population.
3. Providing accurate information about local job availability and occupational outlook.

There are four possible additional goals specific to various settings:

1. Providing exploration or information materials that can be used by faculty in a classroom or in planning units in career development.
2. Providing materials that counselors can use in group career counseling.
3. Providing resources that a client may use to gain experience in the world of work, e.g. job experience kits, lists of volunteer work experiences, or community referral resources.
4. Providing specialized materials for minorities, returning women, midlife career changers, handicapped, or other special populations.

Other goals specific to individual settings could, of course, be added to the list.

CONSIDERATIONS IN THE DEVELOPMENT OF A CENTER

The most difficult aspect of developing a career resource center is likely to be obtaining the necessary resources: money, space, equipment, and personnel. A careful application of the systems approach can be of great help in this task. A useful model for this approach is presented by Hosford and Ryan (1970). The steps in this model are (1) study the environment, (2) define the problem situation, (3) establish the project, (4) design the counseling/guidance intervention, (5) simulate, (6) pilot test, (7) introduce the system, (8) operate the system, (9) evaluate the system, and (10) use feedback to modify, continue, or eliminate the intervention.

Using this model, the counselor may survey existing programs and resources and the career development needs of the clients. This information can be used to develop a program proposal that will meet the needs in the environmental context. The career resource center must be viewed in the context of the larger, comprehensive career development program since neither will be effective without the other.

Using the systems approach to program development provides the counselor with a well-thought-out plan necessary in obtaining approval to proceed with the establishment of a career resource center. The counselor must have an effective case to present when requesting resources from principals, superintendents, university officials, personnel or employee development departments, alumni associations, or other funding agencies. Gaining support from administrators is a key factor. The support of colleagues may be helpful, and the counselor should be prepared to utilize academic politics or public relations skills if necessary. A discussion of the use of the systems approach in developing a career development program is presented by Axelrod, Drier, Kimmel, and Sechler (1977).

Each of the following factors should be considered in the development of a career resource center.

Location

The location of a career resource center will have a major effect on its usefulness. If possible, the resource center should be located in an area that is easily accessible to clients as well as counselors. Particular attention also should be paid to accessibility for the handicapped. The center should be available for browsing and independent use rather than available only to supervised groups. Locating the center in a high traffic area can greatly increase its use. The group of college students surveyed by LeMay and Warnath (1967) indicated overwhelmingly that they would prefer the location of a central library of occupational information in the union. Reardon (1977) reported four times as many contracts for a career center in a student union location than in a student services building "off the beaten path." Realistically, however, the convenient availability of space is usually the most important factor in choosing a location.

The size of the space available will, in general, determine the number of clients who may use the facility at any one time and the equipment that may be accommodated. It is suggested that sufficient space be provided for comfortable seating and/or work space for at least ten clients.

Personnel, Materials, and Equipment

A career resource center needs to be monitored by at least one person whenever it is open. Personnel availability on the site is thus an important consideration. Will one or more counselors be available on the site to assist clients, or will the monitoring duties be given to a well-trained paraprofessional or preprofessional? Whoever is monitoring the career resource center needs to be completely familiar with the materials and information available as well as the operation of all equipment. This individual needs to be able to communicate easily with clients and aware of their perspectives.

In addition to personnel to monitor the resource center, clerical assistance is necessary to obtain and maintain current information. In all but the smallest centers, the services of a librarian are also desirable. Careful consideration should be given to the necessity of providing adequate personnel to provide a quality service.

Decisions need to be made, with the goals as a guide, about what types of information are necessary, e.g. browsing materials, information about careers, educational information, employment outlook, salary ranges, placement information, or career development materials. Next, decisions must be made about the vehicles for presenting this information. This may be accomplished through briefs, pamphlets, monographs, vocational biographies, filmstrips, microforms, films, audiotapes, videotapes, slidetape presentations, or interactive computer programs. Special consideration needs to be given to the degree of motivation necessary, as media materials seem to attract attention more readily than printed materials. This leads to decisions on equipment for use in the center, e.g. filing cabinets, filmstrip projectors, slide projectors, film projectors, audiotape players, videotape players, computer terminals, or microcomputers. Selection of media has to be made within the constraints of money and space available.

Choices need to be made about the necessity of having materials that can be used by groups (films, duplicate materials) or by faculty in planning curriculum units (lesson plans, career education materials). The specificity and reading level of the materials should be carefully selected.

The last question the counselor may want to consider is the advisability of developing some local materials, e.g. community referral resources, taped interviews with people in various professions, or local occupational outlook briefs.

After consideration of personnel, materials, equipment, and materials development needs, the counselor should be able to present cost estimates for the various components of the career resource center.

It is at this point also that priorities need to be set. Assigning priorities to the goals enables the counselor to begin with limited resources, if necessary, or to modify plans if sufficient resources are not available for the program as originally conceived.

At this point, the counselor should have assessed the needs and the environment, considered available resources and additional ones necessary, set priorities, and determined the location, personnel, information, and equipment needs. Zunker (1981) discusses the importance of having an advisory committee for the career resource center. It may be useful at this time to establish an advisory committee composed of individuals both inside and outside of the institution/organization. Parents, teachers, and local business/community leaders would be included on advisory committees for schools; alumni, faculty, and major employers of graduates for colleges and universities; and representatives from related agencies and organizations for noneducational agencies or organizations. It is then appropriate to present the proposal for a career resource center to the person or persons with the authority and resources to establish such a center.

ESTABLISHING THE CENTER

Having developed a plan for the career resource center and having obtained the necessary resources and administrative support, the counselor is ready to begin establishing the center.

After the designations of location, budget, and personnel have been made and existing equipment and resources have been identified, the next step is to identify sources of materials and equipment necessary.

There are several categories of information the counselor may want to consider:

1. Occupational briefs and pamphlets,
2. Books and monographs about specific careers,

3. Basic reference books such as the *Dictionary of Occupational Titles* and the *Occupational Outlook Handbook,*
4. Guides to colleges, universities, technical schools, and graduate schools,
5. Computerized information or career guidance systems (see Chapter 8),
6. Career development books and books on special problems and/or opportunities for minority groups,
7. Motivational or special interest books such as *What Color is Your Parachute, The Three Boxes of Life, The Two-Paycheck Marriage,* etc.,
8. Local, regional, and national labor market information,
9. Current salary surveys,
10. Films, filmstrips, audio- and videotapes, which may be used by individuals or in group presentations, and
11. Materials (printed and media) that may be used as part of the curriculum by teachers or counselors.

The following is a list of possible equipment needs:
1. Filing cabinets,
2. Display shelving or racks,
3. Shelving for books, catalogs, and other materials,
4. Library tables (or study carrels), chairs,
5. Listening-viewing carrels,
6. Cassette tape players,
7. Slide and/or filmstrip projectors,
8. VTR and video monitor,
9. Videodisk player,
10. Computer terminals or microcomputers,
11. Sound-on-slide equipment by 3M® or the Singer Graflex Caramate®,
12. 16mm film projector and screen,
13. Microfiche reader,
14. Monitor's desk,
15. Bulletin boards,
16. Card catalogs,
17. Comfortable, lounge-type seating, and
18. Typewriter.

Reardon (Chapter 3) describes a range of types of occupational information developed by Albert Thompson that may be used as a guide to information the counselor can provide. These types are arranged in order according to the degree of involvement (commitment) a client needs to have in order to use them:

1. Publications (books, monographs, etc.),
2. Audiovisual aids (films, tapes, slides, etc.),
3. Programmed instructional materials (books, workbooks, etc.),
4. Computer-based systems (storage, retrieval, mechanized systems),
5. Interviews with experts (direct questioning of occupational representatives),
6. Simulated situations (career games, role playing, etc.),
7. Synthetically-created work environments (artificial reproduction of work settings),
8. Direct observations (visits to work sites),
9. Directed exploratory experiences (work samples, evaluation tasks, etc.), and
10. On-the-job tryout (casual work or work-study programs).

Several of these categories involve programs that must be developed locally by counselors or others (see Chapters 3 and 11 for additional comments on this topic). The career resource center should have many of these types of information and be able to refer the client to sources for others.

Identifying Sources of Information

Sources of occupational information are indeed numerous. A discussion of some recommended materials and sources of materials follows, and a more complete list of sources is included at the end of this chapter.

The *Dictionary of Occupational Titles* (DOT) is a standard reference for career information. It offers descriptions of careers and a way to identify related careers by numerical categories and worker trait groups. Isaacson (1971) and Hoppock (1976) offer thorough discussions on the DOT and its use in counseling.

The *Occupational Outlook Handbook,* revised every two years, provides information on hundreds of occupations. The *Handbook* discusses the following topics for each occupation: nature of work, places of employment, training, other qualifications, and advancement, employment outlook, earnings and working conditions, and sources of additional information.

Interesting articles describing occupational outlook, the impact of national labor and economic trends on the job market, and the relationship between academic work and getting a job are found in the *Occupational Outlook Quarterly.*

Guides to colleges, universities, and technical schools include the following:

1. *The College Handbook*, College Entrance Examination Board,
2. *Profiles of American Colleges*, Barron's Educational Series,
3. *Guide to Two-Year Colleges*, Barron's Educational Series,
4. *The College Blue Book*, Macmillan Library Services,
5. *The Technical Education Yearbook*, Prakken Publisher, and
6. *The American Trade Schools Directory*, Croner Publications, Inc.

Several commercial companies publish libraries of occupational briefs:

1. Chronicle Guidance Publications, Inc.
   Moravia, New York 13118
2. Careers
   1211 10th Street, S.W.
   P.O. Box 135
   Largo, Florida 33540
3. Vocational Biographies, Inc.
   P.O. Box 31
   Sauk Centre, Minnesota 56378

Updating services — which provide revised occupational briefs, lists of new occupational materials, and professional articles — are available through Chronicle and Vocational Biographies.

Listings of free and/or inexpensive occupational information may be found in the following:

1. *A Counselor's Guide to Occupational Information*
   Superintendent of Documents
   U.S. Government Printing Office
   Washington, D.C. 20402
2. Current issues of *Vocational Guidance Quarterly*
   American Association for Counseling and Development

Membership in the APGA (the American Association for Counseling and Development) and NVGA (the National Vocational

Guidance Association) also can be an asset in keeping current with career guidance materials. "Guidepost," a biweekly publication of AACD, carries an annotated listing of new guidance materials; a subscription to the *Vocational Guidance Quarterly* is included with membership in NVGA. Commercial publishers send advertisements of new materials to AACD and NVGA members.

Books about specific careers may be purchased from these companies:

1. (Vocational Guidance Manuals)
   VGM-Career Horizons
   National Textbook Company
   4255 West Touhy Avenue
   Lincolnwood, Illinois 60646
2. Richard Rosen Press
   29 East 21st Street
   New York, New York 10010
3. ARCO Publishing Co.
   Educational Division
   219 Park Ave. South
   New York, New York 10003

Audiotaped interviews with people in various professions may be obtained from the following:

1. Educational Progress Corporation
   P.O. Box 45663
   Tulsa, Oklahoma 74145
2. Jeffrey Norton Publishing Company
   145 East 49th Street
   New York, New York 10017
3. MacMillan Library Services
   255 B Brown Street
   Riverside, New Jersey 08075

Entire career guidance programs, additional career and occupational information, career guidance materials for classroom use, films and film strips, job experience kits, and other materials may be obtained from commerical publishing companies. A list of some of these companies can be found at the end of this chapter. Catalogs may be obtained on request.

Professional organizations are a good source of occupational information. Of course, information from these sources must be evaluated to determine the degree to which it is recruitment literature and the degree to which it may be helpful to students. A list of professional organizations and labor unions may be found in the Directory of National Trade and Professional Associations, Garrett Park Press, Garrett Park, Maryland, 20766.

Computerized career information or career guidance systems offer an efficient way to identify occupations, educational institutions, or training programs that correspond to the desired characteristics of clients. The good career resource center will have at least one of these systems. Computer hardware will include a printer to enable clients to keep a record of occupations or educational alternatives which meet their needs. Chapter 8 provides a thorough discussion of the different types of systems and criteria for selecting a system.

Layout

Different types of materials should be stored in areas that facilitate their use. Browsing materials and reading materials should be located in or near a lounge area or worktable; media materials should be stored close to audiovisual carrels, tape recorders, or computer terminals. Jacobson (1971) and Zunker (1981) provide examples of layouts.

Ordering and Filing

The actual ordering and filing of materials is a tedious but important process. Files and materials that are well-organized, cross-referenced, and easily accessible encourage use. Moreover, clients are impressed by a complete, well-organized resource center and discouraged when information is lacking or out of place. Simply stated, if clients can't find it, it may as well not be there.

Records need to be kept of materials ordered, date, and source. This enables the staff to check up on materials that may not have arrived after having been ordered for an abnormally long time. These records are extremely important if the counselor works in an institution with no central purchasing department; however, they are not unnecessary even if there is a purchasing unit.

The overall filing plan for a career resource center must be that adapted to local needs. There are, however, some general guidelines that may be helpful:

1. Separate locations need to be available for different types (occupational literature, guides to colleges and trade schools, classroom materials) and forms (briefs, books, films, audiotapes) of information.
2. Information needs to be indexed by both type and subject with the location indicated.
3. Materials should be cross-referenced so individuals may locate all available information about a particular subject, e.g. choosing a college, changing careers.
4. The system should, if at all possible, enable the individuals to use materials on their own, without having to request assistance in finding each piece or type of information.

Many plans for filing information and materials have been developed. Some of them are discussed by Green (1979), Holland (1973), Hoppock (1976), Isaacson (1971), Norris, Zeran, Hatch, and Engelkes (1972), Michels and Kirk (1964), and Smith (1983). One of the most popular filing systems for occupational information is that found in the *Dictionary of Occupational Titles* (DOT). It is easy to understand and use. Many commercial materials have the DOT number printed on them, saving the staff time in filing them. Gottfredson, Holland, and Ogawa (1982) have even cross-indexed the Holland occupational classification to that of the DOT.

Holland (1973) suggests that organizing occupational information using his typology (see Chapter 2) facilitates exploration of many occupations related to the individual's interests. Individuals can find information about many related occupations filed close to each other, thus increasing the probability that they will explore more options. This system is being used in many centers, particularly those that use interest inventories from which the clients get a Holland code.

While these are probably the two most popular filing systems for occupational information, it is important to remember that there is much more material in a career resource center than just occupational information. Green (1979) and Smith (1983) have described systems that cross-reference and integrate all types of information available in the center. Smith reports that keeping the organizational system on a microcomputer has resulted in use of materials that had never been used previously. This supports the notion that the ease with which individuals can access information available influences the extent to which they actually seek information.

The *Standard Occupational Classification* (SOC) is a new filing system that is being used by the SOICC sponsored computerized guidance and information systems. Smith (1983) discusses an SOC based system of organizing information using a microcomputer to access information on specific topics.

Evaluating Materials

Materials may be evaluated on two criteria: the completeness of information presented and the accuracy of that information. To help the counselor evaluate completeness, NVGA has developed *Guidelines for the Preparation and Evaluation of Career Information Literature* and *Guidelines for the Preparation and Evaluation of Nonprint Career Media.*

Counselors must go to other sources for evaluation of the accuracy of information. These sources may include information compiled more recently or the counselor's personal knowledge and experience. When evaluating accuracy of information, especially occupational outlook, counselors may check the information about one or more fields with which they are personally familiar. If this information is consistent with the counselors' own knowledge and experience, they may be relatively sure that the information about other occupations is also correct. If a counselor knows that the information is incorrect, the accuracy of other information in the same volume or published by the same company may be in doubt.

Counselors and clients who use occupational outlook information need to be aware of its limitations. The counselor must convey to clients the unreliability of some printed and media information about national occupational outlook. This information usually describes the job market accurately as of the time it was compiled and projects the future outlook based on current conditions. However, compilation and publication take a year or longer, which frequently makes these statistics and outlook outdated by the time they are printed. Further, a client who is interested in this information frequently will not be ready to enter the job market for a year or more. Thus, individuals should be cautioned against uncritical acceptance of occupational outlook.

This should not be construed as discounting the value of national statistics developed by sources such as the Bureau of Labor Statistics but rather as pointing up the fact that individuals need to understand the realities of the changing job market and to develop some flexibility with regard to planning for the future.

Creating Materials

Local information is very important, especially to counselors in secondary schools, vocational schools, junior colleges, and those that serve a primarily adult clientele. Frequently it is necessary for the center staff to compile this information. Local information needed would include job openings, occupational outlook, and local training opportunities. Examples would include comparative information and sample programs of courses required for specific majors at junior colleges, colleges, and universities. These are typically called advising handbooks. In addition, audio- or videotaped interviews with individuals in specific occupations or with professors discussing what it is like to major in specific fields bridge the gap between written information and personal interviews. They enable clients to receive a personalized account of a major or occupation without the time and effort of finding an appropriate person and arranging an interview. Taped interviews or presentations from special career activities also can provide valuable local information.

Tolbert (1980) provides an excellent discussion of finding and organizing local information. Overs (1967) suggests that the counselor develop a more subjective type of occupational information, which he terms covert occupational information. He describes this information as a knowledge of "how it really is" and describes its five sources:

1. Reports from present and former clients.
2. Informal talks with significant administrators.
3. Observed employment outcomes.
4. Information from professional contacts.
5. Information from nonprofessional areas.

The counselor has a responsibility to develop reliable sources as to "how it really is" in order to best serve clients. One development that has made this easier is the recent establishment of the National

Occupational Information Coordinating Committee (NOICC) and State Occupational Information Coordinating Committees (SOICC). Soon each state will have an SOICC whose purpose is to provide local occupational outlook information and job availability information. Many SOICCs are now operating, and they are excellent sources of local (state) information.

OPERATION AND STAFFING

Beyond the information, stimulation, and exploration materials available in a career resource center, an important aspect of the center is the availability of a professional staff member who might be termed a Career Information Specialist.

Scherini and Kirk (1963) describe the function of an Occupational Information Specialist at the University of California at Berkeley. This full-time staff member spends all of her time collecting information, consulting with other counselors, and gathering current local information. She also serves as liaison with both the placement office and the faculty of the university. She arranges special presentations to the counseling center staff concerning topics such as summer job opportunities, graduate school admissions, and overseas careers.

Hoppock and Novick (1974) conducted a survey of counseling agencies and identified the following duties for the person they call an Occupational Information Consultant:

1. Determines what occupational information teachers and counselors need in order to make instruction and counseling more relevant to the world of work;
2. Identifies entry-level jobs in the community;
3. Serves as a liaison between school and business and industry;
4. Develops opportunities for students to obtain career information;
5. Explores and interprets possibilities in the area of computerized career counseling services;
6. Maintains a library of materials on careers and employment opportunities;
7. Provides teachers with career information to incorporate in

their course content;
8. Assists the guidance staff in organizing and conducting career guidance activities;
9. Organizes and prepares research studies relating to students' career choices and placement;
10. Develops and implements effective ways of publicizing occupational information to all students.

Of course each center will be staffed differently according to the needs of its clients and the sponsoring organization. Current centers are directed by counselors, librarians, former teachers, or others who have taken on the role of career information specialists. In addition, many centers use paraprofessionals (Fredrickson, 1982) or preprofessionals (Reardon & Minor, 1975) to help clients find and use information. Using paraprofessional peers of the primary client groups enables clients to feel more comfortable in the center and make more use of it.

Paraprofessionals used in this way need to be trained in basic helping skills, in how to find and use the resources of the center, and in making appropriate referrals when information or services requested are not available in the center. They need to be able to recognize typical questions of clients and relate those questions to information or resources available. Fredrickson (1982) offers a checklist of skills for paraprofessionals working in career centers. Johnston and Hansen (1981) offer a model for selecting and training paraprofessionals.

As mentioned earlier, clerical assistance in maintaining the center is essential. A career resource center is dynamic: it needs to be constantly monitored, updated, and changed to meet the needs of the clients and to reflect the changes in information available. There is much clerical work to be done in filing, ordering, and keeping up with materials.

In addition, the services of a librarian are useful in developing and maintaining the filing and access systems for materials in the center (Smith, 1983).

EVALUATION

Both process and product evaluations are important for a career resource center. Simple reports of the numbers of users are not sufficient data to evaluate the effectiveness of a center. Reardon, Domkowski, and Jackson (1980), following the suggestions of Goldman (1978), have reported a comprehensive model for the evaluation of the operation of a career center and its impact on clients. An adaptation of their model is presented here.

Process evaluation:

1. Data from sign-in sheets.
    a. Who uses the center? (From what class, department, etc.)
    b. How did clients learn about the center? (From friends, faculty, advertising, etc.)
    c. Why did the clients visit the center? (For career planning information, academic/career information, employability skills, etc.)
    d. How long did the client spend in the center?
2. Participant observation (using career technicians with special training in participant observation techniques.)
    a. In which activities did clients engage? (Reading, writing, listening, observing)
    b. What was the general demeanor of clients entering the center? (shy, confused, cautious, assertive, experienced)
    c. Did the clients interact with career technicians or proceed totally on their own?

Product (Impact) Evaluation

1. Client impact survey, random sample of clients. (Convenience of location, accessibility of materials, physical surroundings conducive to individual work, expertise of career technicians, general satisfaction with assistance received, etc.)
2. Faculty awareness and utilization survey, random sample of faculty. (Are you aware of center? Do you refer clients to it?)
3. Student awareness and utilization survey, random sample of students on campus. (Are you aware of the center? Have you used it? Was it helpful?)
4. In-depth case studies, small sample of clients.

While this is clearly a model for a mature or well-funded center, it indicates the possibilities for evaluating the functions of the center for possible revisions and short-term outcomes for clients. The most highly desirable form of product evaluation, of course, would be a longitudinal study of individuals who have and have not made use of the career center or other career programs. This is difficult but not impossible and should be a goal for the future.

EXPANDED FUNCTIONS OF A CAREER CENTER

A good career center is dynamic — it grows and matures. Jacobsen (1978) and Reardon, Domkowski, and Jackson (1980) have discussed the phenomenon of the evolution of a career center. A center typically begins as an accessible, well organized collection of information. It may be utilized by both individuals on a drop-in basis and by organized groups or classes. Once this information service becomes fully functioning, the center staff may increase its scope of activities to include using and training paraprofessionals and developing additional materials, referral services, and localized information. The evolution continues to include consultation, intervention in the organization on behalf of the center's clientele, and research of the effectiveness of various types of interventions.

The career center can become not only the focal point but also the hub of career services in any organization — providing information, individual counseling and consultation, workshops on decision making, job seeking, resume writing, special needs of women, minorities, handicapped, and others, organizational consultation and advocacy, and research. Indeed, Kerr (1982) found that the career center was a more positive setting for career counseling than either a professional office or a counseling interview room. The center was both more attractive to the clients and produced more career exploratory behavior on their part — making it the preferred location for career counseling.

In addition to expanding their functions, career centers have expanded their audiences. Once found primarily in schools, colleges, and universities, they have now expanded into the community and the work place (Aslanian & Schmelter, 1980; McEver, 1979). Centers in educational settings are increasing their focus to include parents, alumni, potential adult students, and the community at large (Hepper & Olson, 1982). Special materials and/or workshops serve the needs of minorities, the handicapped, women returning to school, and midlife career changers.

This process of evolution can be expected to continue in the future. Career center staffs will attend to the changing needs of their clientele and of the community at large.

SUMMARY

The first step in the process of developing a career resource center is the setting of goals. Important considerations in planning include (1) using the systems approach to develop a well-thought-out plan, (2) determining the most useful available location, (3) determining personnel, materials, and equipment needs, and (4) setting priorities. Establishing the center includes (1) identifying sources of materials and equipment, (2) ordering, (3) setting up a filing system, (4) determining the physical layout, (5) evaluating and creating materials, (6) selecting and training the staff, and (7) evaluation.

BIBLIOGRAPHY

Aslanian, C., and Schmelter, H. *Adult access to education and new careers: A handbook for action.* New York: College Entrance Examination Board, 1980.

Axelrod, V., Drier, H., Kimmel, K., and Sechler, J. *Career resource centers.* Columbus: Center for Vocational Education, Ohio State University, 1977.

Fredrickson, R. *Career information.* Englewood Cliffs, NJ: Prentice-Hall, 1982.

Goldman, L. (Ed.). *Research methods for counselors: Practical approaches in field settings.* New York: John Wiley & Sons, 1978.

Gottfredson, G. D., Holland, J. L., and Ogawa, D. K. *Dictionary of Holland occupational codes.* Palo Alto, CA.: Consulting Psychologists Press, 1982.

Green, D. Managing career information: A librarian's perspective. *Vocational Guidance Quarterly,* 1979, *28,* 83-91.

Heald, J. E. Mid-life career influence. *Vocational Guidance Quarterly,* 1977, *25,* 309-312.

Heppner, M. J., and Olson, S. K. Expanding college career centers to meet the needs of adults. *Journal of College Student Personnel,* 1982, *23,* 123-128.

Holland, J. L. *Making vocational choices: A theory of careers.* Englewood Cliffs, New Jersey: Prentice-Hall, 1973.

Hoppock, Robert. *Occupational information.* (3rd Ed.). New York: McGraw-Hill, 1976.

Hoppock, R., and Novick, B. Occupational information consultant: A new profession? *Personnel and Guidance Journal,* 1974, *49,* 555-558.

Hosford, R. E., and Ryan, T. A. Systems design in the development of counseling and guidance programs. *Personnel and Guidance Journal*, 1970, *49*, 221-230.

Jacobson, T. Career resource centers. In G. Walz and L. Benjamin (Eds.), *New imperatives for guidance.* Ann Arbor: ERIC/Counseling and Personnel Services, University of Michigan, 1978.

Jacobson, T. J. Career guidance center. *Exchange*, 1971, *1* (5), 1-4.

Johnston, J. A., and Hansen, R. N. Using paraprofessionals in career development programming. In V. A. Harren, M. H. Daniels, and J. N. Buck (Eds.), *Facilitating student's career development*, New Directions for Student Services, 14, 1981.

Kerr, B. A. The setting of career counseling. *Vocational Guidance Quarterly*, 1982, *30*, 210-218.

LeMay, M. L., and Warnath, C. F. Student opinion on the location of occupational information on a university campus. *Personnel and Guidance Journal*, 1967, *45*, 821-823.

McEver, C. *A catalog of possibilities: The community career education resource center.* Washington, D.C.: U.S. Gov't Printing Office, 1979.

Michels, E., and Kirk, A. *California plan for classifying occupational information* (Part I). Palo Alto, California: Consulting Psychologists Press, 1964.

Norris, W., Zeran, F. R., Hatch, R. N., and Engelkes, J. R. *The information service in guidance: For career development and planning.* Chicago: Rand McNally, 1972.

Overs, R. P. Covert occupational information. *Vocational Guidance Quarterly*, 1967, *16*, 7-12.

Reardon, R. Campus location and the effectiveness of a career information center. *Journal of College Student Personnel*, 1977, *18*, 240-241.

Reardon, R., Domkowski, D., and Jackson, E. Career center evaluation methods: A case study. *Vocational Guidance Quarterly*, 1980, *29*, 150-158.

Reardon, R., and Minor, C. Revitalizing the career information service. *Personnel & Guidance Journal*, 1975, *54*, 169-171.

Roach, D., Reardon, R., Alexander, J., and Cloudman, D. Career counseling by phone. *Journal of College Student Personnel*, 1983, *24*, 71-76.

Scherini, R., and Kirk, B. A. Keeping current on occupational information. *Vocational Guidance Quarterly*, 1963, *11*, 96-98.

Schlossberg, N. K. Breaking out of the box: Organizational options for adults. *Vocational Guidance Quarterly*, 1977, *25*, 313-319.

Smith, E. Career key: A career library management system. *Vocational Guidance Quarterly*, 1983, *32*, 52-56.

Tolbert, E. L. *Counseling for career development.* (2nd Ed.). Boston: Houghton-Mifflin, 1980.

Zunker, V. *Career counseling: Applied concepts of life planning.* Belmont, CA: Brooks/Cole, 1981.

ADDITIONAL SOURCES

American Association for Counseling and Development
5999 Stevenson Avenue
Alexandria, VA 22304

Barron's Educational Series, Inc.
113 Crossways Park Drive
Woodbury, N.Y. 11797

Bellman Publishing Company
P. O. Box 164
Arlington, MA 02174

B'nai B'rith Career and Counseling Services
1640 Rhode Island Avenue, N.W.
Washington, D.C. 20036

Career Aids, Inc.
8950 Lurline Ave., Department F
Chatsworth, CA 91311

Catalyst
14 East 60th Street
New York, N.Y. 10022

Charles A. Jones Publishing Co.
4 Village Green, S.E.
Worthington, OH 43085

Charles E. Merrill Publishing Co.
1300 Alum Creek Drive
Columbus, OH 43216

College Entrance Examination Board
Publications Order Office
Box 2815
Princeton, N.J. 08541

College Placement Council, Inc.
62 Highland Ave.
Bethlehem, PA 18017

Consulting Psychologists Press, Inc.
577 College Avenue
Palo Alto, CA 94306

Cowles Education Corporation
Look Building
488 Madison Avenue
New York, N.Y. 10022

Croner Publications, Inc.
211-03 Jamaica Ave.
Queens Villiage
New York, N.Y. 11428

Educational Dimensions Group
Box 126
Stamford, Connecticut 06904

E. P. Dutton and Company, Inc.
2 Park Ave.
New York, N.Y. 10016

Garrett Park Press
Garrett Park, MD 20766

Guidance Associates
Communications Park

Box 3000
Mount Kisco, N.Y. 10549

Harper and Row
10 E. 53rd Street
New York, N.Y. 10022

Houghton-Mifflin Company
2 Park Street
Boston, MA 02107

H. Z. Walck, Inc.
19 Union Square, West
New York, N.Y. 10003

Jeffrey Norton Publishers
145 East 49th Street
New York, N.Y. 10017

Julian Messner, Inc.
1230 Avenue of the Americas
New York, N.Y. 10020

The Macmillan Company
866 3rd Avenue
New York, N.Y. 10022

McGraw Hill Book Company
1221 Avenue of the Americas
New York, N.Y. 10020

McKnight Publishing Co.
Box 2854
Bloomington, IL 61701

National Career Consultants
1300 E. Arapaho Road
Richardson, TX 75081

New Careers Development Center
184 Fifth Avenue
New York, N.Y. 10010

Pilot Books
347 Fifth Avenue
New York, N.Y. 10016

Prakken Publishers
P. O. Box 8623
416 Longshore Drive
Ann Arbor, MI 48107

Rand McNally and Company
P. O. Box 7600
Chicago, IL 60680

Science Research Associates, Inc.
259 East Erie Street
Chicago, IL 60611

Ten Speed Press
P. O. Box 7123
Berkeley, CA 94707

Viking/Penguin, Inc.
299 Murray Hill Pkwy.
East Rutherford, N.J. 07073

Vocations for Social Change
P. O. Box 211
Essex Station
Boston, MA 02112

CHAPTER 10

USING COMMUNITY RESOURCES

Janet G. Lenz

THE idea of using community resources in the delivery of career interventions is hardly a novel or unusual concept. A review of the literature in this area reveals frequent emphasis on the need for community collaboration and describes many successful efforts on the part of schools at all levels to establish linkages with persons and organizations in their local areas (Barton, 1976; Ferrin, 1975; Healy, 1976; Hoyt, 1979). However, community linkage does not always come easily, and frequently efforts in this area are crowded out by a counselor's more pressing concerns. Counselors are often overwhelmed by the work load they face on a daily basis. Direct service delivery, responding to the immediate needs of clients, generally takes priority over program development. Career guidance personnel are often unable to look beyond the line of people at their office door or the mountains of paperwork to be processed on their desk.

Ironically, it is just this sort of crunch that makes outreach into the community a vital component of any career services office. As Healy (1976) points out:

> The number of counselors will never be sufficient to offer the necessary counseling and guidance on the broad scale needed. . . . In essence, the inadequacy is inherent in the assumption that by itself one small part of the educational institution can foster the career development of youth. Such development is properly the responsibility of several institutions: family, school, and the community, and will not be achieved until it is recognized that placement officers and counselors can only be part of the solution.

There are excellent resources to be utilized in the improvement of career guidance in schools, and these can be found through contacts with business and industry, parent groups, civic/service organizations, alumni associations, and so forth. As counselors continue to face budget cuts that threaten not only financial resources but personnel resources as well, effective utilization of community-based individuals and organizations becomes a greater imperative. Counselors may feel they're neglecting primary responsibilities by spending time away from the office involved in the many activities that are necessary to generate and sustain community involvement and support. However, the greater gains to be realized from collaboration with community groups will more than justify hours devoted to building and cultivating community networks.

This chapter begins with an outline of the various benefits to be gained from community linkage. No community outreach effort can be successful without planning, consideration of needed resources, and building of contacts. Some points to consider in this regard will be addressed in the second section. The third section will cite specific examples of programs and activities that have resulted in cooperative efforts between counselors and various community groups. Finally, some discussion will be devoted to problems that may arise in attempting to involve employers and other community groups in programs designed to enhance and expand career guidance services in the schools. The reader should note that the term "schools" will be used throughout the chapter to refer to educational institutions at a variety of levels ranging from secondary to postsecondary.

BENEFITS OF UTILIZING COMMUNITY RESOURCES

Cooperative efforts between school and community may be viewed in terms of benefits to the (1) students, (2) the school, and (3) the community. Although one member of this partnership may be a greater contributor at varying times, no one stands to lose through increased cooperation that improves career guidance services in the community.

Student Benefits

An exposure to the work world is valuable to students in that it can provide for several significant educational experiences that are not usually available through traditional classroom activities. First, observation, visitations, volunteer work, work-study arrangements, etc. can provide a testing ground for trying out a career before students commit valuable time to preparing for it. Second, students can learn to appreciate the dignity of many kinds of work and thereby gain a greater understanding of the variety of work roles available to them. Third, students often experience increased motivation as they see a relationship between academic course work and possible careers. Fourth, students may see that a career is not merely a means for earning a livelihood but rather affects one's total life-style. It may influence educational choices, where individuals live, who they marry, the type of friendships they develop, socio-economic status, leisure pursuits, and so forth. Student benefits, then, primarily involve increased opportunities for exposure to the world of work and to experience the consequences of various career decisions under controlled conditions.

School Benefits

Schools have always been and will continue to be an integral part of the communities in which they are located. Career guidance activities, because of the potential external focus, can help the school function as a realistic and integral part of the community rather than as an isolated entity.

Through its placement activities and related work-experience programs, schools stay attuned to the personnel needs of employers. By cooperating with employers to insure an adequate flow of trained workers who understand and appreciate the value of work, schools generate employer support. This support may be demonstrated not only through the hiring of the institutions' graduates but also through tangible and intangible means, including corporate donations of funds/equipment to the school or to the career guidance office directly, participation by corporate representatives in class or workshop presentations, and so forth.

The kind of direct contact with business and industry that results from student placement in full-time or part-time positions serves as a feedback mechanism for the school as it examines its curriculum and its relevance to the world of work. Schools are increasingly being held accountable by students, taxpayers, and legislators for their ability to graduate students with marketable skills. Schools who accept this mandate cannot afford to ignore employer input regarding curriculum development. If there is little demand by employers for the services of a school's graduates, this lack of interest should signal the need for a closer look at the educational preparation of students in relation to the community's manpower needs.

Schools that make a special effort to cultivate productive relations with employers and other representatives of the local community are much more likely to be on the receiving end of job opportunities for their students, financial donations, favorable votes on school-related issues, and related forms of support.

Community Benefits

Finally, the community as a whole receives benefits from collaboration with schools in meeting the career guidance needs of students. Increased funding for schools at all levels has become a sensitive issue in many communities. The types of activities described in this chapter represent a way for parents, employers, and other citizens to make a contribution to schools without investing additional tax dollars. Communities rely on schools to supply them with skilled individuals to meet the labor demands of various organizations. This is particularly true in a community's efforts to attract new industry. These industries want assurance that the types of workers they need will be available. Only through close cooperation with the schools are employers likely to achieve this goal. In addition, employers who participate in work-experience programs get a chance to examine potential employees. With students who seem promising, employers can begin the training process earlier and at a lower cost to themselves. Salaries of student workers are generally below those of full-time permanent employees who are receiving other company benefits, in addition to higher wages. In turn, students who have positive experiences with employers on a part-time or temporary basis while in school are more likely to consider that employer as a first choice upon graduation.

For service clubs and other community organizations, cooperative efforts with the local schools contribute to good public relations for the organization. The individual members of these organizations, as parents and taxpayers, also get an opportunity to have a voice in setting priorities for career guidance services in the schools.

PLANNING FOR COOPERATIVE EFFORTS

Consideration of School Resources

Assuming that a school has decided to become involved in community outreach, it is important to invest time in planning and considering resources that are currently available to support outreach efforts as well as resources that will have to be developed or acquired. The counselor will need access to office space and supplies, a conference room, support staff that may include secretaries, interns, and work-study students, and various directories of community organizations, service clubs, employers, and so forth. If audiovisual materials are to be produced, arrangements should be made with a campus office that provides assistance in this area to insure the best quality possible. In addition to office materials and personnel, consideration should be given to any funds that may be required. Sources to fund community outreach activities may include in-kind contributions from the institution to cover expenses such as postage, duplicating, phone calls, and so forth; other schools have discretionary funds available to support special projects (e.g. one institution received a special allocation from the Chancellor's discretionary fund to underwrite the costs of developing an Alumni Career Network program and a Summer Jobs Fair). Another alternative is the possible availability of grant funds from state and federal agencies and private foundations. Once initial plans have been developed, counselors may want to meet with higher level administrators or guidance supervisors to explain their objectives in seeking community involvement and the benefits mentioned earlier that accrue to students and schools, as well as to encourage administrative support of the counselors' community outreach activities.

Consideration of Community Resources

The second step in planning is the identification of individuals and/or groups who can assist counselors in meeting their objectives or in some instances establishing new objectives not previously defined. The specific methods for involving nonschool personnel in the career guidance process are too numerous to allow for comprehensive coverage in this chapter. The important point to remember is that no community-based guidance project is likely to be successful unless career guidance personnel take the initiative to establish and nurture key individual or organizational contacts in their local area. The quality of planning for career guidance programs is optimized when it is accomplished cooperatively by educational personnel and community representatives (Altschuld, Kimmel, Axelrod, Stein, & Drier, 1978).

Depending on their purposes for establishing a community coalition or advisory committee, counselors may invite different groups or individuals to participate. Some may wish to include alumni of the institution. Some may wish to insure that a wide range of businesses and industries are represented. Others may simply want a good mix of all of the above. A New York group made an attempt to include representatives from a variety of occupational roles — from entry-level to professional — in their community coalition, as well as a representative from each of the county's thirteen school districts. They established an advisory board comprised of two influential members of the county's work force and two of the county's influential educators — the role of the board was to chair coalition meetings, formulate agendas, and provide counsel and direction to coalition members (Keller, 1980).

For other institutions, the preferred method may be to work with previously established groups such as professional associations, civic/service clubs, Chambers of Commerce, and the like. The stimulus for cooperation between these types of groups and the schools may already be present due to the organizations' prior commitments to, or history of, involvement with career guidance activities. In California, the Chamber of Commerce encourages its local members to build close relations with schools, especially high schools and community colleges, both in the spirit of community service and in an effort to insure a steady supply of trained personnel for the companies (Ferrin, 1975). Similarly, Rotary International, the leadership body for Rotary Clubs across the country, identified four general service areas for its local clubs, one of which is "vocational service" (Hoyt, 1978).

There seems to be no universally applicable method for counselors to establish linkages with community individuals and groups. For more information on this, see Hoyt (1979). The primary criteria in selecting community resources should be a demonstrated interest and commitment on the part of the individuals or organizations to meet the career guidance needs of youth and adults.

OUTCOMES OF COOPERATIVE EFFORTS

Printed / Audiovisual Resources

Many community-based career guidance efforts have produced career resources that continue to be useful to students and counselors after the initial project has ended. These resources have been developed through individual initiative on the part of community organizations as well as through cooperative ventures by schools and community groups.

Counselors rely heavily on career information resources in their work with students. Accurate, informative career information is an essential element of the career exploration, career decision-making process. One of the most frequent complaints of counselors and students is the lack of localized career information. Students have for years relied on career information produced by national associations and departments of the federal government. The data contained in these documents are not always accurate pictures of career opportunities or job market conditions for regional, state, and local areas — areas where the majority of graduates from many institutions are likely to live and work. There is a need for state and local career information (Miller, 1982; Tolbert, 1974). In response to this need on the part of counselors and their clients, community personnel can make a direct and immediately useful contribution. The business/industry community can serve as a primary source in providing local information about various occupations and industries, job outlook data, and related forms of career information.

One attempt to provide such information was a survey done by a Chamber of Commerce and a local industry council, with assistance from a nearby research institute (Research Triangle Institute, 1980). The survey queried county employers about their anticipated needs for employees in thirty-four skilled occupations, the conditions of employment in selected occupations in which they employed workers, and their experiences with local training programs. These survey results were to be used in planning the training programs offered by the local technical institute, the public schools, and other manpower programs. The results of the survey were summarized and publicized in a two-page flyer that was distributed to students through a Career Day program and through their school's guidance office. The flyer was received quite positively, particularly by counselors, who previously had not had this type of localized career information to share with their students.

A more comprehensive effort to develop local career information was undertaken by a local chapter of the National Alliance of Business in cooperation with a human service agency (Hoyt, 1978). Their plans called for the establishment and operation of a computer-based system containing 10,000 to 20,000 job descriptions of occupations existing in the Greater Cleveland area as well as the names and addresses of companies that employ persons in these occupations. An additional component of the system included plans for the development of 1,000 audio cassettes of adult workers talking about their occupations.

Audiovisual resources represent another excellent means for counselors and students to increase their understanding of the world of work and local industries. It seems wise, therefore, for counselors to consider working jointly with local organizations to produce multimedia resources — films, videotapes, slideshows — focusing on employers and industries in the community, which could be used over and over again in the schools. Many schools, as well as businesses, have media center personnel who could work with counselors in such endeavors. Several companies have been aggressive in this type of activity and have produced media materials that they are willing to donate to institutions. In many placement offices, videotapes and slideshows are becoming a replacement for, or an adjunct to, the standard company literature. Another means for utilizing media technology to enhance career awareness was demonstrated by the Rotary Club of Gold Beach, Oregon (Hoyt, 1978). As part of their community career education efforts, arrangements were made for high school students to videotape Rotary Club members at their place of work and then these tapes were included in the school's career information library.

Career Days / Employer Panels

The most frequently utilized methods for involving employers and professionals from various career areas in the guidance process are career days, career panels, and other types of presentations in which students can be in direct contact with persons representing their specialization of interest (Tolbert, 1974). Closely related to this are presentations aimed at counselors, who in turn share the information with their students.

One community, as a way of encouraging career exploration, planned a career day in the coliseum with the cooperation of the city school system, the Chamber of Commerce, and the local Youth Council. The event brought together employers in the community who represented the six themes of Holland's theory of career choice (Holland, 1973). Students completed an interest inventory and then were encouraged to discuss their interests with organizations that matched their Holland code profile. For additional reading on communitywide career days, job fairs, and related programs, the reader is referred to Hoyt (1979).

Other programs such as this have put counselors in touch with employers. One example is the Professional Exchange Program (PEP), developed by the Western College Placement Association (WCPA). The exchange program offers opportunities for placement personnel to visit recruiters' offices and for recruiters to visit colleges and universities (McGregor, 1980). The association's Board of Directors created a Professional Exchange Program Committee to organize and direct the activities of the program. Any expenses incurred were paid by the individuals participating or their respective organizations. Activities have included employers in common career areas getting together to provide an overview for their particular industry and in more remote geographic areas educational institutions coming together as a consortium to provide recruiters, over several days time, the opportunity to get a better knowledge of curriculum offerings and career services programs. These programs are organized during the winter and spring, with the exchanges taking place during the summer. Despite some problems with sustaining member interest and participations (particularly from employer members), the PEP program has continued to grow and develop. College participants noted the value of the exchanges in learning about the work environment of the employers to whom they refer students. Employers, on the other hand, gained insights and contacts that went far beyond their usual involvement with career services personnel.

A similar type of program grew out of a community career guidance team's activities. During the team's assessment of career guidance needs in the local community, it was found that counselors in the high schools and post-secondary institutions were interested in obtaining more firsthand information about job opportunities available from local employers. With input from employers on the guidance team and information on occupational areas in demand from the Chamber of Commerce and the local Employment Service Office, ten career areas were identified. Team members then volunteered to contact local employers representing each area who were willing to conduct seminars about careers related to the area. Letters were sent to counselors inviting them to participate; thirty people expressed an immediate interest in attending the seminars. The thirty included counselors from the public schools, a technical institute, colleges and universities, vocational rehabilitation, and the employment service. All seminar presenters focused on the following points: (1) present job opportunities in the field, (2) future possibilities in the field, (3) nature of the work, including salaries, (4) traits, skills, abilities, and attitudes that are needed by potential employees for the present and the future, (5) what schools, colleges, and technical institutes can do to better prepare people for the jobs of now and the future in the field, and (6) what can be done to get more of the counselors' clients placed in jobs in the field. Through the cooperation and support of guidance supervisors, counselors were able to get continuing education credit for their participation. The seminars provided a basis for approaching business and industry about career guidance needs and a means for the employers to make a direct contribution to the counselors' understanding of work opportunities in their immediate geographic area (University of North Carolina at Greensboro, 1982).

Career days and employer visitations also can be used to encourage career guidance activities in the classroom through teacher involvement. Hoyt (1979) cites several of these programs. A Chamber of Commerce in Fort Myers, Florida, cooperated with the public schools to develop the Business Education Exchange Program (BEEP). In this program, educators from area high schools visited members of the business/industry community and then through small group meetings planned ways to incorporate the information learned on these visits into the teaching process. Community collaboration also can bring employers into the classroom. Lockheed Corporation joined forces with counselors and teachers in a San Jose, California, school district on a project that combined teaching units with a career emphasis, classroom presentations by community resource persons, and use of the occupational community as a learning laboratory for students and teachers.

Placement

The most obvious place for a career guidance program to link with the larger community and the world of work has been through its placement activities. For many students, parents, and faculty, finding jobs for graduates is one of the most vital functions performed by career planning and placement professionals. Readers wishing detailed descriptions of the organization and operation of placement services are referred to the resource list at the end of the chapter.

Placement activities have traditionally centered around two main areas as part of helping students. The first is receiving job notices from employers and then using a variety of means to communicate this information to job seekers registered with the placement service. A second major activity is on-campus interviewing with prospective employers.

Recently, however, hard times have taken their toll on the hiring demands of employers. Employers in the private sector are doing more with fewer people. Recruiting visits to schools are being curtailed as companies are faced with the prospect of laying off current employees as well as the increasing costs of recruiting. The number of job notices received in the placement office has dwindled as companies fill their vacant positions through internal promotion and applicants who contact them directly.

These events have prompted career guidance offices to devise new strategies to make job opportunities available. All of these strategies involve reaching out to the larger community, either through cooperative efforts with other institutions or employer visitation/job development activities. Many schools have recognized the benefits to be realized from banding together with neighboring institutions. Examples of typical activities include shared recruiting schedules allowing students from one campus to interview with employers at another exchange of job listings, and career days or job fairs sponsored by two or more schools.

In addition to establishing cooperative programs/services with other schools, counselors can initiate direct contact with employers off-campus as a way of generating work opportunities. Many employers, who would otherwise overlook a particular school when filling a position, may be more inclined to seek candidates from that school when the counselor has taken the initiative to meet the employer and persuade the employer to consider the school's graduates. Counselors, who have a feel for the career interests of the clients they serve, can easily identify employers in the local community who are likely to be productive contacts. Sources to aid in this identification include employer directories, community service organization directories, and related information resources. The Career Planning and Placement Center at the University of North Carolina-Greensboro compiled a list of employers to be contacted and then had each of its counseling staff members sign up to visit an assigned number of employers. The center devised an "employer visitation report" to standardize the information collected. These reports became a source of "covert" career information for students — a useful supplement to other forms of employer literature.

Counselors with placement responsibilities will continue to be held accountable by students, faculty, parents, and legislators for the number of graduates who find employment. Counselors cannot rely solely on traditional sources of job notices, nor can they assume that on-campus recruiting will continue to generate jobs. Only through linkage with other institutions and through direct outreach to employers are they likely to produce results which can positively emerge from the scrutiny of those who have a vital interest in the placement of students.

Experiential Learning

Previously, placement following graduation was for many students their first real exposure to the career field they had decided to enter. Yet, at institutions committed to the career development of students, experiential education throughout a students' academic experience has long been recognized as an essential component of career services programming and an effective means for expanding career awareness (Millett & Dean, 1979). With increasing frequency, career-related and experiential education programs are being linked in ways that well may lead to new combinations of education and work, which means new opportunities for lifelong learning and career development (van Aalst, 1979). Experiential education has taken many forms — including cooperative education, shadowing, internships, and mentor/extern programs. For additional references on exemplary programs and research in this area, see Coleman (1979). Several examples of community-school cooperation to create experiential learning opportunities for students are now discussed.

The University of Nebraska (Lincoln) developed an Experiential Learning Opportunities program (ELO) to offer its students an opportunity to sample careers and gain practical experience in their academic area while serving as volunteers in the community. Over fifty agencies in the Lincoln area responded offering learning opportunities in over forty different academic-career fields. ELO was described as a low-cost, effective career guidance technique that could be implemented on any college campus. It was an excellent way to use community resources to assist students with career decision making while at the same time providing the community with a source of volunteer manpower (Welker, 1981).

Another experiential program for young people was developed by a career guidance specialist in upstate New York. Students had the opportunity on a voluntary basis to enter into individual learning contracts that put them in contact with persons from the business/industry community. They spent two to three hours per week, after school, for an entire semester interacting with community resource persons at their job sites. Program coordinators oriented the "community mentors" prior to their participation to make sure they understood that the purpose of the program was to help youth explore careers, not provide "free labor for employers"(Hoyt, 1979).

Work experience programs have previously been geared to students in more "vocationally-oriented" or technical disciplines. The Vera Christie Project, sponsored by the Western College Placement Association, was designed to address the problem of placing liberal arts graduates in entry level positions in business and industry (Faught, 1979). The project's primary goal was to assess which internship opportunities could be developed in business for liberal arts students. Four universities participated in the project, which produced interviews with eighty business executives and 120 ideas for internship opportunities. The interviews were carried out by four liberal arts students and the responsibilities included researching local businessess and industries, identifying potential organizations to be contacted, and telephoning for appointments with chief executive officers. Although the students received some guidance and instruction from the Project Director and the placement directors at their respective institutions, they assumed the major responsibility.

In the earlier discussion, mention was made of the benefits accruing to employers and students who participate in work experience programs. Some of the best examples of effective program development in this area are the Job Location and Development Programs that have recently come into existence as a result of federal financial aid legislation. The original intent of the legislation was to encourage the development of financial aid support for college students from the local community. On many campuses, however, the programs are designed to make a contribution that goes beyond that of financial aid. The Financial Aid Office at the University of Missouri-Columbia in cooperation with the Career Planning and Placement Center operates a work experience program that provides both income and experience to students and a quality labor pool to the community. While earning money to finance their education, students have opportunities to (1) explore career areas and work settings in which they have an interest and (2) gain valuable experience that will enhance their employability upon graduation (Bazin & Brooks, 1981). Part-time student employment programs, whether offered through a Job Location and Development office, career center, or financial aid office, offer many advantages to students and employers alike. If the role that student employment plays in career guidance has not been clearly recognized and cultivated at an institution, counselors can take the lead in developing and articulating that role.

Given the positive outcomes that have resulted from experiential education efforts on the part of schools and local communities, this type of career awareness activity should continue as a vital component of comprehensive career guidance programs. Experiential learning not only has enhanced the career development of students but also has brought schools and communities together in arrangements that have contributed to increased understanding, produced a source of volunteer manpower for the community, and generated alumni goodwill.

Alumni Networks

Alumni represent a unique group in the community with respect to their potential for making contributions to a school's career guidance program. Alumni involvement in students' career planning and job search activities can take several forms including the following:

(1) *Alumni Career Reports* — information provided on surveys, telephone interviews, cassette tape recordings, or through personal appearances at workshops on career panels; alumni can reveal career paths associated with academic majors and provide advice on educational plans and job search strategies.

(2) *Extern/Intern Programs* — opportunities for students to spend a designated period of time ranging from one day to a semester with alumni at their place of work, observing and/or working.

(3) *Employment* — alumni can provide the career center with specific job openings, encourage their employer to interview and hire students for summer jobs and permanent positions, and provide valuable job-hunting contacts.

Alumni programs reflecting these types of activities are currently in existence and successfully functioning at many schools around the country. Examples include University of Missouri-Columbia Career Planning and Placement Center's ASK program: Alumni Sharing Knowledge (Heppner, 1981), Longwood College Alumni Association's Alumni Assistance Program, University of Iowa Alumni Association's Career Information Network, Harvard University Office of Career Services and Off-Campus Learning's Alumni/ae Career Advisory Service, Illinois Benedictine College Office of Career Planning and Placement's Alumni Center Assistance Network, and University of Texas-Austin Exstudents' Association's Career Contacts. Other examples of schools involved in using alumni to extend career guidance services include Emory & Henry College, University of North Carolina at Greensboro, Swarthmore, Colgate University, University of Virginia, and Furman University. For additional reading on alumni programs see the publications available through the Council for the Advancement and Support of Education (CASE), Suite 400, 11 DuPont Circle, Washington, DC 20036.

PROBLEMS IN DEVELOPING AND USING COMMUNITY RESOURCES

Thus far, the focus of this chapter has been on the benefits of utilizing community resources and the positive outcomes that can be achieved. It would be naive to assume, however, that collaboration and cooperation with community groups can be achieved without problems and obstacles. Problems can occur in the planning phase, during the actual project activity, and while trying to maintain project activities and/or advisory groups. In order for counselors considering community outreach to be forewarned, these problematic areas are now discussed.

Employer Reluctance

In dealing with employers, counselors are likely to hear comments concerning the employer frustration in dealing with educational institutions. Cooperative efforts have been initiated in the past with business and industry that have not been positive. Employers may be reluctant to give additional time to committees, councils, or projects. They may be frustrated with the rate at which educational systems respond to employer requests for changes in curriculum and training programs. They are tired of talking about the problem without seeing steps being taken to correct it. The types of activities that employers participate in with schools may be very beneficial to students, i.e. during a Career Day students may be exposed to a wide variety of occupations and may be able to gather firsthand career information but the benefits to employers are not always apparent. Employers do not always achieve desired outcomes; that is, despite exposure to labor market information and the hiring needs of employers, students do not always choose areas of study that are in line with these needs. Finally, while employers may be sympathetic with the concerns and goals of counselors, they may feel that counselors are not in the best position to improve career guidance services. For significant change to take place in the delivery of career services, discussions and planning must take place at a higher level in the educational hierarchy, i.e. with School Board members, Superintendents, Deans, or Vice-Presidents..

Organizational Priorities

In seeking involvement from service clubs and civic groups, counselors may face the reality that these groups have other commitments and may not consider career guidance a top priority. This is particularly true if the guidance project or program requires some outlay of the organizations' funding.

Serving Diverse Interests

Convening a diverse group of people to form an advisory committee or work-education council/coalition brings with it another set of problems. Often it is difficult to generate interest and commitment on the part of participants, especially if the project or collaborative effort is to extend over a long period of time. It is a major task to bring people from many settings together and insure that all interests and hidden agendas are served. Without any sort of financial remuneration to offer participants, the incentive may not be there to sustain the involvement of individual members. General apathy may develop or committee members may be pulled away because of work responsibilities or involvement in other organizations or clubs. It is not uncommon to find that the types of persons targeted and selected for involvement on community career guidance teams or councils are already heavily committed to a myriad of other responsibilities.

Counselor Responsibilities

In addition, counselors take a greater burden on themselves if they undertake projects to establish linkages with community resources. If they are involved in off-campus meetings, collecting information outside the office, and visitations with employers as part of their outreach efforts, counselors may feel they are neglecting in-house responsibilities, especially if the ratio of counselors to students is extremely high. Because counselors are often the initiators of community networks, leadership and coordination responsibilities often fall to them. These responsibilities may call for not only a great deal of activity on the counselor's part but may also generate a lot of in-house paperwork — minutes of committee meetings to be typed and distributed, community survey results to be collected, career contact forms to be tabulated, and so on. Someone has to assume responsibility for organization and maintenance of these resources to insure that students can utilize them. If a counselor lobbies for the development of career contact files or career day programs and in response to the counselor's request a major effort is undertaken by a service club, an advisory council, or other community group to develop resource files or plan a career day, the counselor cannot avoid some responsibility for insuring that students participate. Similarly, counselors must insure that career contacts are not overburdened with requests for shadowing, internships, or information. With consideration for their institution's priorities, counselors must decide how to best apportion their time between direct client contact and program development activities to arrive at an effective combination of interventions for meeting career guidance needs.

Before undertaking projects that require community participation, the counselor would be wise to consider the above points and plan strategies for reducing or eliminating their impact. If they occur despite a counselor's best efforts to avoid them, having been forewarned, one may find them easier to accept, realizing that they are part and parcel of most community outreach efforts.

SUMMARY

Despite the problems likely to be encountered in building community linkages, counselors cannot afford to be office bound. Counselors are urged to cultivate and expand their networks/personal contacts with employers, training directors, and other community personnel, because these networks will help clients (Healy, 1982). There is a critical need for school and community linkages — without such linkages the counselor does not have career education or career guidance (Treichel, Sanders, Peterson, & Halasz-Salster, 1979). Realistic career planning and satisfying employment for students can be realized only when counselors move beyond the isolated environment of the institutions and into the larger community. Attention to community relations and effective utilization of community resources opens channels that contribute to improved career information and programs, student and counselor awareness of the world of work, and employer and citizen understanding of community limitations that affect the career development of young people, e.g. poor schools, understaffed guidance offices, unfair job entry requirements, and insufficient jobs (Healy, 1982). By joining forces and combining resources to address career guidance needs and community problems, the potential for success in meeting the needs and solving the problems is greater than what might be realized through the efforts of a single organization.

Involvement of community resources to facilitate career development in the schools is not a new idea. Many programs involving community linkage have been operational for a considerable period of time. The points that need to be made here are that (1) there are still many communities where the possibilities for linkages in ways already described have not begun to be explored and (2) there are innovative methods for community collaboration yet to be conceived and implemented by counselors facing the realities of fewer dollars and less personnel support within their institution. What Ken Hoyt said in 1974 is still true for many educational institutions today: "Despite the learning resources available in every community, very few schools have actually begun to make effective use of the many talented individuals residing in the community and willing to be of service to the schools."

BIBLIOGRAPHY

Altschuld, J. W., Kimmel, K. S., Axelrod, V., Stein, W. M., and Drier, H. N. *From idea to action — career guidance plans of rural and small schools.* Research and Development Series No. 148. Columbus, OH: The National Center for Research in Vocational Education, The Ohio State University, 1978.

Barton, P. E. Community councils as an intermediate institution. In H. Silberman and M. Ginzberg (Eds.), *Easing the transition from schooling to work.* San Francisco: Jossey-Bass, Inc., 1976.

Bazin, J. R., and Brooks, G. The work experience program — A collaborative effort between financial aids and the career planning and placement center. *The Journal of Student Financial Aid,* 1981, *11* (3), 5-8.

Coleman, D. D. (Ed.). *Experiential education in the workplace: An annotated bibliography.* Columbus, OH: The National Center for Research in Vocational Education, The Ohio State University, 1979.

Faught, B. *How to develop internships for liberal arts students in business and industry.* Sacramento, CA: Vera Christie Project, 1979.

Ferrin, R. I. *Bridging the gap: A study of education-to-work linkages.* New York: College Entrance Examination Board, 1975.

Healy, C. C. Placement services and career development. In H. Silberman and M. Ginzberg (Eds.), *Easing the transition from schooling to work.* San Francisco: Jossey-Bass, Inc., 1976.

Healy, C. C. *Career development: Counseling through the life stages.* Boston: Allyn & Bacon, Inc., 1982.

Heppner, M. J. Alumni Sharing Knowledge (ASK): High quality, cost-effective career resources. *Journal of College Student Personnel*, 1981, *22*, (2), 173-174.

Holland, J. L. *Making vocational choices: A theory of careers.* Englewood Cliffs, N.J.: Prentice Hall, 1973.

Hoyt, K. B., Evans, R.E., Mackin, E. F., and Mangum, G. L. *Career Education: What it is and how to do it.* (2nd Ed.) Salt Lake City: Olympus Publishing Company, 1974.

Hoyt, K. B. Rotary International and career education. *Monographs on Career education.* Washington, D.C.: U.S. Government Printing Office, 1978.

Hoyt, K. B. Community involvement in the implementation of career education. *Monographs on career education.* Washington, D.C.: U.S. Government Printing Office, 1979.

Hoyt, K. B. National Alliance of Business and career education. *Monographs on career education.* Washington, D.C.: U.S. Government Printing Office, 1978.

Keller, K. E. Schools and community: Making the marriage work. *Vocational Guidance Quarterly,* 1980, *28*, (3), 263-268.

McGregor, W. J. PEP in the West. *Journal of College Placement,* 1980, *40*, (3), 33-35.

Miller, J. M. Career guidance and information: Who is responsible? In A. S. Lancaster (Ed.), *National Vocational Guidance Association Newsletter,* 1982, *21*, (4), 3.

Millett, O., and Dean, S. Expanding career awareness. *Journal of College Placement,* 1979, *40* (1), 50-53.

Research Triangle Institute. *Assessment of employment and training needs in Guilford County.* Report prepared for the Greensboro Chamber of Commerce and the Private Industry Council, Research Triangle Park, NC, 1980.

Tolbert, E. L. *Counseling for career development.* Boston: Houghton-Mifflin Company, 1974.

Treichel, J., Sanders, C., Peterson, M., and Halasz-Salster, I. *Optimizing planning techniques for career guidance: Six case studies.* University of Illinois, Department of Vocational and Technical Education. Urbana-Champaign, IL, 1979.

University of North Carolina at Greensboro. *Guidance team training project.* Final evaluation report. Columbus, OH: The National Center for Research in Vocational Education, The Ohio State University, 1982.

van Aalst, F. D. (Ed.). *New directions for experiential learning: Combining career development with experiential learning.* (No. 5) San Francisco: Jossey-Bass, 1979.

Welker, J. C. An experiential education program for college students. *Journal of College Student Personnel,* 1981, *22* (6), 561.

RESOURCES USEFUL IN THE ORGANIZATION AND OPERATION OF A PLACEMENT SERVICE

Beaumont, A. G., Cooper, A. C., and Stockard, R. H. *A model career counseling and placement program.* Bethlehem, PA: College Placement Services, 1978. Presents a comprehensive model program. Outlines specific student-oriented activities as well as managerial and administrative activities.

Journal of College Placement, College Placement Council, (CPC) Inc. P. O. Box 2263, Bethlehem, PA 18001. Four issues/year. Professional magazine of placement/recruitment featuring articles of interest to the field. The *Journal,* along with other CPC publications, comes as part of the CPC membership fee.

Powell, C. R., and Kirts, D.K. *Career services today.* Bethlehem, PA: The College Placement Council, 1980. Text incorporates with the theory and practice of career counseling and placement. Examines a wide range of activities related to career services. Appendix provides examples of forms used in career planning and placement offices.

Stephens, E. W. *Career counseling and placement in higher education: A student personnel function.* Bethlehem, PA: The College Placement Services, Inc., 1978. A presentation of the fundamentals of career counseling and placement, including philosophy, principles, and rationale as well as the relationship to other functional areas of higher education.

Tolbert, E. L. *Counseling for career development.* Boston: Houghton-Mifflin, 1974. Covers a wide range of career development topics citing practical applications supported by relevant theory and research. Discusses the pros and cons of placement and offers suggestions on organizing and staffing this service.

CHAPTER 11

CAREER PLANNING THROUGH INSTRUCTION

MICHAEL J. GIMMESTAD

COUNSELORS and educators are confronted with increasing demands for effective career guidance and are faced with two major challenges: first, to make career guidance efforts relevant and interesting to their clientele, and second, to increase the delivery of systematic career guidance services while operating under strict cost-efficient constraints. One response to these challenges is discussed in this chapter: instructional, or curricular, approaches to career development. Instructional approaches are defined as systematic efforts to meet career development objectives for groups of students through courses or units of courses offered as a part of the regular school or college curriculum (including credit and non-credit offerings).

Included in this chapter are (1) a discussion of the special needs of client groups as related to curricular approaches to career development, (2) common goals ascribed to by instructional approaches, (3) summaries of selected interventions that are representative of these approaches, (4) an assessment and comparative evaluation of these strategies, and (5) a summary.

CLIENT AND INSTITUTIONAL NEEDS

Instructional approaches can be especially responsive to a wide variety of student needs. Also, they can provide a means for institutions to respond within the constraints of limited financial resources. Ways in which instructional approaches have demonstrated particular responsiveness to those needs follow.

Need for Systematic, Developmental Approaches

Various facets of career development and career guidance have been extensively described in texts on career development theories, occupational/educational information, and vocational guidance (see Chapter 2). Chronological developmental constructs such as Erikson's eight stages of human development (1950) and Levinson's "seasons of a man's life" (1978) are familiar to counselors. Guidance services such as individual appraisal, information services, counseling, placement, and follow-up are described in most standard texts on guidance. Facilitation of career development necessitates the integration of knowledge of human development (including career development) with the offering of student services that are based on principles of individual differences, motivation, and learning as well as interest and ability. The impact of developmental psychology is evident in contributions to career development theory and practice of Jordaan (1974) and Knefelkamp and Slepitza (1976). An increasing number of career planning courses described in the professional literature are identified as "theory-based" (Barker, 1979; Egner & Jackson, 1978; Ganster & Lovell, 1978; Heppner & Krause, 1979; Mackin & Hansen, 1981; Touchton, Wertheimer, Cornfeld, & Harrison, 1977). It is in the breadth and unity provided by the recent developments in instructional approaches that they are different. Careers courses are not new. Holcomb (1966) reported the existence of college-level courses focusing on career guidance as early as 1917, and the high school unit on careers has a long history, generally in the context of either English or social studies classes (Mazzano, 1969). What, then, is new and exciting?

It is the integration of self-assessment, values clarification and other approaches to self-exploration, mastery of microcomputer and other technological contributions to information systems, and the teaching of decision-making skills. It is the design of instructional materials and procedures that respect the wide range of individual differences of students, both in stages of maturation and in interests and abilities. It is in the use of a full range of educational technology and other means of maximizing the motivation and learning of each individual. Traditional instructional approaches that focus primarily on testing, the study of a small number of specific occupations, or preparation for placement cannot adequately respond to the needs of all students. What is demanded is an approach that integrates these and other aspects of career planning in accord with principles of human development and sound instructional methodology.

Need to Legitimize Career Development as Academic Experience

Efforts to facilitate career development in schools and colleges typically have occurred in ancillary services rather than in the mainstream of the academic curriculum. The major exception to this is in vocational education courses, which are considered by many educators to be nonacademic. Borow (1960) traced the growth of career development activities offered within formal college curricula and found significant increases from the early 1930s until the post-Sputnik era, when concern for "pure academics" controlled the curriculum. Recent years have witnessed another turnabout; the public has become disenchanted with education for education's sake and is demanding that public education be more utilitarian. The Career Education movement of the 1970s, though never fully implemented, has given great impetus to career development activities as a legitimate credit-earning aspect of the curriculum. As Reardon (1973) pointed out, "In general the impetus appears to be for the college to provide preparation for making a living as well as living." In the nation's colleges and universities, the last bastion of nonutilitarian academics in a pragmatic world, the receptivity to granting academic credit for career development activities has increased. Erhart and Gilmore (1977) have chronicled some of the difficulties in obtaining approval from curriculum committees for the granting of academic credit for career-planning courses. The success of counselors, placement officials, and concerned faculty in obtaining such approval is evident, however, in the increasing numbers of schools, colleges, and universities offering career development and career-planning courses.

Devlin (1974) identified seventy-two colleges offering academic credit for courses focusing on the teaching of career decision-making skills. Haney and Howland (1978) found a rapid increase in the number of new career development courses offered for credit, from twenty-seven in 1972-73 to 109 in 1975-76, following which the rate of offering of new courses appeared to level off. Their survey, which included both two-year and four-year colleges, identified 353 institutions offering courses for credit. This represented 39 percent of the institutions responding to their survey. In a 1977 survey of thirty-seven college career-planning and placement centers in California, Koehn (1978) found 42 percent of the campuses offering career-planning courses. In a random sample of 20 percent of the four-year colleges and universities in the fifty states, Puerto Rico, and Guam, Reardon, Zunker, and Dyal (1979) found that 29 percent of the 299 institutions responding offered career planning courses for academic credit, and another 29 percent offered structured courses on a noncredit basis. In a more recent survey sponsored by the NVGA Commission on the Career Development of Young Adults, Goodson (1982) found that 64 percent of ninety-eight institutions, representing forty-seven states, offered career classes.

Instructional efforts in higher education have been more widely reported than those in the elementary and secondary schools. However, this does not mean that there is less activity at that level. The findings of Prediger, Roth, and Noeth (1973) have not gone unnoticed. In their nationwide survey of 11th graders, they found that nearly 80 percent indicated that they desired help with their career planning; yet only about half of the students responding had received any assistance in their career planning. Extensive activities have occurred throughout the nation as state departments of education and individual school districts have engaged in planning and implementation of career education programs. Two extensive efforts in developing curricular models for career development are the California model (Cunha, Laramore, Lowrey, Mitchell, Smith, & Wooley, 1972) and the Minnesota model (Tennyson, Hansen, Klaurens, & Antholz, 1975).

Need to Respond to Individual Differences

Regardless of the stage of career development of the client, the counselor must be aware of and responsive to the wide range of individual differences among clients. Many of these differences relate directly to career development: differences in decision-making skills, ability to assimilate and evaluate information, skills in goal setting and priority setting, reading level, ability to understand self and others, and many other differences. Mackin and Hansen (1981), citing Super's (1953) proposition that career development is the implementation of self-concept, are critical of most programmatic efforts at bringing career development into the curriculum. They reported that "of most significance to school counselors is the fact that the developmental stages and tasks of the high school years are primarily focused on exploration (self and career), not preparation, for a career."

Goodson (1981) also supported responsiveness to individual differences when he challenged the assumption that college students who have selected an academic major do not need help in career exploration. He found that approximately half of all entering freshman and transfer students at Brigham Young University indicated that they needed various kinds of help in career exploration. He concluded that "Many students who enter college already having decided upon a major and an occupation have done little research in their chosen field of interest to be well-informed of personal suitability and job opportunities. Many of these students, on learning the realities of their chosen occupation, will often change direction and select a more suitable major that best matches their abilities, interests, and desires."

It is clear that programs designed to address career development needs of all students must be flexible and responsive to individual differences. Instructional approaches to career development and career planning have demonstrated that they can be both systematic in design and flexible in response to the individual needs of each client.

Needs of the Institution

Systematic facilitation of career development implies comprehensive services to all students. No educational institution is likely to underwrite an approach that is based primarily on direct services of professional counselors, either through individual or group counseling, to all its students. The number of additional counseling positions this would require would be prohibitively expensive. Classes in career exploration and career planning provide one way for institutions to make available to all students a systematic approach that carries with it the benefits of credit-generating academic coursework, while minimizing the difficulties of providing all career development services solely with student services staff. Most institutions are funded, at least in part, on formulae that are to a large extent driven by the generation of academic credit. Whether courses are taught by academic faculty or by student services staff, if academic credits are generated the institution benefits.

Adams (1974), in discussing some of the problems inherent in a community college "open-door" admissions policy, indicated that such a policy "has in fact become a revolving door through which colleges process hundreds of thousands of young people whose experience with higher education in the community colleges has been one of frustration, failure, and disillusionment." It is Adams's contention that the high dropout rate in community colleges is not because of the academic inability of students to succeed in the community college setting. He stated that "Most students who drop out cite as their reasons low grades and dissatisfaction with school. However, these reasons can usually be traced to an inappropriate career or educational program choice — or their inability to put together anything that makes sense to them." These assumptions were the impetus for the development of a class in career planning at Everett (Washington) Community College. At a time when most institutions of higher education are seriously concerned about curbing enrollment declines, a high priority is given on most campuses to activities oriented toward increasing the student retention rate. Carver (1982) has demonstrated a strong relationship between activities such as career-planning courses and improved student retention among those students who are not experiencing academic failure. That these concerns exist across all aspects of college and university campuses is partially demonstrated at Pennsylvania State University, where the Career Development and Placement Center offers courses in career development through three of the University's colleges (Swails & Hess, 1977). At Penn State, courses are offered through the College of Liberal Arts, the College of Human Development, and the College of Agriculture — three very different colleges, each with faculty and students with unique academic objectives and priorities.

COMMON PROGRAM GOALS

Among the instructional approaches reviewed here there are a number of common program goals: (1) to facilitate awareness of self, which encompasses a broad spectrum of specific approaches, (2) to facilitate awareness of the world of work, including the identification, evaluation, and use of occupational and educational information, (3) to develop goal-setting and decision-making skills, which typically involves the processing and integration of information from (1) and (2), and (4) the development of a personal career action plan based on sound personalized decision making.

As indicated earlier, notions of career developmental stages and developmental tasks, as well as career maturity, have influenced the specific program goals adopted for students at different levels. Those courses designed for the high school level typically focus more on objectives related to self-awareness and career awareness than on those activities related to making a decision on a specific occupation or actually seeking employment.

Mackin and Hansen (1981) describe the objectives for a class entitled "Career — Thinking About Your Future" offered to juniors and seniors at a Minneapolis high school: "The goals of the curriculum are three-fold: (a) to increase self-awareness; (b) to increase career awareness; and (c) to increase decision-making and planning skills." The "packaged" course for ninth and tenth graders developed by Appalachia Educational Laboratory (AEL, 1978), entitled "Exploring Career Decision-Making" also has emphasis on self-exploration and occupational exploration.

At the college level four types of courses were found. The first type was the course offered by a specific academic discipline, with a straightforward objective of providing students with information regarding career opportunities available to students completing a particular academic major. The second type of course is similar in many respects to those offered at the high school level. In these courses the objectives continue to focus on exploration of self and the world in which we live and work, typically with a heavy dose of decision-making strategies, goal setting, and priority setting. Schrank (1982) provided a typical set of objectives for this type of course:

> to help students (a) learn a decision-making process as it relates to educational and vocational decisions; (b) become aware of past experiences

and how they affect current decisions; (c) explore through various tests and exercises values, personality characteristics, interests, and abilities and how they relate to educational-vocational decisions; (d) become aware of various sources of educational and vocational information and how to use these sources in planning a career; (e) learn how to integrate various kinds of information about oneself and the world of work to establish educational and vocational plans, and (f) choose preferred and alternative educational goals and plans.

These courses tend to be designed to meet the needs of freshman and sophomore students who, according to Heppner and Krause (1979), are "more in need of life-planning skills" as compared to juniors and seniors, who are "more in need of job-seeking and job-getting skills." In an extensive survey that identified 353 two-year and four-year colleges offering career courses for credit, 84 percent indicated that their major emphasis was on "assisting students to develop self-awareness regarding their abilities, interests, needs, and life-styles" (Haney & Howland, 1978).

The third type of course is that which deals with the later stages of career development, involving objectives that focus on attainment of appropriate employment. Such a course at Florida State University has five goals:

(a) assess interests, values, and abilities; (b) develop decision-making strategies for career and leisure planning; (c) explore a career field and interview professionals in that field; (d) learn about the job market and employment outlooks; (e) develop a career plan; and (f) write a resume and develop interviewing skills (Reardon & Regan, 1981).

The fourth type of course is, as might be expected, all of the above. An example of the objectives for a comprehensive career development and career planning course is presented by Barker (1981), in describing the objectives for the course "Career Planning and Decision-Making for College," developed by Appalachia Educational Laboratory:

The six goals of the course are that students will learn to (a) apply the concepts of career and decision making in examining their own experience; (b) establish an occupational preference by integrating knowledge of self and work; (c) identify personally relevant career goals by learning to project their own values into the future; (d) develop a detailed career plan based on their goals, knowledge of college options, and personal criteria; (e) demonstrate ability to decide and act with respect to taking the initial steps of their career plan; and (f) comprehend that planning and deciding is a continual process in controlling and shaping a career.

Additional statements of objectives for career courses may be found in the publications cited as references in the next section.

TYPICAL KINDS OF INTERVENTION STRATEGIES

The instructional approaches include courses, both credit and noncredit, which are offered in schools and colleges, as well as those materials and procedures that comprise an intact "package" for use as a unit within a course. These are to be distinguished from the increasing volume of career guidance materials that are designed for intermittent use or to be interwoven with courses in the regular curriculum.

Instructional approaches are not new. Holcomb (1966) identified a high school course devoted entirely to the study of vocations offered in 1908 and a college course offered in 1917. What is offered in current instructional approaches may best be contrasted with the old by comparing titles: "career development" and "career decision making" as opposed to "the study of vocations" and "the choice of an occupation." The focus is on the career as a dynamic, developing process and on teaching decision-making skills that can be used throughout many career decision points rather than emphasizing the selection of one occupational choice as an outcome of the course. A number of instructional approaches, representing both formal courses and other "packaged" units, at levels ranging from junior high school through adult, have been selected for review. Summaries of these approaches follow.

Instructional Packages

The instructional packages are materials that are available from commercial publishers and that have been designed for implementation as either a self-contained course in career planning or as a unit within a course or as a group guidance activity. A sample of materials for use with client groups ranging from junior high school students through adults is reviewed below.

Deciding and Decisions and Outcomes

These two sets of curricular materials are published by the College Entrance Examination Board (Gelatt, Varenhorst, Carey, &

Miller, 1972,1973). Similar in design, they both focus on the development of decision-making skills on (1) examination and recognition of personal values, (2) knowledge and use of adequate, relevant information, and (3) knowledge and use of an effective strategy for converting this information into action. *Deciding,* designed for junior high school students, consists of three units entitled Values, Information, and Strategy. *Decisions and Outcomes,* for senior high school and college students and adults, has four units: The Starting Point, The Deciding Self, Before Deciding, and Applying Skills. Both are presented in workbook format. Leader's guides accompany both, outlining the "Theory underlying the decision-making process and providing detailed instructions on how to conduct effective group sessions." Both *Deciding* and *Decisions and Outcomes* can be used effectively as the framework for a course in decision making, as major components in counseling and guidance programs, or as units in subject areas such as English, history, human relations, drug education, and health education. Both can be completed in as few as fifteen class sessions or extended to as many as forty-five. Although focusing on personal values clarification and the development of personalized decision-making skills, both rely extensively on peer interaction and group discussion.

Life / Career Development System

This is a set of nine modules developed by Walz and associates (Walz, undated) for use with students in grades nine to twelve and college. Each requires six to nine hours to complete and can be used in large classes or individually. The system is designed for a trained facilitator to present the modules and coordinate the learning experiences of the participants. The modules are not available separately but rather are purchased as part of a kit, including pre-/post-measures, facilitator's manuals, participant journals, telephone consultation with the publisher, and training of facilitators. The nine modules are (1) Exploring Self, (2) Determining Values, (3) Setting Goals, (4) Expanding Options, (5) Overcoming Barriers, (6) Using Information, (7) Working Effectively, (8) Thinking Futuristically, and (9) Selecting Mates.

Exploring Career Decision Making

This is a package of materials developed by the Appalachia Educational Laboratory (1978). A structured course for ninth and tenth grade students is recommended, with options for varied lengths of duration and selection of materials. Among the materials available are a text, activity booklets, and eighteen filmstrip/cassette tape sets. The program is designed for large group instruction at the high school freshman and sophomore level, but individual parts of the set of materials are adaptable for individual use with older clients. The contents of this package cover quite broadly the areas of self-exploration and career awareness.

ACT Career Planning Program

The *Career Planning Program*, published by the American College Testing Program (1976), is a "guidance-oriented system designed to help students identify and explore personally relevant occupation and educational programs." It is intended for use with persons sixteen and over. The system has two primary components: a student assessment instrument, which is scored by ACT and results in the production of an individual student report, and a planning booklet, which is designed for either group or individual usage in working with information generated in the student report. The planning booklet is available in two formats, a student version entitled "Planning: CPP Student's Booklet" and an adult version entitled "Planning Career Changes." The student report presents information on vocational interests, work-related experiences, and abilities, all related to the world of work through a system of eight career clusters and a "World of Work Map." The system is designed to facilitate personal career exploration, with the occupational cluster system cross-indexed to the USOE Career Clusters. The *Career Planning Program* may be used as a format for a course, as a part of a course, or as a noncurricular group guidance program. The program has been extensively researched and revised after field testing and has been adopted for statewide use by the South Carolina Department of Education. The materials provided are extensive: in addition to the test booklets and student planning booklets, a supervisor's manual, a counselor's manual, and a handbook are provided. Sample public relations materials and research reports are also provided, and the opportunity is provided for a school to add up to twelve locally prepared items to the test booklet.

Take Hold of Your Future

This program, also known as the "Personal Life and Career Planning Program," published by ACT (Harris-Bowlsbey, Spivack, & Lisansky, 1982), consists of a leader's manual and a student career planning guide. The program was initially developed by Harris-Bowlsbey and her associates at Towson State University as a systematic career planning course for university students. The general purpose of the program is to increase the vocational maturity of participants. The authors define career maturity as "the ability to cope adequately with the developmental tasks of a given life stage." The program is designed to address six themes of career maturity and is organized into 14 two-hour class sessions. A stated short-range goal is to enable participants to "make a sound preliminary vocational choice and related educational decisions;" a long-range goal is to "develop the ability to use the skills introduced here to cope with career decision making in later life stages." The program is intended for adults of post-secondary age and has been extensively field-tested with undergraduate university students. The program utilizes three instructional modes: lectures, large group activities, and small group interaction. The leader's manual presents a three-part format for each session: (1) a summary indicating the necessary leader preparation and a suggested timetable and materials needed for the session, (2) a detailed description of objectives and suggested activities, and (3) theoretical background material. The program uses the Ability Tests Battery from the *ACT Career Planning Program* and provides an extensive set of materials in the leader's manual for use as handouts and overhead transparencies.

Career Planning and Decision Making for College

This program, developed by the Appalachia Educational Laboratory (1980), is recommended for use as a course for college level freshmen and sophomores. A workbook format is used, organizing student activities for the purpose of developing "a greater understanding of the world of work as a basis for planning and choice" (Barker, 1981). The CPDM is exemplary in its extensive validation. In addition to formative evaluations that contributed to revisions of earlier versions, AEL conducted an extensive summative evaluation during the 1978-79 field tests of the CPDM. Fourteen colleges participated, with 589 undergraduate students involved in fifteen experimental and fifteen control classes. On the *Assessment of Career Decision-Making* instrument (Harren, 1978), students participating in the CPDM classes made significantly greater gains than students in control classes in the following areas:

> (a) progress in selecting a college major, (b) progress toward selecting an occupation to pursue after college completion, (c) knowledge about college majors, (d) knowledge about the relation between college majors and occupations, (e) knowledge about occupations of interest, (f) understanding of self in relation to work, (g) quality of decision-making process, (h) effectiveness that one rated his or her decision-making process, (i) accuracy in defining the terms work and career, (j) ability to identify criteria for evaluating career information, and (k) ability to identify correct course concept definitions. (Barker, 1981)

Careers Courses

A variety of descriptions of courses were reviewed, with considerable overlap in objectives and activities. Calvert, Carter, and Murphy (1964) identified four different types of careers courses: (1) the course on personal-vocational selection or career planning, with emphasis on self-appraisal, (2) introduction to the world of work, involving analyses of occupations and use of occupational information, (3) job-seeking techniques, focusing on actual job placement, and (4) adjustment to careers, examining problems one might expect to encounter in making the transition from school or college to the world of work. Most of the courses reviewed are hybrids of these four types and appear to be based heavily on the Borow (1960) prototype. Highlights of selected courses, representing a variety of institutions at several levels, follow.

Secondary School Level

MINNEAPOLIS PUBLIC SCHOOLS. Although most published reports in the literature describe courses at the college and university level, examples of carefully designed and validated courses at the high school level do exist. Mackin and Hansen (1981) developed an eleven-week course for eleventh and twelfth grade students in the Minneapolis schools. The course, entitled "Career — Thinking about Your Future," is unique, according to Mackin and Hansen "in that it uses career development theory as its reference and consciously selects learning activities related to the student's developmental stage and the broad concept of career." The course is organized around three broad goals: (1) increased self-awareness, with units on "self-concept," "interests," "abilities," and "values and needs," (2) increased career awareness, with units on "career development" and "the future," and (3) increased decision-making and planning skills, with one unit on goal-setting, planning, and decision making.

College and University Level

UNIVERSITY OF NORTHERN COLORADO. A three-quarter hour course entitled "Career and Self-Exploration" is offered at the University of Northern Colorado. This course, offered collaboratively by the Counseling and Career Center and the academic program in College Student Personnel Administration, is designed to meet the needs of lower division students who have not yet selected a major. The objectives of the course are to

> (1) enhance student's understanding of what she/he wants from college, career and life experiences; (2) increase student's skills in setting goals and developing realistic action plans to meet those goals: (3) provide an understanding of and skills in decision making; (4) enable students to assess their abilities, interests, values, needs and skills; (5) provide students with opportunities for contrasting fantasies with realities; (5) expose students to majors available at UNC; (7) broaden students' knowledge of occupational information and job trends; (8) orient students to academic requirements and procedures, e.g. GPA, deadlines, registration, general education requirements, etc.; (9) assist students in learning environment-appropriate survival skills: how to access information; how to know when it's needed; how to benefit from past experience; and (10) introduce the concept of sex role influence on educational and career decisions.*

FLORIDA STATE UNIVERSITY. A three-part course entitled "Career Planning" is offered under the joint auspices of the College of Business and the College of Education and is team-taught by faculty and staff members from the Career Planning Office and the Curricular-Career Information Service (CCIS), a multimedia resource center. This upper division course is offered for variable credit and may be

---

*Fontaine, J. Personal communication, November, 1982.

repeated to a maximum of three quarter credits, depending on the number of units for which a student has contracted. The course is divided into three units:

> Unit I, Self and Environmental Analysis, provides the students with a variety of self-assessment experiences to help them determine their values, skills, and personality characteristics. Students are given tours of the career services offices that are most likely to be important in their career planning. Many occupational information resources are introduced, including the first four modules available in the Curricular-Career Information Service. Unit II, Decision-Making, covers topics such as leisure planning in relation to career development, labor market forecasts and employment information, decision-making models and the development of related skills, interviews with persons in three occupational areas, completion of selected CCIS modules, instructor conferences, and a performance test on relevant academic content. Unit III, Job Acquisition, includes materials related to resume and cover letter preparation, interviewing skills, job negotiation strategies, videotape simulated job interviews, and a panel of personnel recruiters. Two written projects include a career plan project . . . and a goal setting exercise. (Reardon & Regan, 1981)

An extensive process evaluation has been conducted, providing both an indication of student perceptions of several aspects of the course and a comparison of this course with other university courses. Reardon and Regan (1981) found that "The evaluation has provided some valuable information for instructors, students, and administrators. The course . . . may provide an alternative to traditional one-to-one or group career counseling. The evaluation has revealed which features of the course are likely to be most marketable to potential students, and it has shown instructors how some class activities and assignments might be modified. Finally, this process evaluation has shown that the career planning class has measured qualities that enable it to stand on its own with other courses in the academic marketplace."

UNIVERSITY OF MARYLAND. A noncredit course offered since 1970 by the Career Development Center at the University of Maryland became a credit-bearing course in 1975, as that unit joined forces with the academic Department of Counseling and Personnel Services (Touchton, Wertheimer, Cornfeld, & Harrison, 1977). This course is unique among those reviewed in that it is based on a career development model for college students that is adapted from a model of cognitive development (Knefelkamp & Slepitza, 1976). The developmentally-designed course consists of three units, as follows:

> (1) Careers and Who People Are. Topics include why people work, what we need to know about people to think about them in careers, analysis of literary works dealing with people in careers. (2) Knowing Who You Are. Topics include interests, needs, values, integrative skills, and self-assessment. (3) Putting it All Together. Unit includes occupational exploration through (a) visits to the Career Library and Experiential Learning Office, (b) conducting career biographical interviews, and (c) decision-making skills. (Touchton et al., 1977)

Pennsylvania State University. A ten-week course offered in the College of Liberal Arts at Pennsylvania State University for undeclared majors has, in addition to the goals stated for other career planning courses, a goal of "altering students' general orientation (e.g. moving their locus of control from externality to internality)" (Bartsch & Hackett, 1979). The course "Effective Personal and Career Decision-Making" meets for two 75-minute class sessions per week, with one class session and one lab session each week. Themes stressed in the course are importance of self-management, self-direction, and personal responsibility for choice (Bartsch, 1977). Among the specific topics included are goal setting, mental sets and constraining beliefs, values, interests and abilities in career decision making, assertiveness, self-management, and coping skills in making a decision.

University of Oregon. In contrast to the recommended class size of fifteen to twenty found in most descriptions of career planning courses, Ripley (1975) describes a career planning course at the University of Oregan designed for 125 students. The course consists of ten 1-hour sessions, including lectures, written exercises, visual presentations, role-playing demonstrations, and panel discussions, with optional small group sessions to complete exercises.

In addition to the sample of courses described above, the reader is referred to additional descriptions of courses at the University of Alabama (Comas & Day, 1976), Central Michigan University (Gillingham & Lounsbury, 1979), Cornell University (Babcock & Kaufman, 1976), Everett Community College (Adams, 1974), Pennsylvania State University (Bucher, 1980; Swails & Hess, 1977), Purdue University (Ganster & Lovell, 1978), Southern Illinois University (Evans & Rector, 1978), and Washington State University (Parker, Bunch, & Hagberg, 1974).

ASSESSMENT AND COMPARATIVE EVALUATIONS OF THE INTERVENTION STRATEGIES

In the time that passed since the publication of Reardon and Burck's 1975 book, there have been significant changes in the nature of publications regarding instructional approaches to career development. All of the reports of careers courses reviewed at that time were descriptive only. The reports outlined course objectives and structure and discussed strategies involved in obtaining approval from academic authorities to offer such courses for credit. These reports met a need in that relevant information not previously addressed in the literature that was shared. However, no information was provided regarding the effectiveness of such offerings, and the profession could only guess as to the impact of offering careers courses.

A review of the literature since 1974 revealed considerable effort on the part of counselors to evaluate the effectiveness of courses in career planning. Seventy-five percent of the reports reviewed for this chapter included efforts to evaluate the impact of the careers course. A wide range of criteria, as well as research/evaluation designs, were reported. Locally designed questionnaires based on students' expressions of satisfaction and self-ratings on attainment of course goals were frequent. A process evaluation conducted by Reardon and Regan (1981) found that students perceived the Florida State University career planning course to be as demanding as other university courses. The programs developed at Appalachia Educational Laboratory and the American College Testing Program have been extensively validated. Many courses have been evaluated on their ability to increase student scores on the Career Maturity Inventory (Crites, 1973), with a very impressive degree of success. Bartsch and Hackett (1979) reported success in increasing the extent to which students demonstrated an internalized locus of control on Rotter's I-E Scale (Rotter, 1966). Increased scores on Harren's Assessment of Career Decision-Making (Harren, 1978) were demonstrated in evaluations of courses at Southern Illinois University (Evans & Rector, 1978) and in Barker's (1981) evaluation of the

AEL college-level program. Carver (1982) reported significant improvement on the Career Decision Scale (Osipow, Carney, Winer, Yanico, & Koschier, 1976).

Most courses reviewed were quite similar in their general goals and organization. Objectives of increasing self-awareness, increasing awareness of career opportunities, and the development of skills in goal setting, planning, and decision making were universal. Almost all courses focus heavily on student involvement in exercises, discussion, and assignments. Though all courses reviewed utilize lectures and presentations, only the large class at the University of Oregon (Ripley, 1975) relied entirely on the presentation of information to students via lectures and panel discussions, and in that case small group meetings were provided on an optional basis. In most cases the primary audience for whom the course is designed is students who need to engage in self-exploration — typically high school students and students early in their college careers. Rarely, however, were courses found that were specifically designed on a theoretical basis that addressed developmental stages and needs of the specific target group. Notable exceptions were the course in the Minneapolis Public Schools reported by Mackin and Hansen (1981) and the University of Maryland course reported by Touchton et al. (1977). In almost all cases the careers course is a self-standing course, offered by an academic department, occasionally in conjunction with a unit of the student services division of the institution. Those courses that appear to be most successful are those that are designed for a specific client group to meet identified needs. These courses include the full range of goals, from the self-awareness oriented courses to those that focus exclusively on preparation for the job search and placement.

SUMMARY AND CONCLUSIONS

Courses in career and self-exploration and career planning are frequently offered in post-secondary education institutions as well as in secondary schools. This instructional approach to career development reflects a responsiveness to a set of universal developmental needs of students in the areas of increasing understanding of self, awareness of career opportunities, and the development of related skills in goal-setting, planning, and decision making. Academic courses are seen as cost-effective and revenue-generating means of assisting students to meet these career development needs. Evaluation of career development courses in the areas of increasing student levels of career maturity, career decision-making skills, and related measures indicates that such courses are, in general, an effective and efficient means of facilitating career development.

BIBLIOGRAPHY

Adams, G. A. 'Preventative' career counseling — proving that it works. *Journal of College Placement*, 1974, *34*, 26-33.

American College Testing Program. *ACT career planning program (Form H)*. Iowa City, Iowa: Author, 1976.

Appalachia Educational Laboratory, Inc. *Career planning and decision-making for college*. Bloomington, Illinois: McKnight Publishing Company, 1980.

Appalachia Educational Laboratory, Inc. *Exploring career decision-making*. Bloomington, Illinois: McKnight Publishing Company, 1978.

Babcock, R. J., and Kaufman, M. A. Effectiveness of a career course. *Vocational Guidance Quarterly*, 1976, *24*, 261-266.

Barker, S. B. An evaluation of the effectiveness of a college career guidance course. *Journal of College Student Personnel*, 1981, *22*, 354-358.

Bartsch, K. *Instructor's manual: How to teach effective personal and career decision making*. Walpole, Massachusetts: Edupac, 1977.

Bartsch, K., and Hackett, G. Effect of a decision-making course on locus of control, conceptualization, and career planning. *Journal of College Student Personnel*, 1979, *20*, 230-235.

Borow, H. College courses in vocational planning. *Vocational Guidance Quarterly*, 1960, *9*, 75-80.

Bucher, J. P. A career development course for credit. *Journal of College Placement*, 1980, *41(1)*, 25-26.

Carver, D. S. *The effects of a career and self exploration course on the career development and self concept of undeclared freshmen*. Unpublished doctoral dissertation, University of Northern Colorado, 1982.

Comas, R. E., and Day, R. W. College students explore careers. *Vocational Guidance Quarterly*, 1976, *25*, 76-79.

Crites, J. D. *The Career Maturity Inventory*. Monterey, California: McGraw-Hill, 1973.

Cunha, J., Laramore, D., Lowrey, B., Mitchell, A., Smith, T., and Wooley, D. (Eds.). *Career development: A California model for career guidance curriculum k-adult*. Fullerton, California: California Personnel and Guidance Association, 1972.

Devlin, T. C. Career development courses: An important part of the counselor's repertoire. *Journal of College Placement*, 1974, *34(4)*, 62-64.

Egner, J. R., and Jackson, D. J. Effectiveness of a counseling intervention program for teaching career decision-making skills. *Journal of Counseling Psychology,* 1978, *25,* 45-52.

Erikson, E. H. *Childhood and society.* New York: W. W. Norton, 1950.

Erhart, J. F., and Gilmore, R. G. Working together for academic credit. *Journal of College Placement,* 1977, *37(3),* 71-75.

Evans, J. R., and Rector, A. P. Evaluation of a college course in career decision making. *Journal of College Student Personnel,* 1978, *19,* 163-168.

Ganster, D. C., and Lovell, J. E. An evaluation of a career development seminar using Crites' Career Maturity Inventory. *Journal of Vocational Behavior,* 1978, *13,* 172-179.

Gelatt, H. B., Varenhorst, B., and Carey, R. *Deciding.* New York: College Entrance Examination Board, 1972.

Gelatt, H. B., Varenhorst, B., Carey, R., and Miller, G. P. *Decisions and Outcomes.* New York: College Entrance Examination Board, 1973.

Gillingham, W. H., and Lounsbury, J. E. A description and evaluation of a career exploration course. *Journal of College Student Personnel,* 1979, *20,* 525-529.

Goodson, W. D. Do career development needs exist for all students entering colleges or just the undecided major student? *Journal of College Student Personnel,* 1981, *22,* 413-417.

Goodson, W. D. Status of career programs on college and university campuses. *Vocational Guidance Quarterly,* 1982, *30,* 230-235.

Haney, T., and Howland, P. A. career courses for credit: Necessity or luxury? *Journal of College Placement,* 1978, *38(2),* 75-79.

Harren, V. A. *Assessment of career decision-making.* Carbondale, Illinois: Southern Illinois University, Department of Psychology, 1978.

Harris-Bowlsbey, J., Spivack, J. D., and Lisansky, R. S. *Take hold of your future: A career planning guide.* Iowa City, Iowa: The American College Testing Program, 1982.

Heppner, P. P., and Krause, J. B. A career seminar course. *Journal of College Student Personnel,* 1979, *20,* 300-305.

Holcomb, J. R. *College courses in careers: An historical and evaluative treatment.* Unpublished paper. Pittsburgh: Duquesne University, 1966.

Jordaan, J. P. Life stages as organizing modes of career development. In E. L. Herr (Ed.), *Vocational guidance and human development.* Boston: Houghton-Mifflin, 1974.

Knefelkamp, L. L., and Slepitza, R. A cognitive-developmental model of career development — an adaptation of the Perry scheme. *The Counseling Psychologist,* 1976, *6(3),* 53-58.

Koehn, S. Who's doing what? An update survey of career planning programs. *Journal of College Student Personnel,* 1978, *19,* 523-526.

Levinson, D. *The seasons of a man's life.* New York: Alfred A. Knopf, 1978.

Mackin, R. K., and Hansen, L. S. A theory-based career development course: A plant in the garden. *School Counselor,* 1981, *28,* 325-334.

Mazzano, J. A survey of the teaching of occupations. *Vocational Guidance Quarterly,* 1969, *17,* 275-277.

Osipow, S. H., Carney, C. G., Winer, J., Yanico, B., and Koschier, M. *The Career Decision Scale.* Columbus, Ohio: Marathon Press, 1976.

Parker, C., Bunch, C., and Hagberg, R. Group vocational guidance with college students. *Vocational Guidance Quarterly,* 1974, *23,* 168-172.

Prediger, D. J., Roth, J. D., and Noeth, R. J. *A nation-wide study of student career development: Summary of results. (ACT Research Report No. 61).* Iowa City: American College Testing Program, 1973.

Reardon, R. C. The counselor and career information services. *Journal of College Student Personnel,* 1973, *14,* 495-500.

Reardon, R. C., and Regan, K. Process evaluation of a career planning course. *Vocational Guidance Quarterly,* 1981, *29,* 265-269.

Reardon, R. C., Zunker, V., and Dyal, M. A. The status of career planning programs and career centers in colleges and universities. *Vocational Guidance Quarterly,* 1979, *28,* 154-159.

Ripley, T. M. Large career planning classes. *Journal of College Placement,* 1975, *36(1),* 66-70.

Rotter, J. B. Generalized expectancies for internal versus external control reinforcement. *Psychological Monographs,* 1966, *80 (1, Whole No. 609).*

Schrank, F. A. A faculty/counselor implemented career planning course. *Journal of College Student Personnel,* 1982, *23,* 83-84.

Super, D. E. A theory of vocational development. *American Psychologist,* 1953, *8,* 185-190.

Swails, R. G., and Hess, H. R. Human Development 498. *Journal of College Placement,* 1977, *37(2),* 57-59.

Tennyson, W. W., Hansen, L. S., Klaurens, M. K., and Antholz, M. B. *Educating for career development.* St. Paul, Minnesota: Minnesota Department of Education, 1975.

Touchton, J. G., Wertheimer, L. C., Cornfeld, J. L., and Harrision, K. H. Career planning and decision-making: A developmental approach to the classroom. *The Counseling Psychologist,* 1977, *6(4),* 42-47.

Walz, G. *Life/career development system.* Ann Arbor: Human Development Services, Inc., undated.

CHAPTER 12

CAREER DEVELOPMENT OF WOMEN

Jennifer Boretz Kahnweiler

DRAMATIC changes for women have occurred during the past decade. Over half of all women now work outside the home, an increase of over 10 percent from only a decade earlier. This figure is expected to continue to rise dramatically. Also, increasing numbers of women are choosing nontraditional career paths. For example, business and law schools are now equally represented by both sexes. Many would argue, however, that despite the statistics reflecting changes in women's status, most professional and business fields are still male dominated, and women continue to occupy the lowest ranking and paying positions.

The first purpose of this chapter will be to assist counselors in understanding some of the major societal trends that have influenced women and their career development over the past decade. In recent years career counselors have become aware of the special needs of women at different stages of development. A second purpose will be to provide insight into unique career related issues that emerge for women at different points in their lives — from grade school through retirement. Only by understanding these unique dilemmas can counselors hope to assist women to effectively manage their careers.

Many successful individual and group approaches already have been implemented to help all types and ages of women engage in successful career planning. Therefore, a third purpose of this chapter is to identify and describe some representative and validated programs that counselors might incorporate into their work. Future trends and issues are mentioned and a list of resource materials for counselors is also provided at the end of the chapter.

EMERGING CAREER PATTERNS OF WOMEN

In the early 1970s, the women's movement took firm hold in the United States. Its impact continues to be impressive for both women and men. In the work place, women began to enter the job market, citing needs of independence, recognition, and self-fulfillment (Astin, 1976; Kahnweiler, 1980). The women's movement strongly heralded the message that women had choices as to the type of career and life-style they could hold. For the first time, women who aspired toward career and educational goals felt permission to pursue them. More women also began to realize that their earlier career choices often were based on sex role socialization. It was in this climate that counseling services and programs emerged for women reentering the work world.

Aside from personal needs of recognition and self-fulfillment, research indicates that many women return to school or work because of economic reasons (Astin, 1976). A recent dramatic rise in the divorce rate has also been related to the entrance of more women into the job market (Zunker, 1981). Another trend is of married persons both working in order to maintain a comfortable life-style in today's economy. It is simply not desirable for one spouse to remain at home in today's typical middle-class family. The addition of children creates financial pressures that make the dual career family a necessity.

Changes in government policy throughout the past decade also have contributed to opening up new career opportunities for women. Employers were obliged to go beyond passive compliance with the civil rights ban on discrimination and take affirmative action to seek and hire minority employees. Affirmative action programs have forced organizations to promote and hire greater numbers of women from within and outside. More attention has been paid to opening up new management tracks for women within organizations where these tracks never existed before.

The shift in women's values, new economic realities, and government policy changes all have had a significant impact on the workplace. Employment patterns for women have moved increasingly from more traditional to nontraditional occupations. Women are more visible throughout the labor market.

In a trickling down effect, young girls are actively encouraged to enter scientific disciplines (Kreinberg, 1981). Scherrei (1979) found that young women today increasingly express a desire to enter the "pioneer" professions such as business, law, engineering, and science. More working women have been pursuing career paths to management, and the number of women in positions of leadership has dramatically increased (Adams, 1979).

The foregoing pages have provided an overview of some of the forces affecting women's career development in the past decade. It is clear that changes in the number of females working and changes in the nature of their career choice have occurred. New issues have emerged to accompany this progress. The following pages briefly describe some of the challenges that confront modern women at different stages of their career planning. The needs of young girls and high school women, traditional age college women, women returning to school and work, professional and business women, and women at retirement age are all addressed. Key examples of programming strategies and counselor interventions are described.

YOUNG GIRLS AND HIGH SCHOOL WOMEN

Issues

Sex role stereotyping has been defined as attributing behaviors, abilities, interests, values, and roles to a person or group of persons on the basis of their sex (Peterson & Vetter, 1977). It continues to affect the career choice of many girls. Tibbetts (1975) found that children between ages seven and eleven sex-stereotype occupations. Research by Looft (1971) and Siegel (1973) demonstrated that girls in the primary grades desired to be nurses or teachers. Barnett's (1975) research found that girls tended to avoid choosing high prestige jobs whereas boys did not.

Significant numbers of high school women still avoid scientific and technical careers. McLure and Piel (1978) examined over 1,000 talented high school senior women to discover why they did not choose scientific careers. They found that factors such as lack of information, doubts about combining a career and family life, and lack of role models influenced their subjects. Goldman and Hewitt (1976) concluded that weak mathematics-related abilities restrict young women in their career choices. Betz (1976) suggested that women may incorrectly perceive their true ability in math and thereby eliminate possible career choices.

As revealed in earlier research, many counselors tend to hold traditional attitudes about women. Schlossberg and Pietrofesa (1973) found that counselors discourage women from choosing traditionally male roles. Thomas and Stewart (1971) reported that counselors saw females with nontraditional goals as in need of more counseling than those with traditional goals. It is evident that counselor bias can greatly influence impressionable young girls and high school women. Young women perceive the counselor as an expert and may select fields based on the limited, traditional choices these counselors made available to them.

Program Interventions

Efforts have been made at the public school level to combat stereotypical attitudes. The University of Minnesota has developed a comprehensive career development curriculum described by Hansen (1978) that includes a package entitled *Women and the World of Work*. This is a vehicle through which elementary and high school counselors can work with teachers. Here are some sample objectives:

Grades K-3 — Describes how the contribution of individuals both inside and outside the home is important.

Grades 4-6 — Identifies women and men in new or unusual occupations about which one would like to learn more.

Junior High — Identifies compromises a woman or man may have to make in choosing an occupation.

Senior High — Identifies discriminatory practices in the work environment that one might help to change.

Another model program emphasizes science and math career opportunities for young girls. The unique National Science Foundation Women in Science Workshop (Kreinberg, 1981) is designed to create awareness of employment opportunities for women in science and engineering and encourage women to prepare for careers in these fields. Different activities are designed for different ages of girls and women. At the junior high level, girls are encouraged to engage in hands on activities that include doing experiments, trying out new equipment, and solving math problems. High school students are presented with college requirements and recommended college courses in science and engineering and descriptions of a typical day on the job. They also are given the opportunity to meet with a variety of women in these fields.

In addition to subject related programming, efforts to expose young women to female role models appears one means of combatting sex role stereotyping in career choice. Stake (1981) found that female teachers who had close individual contact with girls and who themselves presented a positive image had a significant influence on the career commitment of their female students. Zunker (1981) suggested that girls be encouraged to interview working women and write a summary of their work related experience. He also implied that a girl's role model could become her mentor, assisting her as she enters into and advances in the working world.

Individual Counseling Strategies

As mentioned before, some counselors still tend to typecast young women into certain roles. To combat this problem, Fitzgerald and Crites (1980) encourage counselors to take an activist role by questioning the occupational choices and values of their young clients. They ask counselors to reinforce girls' independent and decision-making behaviors. Fitzgerald and Crites believe that the counselor can ask leading questions (e.g. "How do you think you can find out more about being a reporter?") and reinforce information seeking behavior (e.g. "You really seem to understand that your interests are very similar to those of physicians"). They state that "the counselor who allows young women to ignore their potential and opt for low level careers or no careers at all, on the grounds that they are making a free choice which should be inviolate are simply ignoring reality."

Another key to promoting change is to have counselors informed of federal law requirements such as Title VII, Title IX, and Affirmative Action Legislation. They also should stay in close contact with their school district Affirmative Action Office and federal agencies that produce materials that could be helpful to their clients. By keeping current on mailing lists and up on new readings, they can learn of new training and career opportunities for their young clients.

Another area for counselor sensitivity is that of interest inventories. Zunker (1980) has done an excellent job of documenting the research on sex bias in interest inventories. Birk (1975) has suggested that manuals for counselors might include scoring guidelines for counseling women.

TRADITIONAL AGE COLLEGE WOMEN

Issues

Traditional age college women (between 18 and 22 years of age) have been tremendously influenced by the societal changes of the past decade. In a large scale study of freshmen women, the trend shows them choosing from a wider variety of career fields, including a move toward all facets of business and away from teaching and nursing (Scherrei, 1979). Medicine and law reflect increased numbers of women, though engineering has yet to attract significant numbers of females. As career options increase, choosing a career based on sound decision making becomes more important than ever for the young woman at the college level.

More college women today view work as playing a vital part in their lives. They see career and family roles as equally important (Moore & Veres, 1976). It seems evident that in planning for a career they also must think about how they will integrate their professional and personal lives. Because marriage and career conflicts may confront these students in the future, it seems vital that preventive programming is included at the college level. The good of this programming should be to help college women plan for how they will support themselves for a lifetime and to teach them how to cope with the role conflict dilemmas they will very likely confront.

Program Interventions

Numerous colleges have taken steps to offer career planning programs for women. O'Neil and Cano (1982) describe a videotape developed at the University of Kansas to help women understand how sexism and gender-role socialization affect their career decision making. A section of the tape is devoted to explaining available resources for women at the university. Richardson and Thomas (1978) reviewed the St. Olaf College program, which included a career advisory panel of successful women, a career counselor hired to work with women, and a funded research project on sex role attitudes of men and women at that institution. Montana State University also aimed at reducing sex role stereotyping and bias with regards to career choice (Leiterman-Stock, 1979). This program was targeted at faculty, administrators, and students and focused on self-exploration and recognizing sexual bias and stereotypes.

As has been pointed out, exposing young women to female role models can have a positive impact on their career goal setting. Programs can be structured to facilitate this role modeling. Mount Saint Joseph College, a women's college in Cincinnati, Ohio, has developed this idea and formed a Mentoring Council. All students are invited to attend monthly breakfasts where they have an opportunity to meet with professional women from a wide range of career fields (over 100 women from the local community participate). The mentors discuss their background, how they reached their present position, and how they balance their personal lives and work lives. They offer career advice and encouragement to the young women and often meet with them after the programs.

Workshops on dual career families have been reported in the literature (Gingrich, 1982; Kahnweiler & Kahnweiler, 1980). These programs aim to present possible future dilemmas for couples such as geographic relocation, having and raising children, competition, and sharing household responsibilities. They ask young people to consider these questions and teach skills for handling possible conflicts. One coping mechanism that is repeatedly suggested is open communication within the relationship (Hall & Hall, 1978). Programs like these are valuable career preparation for both young college women and their future spouses.

Individual Counseling Strategies

Since college counselors are now dealing with many women who plan to have both careers and families, they also need to give greater attention to discussing future life-style in individual counseling sessions. It is also important that college counselors be informed as to government regulations that allow for more opportunities in job hiring and advancement. They then can more readily encourage young women to actively seek new avenues and to be aware to possible discrimination in their job-seeking efforts.

It is essential for college advisors to know undergraduate and graduate curriculum requirements. They should be encouraged to network with other campus staff and faculty to whom they can refer young women for accurate and appropriate advice. If they make these efforts, counselors will be more able to do an excellent job of advising women who seek both traditional and nontraditional career paths.

WOMEN RETURNING TO SCHOOL OR WORK

Issues

As colleges and universities lament declining enrollments, they look with anticipation to a new type of student who is swelling their ranks: the returning woman. She has usually had some college and has interrupted her career to raise children. She tends to be a motivated and serious student. These women enroll in school to complete a degree or to obtain skills to make themselves more employable.

Returning female students confront several barriers in school and in the work place. They may lack self-confidence as they see themselves competing with younger people. They may be rusty on "survival skills" such as notetaking and writing papers for classes or writing an effective resume. The real challenge may be how to aptly handle a change within their family from the role of homemaker to student or breadwinner. Balancing the multiple roles of wife, mother, and professional becomes a tremendous challenge. Many of these women believe they must perform superwomen roles (fulfilling all their roles equally well) and find themselves under a great deal of pressure.

Program Interventions

The needs of returning women students have long been recognized at some institutions of higher education. Continuing Education for Women programs began in the early 1960s and rapidly expanded (Astin, 1976; Kahnweiler, 1980). Programs seek to provide returning students with a blend of survival skills and emotional support and recognize that a reentry woman needs special assistance in strengthening her self-concept and clarifying her values and goals (Karelius-Schumacher, 1977).

The Women's Re-entry Project (Prahl, 1980), for example, suggests providing basic skills instruction in some of the following topics: how to communicate and give presentations, how to manage time and juggle schedules, and how to take exams. The National Science Foundation (Kreinbert, 1981) provides information on workshops for reentering the work force. Areas covered include what employers are looking for in new employees, how to assess strengths and weaknesses for the job market, and a review of educational options available for retraining and refining old skills.

Some programs focus on building emotional support and on helping participants to deal with real emotional barriers, such as role conflict. The C.U.E. Program (Khosh, 1977) gives women an opportunity to explore their values, motivators, personality needs, and interests. It also emphasizes skill building in decision making, assertiveness, and resume writing. Other creative approaches have been tried. Brandenberg (1978) reported a unique workshop for returning women and traditional age college women at Queens College, New York, called an Intergenerational Workshop. The purpose was to improve communication and understanding between two generations of women — traditional college women and returning students. This original workshop served to assist the older students in feeling acceptance and approval from the younger generation.

Individual Counseling Strategies

The programs for returning women in colleges and in the community all apply both individual and group counseling as primary intervention modes. Career counseling in individual sessions, with its emphasis on self-awareness, decision making, and goal setting is usually found most appropriate to meet the needs of this population (Seligman, 1981). Groups are offered for information giving, skill building, and support. They are often formed to accommodate the large numbers of potential clients.

PROFESSIONAL AND BUSINESS WOMEN

Issues

Once they enter the work force, it becomes the goal of many women to advance and succeed in their career fields (Nickles & Ashcraft, 1981). Greater numbers of women are choosing to change career directions from traditional to nontraditional career fields. Motivated by such factors as higher salaries and a need for more recognition, teachers are moving into business and social workers are becoming lawyers. Business ownership has become another viable career option for women seeking more independence. Counselors find that a number of psychological and environmental barriers seem to exist for women making these career switches. Some of these are lack of confidence, lack of family support, lack of appropriate skills, possible fear of failure or success, and a reluctance to take risks.

Married business and professional women find themselves as partners in the approximately three million dual career marriages that exist today (Rice & Rice, 1981). Balancing the often conflicting roles of wife, mother, and career person can be a struggle. The research also points to the fact that professional women still tend to assume the burden of domestic and childcare duties (Nordberg, 1982; Young & Shoun, 1981). Other problems that have been associated with the dual career couple are poor communication, dilemmas concerning children (e.g. whether to have children, child care responsibility, etc.), and which partner's career should take precedence. Resolving these conflicts becomes imperative if the relationship is to survive and grow.

Interventions

A plethora of career development training programs and materials for professional women are available in the marketplace. With such titles as "Today's Professional Woman" and "Women on the Fast Track," these seminars promise to teach comprehensive skills. They select from such components as assertiveness, communication skills, time management, stress management, career pathing, organizational dynamics, and image building. The books and seminars also describe use of such advancement techniques as finding a mentor and networking with other women (for support, future job contacts, etc.) (Adams, 1979; Hennig & Jardim, 1977; Scheele, 1979). Though these training programs appear to fill a void, they have yet to be systematically evaluated. It seems apparent that the programs in themselves cannot be sufficient in helping women advance into management or to higher paying positions. Organizations must open up positions for which women can compete, allow women opportunities for growth in their position, and adopt fair hiring and promotion policies. They also can support women in their dual role dilemmas by providing such arrangements as child care and flexible work time. Until organizational changes occur, training programs for women will most likely remain token gestures.

Individual Counseling Strategies

Career changers can find help from workshops and individual counseling offered at agencies and on college campuses. Career counselors can encourage their clients to assess their transferable skills and determine what skills they can apply to other work settings. Career change workshops offer the advantage of support between members (Kahnweiler, 1981). Other members point out what skills and positive traits they hear being expressed. They also share firsthand knowledge about their own career fields in which others may have an interest. Networking can take place as the group can exchange phone numbers, suggest names of other persons to contact, and may even contract to meet again.

Professional and business women can turn to their professional groups and selected readings in order to find help in dealing with such issues as role conflicts and dual career marriages. They can also approach counselors who themselves are aware of the balancing act in which their clients are involved. Counselors can suggest exercises that can be done to help a woman understand the sources of her stress and assist her to develop a plan of stress reduction. This plan may mean taking time for herself, shifting some responsibilities to other family members, or even turning down certain projects at work (Amatea & Cross, 1981).

OLDER WOMEN

Issues

One in nine persons today is sixty-five years or older, and it is predicted that in several decades one in six persons will be that age (Olson, 1980). Counselors are confronted with growing numbers of women who, as workers and spouses, may confront some formidable obstacles as they grow older.

Employers are legally prohibited from firing or forcing older workers to retire before seventy years of age. Yet, many do violate this ban against age discrimination on a regular basis (Gray Panther Network, 1982). Aside from being forced to retire older workers, women, in particular, find themselves in a serious financial situation around retirement age (Olson, 1981). One reason for this may be due to poor financial planning. Another noticeable trend concerns the middle-aged woman who returns to school or work just as her spouse is winding down from long involvement in a career. The husband's desire to engage in leisure activities may conflict with his wife's wish to achieve in her new career field, and this may lead to marital stress.

Career planning should be as important in preretirement as it is at any life stage. In order for a woman to enjoy a successful retirement she must first engage in self-assessment. Her options for this stage can be chosen from among some of the following: a new full-time occupation, part-time work, further education, volunteerism, or leisure activities. Without planning for a creative retirement, however, this time could become an empty unfulfilling period.

Interventions

Companies are slowly beginning to offer preretirement programs. They do limit themselves by stressing the financial, legal, and medical aspects of retirement and unfortunately do not seem to pay much attention to the need for further career planning (Olson, 1981). Organizations such as the American Association of Retired Persons, The Association for Independent Maturity, and the National Retired Teachers Association all publish materials and offer relevant programs. Mithers (1980) describes an employee career guidance program that was successfully adopted for preretirement.

As women continue to enter the work force, counselors will have to gear up for helping them plan for retirement. Being aware of the often dual roles they play as career women and spouses can be helpful. Counselors also must be sure to include spouses in programs and encourage the couples to communicate about the feelings and attitudes they are having during this period.

FUTURE TRENDS AND ISSUES

Although it is difficult to imagine as many changes taking place for women in the next decade as in the past one, many new challenges will present themselves. The role of counselors who work with women should continue to be one of advocacy and support. Practitioners will need to continually examine their own sex stereotypical attitudes and those of the outside world as they encourage women to plan their careers.

Young girls and high school women will have exposure to more nontraditional role models (many of their mothers will serve in these roles). Counselors will need to continue encouraging female students to actively pursue mathematical and scientific subjects.

Counselors need to urge young women to plan for their careers earlier and to help them to set viable goals for integrating their personal and work lives. The next decade of young professionals should be able to avoid the frustrations of many of today's midlife women who are not prepared to reenter the job market.

Returning women students will continue to pursue college degrees, requiring support from institutions of higher learning and student services, in particular. The expertise of this group should be tapped. Counselors can facilitate an ongoing dialogue between different generations of college women so that mutual learning can take place.

As professional and business women gain more positions of leadership and visibility, it is hoped that organizational decisions will be made to accommodate working parents. Policies such as on-site day care and flexible work hours hopefully will soon be more commonplace than the unique situations they are now. Management training programs probably will continue to be offered to career women. It seems likely that they will be forced to deal with technical subjects that will assist females in their quest to get ahead.

As greater numbers of women continue to enter the work force, more women will also be retiring at earlier ages. Counselors should plan on working with both employers and employees to insure that this next stage of life is a well planned for, productive, and fulfilling one.

SUMMARY

This chapter has attempted to bring to light some of the career issues and trends confronting women of the 1980s. It reviewed some of the needs of women during their different life stages and discussed interventions that have been developed to meet those needs. Some future trends and issues are addressed, and the chapter closes with a list of resource materials available for women.

Counselors can best help women by understanding both the professional and personal conflicts they may face throughout their lives. Only then can career planning professionals choose appropriately from the variety of individual and group strategies available to them.

BIBLIOGRAPHY

Adams, J. *Women on top.* New York: Hawthorn Books, 1979.

Amatea, E. S., and Cross, E. G. Competing worlds, competing standards: Personal control for the professional career woman, wife and mother. *Journal of The National Association for Women Deans, Administrators, and Counselors,* 1981, *44,* 3-10.

Astin, H. S. *Some action of her own.* Lexington, Mass: D.C. Heath & Co., 1976.

Barnett, R. C. Sex differences and age trends in occupational preferences and occupational prestige. *Journal of Counseling Psychology,* 1975, *22,* 35-38.

Birk, J. M. Reducing sex bias: Factors affecting the client's view of the use of interest inventories. In E. Diamond (Ed.), *Issues of sex bias and sex fairness in career interest measurement.* Washington, D.C.: National Institute of Education, 1975. Pp. 101-122

Brandenberg, J. B. Intergenerational workshops for college women. *Journal of The National Association of Women Deans, Administrators, and Counselors,* 1978, *44,* 109-112.

Fitzgerald, L. F., and Crites, J. O. Toward a career psychology of women: What do we know? What do we need to know? *Journal of Counseling Psychology,* 1980, *27,* 44-62.

Gingrich, D. D. The dual career couple dilemma. *Journal of College Placement,* 1982, *42,* 26-30.

Goblman, R. D., and Hewitt, B. N. The Scholastic Aptitude Test "explains" why college men major in science more often than college women. *Journal of Counseling Psychology,* 1976, *23,* 50-54.

Gutek, B. A. *New directions for education, work and careers: Enhancing women's career development.* San Francisco: Jossey-Bass, Inc., 1979.

Hall, F., and Hall, D. T. *The two career couple.* Phillippines: Addison-Wesley Publishing Co., Inc., 1979.

Hansen, L. S., and Rapoza, R. S. *Career development and counseling of women.* Springfield, IL: Charles C Thomas, 1978.

Hennig, M., and Jardim, A. *The managerial woman.* New York: Doubleday, 1977.

Kahnweiler, J. B. So you've been a teacher, now what? *Vocational Guidance Quarterly,* 1981, *29,* 164-171.

Kahnweiler, J. B. A midlife developmental profile of the returning woman student. *Journal of College Student Personnel,* 1980, *21,* 414-418.

Kahnweiler, J. B., and Kahnweiler, W. M. A dual-career family workshop for college undergraduates. *Vocational Guidance Quarterly,* 1980, *28,* 225-230.

Karelius-Schumacher, K. L. Designing a counseling program for the mature woman student. *Journal of the National Association of Women Deans, Administrators, and Counselors,* 1977, *41,* 28-31.

Khosh, M. N. *A career planning program for women: The experience CUE.* Ann Arbor, MI: ERIC, 1977.

Kreinberg, N. *Ideas for developing and conducting a women in science career workshop.* Washington, D.C.: National Science Foundation, 1981.

Leiterman-Stock, P. *Reduction of sexual stereotyping and bias with regards to career choice: Land grant institution of higher education.* Bozeman, MT: Montana State University, 1979. (ERIC Document Reproduction Service No. ED 189 434)

Looft, W. R. Sex differences in the expression of vocational aspirations by elementary school children. *Developmental Psychology,* 1971, *5,* 366.

McClure, B. T., and Piel, E. College bound girls and science careers: Perceptions of barriers and facilitating factors. *Journal of Vocational Behavior,* 1978, *12,* 208-216.

Mithers, J. Turn your employee career guidance program into an effective preretirement vehicle. *Personnel Administrators,* 1980, *25,* 49-51.

Moore, K. M., and Veres, H. C. Traditional and innovative career plans of two year college women. *Journal of College Student Personnel,* 1976, *17,* 34-38.

Mundy, J. Charges of age discrimination on the rise. *Grey Panther Network,* March/April, 1982, p. 2.

Nickles, E., and Asheraft, L. *The coming matriarchy.* New York: Seaview Books, 1981.

Nordberg, O. S. In a class by ourselves. *Savvy,* March, 1982, 43-54.

Olson, S. K. Current status of corporate retirement preparation programs. *Aging and Work,* 1981, *4,* 175-187.

O'Neil, J. M., and Cano, L. Facilitating women's understanding of sexism, gender roles and factors affecting career decision-making. *Journal of College Student Personnel,* 1982, *23,* 167-169.

Peterson, M., and Vetter L. *Sex fairness in career education.* Columbus, OH: ERIC, 1977.

Prahl, E. *Confidence and competence: Basic skills programs and refresher courses for re-entry women.* Washington, D.C.: Association of American Colleges, 1980.

Rice, D. *Dual career marriage: Conflict and treatment,* New York: Macmillan, 1979.

Richardson, J. M., and Thomas, A. M. *Evaluation of "Women in Careers" Program.* Northfield, MN: St. Olaf College, 1978. (ERIC Document Reproduction Service, No. Ed 170 481)

Scheele, A. *Skills for success.* New York: William Morrow & Co., 1979.

Schlossberg, N., and Pietrofesa, J. Perspectives on counseling bias: Implications for counselor education. *The Counseling Psychologist,* 1973, *4*, 44-54.

Scherrei, R. Changes in career aspirations of women entering college. In B. A. Gutek (Ed.), *New directions for education, work, and careers: Enhancing women's career development.* San Francisco: Jossey-Bass, 1979.

Seligman, L. Outcomes of career counseling with women. *Journal of the National Association of Women Deans, Administrators, and Counselors,* 1981, *4*, 25-32.

Siegel, C. L. F. Sex differences in the occupational choices of second graders. *Journal of Vocational Behavior,* 1973, *3*, 15-19.

Stake, J. E. The educator's role in fostering female career aspirations. *Journal of the National Association for Women Deans, Administrators and Counselors,* 1981, *45*, 3-10.

Thomas, A., and Stewart, N. Counselor response to female clients with deviate and conforming career goals. *Journal of Counseling Psychology,* 1971, *18*, 352-357.

Tibbetts, S. L. Sex role stereotyping in the lower grades: Part of the solution. *Journal of Vocational Behavior,* 1975, *6*, 255-261.

U.S. Dept. of Labor. *Manpower report to The President.* Washington, D.C.: U.S. Government Printing Office, 1975.

Young, D., and Shoun, S. Equity in dual career marriages. *Journal of the National Association for Women Deans, Administrators and Counselors,* 1981, *44*, 9-12.

Zunker, V. G. *Career counseling: Applied concepts of life planning.* Monterey, CA: Brooks/Cole Publishing Co., 1981.

ADDITIONAL SOURCES

Write or refer to the following for current resource materials in women's career development.

Bibliography on Adult Students, *Journal of The National Association of Women Deans, Administrators and Counselors,* Spring, 1979, *42*, 33.

Bibliographies About Women in *Career development and counseling of women,* L. S. Hansen and R. S. Rapoza, Springfield, Illinois: Charles C Thomas, 1978.

Catalyst Publications, 14 East 60th St., New York, New York 10022.

Project on the Status and Education of Women, *Publications List,* Association of American Colleges, 1818 R Street, NW, Washington, D.C. 20009.

Women's Educational Equity Act Program, c/o Education Development Center, 55 Chapel St., Newton, Mass. 02160

Woman's Educational Equity Communications Network Publications, Far West Laboratory, 1855 Folson St., San Francisco, California 94103.

Sample Programs for Women

A career planning program for women: The experience CUE by Mary N. Khosh, 1977, ERIC Counseling and Personnel Services Information Center, School of Education, The University of Michigan, Ann Arbor, MI 48109.

HERS, leadership and management seminars, HERS, Mid-Atlantic, 3601 Locust Walk/C8, Philadelphia, PA 19104.

Hansen, L. S. Project born free: A collaborative consultation model for career development and sex role stereotyping. *Personnel and Guidance Journal,* 1978, *56,* 395-99.

Books

This is a listing of sample books to use with women. Numerous others can be found in Career Placement Offices on college campus and in local programs for women. Others can be found in this chapter's bibliography. Writing to professional organizations will also yield materials aimed specifically at women.

Berman, E. *Re-entering: Successful back to work strategies for women seeking a fresh start.* New York: Crown Publishers, 1980.

Catalyst staff. *What to do with the rest of your life: The catalyst career guide for women in the 80's.* New York: Simon & Schuster, 1980.

Fabel, M., and Wikler, N. *Up against the clock.* New York: Random House, 1979.

Hennig, M., and Jardim, A. *The managerial woman.* New York: Pocket Books, 1977.

Higginson, M., and Quick, T. *The ambitious woman's guide to a successful career.* New York: Amacom, 1980.

Loring, R. K., and Otto, H. (Eds.). *New life options: The working woman's resource book.* New York: McGraw Hill, Inc., 1976.

Mitchell, J. S. *I can be anything: Careers and colleges for young women.*

New York: Bantam Books, 1978.

Schwartz, F. *How to go to work when your husband is against it, your children aren't old enough and there's nothing you can do anyhow.* New York: Simon And Schuster, 1972.

CHAPTER 13

SERVICES FOR DISABLED PERSONS

E. JANE BURKHEAD

THE career development needs of disabled persons have received much attention during the last decade. Career development programs for special populations have proliferated at all levels within education and community organizations. Federal legislation of the 1970s focused on providing equal rights and equal opportunities for disabled persons to facilitate their integration into society as fully functioning members. The Education for All Handicapped Children Act, PL 94-142, enacted in 1975, guarantees free, appropriate public education to all handicapped. Sections 503 and 504 of the Rehabilitation Act of 1973 were designed to eliminate discrimination against disabled persons in business and industry, education, health care, and social service agencies. The provision of opportunities and services necessary for the disabled person to reach maximal functional potential and the removal of barriers to the disabled person's functioning in various life roles became a priority. Because successful career development facilitates the mainstreaming of persons with disabilities, career development programs have been viewed as important components in the habilitation and rehabilitation of persons with disabilities.

This chapter covers the following areas related to career development services for disabled persons: special needs and concerns of disabled persons, common program goals, and specific intervention strategies of selected programs. Because of the need to limit the number of programs discussed in the chapter, only career development programs for physically disabled persons, mentally disabled (mentally retarded) persons, and multiply disabled persons are considered. Before the discussion of the above areas, there is a need to define the terms "disabled" and "handicapped" as they are used in this chapter.

In rehabilitation, a distinction typically is made between the terms disabled and handicapped. Disabled refers to having ". . . a long-term or chronic condition medically defined as a physiological, anatomical, mental, or emotional impairment resulting from disease or illness, inherited or congenital defect, trauma, or other insult (including environmental) to mind or body" (Wright, 1980). Handicapped connotes having ". . . a disadvantage, interference, or barrier to performance, opportunity, or fulfillment in any desired role in life (e.g., vocational, social, educational, familial), imposed by limitation in function or by other problems associated with disability and/or personal characteristics in the context of the individual's environment or roles" (Wright, 1980). According to these definitions, a person may be disabled but not handicapped. For example, a paraplegic person using a wheelchair is disabled but would not be handicapped in an accessible environment with modifications such as ramps to buildings, wide doorways, and wheelchair lifts on public transportation. This distinction in terms has significant implications for practitioners since interventions should be and are designed to reduce or eliminate handicaps. The term disabled is used throughout this chapter to refer to target populations; the only exceptions to this are when specific programs use handicapped.

SPECIAL NEEDS AND CONCERNS

Although many career issues are the same for both disabled and nondisabled persons, there are needs and concerns unique to disabled people that should be considered in the planning and implementation of career development services.

Unemployment and Underemployment

Evidence abounds that disabled individuals are unemployed and underemployed at consistently higher rates than nondisabled persons. Levitan and Taggart (1976) reported that only 40 percent of disabled persons are employed compared to 75 percent of nondisabled people. Similarly, of 161 disabled persons surveyed in a needs assessment study, only 35 percent were employed (Shoepke, 1979). Davis and Weintraub (1978) reported that 62 percent of people with cerebral palsy are unemployed. Underemployment, or employment below one's skill level, is illustrated by findings that the average weekly earnings of employed disabled males are 22 percent lower than those of nondisabled males (Levitan & Taggart, 1976). Biklen and Bogdam (1978) reported that 85 percent of employed disabled people had annual incomes of less than 7000 dollars and 52 percent had incomes less than 2000 dollars. Lonnquist (1978), in a follow-up study of disabled former college students, found significantly higher rates of unemployment and underemployment among disabled subjects compared to matched, nondisabled control subjects.

Disabled persons apparently have more difficulty than nondisabled persons in obtaining and maintaining employment. The reasons for this situation are complex. The barriers discussed below are generally believed to be largely responsible. However, whatever the reasons for this situation, helping professionals must be aware that disabled clients are encountering more problems in finding and keeping appropriate jobs than nondisabled clients.

Barriers to Employment

Transportation

Accessible economic transportation is a pressing need of disabled persons. Although statutes have existed since 1970 requiring accessibility of public transportation, little progress has been made in making low-cost public transportation available to disabled persons (DeLoach & Greer, 1981).

Goodkin (1977) reported findings of a comprehensive needs study of severely handicapped persons, mandated by the Rehabilitation Act of 1973, which clearly demonstrate the problem. Two groups, patients in a medical rehabilitation facility and persons rejected by Vocational Rehabilitation Placement Agencies as too severely disabled, were studied. In the rehabilitation group, 60 percent of those needing transportation to go to work did not have it. This group indicated that transportation was their greatest need.

Persons in both groups indicated that lack of transportation was a major reason for not working.

In addition to the problem of availability of transportation, disabled persons also may have higher transportation expenses than nondisabled persons. For those who drive, it may be impossible to use fuel-efficient, less expensive smaller cars because of the need for room to store mobility aids such as wheelchairs. Also, costly modifications such as wheelchair lifts or special controls may be needed. Those who cannot drive often have no alternative except higher cost taxi service. Goodkin (1977) reported that 14 percent of trips of disabled persons are by taxi compared to 2 percent of the trips of the population as a whole.

The importance of transportation to rehabilitation was demonstrated by a study of 111 spinal cord injured persons two years after discharge from medical rehabilitation centers (DeJong, 1981). Transportation was one of the strongest predictors of productivity. Those persons who had fewer transportation barriers tended to be more productive, as measured by participation in work or school/training, organizations, homemaking, and leisure activities.

Architectural

Although progress has been made through federal and state legislation in eliminating barriers, architectural accessibility is still a major concern of disabled persons (Nugent, 1977). Disabled workers need both accessible housing and accessible work places. DeLoach and Greer (1981), in explaining what architectural barriers are, classify barriers into three types: approach barriers, entrance barriers, and functional or total-use barriers. Approach barriers include parking and walkway barriers. Stairs to entrances, narrow doors, and doors with pressure closers are examples of entrance barriers. Functional or total-use barriers are features that prevent persons from making full use of a facility; they include narrow bathroom doors and stalls, inaccessible drinking fountains, and lack of Braille elevator markings or building directories. These barriers effectively prevent persons with disabilities from participating in community life.

The negative impact of home barriers was illustrated in DeJong's (1981) study of 111 spinal cord injured persons. Of these 111 people, 29.7 percent indicated that they had barriers to getting into and out of their homes. DeJong (1981) speculated that these housing barriers may partially account for the high degree of social isolation in the study group. His findings indicated that 21.8 percent never left their homes during the period of a week, and 46.4 percent went out three times or less during the period of a week. The removal of home barriers is obviously a vital component of a program to facilitate independent functioning and employment.

Negative and Stereotyped Attitudes

Attitudinal barriers place subtle but substantial limitations on the functioning of disabled persons. Negative and stereotyped attitudes about the potential of disabled persons exist in all sectors of society, but perhaps the impact is greatest when these attitudes are present in employers, helping professionals, and educators. If an employer, for example, views disabled persons as incapable of performing satisfactorily, a disabled applicant will not be hired, no matter how job-ready.

Opportunities for career development experiences can be greatly curtailed by attitudinal barriers among helping professionals and educators (Fair & Sullivan, 1980; Humes, 1982). Jordan (1976) and Fair and Sullivan (1980) pointed out the problem of job stereotyping in educational programs, stating that disabled students are typically guided toward skilled or unskilled work. Humes (1982) described specific negative and erroneous assumptions of helping professionals about the career development of disabled persons. According to Jordan (1976), "too few handicapped individuals have been assisted in their own choices or in their own efforts to pursue higher education and/or go into a broad range of career choices."

Personal

Personal barriers arise when disabled persons have not learned skills necessary for community and vocational adjustment. Research on adjustment has demonstrated that problems occur primarily in the areas of daily living skills, social behaviors, leisure time management, and other self-management skills (Appell, 1977; Brolin, 1972; Sprafkin, Gershaw, & Goldstein, 1978; Wilkinson, 1975). Although individuals may have job-specific skills, they may not be able to maintain employment if they are unable to cope with other aspects of their lives. These personal skills are often taken for granted by nondisabled persons because they seem to involve "simple" tasks. However, tasks such as dressing, eating, grooming, or managing money, which are basic to overall functioning, are sometimes major obstacles for disabled individuals.

Skills related to vocational decision making and vocational preparation also may be limited due to restricted exposure to careers and career-related experiences. Some disabled people have not had the opportunity to explore their abilities as they relate to careers or to explore the world of work, resulting in inappropriate career choices. Also, because work experience is often lacking, the disabled individual may not have learned required work behaviors, such as getting to work on time or accepting supervision. In order for the person with a disability to be job-ready, deficits in vocational and daily living skills must be assessed and intervention strategies planned to remediate these deficits.

PROGRAM GOALS

Goals of career development programs for disabled persons vary greatly. Some programs are comprehensive, attempting to meet a broad range of needs, while others are narrow in scope, focusing on specific aspects of career development. There are, however, some discernible common program goals.

(1) *To facilitate the disabled client's optimal level of independent functioning.* This goal is reflected in the self-help orientation of many programs. Responsibility is placed on the client to set individual goals and complete activities designed to accomplish goals. Clients are co-managers of their programs to the extent that their capabilities will allow.

(2) *To consider the needs of the whole person in the provision of a program of services.* All programs do not have the resources to address directly all needs, but there typically is a holistic approach to the individual. Daily living skills, socialization skills, and leisure skills as well as vocational skills are recognized as vital to adequate career development.

(3) *To educate community and business leaders about architectural and transportation barriers and about legislation pertaining to elimination of these barriers.* The ultimate goal is to enlist the cooperation of these leaders

in making community life fully accessible to all people.

(4) *To educate employers about disabled workers and about legislation pertaining to employment of disabled persons.* These educational efforts are designed to eliminate or reduce attitudinal barriers of employers.

(5) *To facilitate the disabled client's exploration of career alternatives, assist in clarifying career goals, and to provide services required to reach career goals.* This is the primary goal of most career development programs, whether for disabled or nondisabled persons. It is a particularly important goal for disabled people, however, in light of their needs for expanding career experiences discussed above.

INTERVENTION STRATEGIES

Life Centered Career Education

Life Centered Career Education is a competency-based model of career education developed for grades K-12 (Brolin, 1978). Within this model, career is defined broadly to include all life roles: worker, learner, consumer, family member, and social-political being (Brolin, 1978; Gordon, 1973). The career education curriculum is designed to prepare the student for each of these roles. Therefore, learning experiences are organized into three domains: daily living skills, personal-social skills, and occupational guidance and preparation. Within each domain are individual competencies that the student must master to achieve successful career development. Daily living skills include skills such as managing family finances, caring for personal needs, and buying and preparing food. Examples of personal-social skills are achieving self-awareness, acquiring self-confidence, and achieving problem-solving skills. Knowing and exploring occupational possibilities, selecting and planning occupational choices, and obtaining a specific skill are examples of the occupational guidance and preparation domain.

Brolin (1982, 1978) suggested infusion of career education into the school curriculum. This is accomplished by applying the competencies throughout the student's program rather than devising a lesson or course based on the competencies. For example, a teacher can write one career education objective, based on the students needs,

tion Plan (Brolin, 1982).

In order to facilitate the student's mastery of the competencies, the teacher should utilize the resources of the school, family, and community to provide learning experiences. In acquiring the competency of knowing and exploring occupational possibilities, for example, the following resources are recommended (Brolin, 1982): field trips to local businesses/industries, job tryouts, employers' and former students' presentations about companies and jobs, speeches by manpower and rehabilitation agency caseworkers, audiovisual materials, occupational literature, parents' presentations about their jobs, school counselors' assistance on occupational exploration, and teachers in every area relating instruction to careers.

The Lifelong Career Development Model

The Lifelong Career Development (LCD) model (Brolin & Carver, 1982) is a method of coordinating and providing services to disabled persons with the goal of helping them to achieve and maintain their optimum level of independent functioning throughout the life span. The program can be based in a community college, vocational-technical school, independent living center, rehabilitation agency, or other community agency. Personnel required to operate the program are an LCD coordinator, team, and advisory committee. The coordinator, ideally a member of the agency or school where the program is based, is responsible for program development and administration. The team, composed of disabled consumers and/or family members and school and community agency staff, provide the manpower to implement the program. The advisory committee includes people from local agencies, business, and consumer groups. Its functions are to assist in linkage of existing community services, to act as consultants to team members, to provide manpower and expertise to program acitivities, to provide information on local, state, and national resources, and to increase community support for the program.

There are seven services offered by the LCD program:
1. training for educational and helping professionals and other community members to help provide effective services to disabled persons;
2. instruction for adults with disabilities;

3. career assessment based on evaluation of the disabled person's skills and interests relative to Brolin's (1978) life-centered competencies;
4. life-centered career development planning based on the individual's training interests and needs and the options available in the community;
5. resource collection available to community members, professional staff, and disabled persons;
6. information service to community members, professional staff, and disabled persons; and
7. advocacy, focusing on preparing disabled persons to be self-advocates.

It should be noted that three of these services, training, information service, and resource collection, are provided to human service professionals, family members, and other relevant community groups in addition to disabled persons. This program component is based on the concept that it is as important to work with individuals who may provide services to disabled people as it is to work with disabled persons.

Larson (1982) described the implementation of the LCD model at Iowa Central Community College (ICCC), one of four midwestern community colleges where it was field tested (Brolin, 1982). The director of the ICCC Special Needs Program serves as the LCD Coordinator, devoting about twenty hours per month to working with team members for programming purposes. The LCD team has seven members: a vocational education instructor, a representative of the administration of the college, a representative of the administration and a consultant to the Arrowhead Education Agency, a Vocational Rehabilitation Counselor, the ICCC Assessment Center Coordinator, and a teacher of handicapped persons in a special program.

The program of services developed at ICCC follow:

1. *LCD planning.* Planning sessions or staffing conferences, involving two to three team members, are used to study each client's personal data in relationship to program availability to develop an individual LCD plan.

2. *Special program offering.* ICCC instituted a series of short-term

special courses for disabled persons in addition to the regular vocational program. Special courses were Managing Family Finances; Planning, Buying, and Preparing of Food; Planning, Buying, and Caring for Clothing; Utilizing Recreation and Leisure; Family Living and Raising Children; and Achieving Economic Independence.

3. *Advocacy.* Team members focused on activities that prepared individuals to be self-advocates. In addition to these services, a resource collection was established in the Special Needs Coordinator's library. To receive services from the LCD program, a prospective client would contact the LCD coordinator's office. The client is then assigned to a staffing conference, where decisions regarding referral to the assessment center and/or other services are made. Service referrals may be to local agencies, to the ICCC vocational program, or to the ICCC special program for disabled adults. Larson (1982) concluded that the LCD program was effective in delivering career development services to disabled adults and in increasing knowledge and awareness of disabled persons' needs and abilities among college staff and faculty.

The Career Development for the Handicapped Project

The Career Development for the Handicapped Project was a three-year, grant-funded program designed to provide career services to physically disabled adults in Florida (Hicks, McGreevy, & Broderick, no date). The project included a two-year demonstration program and one year of technical assistance to post-secondary institutions. During the first two years of the program, career counseling centers were established in six Florida communities (Anderson & Reardon, 1981). The project was responsible for developing materials, purchasing equipment, and staffing the centers by providing to selected disabled adults training/employment programs in paraprofessional career guidance. The self-directed career planning program of the Florida State University Curricular — Career Information Center was used as a model for the materials developed (White, Reardon, Barker, & Carlson, 1979). At the end of the demonstration program, the six career centers were incorporated into ongoing institutions such as community colleges.

To meet the needs of adults with physical disabilities, Hicks et al. recommended five additions to the typical services of vocational

assessment, counseling, and placement offered by career counseling and placement centers:
1. knowledgeable personnel who have explored their own attitudes toward disability.
2. an accessible facility and accessible materials.
3. placement services, including internship or work study programs, designed especially for disabled persons.
4. a strong network of private and public agencies serving disabled community members.
5. specialized information and services for disabled persons.

In providing specialized information and services, the major goals are to help the disabled person develop a positive self-concept, to provide a broad base of occupational information, and to provide training in self-advocacy in the job market. Hicks et al. proposed the following specific intervention strategies:
1. provide up-to-date information on legal rights in education and employment through workshops and training sessions.
2. provide up-to-date information about adaptive equipment and possible job accommodations through workshops and training sessions.
3. design activities for training in job search skills that address the special needs of disabled job-seekers.
4. investigate existing systems for analyzing job functions and providing information about physical requirements.
5. interviews with disabled adults in nonstereotypical occupations available on audiotape, in Braille, large type, and regular type.
6. construct a community service network.
7. form an advisory council of public and private employers to meet with disabled persons to offer training in self-advocacy and to provide group support, occupational information, and resources for job search.
8. develop a panel of disabled adults to talk about their own career development, including successes and failures, obstacles, and strategies for success.
9. locate disabled alumni to serve as resources for disabled persons on an individual basis.

10. establish an advisory council of disabled persons to assess the career center and recommend needed changes.

Placement Services

Job Finding Club

The Job Finding Club (Azrin, Flores, & Kaplan, 1977) is a structured, skill-oriented, group approach to job seeking. A "buddy system," which allows for the sharing of transportation and job leads and for mutual encouragement, is the basic component of the program. Also, group sessions are used for training in interview behaviors, resume preparation, methods of obtaining job leads, and appropriate dress and grooming. Clients are required to be involved in full-time job seeking. To encourage family support, program staff may send a letter to a family member or friend living with the job seeker, offering suggestions for helping with the job-finding process. Suggestions include limiting use of family phone, helping with transportation, job leads and suggestions, emotional support and encouragement, and understanding of the great amount of time needed for job-seeking. This program is effective in helping persons obtain jobs. Azrin et al. reported that within two months, 90 percent of the experimental group obtained employment compared to 55 percent of the noncounseled control group.

Job Seeking Skills

Job Seeking Skills (Multi-Resource Center, 1971) is a method of teaching job-ready clients how to seek and obtain employment. Clients learn how to write resumes, complete job applications, and how to behave during a job interview. In teaching interview behavior, emphasis is on anticipating questions and developing answers to "problem" questions. Job Seeking Skills training may be done in groups or individually. However, because role-playing of interviews is used extensively, group training may be more effective by providing peer as well as staff feedback. Also, group sessions are more efficient in use of staff time.

The Michigan Model

The Michigan Vocational Rehabilitation Agency established a

systematic approach to placement (Molinaro, 1977). There are five major components of the system:

1. An account system. Every Vocational Rehabilitation Counselor was responsible for establishing a relationship with at least one major employer, becoming familiar with hiring practices, job descriptions, and job sites. This has been an effective method of developing jobs and learning about openings.
2. A skill bank, a group of job-ready clients, from which can be drawn persons to fill job vacancies.
3. A job bank, a collection of job vacancies.
4. Job seeking skills training.
5. Employer services. Assistance is provided to employers in the areas of worker's compensation, second injury certification, Affirmative Action consultation and implementation, awareness training, selective placement, and troubled employees.

This systematic approach to placement ensures that specific agency staff have responsibility for placement activities and provides a mechanism for coordinating these activities.

Work Experience Program

The Academic Internship Program for Handicapped Students at the University of California, Riverside, was designed to help physically disabled students overcome the problems of lack of work experience and exposure to a narrow range of careers and to reduce prejudice and stereotyping by employers. Students are placed in part-time paid and volunteer internships related to their career interests. They also receive instruction in writing resumes, interviewing, and other job seeking behaviors. In addition to demonstrating to employers the abilities of disabled persons, the program also educates employers about hiring disabled people by conducting workshops and informally sharing information with them. This internship program has benefitted disabled students, employers, and the University (*An Experiential Learning Model, 1980*).

Postemployment Services

Group support techniques are effective in helping disabled persons adjust to and maintain employment. The job retention club, used by the Minneapolis Rehabilitation Center, is an ongoing, social support group that meets once per week with a rehabilitation counselor ("Teaching Placement Skills," 1978). The sessions are divided into two parts. The first part is used for group discussion of problems on the job and possible solutions. During the second part, participants socialize informally and have refreshments. A buddy system can also be instituted. The "job buddy" may be a friend or acquaintance from work or someone else the client met in earlier phases of rehabilitation ("Teaching Placement Skills," 1978). Social or alumni clubs, groups of clients who have completed the rehabilitation process and are working, are another alternative for providing clients with support during the transition from client to worker ("Teaching Placement Skills," 1978).

SUMMARY AND CONCLUSIONS

A wide range of services currently are being offered to meet the career development needs of persons with disabilities. Specialized services are available for all ages, from early childhood throughout the adult years. The variance in goals, specific intervention strategies, and target groups is demonstrated in the selected programs reviewed in this chapter. Some programs, such as Life Centered Career Education, take a comprehensive approach to career development while others, such as work experience programs, are designed to meet an individual's needs in a specific area of career development. Some programs include groups such as employers, helping professionals, and family members in addition to disabled persons in their target groups. The Lifelong Career Development Model and the internship program at the University of California, Riverside, are examples of this. These programs recognize that societal barriers need to be reduced or eliminated to facilitate disabled persons' reaching their maximum potential.

Successful career development is important for the integration of persons with disabilities into society. Career development programs have focused on preparing disabled individuals for the world of work and on educating employers and other community people about disabled workers. Transportation and architectural barriers continue to be significant handicapping factors for persons with disabilities.

Further efforts are needed to remove these barriers so that disabled persons will have the opportunity to participate fully in community life.

BIBLIOGRAPHY

Anderson, J., and Reardon, R. Self-directed career planning for persons with disabilities. *Journal of Employment Counseling*, 1981, *18*, 73-80.

Appell, M. Some policies and practices in the federal sector concerning career education for the handicapped. *Journal of Career Education*, 1977, *3*, 75-91.

Azrin, N. H., Flores, T., and Kaplan, S. J. Job finding club: A group assisted program for obtaining employment. *Rehabilitation Counseling Bulletin*, 1977, *21*, 131-140.

Bilklen, D., and Bogdam, R. Handicapism in America. *Win*, October 28, 1978.

Brolin, D. E. Value of rehabilitation services and correlates of vocational success with the mentally retarded. *American Association on Mental Deficiency*, 1972, *76*, 644-651.

Brolin, D. E. *Vocational preparation of persons with handicaps*. Columbus, OH: Charles E. Merrill, 1982.

Brolin, D. E., and Carver, J. T. Lifelong career development for adults with handicaps: A new model. *Journal of Career Education*, 1982, *8*, 280-292.

Davis, S. A. and Weintraub, F. J. Beyond traditional career sterotyping. *Journal of Career Education*, 1978, *5*, 24-35.

DeJong, G. *Environmental accessibility and independent living outcomes: Directions for disability policy and research*. East Lansing, MI: University Center for International Rehabilitation, Michigan State University, June 1981.

DeLoach, C., and Greer, B. G. *Adjustment to severe physical disability: A metamorphosis*. New York: McGraw-Hill, 1981.

An experiential learning model for students with disabilities: Internships and career development. Berkeley: University of California, 1980. (ERIC Document Reproduction Service No. ED 185790).

Fair, G. W., and Sullivan, A. R. Career opportunities for culturally diverse handicapped youth. *Exceptional Children*, 1980, *46*, 626-631.

Goodkin, H. F. Transportation accessibility. In *White House Conference on Handicapped Individuals, Volume one: Awareness papers*. Washington, D. C.: U. S. Government Printing Office, 1977.

Gordon, E. W. Broadening the concept of career education. In L. McClure and C. Buan (Eds.), *Essays on career education*. Portland, Oregon: Northwest Regional Educational Laboratory, 1973.

Hicks, L. C., McGreevy, J. G., and Groderick, C. A. *Empowering diversity: Resources for developing career counseling and placement programs for college students with physical disabilities*. Tallahassee: United Cerebral Palsy of Florida.

Humes, C. W. Career guidance for the handicapped: A comprehensive approach. *Vocational Guidance Quarterly*, 1982, *30*, 351-358.

Jordan, J. B. (Ed.). *Exceptional child education at the bicentennial: A parade of progress.* Reston, VA: The Council for Exceptional Children, 1976.

Larson, C. H. A community college service model of lifelong career development for adult persons with handicaps. *Journal of Career Education,* 1982, *8,* 293-300.

Levitan, S. A., and Taggart, R. *Jobs for the disabled.* Washington, D. C.: George Washington University Center for Manpower Policy Studies, 1976.

Lonnquist, D. E. The handicapped in college and afterwards: A survey of the severely physically disabled and matched able-bodied students at Missouri (Doctoral dissertation, University of Missouri, 1977). *Dissertation Abstracts International,* 1978, *39,* 2-A. (University Microfilms No. 782).

Molinaro, D. A placement system develops and settles: The Michigan model. *Rehabilitation Counseling Bulletin,* 1977, *21,* 121-129.

Multi-Resource Center. *Job seeking skills reference manual.* Minneapolis: Minneapolis Rehabilitation Center, Inc., 1971.

Nugent, T. J. Architectural accessibility. In *White House Conference on Handicapped Individuals, Volume one: Awareness papers.* Washington, D. C.: U. S. Government Printing Office, 1977.

Shoepke, J. *Lifelong career development needs assessment study.* Columbia: University of Missouri, 1979.

Sprafkin, R. P., Gershaw, N. J., and Goldstein, A. P. Teaching interpersonal skills to psychiatric outpatients: Using structured learning therapy in a community based setting. *Journal of Rehabilitation,* 1978, *44,* 26-29.

Teaching placement skills to severely disabled clients. *Rehab Brief,* September 8, 1978, *1,* (12).

White, P., Reardon, R., Barker, S., and Carlson, A. Adapting a university career center for use by the blind. *Personnel and Guidance Journal,* 1978, *58,* 292-295.

Wilkinson, M. W. Leisure: An alternative to the meaning of work. *Journal of Applied Rehabilitation Counseling,* 1975, *6,* 73-77.

Wright, G. N. *Total rehabilitation.* Boston: Little, Brown and Company, 1980.

CHAPTER 14

SERVING ETHNIC MINORITIES

Winifred O. Stone

"There is very little difference between one man [person] and another; but what little [difference] there is, is very important."

— William James

UNDERSTANDING cultural and ethnic group differences is important, if not essential, to the helping relationship in facilitating career development. With this realization, if career development strategies are to be of value to ethnic groups, they must be facilitated by helpers who understand the educational, sociocultural, and psychological aspects of human relations; moreover, they should be aware of the economic, political, and legal issues that impact employment and, thus, the quality of life of ethnic groups in our society.

Because of differences among various ethnic groups, multicultural perspectives of career development are necessary. During developmental processes, they are also necessary because the importance of cultural and ethnic differences continue to be denied, overlooked, and underestimated.

An essential element in career development facilitation is the ethnic factor. Concurring with this perspective, Garcia proposes that the ethnic-cultural factor is "not just another teaching-learning complication. Cultural and ethnic differences have always existed . . . [Career development] activities and factors — [career] classroom management techniques, instructional strategies, and, of course, self-concepts — operate on assumptions which are embedded in cultural values, attitudes, and beliefs. There is no such thing as a culturally neutral or culturally free [career development] activity" (1982).

In consideration of Garcia's proposal, if barrier free career development is to become a reality for ethnic groups in the foreseeable future, our approach to education and career development must change so that the ethnic-cultural factor is no longer ignored. Thereby, the tendency to exhibit diminished attitudes, feelings, and behavior by the larger society toward the ability, performance, and potential of ethnic groups may be modified in more positive directions.

Although multifaceted problems exist in our understanding of the diversity of American ethnic groups, multicultural and cross-cultural training are effective and systematic methods for increasing multiethnic and transcultural awareness (Pedersen, 1978). In 1982, the National Council for Accreditation of Teacher Education (NCATE) established new education standards. Now, NCATE mandates "multicultural education" for basic and advanced programs for all professional school personnel:

> Multicultural education is preparation for the social, political, and economic realities that individuals experience in culturally diverse and complex human encounters. These realities have both national and international dimensions. This preparation provides a process by which an individual develops competencies for perceiving, believing, evaluating, and behaving in differential cultural settings. Thus, multicultural education is viewed as an intervention and an on-going assessment process to help institutions and individuals become more responsive to the human condition, individual cultural integrity, and cultural pluralism in society.
>
> Multicultural education could include but would not be limited to experiences which: (1) promote analytical and evaluative abilities to confront issues such as participatory democracy, racism and sexism, and the parity of power; (2) develop skills for values clarification including the study of the manifest and latent transmission of values; (3) examine the dynamics of diverse cultures and the implications for developing teaching strategies; and (4) examine linguistic variations and diverse learning styles as a basis for the development of appropriate teaching strategies. (NCATE, 1982)

These new multicultural standards mandate that institutions must provide multicultural education in the general, professional, and advanced studies components for teacher education curricula. They include the content and theory for specialities, the humanistic and behavioral studies, direct, and simulated experiences. Such curricula should be appropriate to the professional roles for which candidates are being prepared; additionally, they should differentiate by the degree and certificate level for which candidates are being prepared (NCATE, 1982).

Farley, too, sees a need for such a mandate because one of the debilitating effects of the current "educational system is to preserve inequalities rather than to reduce or eliminate them. Since economic inequality in the United States falls logically along racial and ethnic lines, education may well be acting in ways that preserve racial and ethnic inequality. . . " (1982). Thus, in accord with enabling legal statutes that are pertinent to the handicapped, civil rights, sex discrimination, and equal opportunity compliance, in both education and employment, the strategy of multicultural education appears to be a realistic goal for the facilitation of career development.

To aid transcultural facilitators, proposals offered by Vontress (1969, 1973, 1979) have made significant contributions toward overcoming ethnic encapsulation and ethnocentrism, while bridging cultural differences. In addition to Vontress, several other theorists and practitioners have also contributed significantly toward multiculturalism (*Native Americans:* Trimble & Lee, 1981; Darou, 1980; Hayes, 1979; *Hispanic-Americans:* Arredondo-Dowd & Gonsalves, 1980; Aryes, 1979; Martinez, 1980; *Asian-Americans:* Ching & Prosen, 1980; Sue, 1977, 1978; Yu, 1976; *African-Americans:* Harper, 1973, 1974; Beck, 1973; Harper & Stone, 1974; Gunnings & Simpkins, 1972; *Ethnic Minorities:* Parker & McDavis, 1979, Lennon, 1979). It must be noted, however, that the counseling processes have greatly influenced career development practices and techniques, especially in terms of theoretical approaches, career development processes, and the evaluation of outcomes. Yet, a basic need exists for career development facilitators and practices that are effective for multicultural groups.

The identification of additional appropriate models, methods, and strategies remains a challenging issue in career counseling as well as career development (Crites, 1981). While some progress has been achieved in this realm, it is evident that the conceptual framework for career development theories exhibits a limited application for ethnic groups (Smith, 1981).

Moreover, this chapter will focus on (1) functional definitions of concepts that are often used in reference to multiethnic groups, (2) multicultural career development issues, (3) stages of unemployment, and (4) multiethnic phases of development — relating to the readiness for career development experiences in multicultural settings.

While the above concerns will be addressed, it is important to understand that systematic and evaluative research regarding multicultural career development practices must be continuous if it is to produce significant differences in the career development process and the resultant effect of parity in multiethnic employment. This systematic and evaluative research may provide the empirical bases specifying (a) contrasting parameters of interventions and (b) demographic and psychological characteristics of participants that may moderate the effectiveness of diverse types of interventions (Fretz, 1981). Lastly, rather than proven research outcomes, career development methods, programs, and resources are included in this chapter as suggested guides while research continues.

MULTICULTURAL CONCEPTS

It is imperative that career development facilitators understand and employ the appropriate meaning for concepts that are associated with ethnic groups. "There are advantages and disadvantages in writing about ethnic identity, and they stem from the same characteristic: ethnic identity is a powerful phenomenon. It is powerful both at the affective level, where it touches us in ways mysterious and frequently unconscious, and at the level of strategy where we consciously manipulate it" (Royce, 1982). Many concepts, therefore, are used to identify the various ethnic groups and their relations with other groups. Often these concepts are global in meaning, unclear in definition, and fail to recognize distinct facets of ethnicity and culture. The following multicultural concepts address this issue:

Culture: "A system of beliefs, values, customs, and institutions that when combined serves as a cluster to provide a person meaningful ways for [living]" (Garcia, 1982).

Ethnicity: It is a social quality. Unlike race, however, physical traits are not necessarily a part of ethnicity (Farley, 1982). Ethnicity, then, refers to social-cultural characteristics: (1) community of language, (2) common religious beliefs, (3) similarity of customs, and (4) common political community.

Ethnic Group: Ethnic group refers "to a group of people who are generally regarded by themselves and/or others as a distinct group, with such recognition based on social or cultural characteristics such as nationality, language, and religion" (Farley, 1982). Other social scientists agree that the concept, ethnic group, denotes a social grouping that the majority population considers unique — in religious, linguistic, and cultural characteristics (Gordon, 1964; Rose, 1976; Parrillo, 1980; Banks, 1979).

Race: A social and biological concept rather than simply the results of biogenetic determination. More often, however, race is viewed as a similar grouping such as skin, hair, eyes, nose, and stature.

Ethnic Minority Group: The concept refers to a group of people generally identified as lacking in societal status, "numerical representation," and economic, political, and/or social influence. The group tends to vary from the majority group in appearance and/or customs. In America, primary ethnic minority groups include Afro-Americans (or African Americans), Latinos (or Hispanic Americans, including Cuban Americans and Puerto Ricans as well as Mexican Americans), Indian Americans (or Native Americans, including Hawaiians and Alaskan Eskimos), and Asian Americans, including Japanese Americans, Chinese Americans, and Filipino Americans among several others. Each ethnic minority group classification includes subgroups with very different intergroup and intragroup characteristics. Therefore, sensitivity and care are required to guard against the tendency to generalize or stereotype ethnic minority characteristics (Parrillo, 1980).

Multiethnic and Multicultural: The concepts multiethnic and multicultural are used frequently as collective references. These concepts, therefore, are used interchangeably to infer more than two ethnic groups, cultures, and/or experiences.

Transcultural: Traditionally, the concept "cross-cultural" refers to the study and research of international differences of cultural factors (Pederson, Lonner, & Draguns, 1976), but in this analysis, the concept "transcultural" has been substituted for the concept cross-cultural, for we are comparing and contrasting different cultures within the United States. In this regard, the transcultural helping relationship is one in which interaction occurs between a facilitator and an ethnic client who are affected by different intercultural, subcultural, and ethnic experiences (Stone & Brooks, 1979).

Multicultural Career Development: Multicultural career development is an intervention and continuous assessment process that prepares institutions and individuals to experience the realities of life, work, and leisure in a culturally diverse environment. In particular, multicultural career development considers the effect of and relationship among career options, ethnic-cultural demographics, and psychosocial factors that impact an individual's occupational choices in a pluralistic society.

The definition of multicultural career development conforms in many respects to NCATE standards for multicultural education; furthermore, it encompasses the precarious relationships that exist among the institution, facilitator, and client. Similarly, it considers the ethnic-cultural demographics and psychosocial dynamics of the environment that enhance as well as impede career choices. Thus, multicultural career development is for everyone — Anglo-American, African American, Native American, Hispanic American, and Asian American ethnic groups. In essence, multicultural career development, a subcategory of multicultural education, is for all people irrespective of national origin, race, sex, religion, language, or ethnic group identification.

As a result of this definition, multicultural career development clearly mandates a reconceptualization of career development programs and practices beginning with the understanding of multicultural concepts and language usage.

The effective and accurate use of language is essential in communication. Accordingly, a facilitator's understanding and success are enhanced when functional definitions convey a common meaning for the same multicultural concept. As a consequence, throughout the career development process, facilitators must acquire a sensitivity to the possibility of poor communication and the manner in which it negatively impacts the achievement potential of ethnic clients. Conversely, the appropriate use of multicultural and multiethnic concepts can cultivate a positive client-facilitator relationship.

The following multicultural competency strategies and suggestions can be employed effectively to increase awareness, sensitivity, knowledge of ethnic-cultural groups, and the common usage of multicultural concepts:

1. Acquire a knowledge and application of multiethnic and multicultural concepts (e.g. ethnic group, race, minority, culture).
2. Develop a knowledge of onomastics (the study of surnames).
3. Become acquainted with ethnic and cultural demographics (statistical data regarding population, income, employment, education, fertility, morbidity, mortality rates).
4. Demonstrate the ability to compare and contrast predominant ethnic religions (Shintoism and Catholicism, Baptist and Judaism).
5. Cultivate an awareness of ethnic folkways (food, dress, dance, medicine, folklore, folk music).
6. Study ethnic literature, art, music, history, and drama (Indian art, Jewish literature, African-American dance, Mexican-American history).
7. Become knowledgeable about significant ethnic, cultural, and historical dates, events, and holidays.
8. Administer and evaluate an objective test demonstrating an optimum and functional ethnic literacy quotient (ELQ).
9. Participate in multiethnic and multicultural, peer, personal growth, and encounter group experiences.
10. Demonstrate multicultural competencies in facilitator-client relationships during practica, simulation, laboratory, and field experiences.

MULTICULTURAL CAREER DEVELOPMENT ISSUES

For career development and related vocational studies, the issues of assessment, aspiration, choice, adjustment, and intervention reflect some of the established categories for critical exploration. For example, of the literature published about multiethnic groups and their relationship to career development issues, annual reviews of vocational behavior and career development reflect a significant disparity in quantity and comprehensiveness (Walsch, 1979; Garber & Stover, 1980; Bartol, 1981; Fretz & Leong, 1982). Apparently, there is an inclination and trend whereby only select attention has been given to career development concerns of multicultural groups. As a result, Smith (1981) has called for increased research relative to multicultural career development. In addition, some social scientists advocate that this particular issue can be best addressed by planned, short-term, intermediate, and longitudinal studies in the respective fields of vocational psychology, sociology, and organizational behavior. Despite the lack of critical attention in the area of multicultural career development, there has been an increase in the number of publications indexed for multiethnic groups in the following areas: career counseling, vocational guidance, and career education. These additional publications, moreover, considered African Americans, Hispanic Americans, Indian Americans, and Asian Americans.

In recent years, vocational and career development centers across the country have been federally funded to support career development approaches for disadvantaged youths and adults. Unfortunately, many federally funded programs have been eliminated or severely curtailed. Moreover, the success and continuation of federally funded programs normally are too dependent upon unstable political and other economic priorities. Thus, consistent multicultural career development intervention should not rely largely on federal funding. Consequently, other combinations of economic and programmatic intervention for multicultural career development should be rigorously investigated. During such investigations, the enterprises of education, industry, government, and community opportunities industrialization centers should jointly assess multicultural career development needs, plan and design career program models, and implement appropriate career strategies. Synergetic, comprehensive, and systematic evaluations become imperative to determine the effectiveness of multicultural career development program goals as well as competency-based behavioral objectives.

Osipow (1975) brings still another issue to our attention; he contends that career development theories fail to aid in understanding the life stages of disadvantaged youth and adults who experience "unique" treatment in our society. Responding to Osipow's observation, Crites (1981) proposes a taxonomy model, consisting of methods and materials specifically directed to ethnic minorities. His chief goal is to replace the speculative and experimental efforts of past decades. With appropriate modifications for the development of a comprehensive model, Crites's approach includes the expertise accumulated as a part of the taxonomy model. More appropriately, he even considers the critical factors of intervention relationship and communication as major problems experienced in the client-facilitator encounter. To implement his diagnosis, Crites also has devised a process and outcome model for culturally different groups. Primarily, it indicates that the facilitator should demonstrate exceptional levels of self-understanding, client-acceptance, and client-empathy in order to make the most appropriate application of the career development process. Clearly, Crites has wisely applied career process goals as suggested by Sue (1977). Continuing, Crites's taxonomy model stratifies counseling into (1) preentry, (2) entry, and (3) outcome levels. At each level, the process and goals take into consideration four conditions of career development for the culturally different: (1) cultural values, (2) class values, (3) language factors, and (4) unique, common experiences (Sue, 1977).

Fulfilling the requirements of both Crites's taxonomy and Sue's viewpoint that one must be aware of cultural and class values, language factors, and life experiences, Wernick, in "The Ethnic Imprint of Career Options" (1982), presents an interesting program proposal. His approach induces the concept of ethnic imprinting on career options for Hispanic-American youth. Developed in collaboration with a summer migrant program, Concentrated Employment Training Program Act (CETA), State Board of Education, a state migrant council, and ten other interested agencies, Wernick developed and organized a comprehensive career model, involving educational institutions, the family, ethnic community, and business communities. The foundation of Wernick's ambitious project is what he terms as life-centered career development. As such, the project's primary goal was to minimize the "loss of identity, self-hood, and human communion" (1982). Another integral guideline was the creation of open communication between the project and the youth's family and culture. Clearly, several benefits were derived from Wernick's project, but he hastens to add that it is not a panacea. It does, nevertheless, exist as a potential educational and cultural bridge in future multicultural career development models and programs.

Although the biogenetic concept, imprinting, is used by Wernick to convey beliefs and perceptions about unique aspects of the Hispanic American culture, ethnic imprinting is a biocultural concept employed to explain variations in career, cultural, and human behavior of the Hispanic American worker. Consequently, "these variations should be understood as variations in learned patterns of behavior rather than biologically inherited characteristics" (Arewa, 1977).

Still, we must remember that such intervention programs must be planned with more than the client's personal abilities, desires, or career options in mind. Since the life-centered method does not ignore a client's personal success or job satisfaction in the work place, facilitators must also delve into the ethnic client's perceptions of his/her aspirations as well as the requirements of each vocational choice in order to plan realistically for careers. Lest we forget, the final outcome of the life-centered project is to interface ethnic youths and adults successfully into the larger culture as well as the free enterprise system, while maintaining their individual and cultural integrity.

Indeed, we see the dire need for further experimentation, such as Wernick's life-centered career development program. Additionally, we need increased scholarly research regarding the process and outcomes of multicultural career development models.

UNEMPLOYMENT AND CAREER DEVELOPMENT

While a constellation of subtopics is applicable to each main topic, career development literature has focused extensively upon aspects of theory, practice, and research. Usually, the sequence of career development experience, job search, and subsequent employment depicts the career process in an idealized fashion; however, this has never been true for large segments of ethnic populations. The goal of full employment in America has suffered a severe setback as a result of the economic recession. During the past twenty years, we have seen unemployment increase from three percent to a high of twenty percent in some areas. Unemployment is no longer just a problem for the unskilled worker but also for the skilled and professional worker. Similarly, the displaced worker has become a national problem, permeating the complete spectrum of the labor force — youthful, middle-aged, and older clients: "The displaced worker is an individual who has been laid off from a job and has little or no hope of returning to that particular position" (Miller, 1982). Today, displacement as well as unemployment affects even the most respected professions such as business, education, and performing arts.

Unemployment, as experienced by ethnic minorities, is two or three times the rate of the general population. For minority adults, the rate is approximately eighteen percent, and for minority teenagers, the rate is approaching fifty percent, especially in urban areas. For some minority and ethnic groups, epidemic proportions of unemployment exist. For example, the unemployment rate on Indian reservations may affect seventy to eighty percent of a tribe. As a result of such high unemployment, many psychological and physiological problems tend to surface. An unemployed worker describes his status: "To be unemployed is to feel the disintegration of your confidence as a person and your ability to protect your family from economic disaster . . . it is to realize the simple stunning fact that you are without meaningful representation in this [American] society"(Hesson, 1978).

Since unemployment is a reality in the free enterprise system, it seems pragmatic that career development, especially multiethnic career development, should include the topic of unemployment and how to cope effectively with this newly acquired status. In this direction, Kaufman (1982) provides helpful guides that display four unemployment stages, including estimates of their duration. Figure 14-1 represents the primary characteristics of each stage.

Primary sources for Kaufman's stages of unemployment are the adaptations of research by Powell and Driscoll (1973). These unemployment stages describe the basic psychological effects that are experienced during progressive stages of unemployment. Not included in Figure 14-1, however, are subsets that further describe the deterioration of individual stages. Occurring in three stages, the inclusion of behavioral and physiological manifestations complete the table. Kaufman's stages of unemployment can be helpful in enhancing career multicultural development strategies that are relevant to expectations when unemployed. Just as it was once predicted that a

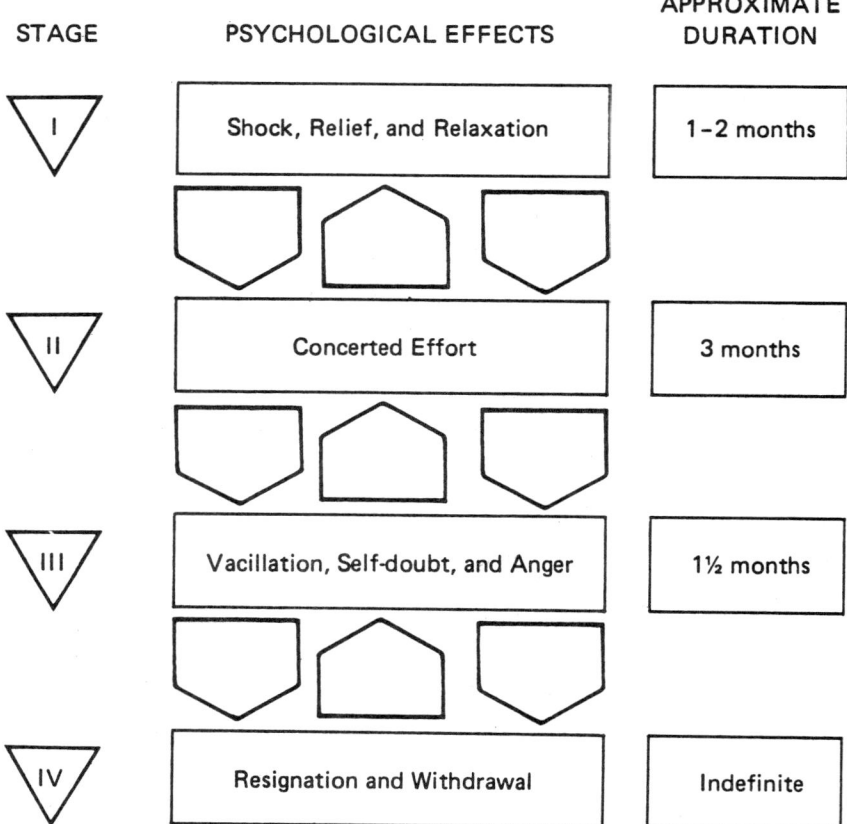

Figure 14-1. Stages of Unemployment. Adapted from Kaufman, 1982.

person could anticipate holding between five and seven positions in a lifetime, it seems equally feasible that we must now teach multiethnic clients that the possibility of having to cope with sustained unemployment may exist as a real event for which they must be prepared.

Usually, intervention is provided after the client has become unemployed or displaced. However, there is a critical need for preunemployment strategies. While the prevention of unemployment and/or displacement is not possible, career development facilitators and employers can institute specific preunemployment action-steps to lessen the impact of unemployment, therefore making the shock, transition, and stress less debilitating. As a result, from a multi-

cultural prespective, the following unemployment needs and strategies have been identified for the preunemployed, unemployed, or displaced client:
1. Employers should provide early notice of layoffs, job terminations, and/or job displacement.
2. Implementation of preunemployment and unemployment action-steps:
   a. Conduct intake screening.
   b. Form clubs, committees (councils), peer, encounter, and developmental groups.
   c. Inventory individual and/or family needs.
   d. Assess the need for psychological, outplacement, and/or employment counseling regarding job loss and stress.
   e. Provide information and job seeking assistance including job relocation and retraining.
   f. Identify local, state, and federal human resource services that provide assistance.
   g. Review financial obligations and income options.
   h. Consider health benefits and insurance for the unemployed.
   i. Develop a comprehensive preunemployment and unemployment profile for each client.
3. Review and assess the ethnic-cultural demographics of the preunemployment profile and the psychosocial factors that impact unemployment.
4. Provide systematic follow-up services for preunemployed, unemployed, or displaced workers.

ETHNIC STAGES AND CAREER DEVELOPMENT

Banks (1976), Sue (1977), and Harren (1981) have devised meaningful paradigms that explain the progression of human growth in career development. Banks charts the emerging stages of ethnicity in a preliminary typology; Sue's "Graphic Representation of World Views" examines clients' locus of control and responsibility; and Harren's model reveals what he believes to be the four stages of career decision making.

While there is a similarity between Banks's typology and other developmental paradigms, his multicultural typology considers the impact of pertinent life experiences upon the social-psychological dynamics that relate to ethnicity. These pertinent life experiences significantly shape the ethnic client's view of environment, the

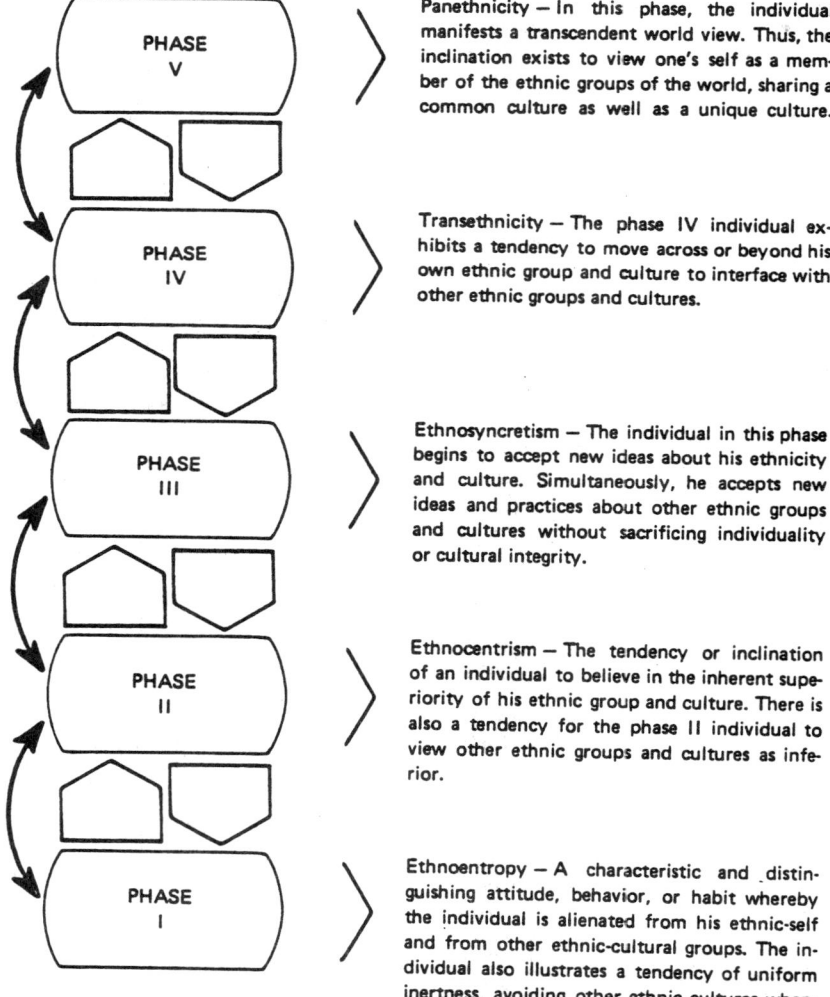

Figure 14-2. A Paradigm of Multiethnic Phases of Development. Adapted from Banks, 1979.

ethnic client's interpersonal world, and the ethnic client's innerworld. Believing this to be the case, Banks implies that facilitators should be aware of the stages of ethnicity in order to insure greater success with multiethnic clients who possess multicultural backgrounds. He has identified five stages of ethnicity: (1) ethnic psychological captivity, (2) ethnic encapsulation, (3) ethnic identity, (4) biethnicity, and (5) multiethnicity. Figure 14-2 modifies Banks's typology, emphasizing multiethnic phases of development.

The paradigm of multiethnic phases of development, a major modification of Banks's typology, reflects the individual's state-trait (Spielberger, Gorsuch, & Luschene, 1969) status, both in a general way and in the present moment continuum of time. The term *phase* is used in place of "stages" because it infers the fluid process of continuous change; thus, ethnic clients fluctuate from one phase to another as they are continuously affected by ethnic-cultural conditions within their environment. Further examining these phases, we see that they may prove useful for ethnic clients who may be isolated — economically, geographically, psychologically, and culturally. In the process of providing career development services and employment assistance to these multiethnic groups, facilitators can use these stages to assess readiness for career development experiences and to reconcile inappropriate attitudes and counterproductive behavioral patterns — when and wherever appropriate.

Cognizant of the stage of one's ethnic development prior to attempting the implementation of systematic career development models, appropriate methods and resources, such as Sue's locus of control and responsibility, may improve intervention success. Examining Sue's method, one discovers that it provides insight relative to an ethnic framework of readiness for career development experiences. Since each quadrant represents a different world view, Sue (1979) infers that the manner in which ethnic clients perceive their relationship to the world is highly correlated to their cultural development and life experiences. Therefore, ethnic clients' world views tend to be reflected in their locus of control and responsibility beliefs. Accordingly, in Figure 14-3, Sue postulates that both the locus of control and responsibility exist on intersecting planes.

Just a brief graphic explanation of Sue's viewpoint shows the latent possibilities for use. Measures in four quadrants represent different world views. In quadrant I, internal control-internal responsi-

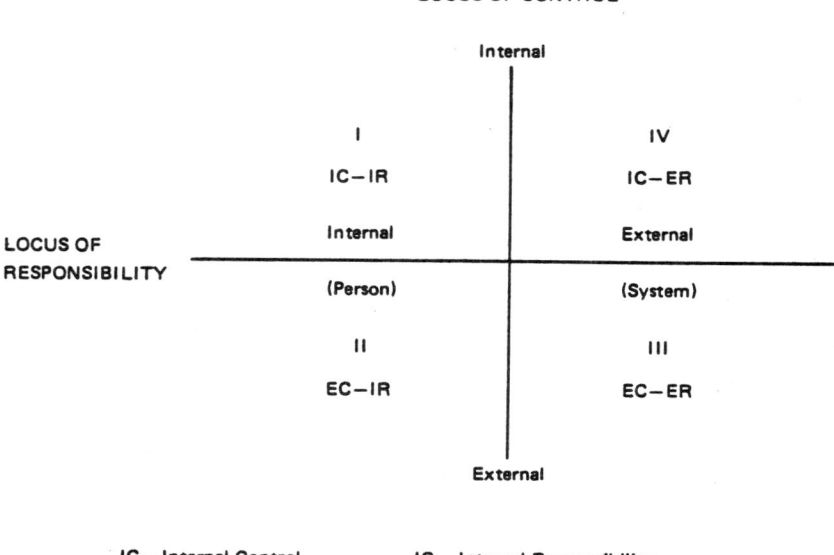

Figure 14-3. Graphic Representation of World Views. Adapted from Sue, 1978.

bility, clients reflect dominant middle-class values. In quadrant II, ethnic clients are more likely to accept the dominant culture's definition for self-responsibility, but they have little real control over how they are defined as marginal persons. In quadrant III, external control-external responsibility, clients are high in system blame and external control. Life, for them, is viewed relatively fixed. In quadrant IV, internal control-external responsibility, clients believe in their ability to shape events in their own life, if they are given the opportunity. Clearly, Sue's locus of control and responsibility can be used transculturally, but it is especially appropriate for ethnic clients who have been identified and assigned minority status.

The Harren model of career decision making contains four important stages of development for the "rational" client: awareness, planning, commitment, and implementation. Lastly, when used in appropriate situations with multiethnic clients, Harren's model promotes multicultural career development as a lifelong process of assessing and integrating knowledge of the self and the work-world as both change over the life span (Daniels & Buck, 1981). A major benefit of Harren's model is that the client-student learns how to make decisions that lead to self-confidence and independence.

Perhaps the models (Banks's paradigm of multiethnic phases of development, Sue's locus of control and locus of responsibility, and Harren's model of career decision making) hold promise as effective approaches to initiate multicultural career development if they are used collectively rather than individually. Indeed, the paradigm of multiethnic phases of development and Sue's model complement Harren's cognitive approach. Although Harren's model does not specifically consider the life expriences of the culturally different client, his approach does consider the four stages of decision making, an integral factor in a successful career development plan.

SUMMARY AND REVIEW

In this chapter, multicultural career development has been defined as a life-work-leisure process (Bolles, 1983) in which facilitators of vocational behavior and practices consider the effect of and the relationship among career options, ethnic-cultural demographics, and psychosocial factors that impact ethnic clients in a pluralistic society. Thus, ethnic clients, career development facilitators, and the multicultural milieu can benefit from the implementation of this concept.

The perspectives discussed in this chapter — ethnic-cultural differences, definitions of multicultural concepts, career development issues, multiethnic phases of development, unemployment stages, and multicultural intervention resources — provide focused direction and positive outlook for the renaissance of career and vocational development.

Facilitators and clients may experience some cognitive dissonance and affective discomfort when considering multicultural perspectives of career development. However, they must realize that "the ground beneath ethnic identity shifts constantly, and one has to be ready to make the mental leaps to more solid ground or to ignore the temporary unease of standing in shifting sands" (Royce, 1982).

BIBLIOGRAPHY

Arredondo-Dowd, P. M., and Gonsalves, J. Preparing culturally effective counselors. *Personnel and Guidance Journal,* 1980, *58,* 657-661.

Aryers, M. E. Counseling Hispanic Americans. *Occupational Outlook Quarterly,* 1979, *23,* 2-8.

Astin, A. W., Astin, H. S., Green, K. C., Kent, L., McNamara, P., and Williams, M. R. *Minorities in American higher education.* San Francisco, California: Jossey-Bass Inc., 1982.

Atkinson, D. R., Morton, G., and Sue, D. W. *Counseling American Minorities: A cross-cultural perspective.* Dubuque, Iowa: William C. Brown Company Publishers, 1979, 1982.

Banks, J. A. *Teaching strategies for ethnic studies.* Boston: Allyn and Bacon, Inc., 1979.

Bahr, H. M., Chadwick, B. A., and Stauss, J. H. *American ethnicity.* Lexington, Kentucky: D.C. Heath Company, 1979.

Bartol, K. M. Vocational behavior and career development, 1980: A review. *Journal of Vocational Behavior,* 1981, *19,* 123-162.

Beck, J. The counselor and black/white relations. *Guidance Monograph Series, Series 7: Special Topic in Counseling.* Boston: Houghton-Mifflin, 1973.

Bolles, R. Where is career counseling going? A lecture presented at the 1983 American Personnel and Guidance Association Annual Convention, Washington, D.C., March 22, 1983.

Career counseling materials and techniques for use with Vietnamese. San Jose, California City College, 1981 (ERIC Reproduction Service No. ED 206758).

Castro, R., et al. *Resource guide for career counseling Spanish-speaking and Chicano students.* San Jose, California: San Jose City College, 1981 (ERIC Reproduction Service No. ED 205695).

Ching, W., and Prosen, S. S. Asian-Americans in group work. *Journal for Specialists in Group Work,* 1980, *5,* 228-232.

Crites, J. O. *Theory and research handbook: Career maturity inventory.* Monterey, California: CTB/McGraw-Hill, 1973.

Crites, J. O. *Career counseling: Models, methods, and materials.* New York: McGraw-Hill Book Company, 1981.

Curriculum and instruction: Cultural issues in education. Los Angeles, California: National Dissemination and Assessment Center, 1978 (ERIC Reproduction Service No. ED 188816).

Darou, W. G. Experiencing native American culture. *Counseling and Values,* 1980, *25,* 3-17.

Dillard, J. M., and Campbell, N. J. Influences of Puerto Rican, Blacks, and Anglo parents' career behavior on their adolescent children's career development. *Vocational Guidance Quarterly,* 1981, *30,* 139-148.

Farley, J. E. *Majority-minority relations.* Englewood Cliffs, New Jersey: Prentice-Hall, Inc., 1982.

Fraser, B. S. *The structure of adult learning, education and training opportunity in the United States.* Washington, D.C.: National Institute for Work and Learning, 1980.

Fretz, B. R. Evaluating the effectiveness of career interventions. *Journal of Counsel-*

ing Psychology Monograph, 1981, *28*, 77-90.

Fretz, B. R., and Leong, F. T. Vocational behavior and career development, 1981: A review. *Journal of Vocational Behavior*, 1982, *21*, 123-163.

Garbin, A. P., and Stover, R. G. Vocational behavior and career development, 1979: A review. *Journal of Vocational Behavior*, 1980, *17*, 125-170.

Garcia, R. L. *Teaching in a pluralistic society: Concepts, models, strategies.* New York: Harper and Row Publishers, 1982.

Gunnings, T., and Simpkins, G. A. A systemic approach to counseling disadvantaged youth. *Journal of Non-White Concerns in Personnel and Guidance*, 1972, *1*, 4-8.

Harper, F. Self-actualization and three Black protestors. *Journal of Afro-American Issue*, 1974, *2*, 303-319.

Harper, F. What counselors must know about the social sciences of Black Americans. *Journal of Negro Education*, Spring, 1973.

Harper, F., and Stone, W. Toward a theory of transcendent counseling with Blacks. *Journals of Non-White Concerns in Personnel and Guidance*, 1974, *2*, 80-85.

Harren, V. A., Daniels, M. H., and Buck, J. N. (Eds.), *New directions for student services: Facilitating students' career development.* San Francisco, California: Jossey-Bass Inc., 1981.

Hayes, S. The counselor aid: Helping services for native American students. *Journal of American Indian Education*, 1979, *18*, 5-11.

Henderson, G. *Understanding and counseling ethnic minorities.* Springfield, Illinois: Charles C Thomas Publishers, 1979.

Hesson, J. D. The hidden psychological costs of unemployment. *Intellect*, April 1978, 389-390.

Hollingshead, A. B. *Two factor index of social position.* Unpublished manuscript, 957 (Available from 1965 Yale Station, New Haven, Connecticut).

Jackson, R. L., Weisen, J. P., and Nieves, L. R. A. Approach for identifying and minimizing bias in standardized tests: A set of guidelines. Monograph prepared by the Office for Minority Education. New Jersey: Educational Testing Service, 1980 (Monograph No. 4).

Jenkins, A. H. *The psychology of the Afro-American: A humanistic approach.* New York: Pergamon Press, 1982.

Kaufman, H. G. *Professionals in search of work: Coping with the stress of job loss and unemployment.* New York: John Wiley and Son, 1982.

Lennon, T. C. Guidance needs of special populations. Information Series No. 145. National Center for Research and Vocational Education. Ohio State University, Columbus, OH, 1979 (ERIC Reproduction Service No. ED 173535).

Martinez, L. M. Chicanos counseling Chicanos: Is it necessary? Paper presented at the Annual Conference on Ethnic and Minority Studies (LaCrosse, WI. April 23-26, 1980) (ERIC Reproduction No. ED 191610).

Miller, J. Displaced workers. *ERIC Overview: Fact Sheet No. 21.* Columbus, Ohio: The National Center for Research in Vocational Education, 1982.

Miller, J. V. Lifelong career development for disadvantaged youth and adults. *Vocational Guidance Quarterly*, 1982, *30*, 359-366.

National Education Association. *Multiethnic education in-service training aids* (Brochure-no date). National Education Association, 1201 Sixteenth Street,

N.W., Washington, D.C. 20036.

Nieves, L. *College achievement through self-help: A planning & guidance manual for minority students.* New Jersey: Educational Testing Service, 1978.

Osipow, S. H. The relevance of theories of career development to special groups: Problems, needed data, and implications. In J. S. Picou and R. E. Campbell (Eds.), *Career behavior of special groups.* Columbus, Ohio: Merrill, 1975.

Parker, W. M., and McDavis, R. J. Using four career guidance strategies with ethnic minorities. Module 45. American Institutes for Research in the Behavioral Sciences, Palo Alto, California, 1979 (ERIC Reproduction Service No. ED 183996).

Parrillo, V. N. *Strangers to these shores: Race and ethnic relations in the United States.* Boston, Massachusetts: Houghton-Mifflin, 1966.

Pedersen, P. Four dimensions of cross-cultural skill in counselor training. *Personnel and Guidance Journal,* 1978, *56,* 457.

Pederson, P., Lonner, W., and Draguns, J. *Counseling across cultures.* Honolulu, Hawaii: University of Hawaii Press, 1976.

Powell, D. H., and Driscoll, P. F. Middle-class professionals force unemployment. *Society,* 1973, *10,* 18-26.

Powell, D. H. The effects of job strategy seminars upon unemployed engineers and scientists. *Journal of Social Psychology,* 1973, *91,* 165-166.

Reardon, R. C., and Burck, H. D. (Eds.). *Facilitating career development: Strategies for counselors.* Springfield, Illinois: Charles C Thomas Publisher, 1975.

Rotter, J. B. Generalized expectancies for internal versus external control of reinforcement. *Psychological Monographs,* 1966, *80,* (1, Whole No. 969).

Royce, A. P. *Ethnic identity: Strategies on diversity.* Bloomington, Indiana: Indiana University Press, 1982,

Sanchez, A. *Counseling the bilingual student: An information analysis paper,* Searchlight Plus 54+. Ann Arbor, Michigan: ERIC Counseling and Personnel Services Clearinghouse, 1981.

Seligman, L. Haitians: A neglected minority. *Personnel and Guidance Journal,* 1977, *55,* 390-396.

Smith, E. J. Career development needs of special populations. Chapter in *New directions for student services: Facilitating students' career development.* Harren, V. A., Daniels, M. H., and Buck, J. N., (Eds.). San Francisco, California: Jossey-Bass Inc., 1981.

Smith, P. C. *Bowling Green State University study of work values.* Bowling Green, Ohio: Bowling Green State University, 1975.

Spielberger, C. D., Gorsuch, R. L., and Luschene, R. E. *The State-Trait Anxiety Inventory (STAI) Test Manual for Form X.* Palo Alto, California: Consulting Psychologist Press, 1969.

Stone, W. O., and Brooks, C. C. *Cross-cultural counseling: Practitioner training and methods.* Proposal submitted to the Fund for the Improvement of Post Secondary Education, Department of Health, Education and Welfare. Washington, D.C.: (unpublished), 1979.

Sue, D. World views and counseling. *Personnel and Guidance Journal*, 1978, *56*, 458-462.

Sue, D. W. Counseling the culturally different: A conceptual analysis. *Personnel and Guidance Journal*, 1977, *55*, 422-425.

Trimble, J., and Lee, D. J. Counseling with American Indians: A review of the literature with methodological considerations. Paper presented at the American Educational Research Association (Los Angeles, CA. April 15, 1981) (ERIC Reproduction Service No. ED 201448).

Vontress, C. E. Cultural barriers in the counseling relationship. *Personnel and Guidance Journal*, 1969, *48*, 11-17.

Vontress, C. E. Counseling the racial and ethnic minorities. *Focus on Guidance*, 1973, *5*, 1-10.

Vontress, C. E. Cross-cultural counseling: An existential approach. *Personnel and Guidance Journal*, 1979, *58*, 117-121.

Walsh, B. W. Vocational behavior and career development, 1978: A review. *Journal of Vocational Behavior*, 1979, *15*, 119-154.

Weissberg, M., Berentsen, M., Cole, A., Cravey B., and Heath, K. An assessment of the personal, career, and academic needs of undergraduate students. *Journal of College Student Personnel*, 1982, *23*, 115-122.

Wernick, W. The ethnic imprint of career options. *Journal of Career Education*, 1982, *8*, 169-172.

Yu, C. Y. The 'others': Asian Americans and education. *Civil Rights Digest*, *1976*, *9, 44-51.*

MULTICULTURAL INTERVENTION RESOURCES

For multicultural career development, there are selected career development intervention resources that seem to offer promise as effective approaches for meeting the needs of clients and facilitators. In general, Fretz (1981) believes that progress will be significantly slow in improving the effectiveness of career intervention because of a lack of systematic and comprehensive evaluations of current strategies. When considering the diversity of multiethnic groups, specific recommendations for career development are difficult. Apparently, this situation exists because the norming process and status of populations used to develop methods, models and materials tend to vary greatly from the backgrounds of the culturally different (Crites, 1981). In assessing these resources for usage, career development facilitators should display creativity and sensitivity rather than stereotypic intervention. It is obvious, however, that for some members of multiethnic groups with excellent environmental advantages a modification of existing intervention resources and other intervention techniques may not be necessary. Nevertheless, it is probable that modifications in methods, models, and materials will be required to work effectively with some multicultural groups. While the career intervention resources cited below may not be equally effective for all ethnic groups, they may spark insight for further innovation, variation, and application.

1. "The Ethnic Imprint of Career Options" (Wernick, 1982).

The article presents an example of comprehensive career development for migrant youth. The approach involved school, local, and state agencies cooperating in an action setting to achieve a life-centered focus for career planning and implementation. The approach focused attention on ethnic heritage, cultural values, family members, educational curriculum, and interview exchanges with adult workers in the community.

2. "Lifelong Career Development for Disadvantaged Youth and Adults" (Miller, 1982).

A valuable reference from a senior research specialist at the National Center for Research in Vocational Education (Ohio State University, Columbus). This publication provides significant information about available directories of career development services, programs, and training opportunities for the disadvantaged. References and reviews about career development and adulthood, career guidance needs of the disadvantaged, and career guidance models are provided.

3. *Resource Guide for Career Counseling Spanish-Speaking and Chicano Students* (Castro et al., 1981).

This guide contains general and specific career development strategies for working with persons from Latin/Hispanic cultures. An annotated bibliography is included for guidance in counseling Chicano and Spanish-speaking students.

4. *Career Counseling Materials and Techniques for Use with Vietnamese* (San Jose City College, 1981).

A reference that is sensitively written and designed to convey understanding about Vietnamese people and their culture, especially recent refugees. Career counseling materials and techniques are provided because the American society is vastly different in culture and values; hence, language problems, cross-cultural misunderstandings, and conflicts are anticipated. This reference is designed to anticipate conflicts and to reduce misunderstandings in the career development process.

5. "An Assessment of the Personal, Career, and Academic Needs of Undergraduate Students" (Weissberg, Berentsen, Coté, Cravey, & Heath, 1982).

A survey consisting of sixty-five items was devised to evaluate academic, career, and personal needs of students enrolled as undergraduates at the University of Georgia. The findings of the study infer minimum sex and class differences in response to the items; however, African-American students indicated significantly stronger needs than Anglo-American students on the three dimensions measured. The results of the survey were shared with student groups, schools, and colleges of the University of Georgia, as well as the student affairs area to assist in the design of programs to address the identified needs of all students.

6. "Influences of Puerto Rican, Black, and Anglo Parents Career Behavior on Their Adolescent Children's Career Development" (Dillard & Campbell, 1981).

This intervention study is unique because it was designed to analyze the relationship among three adolescent groups (two minority) for career aspirations, expectations, and maturity in comparison to the parents' career values and aspirations for their children. Instruments used in the study were the "Two Factor Index of Social Position" (Hollingshead, 1957), "Survey of Work Values" (Smith, 1975), and the "Career Maturity Inventory (ATT-CMI)" (Crites, 1973). Regarding the influence of parents' and their children's career development, differential results were produced by the study. Effects of influence were moderately apparent for African-American and Puerto Rican children. In working with adolescents, especially minorities, career development facilitators should consider parental aspirations for their children.

7. *Professionals in Search of Work: Coping with the Stress of Job Loss and Underemployment* (Kaufman, 1982).

An excellent book that will assist counselors and career development specialists in serving the unemployed and underemployed. Although the title suggests professionals as the target population, paraprofessional, managerial, clerical, skilled, and semiskilled persons can also profit from the contents by simply understanding the psychological and physiological stages experienced as a result of unemployment. Regarding barriers faced in seeking work, cross-cultural and ethnic comparisons are provided. Additional data is presented regarding stress, job search methods, employability, unemployment adjustment, societal responses, and directions for future policy and programs.

8. *College Achievement Through Self-Help: A Planning and Guidance Manual for Minority Students* (Nieves, 1978).

This publication was sponsored by the Graduate Record Examinations Board and the Office for Minority Education of Educational Testing Services. The manual is designed to encourage minority students to acquaint themselves with the array of skills and competencies needed to maximize success in college. Self-assessment, managing anxiety, and career decision making are among the college achievement exercises. This self-help booklet is also available in Spanish.

9. *An Approach for Identifying and Minimizing Bias in Standardized Tests: A Set of Guidelines* (Jackson, Weisen, & Nieves, 1980).

This monograph is the third in a series prepared by the Office of Minority Education and Educational Testing Service (Princeton). The Division of Personnel Administration of the Commonwealth of Massachusetts collaborated on this publication of current issues in fair testing and the reduction of bias and offensiveness in tests. Additional subtopics are concerned with guidelines for test reviews, criterion problems, and suggestions for workshops.

10. *Understanding and Counseling Ethnic Minorities* (Henderson, Ed., 1979).

A required source book for facilitators who wish to gain information about the diverse backgrounds and counseling needs of ethnic groups — African Americans, Hispanic Americans, Puerto Ricans, Native Americans, and Asian Americans.

11. *Counseling American Minorities: A Cross-Cultural Perspective* (Atkinson, Morten, & Sue, 1979, 1982).

A book of readings designed to increase the awareness of professionals about multiethnic groups — Native Americans, Asian-

Americans, African-Americans, and Hispanic-Americans. Counseling approaches in need of minority group/transcultural research are identified.

12. *The Psychology of the Afro-American: A Humanistic Approach* (Jenkins, 1982).

An interesting humanistic analysis of psychology that views African-Americans as determiners of their destiny in spite of repressive circumstances. This publication is a significant humanistic contribution to the field of psychology.

13. *Minorities in American Higher Education* (Astin, 1982).

Minorities remain underrepresented in all career fields and specialities in higher education. Astin presents substantial information regarding academic factors that adversely affect career choice and retention. Numerous recommendations are offered to correct the existing inequalities.

14. *Teaching in a Pluralistic Society: Concepts, Models, Strategies* (Garcia, 1982).

The textbook addresses the relationship that exists between culture and ethnicity and the manner in which these factors interact with the teaching-learning process. While it is also designed to provide specific guidelines for compliance with the NCATE multicultural education standards, the text provides significant assistance for facilitators in the implementation of multicultural career development programs. Users will discover that suggested concepts, models, and strategies are especially helpful.

CHAPTER 15

PROGRAMS IN ORGANIZATIONS

Dorothy Domkowski

Frank Endicott just received a job offer from a newly created microelectonics firm. That offer totals four that he has received this year. He has already changed companies twice and is beginning to wonder if another change is right at this time.

Joyce Robinson is forty-three and has been a secretary ever since she can remember. While her performance evaluations have always been excellent and she enjoys what she is doing, she often wonders if maybe there are other jobs she would like even better. Now that her children aren't home anymore, she even could take some courses.

Henry Martin has been fired. Although the economic situation of the organization looks good, top management feels he hasn't done enough to increase profits of his marketing group. He must find another position, but how?

THINGS have changed. As recently as five to ten years ago, the above fictional characters would have sought assistance for their career concerns from community-based counseling agencies, educational institutions, or private career development practitioners. Now, they might seek such assistance from their own organizations. The recent proliferation of conferences, courses, journals, and books and even films devoted to the topic of career development in organizations can be overwhelming, even to an experienced human resource professional.

Times have changed. As today's college students compete for limited spaces in colleges of business, many nurses, teachers, and engineers are enrolling in the ever increasing number of MBA programs. It is only natural for counselors and career development specialists to look also to the private sector for employment. Meanwhile, these employers, as well as public sector employers, are changing their organizations. Organizational Development (OD) focuses on improving the effectiveness and healthy operation of an organization (Beckhard, 1969). Career development as an OD intervention fits naturally into this framework and thus naturally into an organizational setting. This union of career development with organization development also provides a solution to the problem Hall (1976) identified, that is, a bridge between the separate but related literature in counseling psychology, industrial/organizational psychology, and sociology.

The focus of this chapter is career development programs in organizations. The goal is to identify the specific issues in and components of such programs. Additionally, intervention strategies will be explored and, finally, evaluation will be addressed. The reader should (1) develop a sense of what may need to be considered in the design, implementation, and evaluation of a career development program within an organizational setting and (2) become more knowledgeable about some of the models, resources, and practices from which to draw and build future programs.

ISSUES IN AN ORGANIZATIONAL SETTING

In developing career development programs within an organizational context, three main elements are involved — the organization, the individual, and the career development concept. Understanding the interrelationships of these elements is paramount if any career development intervention is to be developed, implemented, and evaluated. The more information practitioners have about these relationships, the more effective they will be. The following pages will examine each of these elements separately and their relationships to each other. The practitioner's role will also be examined.

The Organization

Some of the keys to understanding the workings of organization can be found using a systems model. In viewing an organization, one can look both at external and internal components. Externally, the organization has many choices and constraints working on it, i.e. government regulations, new technological advancement, and clientele. Internally, the organization's structure, policies, personnel, and technological state can affect the behavior of employees in the organization that in turn affects the quantity and quality of services and products. In a career development context, any of these components can similarly act as a choice or constraint both on the individual and practitioner. Starting and working with only the individual employee may be possible, but effective career change or development in an organizational framework must use a systems approach (Hanson, 1981; Leibowitz, Farren, & Kaye, 1983).

The Organization-Career Development Relationship

Defining the organization-career development relationship is dealing with the whats, whys, and hows of the situation. Clarifying each of these points is critical in the design of any program, and failure to do so can result in unmet expectations for the individual, organization, and practitioner. To help in this clarification process, several guidelines, conditions, or practices have been identified (Alpin & Gerster, 1978; Leibowitz, 1979; London & Stumpf, 1982; Morgan, Hall, & Martier, 1979; Walker & Gutteridge, 1979). Three other resources have been developed that may prove useful in designing the career development program:

1. *A Guide for Career Development Inquiry* (Storey, 1979). It is designed to stimulate practitioners simply to ask the right questions in the design, execution, and communication of results of programs, including risks and benefits.
2. *A Career-Development Program Model* (Kaye, 1979). The model describes six stages: Inception/Preparation, Profiling, Targeting, Strategizing, Execution, and Integration. While the model serves to describe the activities of individuals and organizations in the career development process, the Preparation stage includes the same six stages in designing a program (Kaye, 1982).
3. *A Career Planning System Audit* (Burack & Mathys, 1979). Designed for practitioners interested in "installing or modifying" a career planning system, the form consists of thirteen broad human resource categories and fifty-two specific activities that can provide a valuable support to a comprehensive career development program.

In using the above or other resources, some of the whats, whys, whos, and hows will be answered.

What is career development? As practitioners in school environments have had to distinguish career planning, career education, and career development, the same need to define what one is discussing is important in other organizational settings. Add to these terms career pathing, career management, and organizational career management. Career planning still can be defined as the process the individual undertakes involving self-awareness, goal-setting, and action. The action the individual takes is career pathing. Career management is defined by Storey (1979) as "an on-going process of preparing, implementing, and monitoring career plans undertaken by the individual alone or in concert with the organization." The same definition could be used for organizational career management (Burack & Mathys, 1979). In working within an organizational framework, the consideration and application of functions such as management are important. Career development is still the result of the individual's planning and action, managed or not managed.

Walz (1982) has conceptualized and diagrammed a "Career Development Diamond," which depicts the categories of Career Catalyzing, Career Management, Career Pathing, and Career Exploration, and the activities encompassed in each.

Further complicating the "what" question is what organizations define as a career development activity (Lancaster & Berne, 1981). Career development in organizations has come to mean a variety of activities, and these have been reported by Morgan, Hall, and Martier (1979), Seybolt (1979), and Walker and Gutteridge (1979). One survey ("Career Development Activities: Practices, Focuses, Concerns," 1979) reports twenty-five different activities organizations conduct under the aegis of career development, including tuition-aid programs, assessment centers, job diagnostic surveys, job posting, and individual self-analysis. Many of the fifty-two items on the Burack-Mathys Career Planning System Audit are the same or related activities.

The need regarding the "what" issue may be whether career development is another activity or the umbrella for many human resource activities.

Why career development? General statements for an organization's involvement in career development balance needs of an organization with needs of an individual. Lancaster and Berne (1981) and Miller (1979) list a number of reasons based on changing work values and work ethics; however, most reasons center on the perceived benefits to the organization (Bolyard, 1979; Cohen & Meyer, 1979; Kaye, 1982; Morgan, Hall, & Martier, 1979; Walker & Gutteridge, 1979).

These benefits include a desire (1) to improve worker performance and productivity, (2) to decrease turnover, (3) to develop needed management talent, (4) to develop employees in line with organizational goals, (5) to decrease training costs, (6) to increase levels of employee commitment, involvement, and satisfaction, (7) to obtain more efficient attainment of affirmative action policies, (8) to better match individuals and jobs, (9) to increase motivation, (10) to obtain employee information for modifying resource management, (11) to identify options other than vertical mobility, (12) to attract new employees, (13) to avoid or address union activities, and (14) to link existing human resource activities.

Engaging in career development also creates some problems to the organization. These include (1) loss of some productive employees, (2) raised expectations by employees that may not be able to be met, (3) demand for increased fringe benefits, (4) demand for additional training and development programs, (5) increased movement within the organization, and (6) change in organizational policies or procedures.

Answering the question "why" can identify the motivation and commitment issues and may help answer the "who" and "how" questions.

Who is responsible for career development? The next section will explore the organizational and individual responsibility in the career development process. For program design, implementation, and evaluation purposes, responsibility could reside with a person or unit inside or outside the organization or a combination of both. Some organizations employ full-time professionals while others use staff who may have other functions to perform. Employee supervisors are of paramount importance in the career development program. Their involvement is so critical that many career development efforts have focused on them not only to provide an individual with feedback on current performance but also as a vehicle for the career development program (Gambill, 1979; Hanson, 1980; Jones, Kaye, & Taylor, 1981; Leibowitz & Schlossberg, 1979, 1981;

Meckel, 1981; Miller, 1980; Storey, 1976; Walker & Gutteridge, 1979). One such program at General Electric will be elaborated in another section.

Who participates in career development? The organization may have a clear idea of who program participants will be. They may be a specific population, i.e. women, minorities, "fast-trackers," the engineering division, etc. Whether the participant is a volunteer or volunteered also may be important. Morgan, Hall, and Martier (1979) found in their survey that more than 80 percent of participants in existing programs were nominated by others. Whether employees and their supervisors both participate together in a program also may be a critical factor. Knowing "who" enables practitioners to select appropriate interventions.

Resolving the "who" questions should address needs issues as well as an accountability factor. To whom is the career development effort accountable?

How is career development to work? If all of the above questions have been answered, identification of program goals, interventions, resources, and time frame can be developed. Regarding time, organizations may allow employees varied amounts of company time to participate in career development activities. How much time may be a cost-benefit decision. An additional "how" question is how is information to be used? The answer may address a confidentiality issue. Both organizations and individuals often make decisions about each other without communicating the decision. Models for the presentation of these decisions in the career development process will be presented in another section.

If a fairly clear picture of the organization-career development relationship exists, development of a career development program should proceed smoothly.

Organization-Individual Responsibility

Irrespective of the role any career development specialist may play in the career development program, for the *career development process* to work necessitates a shared responsibility on the parts of both the organization and the individual. As program models are designed, they usually consider this shared responsibility (Benson & Thornton, 1978).

An individual and the organization already have a relationship, as can be depicted by a model developed by Schein (1971). An organization can be viewed as a cone and the individual a point within the cone. Movement the individual may make, as in career changes, could be along any or all of three planes: (1) vertically, to various levels in the system, (2) radially, to various degrees of influence, and (3) circumferentially, to various functional areas.

Kaye (1982) presents another way to view the organization-individual relationship with regard to any career changes that might be made. She refers to these as "options" or "levers" that either party might use. The six possibilities for the individual are (1) lateral, movement to another equal position, (2) vertical, movement up to a higher position, (3) enrichment, assumption of new or different responsibilities, (4) exploratory, action that may provide new information, (5) realignment, movement down to a lower position, and (6) relocation, movement out of the organization.

The career development process depends on the relationship between the organization and the individual. The models above can serve to identify where individuals are and where they want to go (career planning), as well as where organizations see individuals and where they would like to see them move (organizational planning). Much of this planning is dependent upon information that both may have or need to know. The exchange of this information is a key ingredient in the career development process and in any career development program in an organization.

Several models showing the critical exchanges of information between an individual, an organization, as well as the related career development/human resource activities have been developed (Alpin & Gerster, 1978; Ginsburg, 1977; Schein, 1978). Figure 15-1 incorporates many of the similar elements of these models so practitioners can understand and appreciate the unique responsibilities organizations and individuals play in the process and, subsequently, in the importance of any career development program.

In addition to these general models, several other specific models have been created. Miller (1980) presents a career management process identifying both the employee and manager's responsibilities. Cohen and Meyer (1979) present a career planning model for non-management and lower-management personnel where organization's key career-related functions are shown.

Programs in Organizations

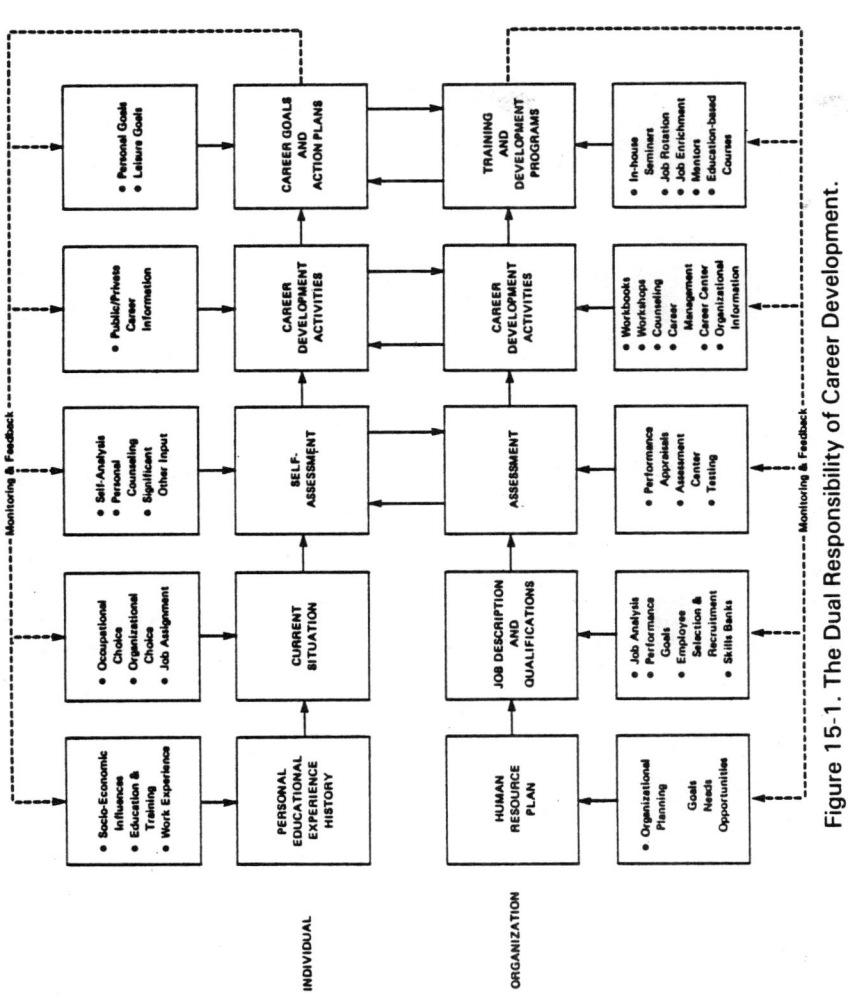

Figure 15-1. The Dual Responsibility of Career Development.

The Individual

One cannot ignore one of the key elements in any career development program, namely the individual. There will be no reference here to the theories and research regarding the career development of an individual; however, the practitioner is encouraged to draw upon that knowledge in designing, implementing, and evaluating programs. What will be considered in this section are some of the more relevant issues about individuals as they relate to an organizational setting.

Adult career development. Many theories and much information has already been disseminated about adult life cycles and the important issues adults face as they become older. Summaries of the work of Erickson, Gould, Valliant, Levinson, and Havighurst can be found in popular as well as professional literature. Implications for the work environment are obvious as adults try to get in, stay in, or get out of work. Three models of this individual-work relationship can be examined. Hall (1976) identifies three basic stages an individual develops within an organization: (1) early stage, becoming established, (2) mid-stage, career maintenance and reexamination, and (3) late stage, approaching retirement. Schein (1978) describes "career anchors" in which an individual develops an occupational self-concept based on self-perceived talents and abilities, motives and needs, and attitudes and values. Hall (1976) presents another model that accounts for the specific situation of an individual in an organization — the factors that influence a person, i.e. job, peers, boss, organizational policy, practices, rewards.

Individual risks and benefits. The individual can take risks and reap benefits by participating in a career development program (Kaye, 1982; Morgan, Hall, & Martier, 1979). Self-awareness, goal setting, and changes are some outcomes of individual career planning. In an organizational setting, individuals also can (1) increase visibility and involvement, (2) develop an organizational identity, (3) clarify what is available, and (4) at the same time identify their own limitations, weaknesses, uncertainties, and inadequacies.

Special populations. As organizations consider career development programs, attention is often given to special populations. The emphasis on supervisors has already been discussed. Other populations that have programs designed with their unique issues in mind are high performers (Dalton, Thompson, & Price, 1979), women (Epstein, 1980; Fort & Codisco, 1981; Jelinek, 1979), young managers (Webber, 1980), middle-aged managers (Levinson, 1980), older workers (Sonnenfeld, 1980), plateaued employees (Stoner, Ference, Warren, & Christensen, 1980), dual-career couples (Hall & Hall, 1980), and the outplaced (Morin & Yorks, 1982; Sweet, 1975).

Motivating the individual to participate is as critical in an organizational setting as elsewhere. Oliver (1981) addresses some of the issues revolving around "Career Unrest" and, consequently, what might motivate individuals to engage in career development programs.

The Career Development Specialist

Central to the career development program in any organization is the career development specialist. Certain factors already have been addressed: specifically, who the specialist may be. As for knowledge, practitioners need to know the career development process for adults, general career information, and organizational career information. Regarding skills, they should have human relations skills and management skills. Most importantly, practitioners need to be able to understand an organization, use its jargon, and navigate its system. Roles other than program designer, implementer, and evaluator could be trainer, counselor, integrator, resource developer, and counsultant. The film *Career Development: A Plan for all Seasons* (1978) profiles Beverly Kaye, a career development consultant, working with both employees and management in a career development effort at Collins Foods. Practitioners wishing professional affiliations and networking opportunities can join the American Society for Training and Development, Career Development Division, and the National Vocational Guidance Association and subscribe to the *Career Planning and Adult Development Newsletter* published by the Career Planning and Adult Development Network, 1190 South Bascom Avenue, Suite 211, San Jose, CA, 95128.

INTERVENTION STRATEGIES

If the issues of the organizational situation have been appropriately assessed, identification of program goals, strategies, and activities will follow. The goals may be very unique to an organization or generalizable to many organizations. Similarly, activities may be unique or common but with organization-specific information. Again, many different activities have become known as career development programs. Figure 15-2 identifies some of the most common activities.

Individual Career Counseling
    Career planning by: career development specialist, personnel staff, supervisors, peers, outside counselor-consultants
    Career Planning by self through workbooks

Group Career Counseling
    Career planning workshops
    Special topics seminars: preretirement, self-analysis, mid-careers, new employees, moving up

Assessment
    Performance appraisals and reviews
    Psychological, interest, and skill testing
    Assessment centers

Career Information
    Career resource center
    Career paths and career ladders
    Job posting
    Information on: personnel policies, training and development activities

Training and Development
    Job enrichment, job rotation
    Dual-career ladders
    Career sabbaticals
    Supervisory training in career counseling
    In-house and outside seminars, workshops, and training experiences

Organizational Career Planning
    Manpower planning and projections
    Skills banks of employees

Special Populations

Minorities	Young managers
Women	High performers
Disabled	Management trainees
Preretirees	Dual-career couples
Plateaued	Scientific/Technological
Outplaced	Support staff

Figure 15-2. Career Development Activities

Model Programs

Three model programs are described as follows.

Lawrence Livermore National Laboratory. This program is probably the most well-known, well-cited, and comprehensive of existing career development programs (Knowdell, 1982; Hanson, 1980, 1981, 1982). The Career/Life Planning Program consists of an orientation session, a career assessment workshop, individual career counseling, and a career information center. Some of the unique features of the program are (1) previous program participants who serve as adjunct counselors in addition to their primary roles as engineers, laboratory assistants, etc., (2) Livermore Achievement Motivation Process (LAMP) skills assessment, and (3) immediate, short-term, and long-term (eight years) evaluation activities.

General Electric. Begun in 1969, the General Electric Program is also well documented (Jones, Kaye, & Taylor, 1981; Storey, 1976). While the variety of programs vary to cover a diverse employee population, the two unique features of the G. E. program are (1) *Career Dimensions,* which consists of three self-help career planning workbooks for individuals and a self-help career management workbook for supervisors, and (2) a *Managing Career Conversations* workshops, designed to help supervisors develop career management skills as they assist their supervisees.

Virginia Polytechnic Institute and State University. Although a relatively new program, the Employee Career Development Program is beginning to gain attention (Hesser & McDaniels, 1982). This program incorporates workshops, counseling, manager consultation, and an advisory council. The unique feature is the Employee Career Resource Center, which contains four self-managed, self-paced stations: (1) Understanding Self, (2) Understanding Environment, (3) Taking Responsible Action, and (4) Life Management.

EVALUATION

When compared to other settings, e.g. education, little evaluation has been done on career programs in organizational settings, although the situation is changing. The reasons often cited for this paucity of evaluation include (1) the newness of the activity, (2) problems associated with identifying what exactly constitutes a career development program, (3) the focus on goals such as increased productivity, profits, and job satisfaction, (4) lack of evaluation methodology by practitioners, (5) focus on process rather than interventions, and (6) barriers in the field caused by practitioners who differ in wants from academics (those who traditionally do research) (Hall, 1980; Lancaster & Berne, 1982; Morgan, Hall, & Martier, 1979; Walker & Gutteridge, 1979). Also, some practitioners with little or no knowledge of career development have been directed to begin programs. Their focus is often to gain knowledge rather than perform evaluations.

However, evaluation has been and is being done. *The Career Development Bulletin* consists entirely of research and evaluative studies relating to organizations. Designed for the career practitioner, this publication presents all information in a brief, easy-to-read, easy-to-understand format. It is published by the Center for Research in Career Development, Graduate School of Business, Columbia University, New York, New York, 10027.

Also, there are several studies that report the state-of-the-art of career development in organizations with regards to evaluation or research issues. Lancaster and Berne (1982) identify methodology problems in surveys they reviewed and summarized. Hall (1980) cites needs for (1) research on interventions, (2) field experiments, (3) attention to greater variety of career outcomes, (4) more theory-testing, and (5) "research on the career-decision-making process."

Of actual practices, Stump found most programs include "retrospective" self-assessment, "prospective" self-assessment, and "integration" of self-assessment with goal setting, as well as information about opportunities. He reports several positive career development efforts. In their survey, Walker and Gutteridge (1979) found, in addition to other things, the more common practices to be informal counseling by personnel staff (89%), career counseling by supervisors (56%), and workshops on interpersonal skills (49%). Gutteridge and Otte (1983) report career planning seminars or workshops (78%), career counseling by staff counselors (70%), job posting (45%), and career workbooks (40%) as the most common activities. Their survey also reports the seminars as the most effective activity. Morgan, Hall, and Martier (1979) have also reported some useful information regarding types of programs, program initiation, commitment of top management, integration into organizational structure, and evaluation.

Regarding a specific program, Kabrosky (1979) reports the results of the program at Crocker National Bank. Analysis of various data on program participants revealed a cost savings of almost 2 million dollars in a year's time. Turnover had been reduced 65 percent, and performance increased 85 percent. There was also a 75 percent change in jobs.

In another study, Kapurch (1983) reports a follow-up of a career/life planning program at the Naval Underwater Systems Center. This study revealed that 87 percent of the program participants were still employed at the Center. While 63 percent of the respondents agreed that another type of work might be more satisfying, they also stated that they were either taking actions to rectify or willing to accept their current situation. Changes reported by individuals were primarily within the organizational setting. Summaries of other programs are reported by London and Stumpf (1982), Hanson (1982), and Lancaster and Berne (1982).

The few studies reported counter the once often-expressed fear — that employees would be exiting organizations in greater numbers. In fact, the opposite seems true. Career development programs are providing a vehicle for important information about the individual and the organization to be explored and, consequently, for better decisions to be made. These positive "feelings" about early career development efforts seem to be supported also by the increased numbers of organizations engaging in such activities. Informal network and grapevine communications are positive and growing.

The task now is to formalize and document more of these career development activities. Several key contributions have been made to assist practitioners with evaluation efforts: needs and methods have been proposed (Hall, 1976, 1980), purposes have been defined (Storey, 1976), and techniques have been suggested (see Chapter 16). In addition, Leibowitz and Schlossberg (1979) advise that "If program decision makers are interested in improving a program, reaction and learning data are probably most relevant. On the other hand, if evaluation data is to be used to make decisions regarding the future of the program, behavior and organizational change data are important."

SUMMARY

Although still a relatively new phenomenon, career development in organizations is increasing in acceptance as a viable organization-implemented activity. Several trends have emerged and are being addressed. These include (1) the need to identify options other than vertical movement for employees, (2) emergence of multiple-career paths, (3) dual-career couples issues, (4) focus on supervisor career management training, (5) greater attention to plateaued employees, (6) provision of more varied career information delivery systems, and (7) use of professional career development specialists.

For those practitioners and organizations in the forefront of the field, the experiences have proven to be very positive, exciting, and challenging.

BIBLIOGRAPHY

Alpin, J. C., and Gerster, D. K. Career development: An integration of individual and organizational needs. *Personnel*, 1978, *55* (2), 23-29.

Beckhard, R. *Organization development: Strategies and models.* Reading, Mass.: Addison Wesley, 1969.

Benson, P. G., and Thornton, G. C. A model career planning program. *Personnel*, 1978, *55* (2), 30-39.

Bolyard, C. What's happening? Career development in business. *Commission VI Career Counseling & Placement*, August 1979, p. 4.

Burack, E. H., and Mathys, N. J. *Career management in organizations: A practical human resource planning approach.* Lake Forest, IL: Brace-Park Press, 1979.

Career development: A plan for all seasons. New York: McGraw-Hill, 1978 (Film).

Career development activities: Practices, focuses, concerns. *Career Development Bulletin*, 1979, *1* (1), 5-10.

Cohen, S. L., and Meyer, H. H. Toward a more comprehensive career planning program. *Personnel Journal*, 1979, *58*, 611-615.

Dalton, G. W., Thompson, P. H., and Price, R. L. The four stages of professional careers: A new look at performance by professionals. In M. Jelinek (Ed.), *Career management: For the individual and the organization.* Chicago: St. Clair Press, 1979.

Epstein, C. F. Institutional barriers: What keeps women out of the executive suite? In M. A. Morgan (Ed.), *Managing career development.* New York: D. Van Nostrand, 1980.

Fort, M. K., and Cordisco, J. H. Career development for women in industry. *Training and Development Journal*, 1981, *35* (2), 62-64.

Gambill, T. R. Career counseling: Too little, too late. *Training and Development Journal*, 1979, *33* (2), 24-27.

Ginsburg, L. R. Career planning: Help your organization grow. *Supervisory Management*, 1977, *22* (6), 9-16.

Gutteridge, T. G., and Otte, F. L. Organizational career development: What's go-

ing on out there? *Training and Development Journal,* 1983, *37* (2), 22-26.
Hall, F. S., and Hall, D. T. Dual careers — How do couples and companies cope with the problems? In M. A. Morgan (Ed.), *Managing career development.* New York: D. Van Nostrand, 1980.
Hall, D. T. *Careers in organizations.* Santa Monica, CA: Goodyear Publishing Co., 1976.
Hanson, M. C. Training employees and managers for their roles in career development. In R. V. Hanle (Ed.), *Career management: Implications for organizations and individuals.* Madison, Wis: ASTD, 1980.
Hanson, M. C. Implementing a career development program. *Training and Development Journal,* 1981, *35* (7), 80-90.
Hanson, M. C. Career/life planning workshops as career services in organizations — are they working? *Training and Development Journal,* 1982, *36* (2), 58-63.
Hesser, A., and McDaniels, C. Career services for adult workers at Virginia Tech. *Career Planning and Adult Development Newsletter,* 1982, *4* (11), 1-2.
Jelinek, M. Career management and women. In M. Jelinek (Ed.), *Career management: For the individual and the organization.* Chicago: St. Clair Press, 1979.
Jones, P. R., Kaye, B., and Taylor, H. R. You want me to do what? *Training and Development Journal,* 1981, *35* (7), 56-62.
Kabrosky, K. Career planning at Crocker National Bank, *The Career Development Bulletin,* 1979, *1* (3), 3-4.
Kapurch, L. Following up on the effects of a goals workshop. *Training and Development Journal,* 1983, *37* (2), 48-52.
Kaye, B. The design of career development programs: A six stage model. *Group and Organization Studies,* 1979, *4* (3), 301-308.
Kaye, B. L. *Up is not the only way: A guide for career development practitioners.* Englewood Cliffs, N.J.: Prentice-Hall, Inc., 1982.
Knowdell, R. L. Comprehensive career guidance programs in the workplace. *Vocational Guidance Quarterly,* 1982, *30,* 323-326.
Lancaster, A. S., and Berne, R. *Employer-sponsored career development programs.* Information series IN 231, ERIC Clearinghouse on Adult, Career, and Vocational Education, Columbus, Ohio, 1981.
Leibowitz, Z. Career development in business and industry. *Commission VI Career Counseling & Placement,* August 1979, p. 5.
Leibowitz, Z. B., Farren, C., and Kaye, B. Will your organization be doing career development in the year 2000? *Training and Development Journal,* 1983, *37* (2), 14-20.
Leibowitz, Z., and Schlossberg, N. *Designing Career Development Programs for Business and Industry* (Module 41). Washington, D.C.: National Consortium on Competency-Based Staff Development, 1979.
Leibowitz, Z. B., and Schlossberg, N. K. Training managers for their role in a career development system. *Training and Development Journal,* 1981, *35* (7), 72-79.
Leibowitz, Z. B., and Schlossberg, N. K. Critical career transitions: A model for designing career services. *Training and Development Journal,* 1982, *36* (2), 12-19.
Levinson, H. On being a middle-aged manager. In M. A. Morgan (Ed.) *Managing*

London, M., and Stump, S. A. *Managing careers.* Reading, MA: Addison-Wesley, 1982.

Meckel, N. T. The manager as a career counselor. *Training and Development Journal,* 1981, *35* (7), 65-69.

Miller, D. B. Career planning and management in organizations. In M. Jelnick (Ed.), *Career management: For the individual and the organziation.* Chicago: St. Clair Press, 1979.

Miller, D. B. Training managers for their role in career development in R. V. Hanle (Ed.), *Career management: Implications for organizations and individuals.* Madison, Wis: ASTD, 1980.

Morgan, M. A., Hall, D. T., and Martier, A. Career development strategies in industry — Where are we and where should we be? *Personnel,* 1979, *56* (2), 13-30.

Morin, W. J., and Yorks, L. *Outplacement techniques: A positive approach to terminating employees.* New York: AMACOM, 1982.

Oliver, R. *Career unrest: A source of creativity.* New York: Center for Research in Career Development, Columbia University, 1981.

Schien, E. The individual, the organization and the career: A conceptual scheme. *Journal of Applied Behavioral Science,* 1971, *7,* 401-426.

Schein, E. *Career dynamics: Matching individual and organizational needs.* Reading, Mass.: Addison-Wesley, 1978.

Seybolt, J. W. Career development: The state of the art among the grassroots. *Training and Development Journal,* 1979, *33* (4), 16-20.

Sonnenfeld, J. Dealing with the aging work force. In M. A. Morgan (Ed.), *Managing career development.* New York: D. Van Nostrand, 1980.

Stoner, J. A., Ference, T. P., Warren E. K., and Chritensen, H. K. *Managerial career plateaus: An exploratory study.* New York: Center for Research in Career Development, Columbia University, 1980.

Storey, W. D. *Career Dimensions IV.* Crotonville, New York: General Electric Company, 1976.

Storey, W. D. *A guide for career development inquiry.* Madison, Wis: ASTD, 1979.

Stump, R. W. Follow-up information on career development programs in organizations. Unpublished manuscript, 1982. (Available from Robert W. Stump, 2208 N. Quintana Street, Arlington, VA, 22205.)

Sweet, D. H. *Decruitment and outplacement: A positive approach to terminations.* Reading, Mass: Addison-Wesley, 1975.

Walker, J. W., and Gutteridge, T. G. *Career planning practices.* New York: AMACOM, 1979.

Walz, G. R. *Career development in organizations.* Ann Arbor, MI: The University of Michigan, 1982.

Webber, R. A. Career problems of going managers. In M. A. Morgan (Ed.), *Managing career development.* New York: D. Van Nostrand, 1980.

CHAPTER 16

ACCOUNTABILITY: A PRACTICAL MODEL

Gary W. Peterson

THE hue and cry for accountability in public education and human service programs has been heralded since the early 1970s when the long growth trend in tax dollars made available to human services began to level off and even decline. In spite of the continuing public demands for accountability,* there has been little progress made in the development of accountability models that enable programs to collect and aggregate data that effectively relates resources to results. A major difficulty behind this apparent lack of progress has been the absence of conceptual and operational constructs that define the outcomes or "products" of human service intervention. Stated in more familiar terms, career counselors have failed to specify how career development services effectively change the minds and hearts of people so that they may lead more satisfying and productive lives. This chapter presents an accountability model based on cognitive development that seeks to define more clearly the "products" of career development programs so that more precise linkages can be made among resources invested in programs, intervention strategies, and the ensuing results.

Accountability in career development has been and may well continue to be both an illusive and troubling issue. It seems as though the mere defining of what is meant by career development

---
*Accountability may be defined in terms of the establishing of responsibility for certain outcomes given a set of human and nonhuman resources (Crabbs & Crabbs, 1977; Henderson & Shore, 1974; Knapper, 1978).

less accountability) seems to be confusing. According to Pietrofesa and Splete (1975), career development is defined as "an on-going process that occurs over the life span and includes home, school, and community experiences related to an individual's self-concept and its implementation in life styles as one lives life and makes a living." Gysbers and Moore (1975) define career development as "self-development over the life span through the integration of the roles, settings, and events of a person's life." Given such rather nonlimiting definitions of career development, career programs ostensibly provide services that facilitate whatever Pietrofesa and Splete or Gysbers and Moore refer to as "career development," but with such global definitions, how does a counselor establish accountability for services rendered with any degree of defensible precision?

Perhaps another reference point for attempting to understand the phenomena of career development may be from an analysis of the activities counselors typically perform when career development services are offered. According to Drier (1977), Splete (1978), and Hoyt (1979), career development activities include (1) developing and clarifying self-concepts, (2) relating occupational information to self-information, (3) "teaching" decision-making skills, (4) providing opportunities for occupational reality testing, and (5) assisting individuals in educational and occupational placement processes. However, at this point a question still remains: for what are the counselors who perform such activities held accountable?

Yet a third avenue for pursuing the meaning of career development may be in analyzing statements pertaining to the outcomes of career development services. Campbell, Walz, Miller, and Kriger (1973) ask, Does a career development program meet the needs of students at a reasonable cost? The National Vocational Guidance Programs (1979) include one standard relevant to the intent of this chapter: "Students demonstrate increased competencies in self-understanding of the worlds of work and leisure, career planning, decision making, and ability to take action." Drier (1977) suggests the following outcome criteria: (a) increased use of community resources, (b) decreased dropout and absenteeism from school, (c) increased involvement of parents and teachers in guidance delivery, (d) increased work-related experiences, and (e) increased use of counseling services.

While such outcome criteria may be helpful for the formulation of career development service goals, one important dimension of outcomes consistently appears to be omitted, namely those changes in perceptual and cognitive thought processes (competencies) that enable individuals to make satisfying and informed career choices commensurate with their intellectual, social, and moral development. In other words, while much attention has been devoted to describing how counselors intervene and the ensuing general effects, the cognitive capacities that clients acquire as a direct result of career development interventions have yet to be clearly conceptualized and articulated. The central point of this chapter is that the development of certain cognitions, herein called "generic competencies," should lie at the core of any career development program and should form the nucleus of an accountability system (Peterson & Burck, 1982).

In a competency approach to accountability in career development, client changes are assessed first in terms of the skills, knowledge, and attitudes (SKAs) acquired as a direct result of career interventions. These are the *primary effects*. Criteria such as job satisfaction, satisfaction with services, job acquisition rates, ventures in career exploration, or successful placement in schools or jobs are viewed as *consequential* or *secondary effects* of intervention. A competency approach is therefore based on the assessment of two levels of outcomes, primary client changes, which concern the development of new cognitive capabilities, and secondary changes, which relate to the manner in which these newly acquired capacities are applied to making effective career and life-style decisions. This two-stage approach to defining outcome criteria permits stronger, more precise linkages between resources invested in a career development program and the ensuing results. In economic terms, the primary programmatic effects may be considered as *outputs* while the secondary effects may be labeled *outcomes* (Kaufman & English, 1979).

ASSUMPTIONS AND PROPOSITIONS

Ultimately, the aim of career development interventions should be to foster changes in the ways clients perceive themselves and the world of work and in the ways clients incorporate such perceptions in the service of generalized problem-solving skills (see Weitz, 1964). In order to demonstrate the linkages among resources invested in human service programs, cognitive development, and consequent results, the following set of assumptions are necessary:

1. A set of fundamental cognitive abilities (i.e. generic competency skills) and knowledge undergird effective career decision-making and problem-solving processes. These include such subordinate skills as Communication, Analysis, Synthesis, Valuing, and Planning.
2. A career development intervention is viewed as a learning process in which generic competency skills are mastered and applied to making career decisions, executing them, and achieving satisfaction with jobs and life in general.
3. There is a causal linkage between the acquisition of generic competency skills acquired in career development programs and subsequent career and life adjustment.
4. Costs for program delivery are determined by accounting for all resources (in monetary terms) required to administer interventions that enable clients with common career problems (criterion groups) to achieve desired levels of proficiency in targeted generic competency skills and areas of knowledge.

A FIVE-STEP ACCOUNTABILITY MODEL

The competency accountability model involves the following stages: (a) a *diagnosis* of client needs, (b) a *prescription* of activities to help a client address such needs, (c) the documenting of activities and plans that form the *processes* of intervention, (d) the *outputs* or primary effects of service, and (e) the resultant effects or *outcomes* of primary changes. Basically, the proposed approach involves the identification of skills and knowledge to be acquired in a program, the prescribing and documenting of services to help clients achieve them, and measuring the attainment of new perceptions and cognitions and then determining whether changes are manifested in subsequent life-adjustment outcomes.

Diagnosis. In a competency approach, client problems are defined in terms of *needs* (Kaufman, 1972) that are the discrepancies or gaps between existing levels and desired levels of competency skill development. The goals and objectives of career development programs are derived from a group of individuals who share common needs (Burck & Peterson, 1975). The demonstration of accountability at the diagnostic stage includes the determination of client generic competency needs, the formulation of program goals, and the documentation of measures and entry level performances of a criterion group (which may be a group of sixth graders in a career education class, a group of housewives returning to the world of work after a "stop-out" to have children, etc.). Examples of diagnostic data are presented in Table 16-1.

Prescription. This stage involves the development of a plan of counselor and client activities that is designed to remove diagnosed needs, i.e. competency skill gaps. Since the development of specified generic skills and knowledge areas is the goal of career development services, learning activities to engender SKAs can be developed through a task analysis (Gagne, 1977) to arrive at a series of learning activities that lead clients from simple to complex skills. The mastery of a content domain, which procedes cognitive skill development, may be structured through content analyses in which clients master certain sets of facts, concepts, rules, or operations on which to base higher order competency skills. For example, career development program concepts for the intervention described in Table 16-1 might include defensiveness, assertiveness, and aggressiveness, factors affecting the supply of applicants and demand for work in a given job classification, the relationship among education, training, and job requirements, and factors affecting motivation. For children and adolescents, learning activities may be structural along cognitive and moral developmental lines as proposed by Inhelder and Piaget (1958) or Kohlberg (1969).

Process. Therapeutic and educational processes are the series of activities, both planned and unplanned, performed by *both* the client and the counselor to bring about change in diagnosed competency skill and knowledge gaps. Here, for accountability purposes, it is important to note accurate and detailed descriptions of counselor and client activities, the attainment of milestones leading to the acquisition of desired skills and knowledge, the accomplishing of prescribed tasks or experiences, or scores on progress tests or inventories. The most important data to collect are those that indicate progress made toward the development of skills or the mastery of new knowledge.

Outputs. The outputs of a successful career development program

Table 16-I

Examples of Generic Skill Diagnostic and Output Data for a Group of Unemployed Adults Seeking Career Counseling.

Generic Competency Skills	Assessment Technique	Entry Level of Development	Desired Level of Development	Actual Level of Development
1. Problem-solving skills	Success & failure incidences; career choice scenarios; selected TAT cards; Piagetian tasks.	70% described a trial and error strategy for securing a job	80% could apply a 5-step problem-solving model to career selection & job identification.	90% could apply a 5-step problem-solving model to career selection.
2. Communications skills	Written free response to simulated job interview questions; Job interview role-playing situation.	25% were able to demonstrate effective assertive responses to written employer challenges; 35% consistently gave assertive responses in a simulated job interview.	80% demonstrate mastery of assertive responses to written employer challenges; 80% give assertive responses in a simulated job-interview questions.	95% could write assertive responses to interview questions; 80% mastered assertive responses in a role play.
3. Analytical skills	Open-ended question asking clients to list *why* they have difficulty securing a job from most important to least important reason.	75% list first reason in terms of factors outside of their control, e.g. prejudice of employers or no work available, indicating lack of responsibility.	90% will list first reason in terms of their own lack of job competence skills, job seeking skills, lack of information about new jobs, adequate educational experience, etc.	85% gave first reason on terms of factors over which they have control.
4. Synthesis skills	List most suitable occupations; list educational or training opportunities for above list in community.	60% listed no more than 2 suitable occupations, 10 listed one; 50% could not list appropriate training opportunities.	80% could list at least 5 "suitable" occupations 80% could list at least one training/educational facility in community for each occupation.	85% could list at least 5 "suitable" occupations; 95% could list appropriate training opportunities.

5. Valuing (interests, abilities, values)	List likes & dislikes, strengths & weaknesses; conflict scenarios; work value inventories; standardized achievement tests.	50% rated 50% of their likes & dislikes as uncertain; 45% had "significant discrepancies between self-rated abilities & tested abilities; 50% indicated differences between stated & tested values.	85% feel certain of stated interests, abilities & values.	85% feel certain about interests, abilities & values.
6. Planning	Given a plausible job for which most members of the group could perform with less than 1 year of additional training or education, list steps one would take to attain employment.	80% listed fewer than four steps to reach the goal indicating a very superficial level of job planning skills.	90% will list at least ten steps to take in preparing, seeking, and securing a job placement.	95% listed ten or more discrete steps to be taken in securing employment.

are the new skills and knowledge acquired that enhance the career development process, which may include development of communication skills, newly acquired capacities for analyzing career problems, the ability to formulate plausible courses of action, clearer understanding of one's own values and the values operating in a social or work environment, and increased planning skills that lead to the successful attainment of self-determined goals. These are viewed as the primary client changes, which are the direct result of career service interventions. Accountability for output should be demonstrated by documenting the gains made in generic competency skill dimensions from entry to exit performance levels. Examples of output data for a career development program are presented in Table 16-1.

Outcome. The outcomes of a career development program are the resultant effects or consequences of having acquired new cognitive or perceptual capacities (i.e. outputs), which may include a more focused and organized plan for career exploration, reduced fear of success or failure, greater toleration and understanding of temporary career indecision, successful job placement, greater satisfaction with a chosen college major, greater job satisfaction, greater harmony among work, family, and leisure responsibilities, reduced absenteeism from school or work, and increased performance in school or work. While there are some published instruments available to measure life satisfaction (Justice & McBee, 1978), career indecision (Osipow, Carney, & Barak, 1976), or even life functioning in general (Carter & Newman, 1976; Endicott et al., 1976), for most purposes, a "home-made" instrument that is more directly related to the aims, goals, and objectives of a given program may provide more valid information with which to make evaluative judgments concerning the effectiveness and worth of a program. Further, the inclusion of open-ended questions may provide the counselor with valuable qualitative information about the program as well. Critical incident methods (Flanagan, 1954) in which clients report success and failure incidents following a career service intervention may be extremely helpful. In order to assess the enduring effects of a career development program, one-month, six-month, and one-year follow-up studies are recommended.

THE DETERMINATION OF COSTS

The determination of costs to conduct career development programs can be an exceedingly complex endeavor if one is to attempt to employ a full-cost model. Further, the difficulty of making causal linkages between resources to results in career development programs also may be fraught with unjustifiable assumptions (Peterson & Burck, 1982). Nevertheless, with the projected long-term trend of diminishing resources with which to deliver human service programs, the determination of cost-effectiveness becomes exceedingly important, if not mandatory.

Without going into a great deal of detail regarding the determination of costs for the present chapter, the cost of a career development program based on a competency approach can be determined by summing the costs for personnel, materials and supplies, and overhead (administrative and custodial expenses, utilities, etc.) for each step in the proposed five-step model (Haller, 1974). For example, the direct costs for diagnostic procedures for a career development program include counselor time for intake interviews and case write-ups, assessment materials, proctoring and scoring tests, plus overhead or indirect costs. Similarly, the direct costs for prescription activities include counselor time for interviews, developing plans for activities, reviewing plans with colleagues, materials and supplies, and overhead. Costs for process, output assessment, and outcome analysis can be determined in the same way. By using intact groups, unit costs (i.e. cost per client) also can be determined.

Once the costs for a program are determined, they can be related to gain scores in knowledge and skill attainment (output). A basic cost/effectiveness (i.e. efficiency) ratio of the amount of client gain per dollar is then derived. This ratio (output/cost) may be compared with other career development programs with similar goals, objectives, and client characteristics to ascertain whether some interventions and personnel configurations are more effective (i.e. promote more client gain) or more efficient (i.e. more gain for the dollar) than others (Knezevich, 1973).

REQUIREMENTS TO IMPLEMENT THE APPROACH

There are three fundamental requirements to implement a competency approach to accountability in career development programs: (1) a knowledge of skills and content domains that underlie rational career decision-making processes in certain contexts, (2) a knowledge of conditions that bring about the development of cognitive, perceptual, and psychomotor abilities in volunteer clients, and (3) valid and sensitive measures to detect subtle changes resulting from career development service interventions. These three requirements indeed may be formidable challenges to meet. They demand that counselors become familiar with new research findings in cognitive and developmental psychology as well as with methods of measuring changes in cognition and perception. Unfortunately, these are areas of study that are typically given very little emphasis in the training of career

reer development experiences throughout life instead of merely providing experiences to move individuals to the "next step" in a career development schema, attention to cognitive development becomes imperative.

CONCLUSIONS AND IMPLICATIONS

The proposed accountability model provides a paradigm for more clearly defining the results of career development by drawing a distinction between outputs, i.e. the direct changes in individuals as a result of service, and outcomes, i.e. the ways in which such client gains are actualized in daily living. This distinction provides a more precise perspective as to for what counselors can be held accountable. Counselors can be held far more accountable for the new kinds of knowledge and skills clients acquire in service programs than for the ways in which changes are implemented in the course of daily living, which may be influenced by a host of capricious environmental factors. Paradoxically, at the programmatic level, a cohort of clients with similar career development problems should demonstrate salutary effects at the outcome level if the program is to be considered effective. Said more concretely, counselors can help clients evaluate their abilities and interests, clarify goals and values, learn to market their skills and knowledge; however, they cannot (and perhaps should not) be held accountable for whether an individual secures a job in a specified length of time.

Perhaps more importantly, the model compels a rethinking of the aims of career development programs. In addition to focusing career service on such issues as career information, job search strategies, interviewing skills, etc., which are some of the important enablers in career development, career counselors should also view their interventions from the wider perspective of enhancing problem-solving skills so that individuals acquire the capability for seeking and processing information, analyzing career problems, formulating creative solutions, choosing the most promising ones, and implementing plans of action to accomplish objectives to reach long-term goals. Perhaps a time-worn allegory is appropriate here: "A person who is given a fish eats for a day, but a person who is taught how to fish eats for a lifetime." If counselors can go beyond helping individuals sur-

fish eats for a lifetime." If counselors can go beyond helping individuals surmount immediate career problems or crises and help individuals acquire the capabilities to manage their own career development over a lifetime, perhaps then a truly valuable service will have been provided. Also, by demonstrating that clients have acquired new capabilities and can apply them to their daily lives, accountability will have been demonstrated as well.

BIBLIOGRAPHY

Burck, H., and Peterson, G.W. Needed: More evaluation, not research. *Personnel and Guidance Journal*, 1975, *53*, 563-569.

Campbell, R., Walz, G., Miller, J., and Kriger, S. *Career guidance, A handbook of methods*. Columbus, Ohio: Charles Merrill, 1973.

Carter, D.E., and Newman, F.L. *A client-oriented system of mental health service delivery and program management: A workbook guide*. Washington D.C.: U.S. Government Printing Office, 1976, (DHEW Publication No. ADM 76-307).

Crabbs, S.K., and Crabbs, M.A. Accountability: Who does what to whom, when, where, and how? *School Counselor*, 1977, *25*, 104-109.

Drier, H.N. *Programs of career guidance, counseling, placement, follow-up, and follow-through: A future perspective*. Columbus, Ohio: National Center for Research in Vocational Education, Ohio State University, 1977.

Endicott, J., Sptizer, R.L., Fleiss, J.L., and Cohen, J. The global assessment scale: A procedure for measuring overall severity of psychiatric disturbance. *Archives of General Psychiatry*, 1976, *33*, 766-771.

Flanagan, J.C. The critical incident technique. *Psychological Bulletin*. 1954, *51*(4), 327-358.

Gagne, R.M. *Conditions of learning* (3rd ed.). New York: Holt, Rinehart and Winston, 1977.

Gysbers, N., and Moore, E. Beyond career development — Life career development. *Personnel and Guidance Journal*, 1975, *53*, 647-652.

Haller, E.J. Cost analysis for education program evaluation. In W.J. Popham (Ed.), *Evaluation in education: Current applications*. Berkeley, Calif.: McCutchen, 1974.

Henderson, R., and Shore, B. Accountability for what to whom? *Social Work*, 1974, *19*, 387-88, 507.

Hoyt, K. The career education treatment. *Journal of Research Development in Education*, 1977, *12*, 1-20.

Inhelder, B., and Piaget, J. *The growth of logical thinking from childhood to adolescence*. New York: Basic Books, 1958.

Justice, B., and McBee, G. A client satisfaction survey as one element in evaluation. *Community Mental Health Journal*, 1978, *14*, 248-252.

Kaufman, R., and English, F. *Needs assessment: Concept and application*. Englewood

Cliffs, N.J.: Educational Technology Publications, 1979.
Knapper, E.Q. Counselor accountability. *Personnel and Guidance Journal,* 1978, *57,* 27-30.
Knezevich, S.J. *Program budgeting (PPBS).* Berkeley, Calif.: McCutchan, 1973.
Kohlberg, L. Stage and sequence: The cognitive development approach to socialization. In D. Goslin (Ed.), *Handbook of socialization theory and research.* Chicago: Rand McNally, 1969.
National Vocational Guidance Association Commission on Criteria for Guidance Programs. Guidelines for a quality career guidance program. *Vocational Guidance Quarterly,* 1979, *28,* 99-100.
Osipow, S.H., Carney, C.G., and Burck, A. A scale of educational-vocational undecidedness: A typological approach. *Journal of Vocational Behavior.* 1976, *9,* 233-243.
Peterson, G.W., and Burck, H. A competency approach to accountability in human service programs. *Personnel and Guidance Journal,* 1982, 60(8), 491-495.
Pietrofesa, J., and Splete, H. *Career development theory and research.* New York: Grune and Stratton, 1975.
Splete, H. *Career development counseling.* Boulder, Co.: University of Colorado, 1978 (Colorado Career Information System Monograph).
Weitz, H. *Behavior change through guidance.* New York: John Wiley, 1964.

CHAPTER 17

PROFESSIONAL AND ETHICAL ISSUES

DANIEL J. MONTGOMERY AND JAMES P. SAMPSON, JR.

IN spite of the interest of other helping professions, such as psychotherapy, career counselors generally have ignored issues pertaining to professional ethics. Although the National Vocational Guidance Association (1979, 1982) has taken some significant steps in the development of standards for career guidance programs and career counselors, a review of the literature suggests that only marginal attention has been devoted to discussing the ethical problems of career counselors, their solution, and their prevention. There may be several reasons for this: (1) career counselors use interventions that are less risky than psychotherapy and consequently may not produce negative effects, (2) individuals who seek the help of career counseling may be less disturbed than individuals seeking therapy and therefore are not as likely to present management problems, (3) career counseling does not tend to foster the dependent client-therapist relationship encouraged by some schools of therapy and as a result career counselors are not as likely to become inappropriately involved with their clients, and (4) the incidence of lawsuits and other forms of litigation is probably lower in career counseling than therapy. Although this may be changing as governmental bodies such as New York City crack down on fraud and misrepresentation in the career counseling industry (Kerr, 1982).

For these reasons, career counselors have been able to conduct their practice with only minimal concern for professional ethics. This is not to suggest that career counselors are unethical but rather that because of the nature of their practice they have not had to face ethical and legal dilemmas that are now common in psychotherapy. However, the absence of client litigation does not excuse career counselors from their responsibility to protect clients. As professionals, career counselors, as do therapists, need to make every effort to protect their clientele from unethical, unprofessional, and incompetent treatment.

The American Psychological Association (1981) and the American Personnel and Guidance Association (1981) standards of ethical conduct provide a set of principles applicable to both counseling and career counseling. The National Vocational Guidance Association(1982) has established minimal educational and training standards for career counselors. Together, these documents provide the basis for ethical practice.

Unfortunately, these guidelines do not alert career counselors to the types of ethical problems they may encounter and how they might prevent them. The purpose of this chapter is to discuss some of the ethical problems that career counselors may face and to suggest potential preventive and corrective measures. The objective is neither to rewrite existing ethical standards nor is it to set forth a separate code for career counselors.

For the purpose of this discussion, ethical problems and potential corrective measures have been categorized as follows: (1) problems caused from lack of training, (2) problems created by counselor conflict of interest, (3) problems created by the client's failure to receive the information needed to make an informed decision regarding counseling, (4) problems arising from counselor's failure to obtain client consent before proceeding with counseling, (5) problems created by the application of computer technology, and (6) problems related to testing.

PROBLEMS STEMMING FROM LACK OF TRAINING

Many counselors and therapists view career counselors and the field of career counseling with contempt. They see career counseling as a second-rate profession, using an outmoded trait-factor model of human personality, comprised of individuals who have neither the intelligence nor the skill or training to do psychotherapy.

Given this attitude, it is not surprising that professionals have ignored the fact that career counseling has become a specialized field with unique training requirements and its own set of professional standards. According to the National Vocational Guidance Association, the competency areas for vocational/career counseling include (1) general counseling skills, (2) information, (3) individual and group assessment, (4) management and administration, (5) implementation, and (6) consultation (1982).

Individuals who do not meet these standards and practice career counseling are not only violating professional ethics but also are quite possibly jeopardizing their client's well-being. The APA and APGA clearly state that a counselor or therapist should not work outside of their area of training. To do so is a violation of professional ethics: Principle 2 (AGA, 1981) and Section A;4 & 7 (APGA, 1981).

In career counseling, the professional is, in many instances, helping the clients decide how to spend approximately one third of their adult life, and as a result the potential for error is great. For example, the counselor might provide outdated or misleading information, incorrectly assess client aptitude and training, distort the nature of the job market, or fail to help the client evaluate alternatives.

Potential Corrective Measures

Increased counselor awareness of the minimum requirements for practicing career counseling is an important first step. The National Vocational Guidance Association and other professional groups need to make a concerted effort to inform professionals and the lay public of the nature of the field and the necessary requirements for professional practices. This means not only actively promoting a new image for career counselors by stressing the increasingly specialized nature of the field but also taking steps toward educating professionals regarding minimum training standards and lobbying for certification or licensure.

In order to remedy the negative image associated with this field, career counseling might consider changing its title to a name that has fewer negative connotations. Such a change would help separate the profession from commercial and government agencies that are presumably staffed by "career counselors" but in reality utilize untrained personnel. Some alternative titles might include "licensed" or "certified career consultant" or a title that might reflect specialities in career counseling such as "information specialist" or "career psychometrist."

Admittedly, terms like consultant and specialist have been used inappropriately, but a change of title would be one way the profession could enhance its image. As it stands now, the term "counselor" refers to such a wide variety of occupational groups with varying educational levels that it is meaningless. There are real estate counselors, loan counselors, counselors at law, camp counselors, church counselors, family planning counselors, to mention only a few. The titles "career counselor" and "counselor" are used so glibly that the public is left with the impression that anyone can be a counselor.

Together with the change of titles, the profession needs to make a concerted effort to obtain certification and possible licensure — although certification would probably suffice. With certification, professionals can help consumers discriminate between professional and lay services as well as limit the usage of "counselor" titles to qualified professionals. Furthermore, certification would help consumer groups monitor career counseling practices and help potential clients make informed decisions when seeking help.

Certification would also help establish a standard curriculum for career counselors. To be certified, counselors would need to demonstrate that they have received training in specified areas. This in turn would pressure counselor education programs to develop specialty areas in career counseling.

PROBLEMS CREATED BY CONFLICT OF INTEREST

Anytime counselor interests are in conflict with client interests, ethical problems can occur. In career counseling, there are several areas where a conflict of interest is likely to arise: conflicts created by third parties such as employers, family, and government agencies, conflicts created by counselor beliefs, attitudes, and values, and conflicts created by the concept of confidential communication.

Third Party Conflicts

Unlike private clinicians, career counselors usually work for a third party. The third party may be a school, a university, a government agency, a corporation, or in the case of a minor, a family. Because counselors are employed by one party to serve the needs of another, they must face the possibility that third party interests may conflict with client needs.

Third party conflicts are most likely to occur when the counselor's employer has a vested interest in the outcome of the counseling process. Examples would include placement agencies whose existence depends on the number of clients obtaining jobs, government agencies whose function is to direct human resources into particular sectors of the economy (e.g. government need for engineers or the armed services effort to "counsel" students into particular career paths), corporation personnel departments that have a vested interest in the career decisions of their employees, and families trying to push sons or daughters into a particular occupation or profession.

Under these circumstances, career counselors face a serious ethical question: "Who is my client? The U.S. Government, the corporation, the university, the referring family, or the individual seeking help?" The answer to this question is critical to the outcome of counseling. Without the counselor knowing whose interests are to be represented, it is difficult to decide on the goal of treatment or an appropriate treatment plan. If, for example, the counselor represents a third party that is committed to recruiting scientists, the counselor is likely to direct clients to information that makes such a career seem attractive, while at the same time downplaying related professions. Affirmative Action Programs may create similar dilemmas. A career counselor faced with the task of recruiting minorities may in the interest of his or her employer or in the interest of long-term source objectives encourage individuals to make career decisions that are not in the best interest of the client.

Many counselors will represent the interest of whoever pays the bills — even at the expense of the client. Granted that some counselors are objective enough to overcome third party pressure; however, the incentive is to represent the paying party, which in turn creates a conflict of interest with the client.

Unfortunately, third party pressures are often subtle. So much so that many counselors are unaware that they tailor their activities to please their employers rather than to help their client. Who can say how many unsuspecting individuals have been directed into careers that were other than their choosing by "objective, well-meaning" career counselors.

Value Conflict

Another form of conflict of interest exists when counselor values conflict with client interests. Just as counselors may place agency, corporation, or government interest above the interests of their clientele, counselors may knowingly or unknowingly influence their clients to subscribe to a particular set of beliefs or attitudes. For example, counselors with a strong religious or political orientation may steer clients away from occupations that they deem offensive or personally unsuitable (e.g. a pacifist counselor may have difficulty with a client seeking employment with the Atomic Energy Commission). In these instances, client interests may be undermined by counselor values.

Conflicts may also occur when counselors unknowingly project their values onto their clients. Examples include counselors who have never realized their own professional goals (e.g. the counselor who was not accepted into medical school) and now want clients to compensate for their failures or, alternatively, counselors who had an especially disagreeable encounter with a particular profession may steer a client toward an alternative occupation (e.g. the counselor who despises insurance salesmen).

As in the case of the third party interests interfering with counseling, most career counselors would deny that they indirectly or directly influence their clientele, but research suggests the contrary. A variety of studies have shown that even the most nondirective counselors influence their clients and that counselors need to be aware of their influence and take steps to protect their clientele (Rosenthal, 1955).

Confidentiality

Confidentiality also is likely to create conflict of interest problems. Career counselors are, as are other mental health professionals, ethically bound to keep client information confidential except in instances of "clear and present danger" and when clients waive their rights and/or the information is subpoenaed by a court of law (Everstine, Everstine, Heymann, True, Frey, Johnson, & Seiden, 1980).

Because much of the information shared in career counseling is not as sensitive as the type of information shared in therapy, career counselors may not take the necessary precautions to protect client rights. Counselors may not secure files, they may store data in a manner that it can be accessed by unauthorized parties, or without consent they may discuss information acquired in confidence with the client's employers, family, etc.

Moreover, career counselors may be more likely to succumb to third party requests for confidential information. Because some of the information clients share with career counselors may seem inconsequential, an unprofessional or naive counselor can easily rationalize a breach of confidentiality. Sharing a Kuder score with a parent does not seem as egregious a violation of ethics as the telling of a wife of her husband's infidelity. This, however, is not the case. Confidentiality is the client's right and not the counselor's. It is the client who decides what the counselor can say and to whom — except in the instances already mentioned. A confidential communication must be kept in confidence, regardless of whether the counselor thinks the information is important.

Possible Corrective Measures

Whether the problem involves a conflict between the client's interests and an agency, the self-interest of the counselor and a government policy, or involves a question of confidentiality, an ethical dilemma exists, and it is the counselor's responsibility to recognize and resolve it.

There are at least two approaches counselors can take to prevent potential conflict of interest problems. Both start from the premise that the values, beliefs, and vested interests of counselors and the parties they represent influence the career counseling process. One stresses professional awareness of the problem as a primary means of prevention, and the other stresses the use of built-in safeguards to prevent conflicts before they occur. To protect client rights, both approaches are required. Counselor awareness of how their allegiances and interests affect clients is an essential first step, but it needs to be augmented with changes in current counseling practices.

COUNSELOR AWARENESS. Since many research studies reveal that counselors, knowingly or unknowingly, transmit their values to their clients, the profession has been concerned with the problem of protecting clients from inappropriate counselor influence (Krasner, 1962; Bandura, 1969). For the most part, professional attention has focused on ways of increasing counselor awareness — the assumption being that if counselors are aware that their value systems, third party allegiances, etc. might lead to a conflict of interests, they in turn can act to prevent it. Consequently, the profession has urged counselors to become more aware of their value systems, evaluate them, and subject them to empirical validation (Bergin, 1980; Walls, 1980; Ellis, 1980).

For the competent, well intentioned professional, greater awareness may help prevent undesirable counselor influence. However, increased counselor awareness will not prevent unethical, misguided, or unintentional abuses from occurring. Additional safeguards are needed.

ALTERNATIVE SAFEGUARDS. A more practical solution would be for the profession to develop client safeguards that would be less dependent on the goodwill and professionalism of the counselor. Ideally, the profession needs a three-fold approach. The profession needs to develop and mandate procedures that would (1) make consumers aware of their rights and show them how to exercise these rights in the selection of services, (2) help counselors make the client's right to know an integral part of the treatment process, and (3) insure that agencies, institutions, and counselors provide clients and counselors with whatever is necessary to protect client rights.

Such an approach would make protection of consumer rights a responsibility of the profession, the agency and counselor, and the client. Each party would be given a specific set of responsibilities. The professional associations, NVGA, APGA, and APA, would have the responsibility of insuring that counselors are knowledgeable of client rights and that accrediting agencies and licensed or certified career counselors exercise the necessary safeguards. Career counselors and agencies, on the other hand, in order to maintain their professional credentials, would have to enact the procedures established by their professional association. Clients, once informed of their rights, could unilaterally exercise their freedom to choose by patronizing agencies that subscribe to prescribed standards and they can retain the services of consumer groups, government, or legal counsel to insure that their rights were protected.

To implement this approach, career counselors, agencies, and professional groups such as NVGA could make consent forms an integral part of the career counseling process. Consent forms include procedural services agreements outlining terms of treatment (e.g. fees, number and length of sessions, etc.), client rights; statements informing clients of what they have a right to expect from treatment as well as what they can do to exercise these rights (e.g. the right to full disclosure of procedures and the right to terminate if the counselor refuses), the informed consent form outlining the procedures to be utilized and the potential benefits and risks, and the treatment contract that details not only goals and treatment plan but also the obligations of both parties in executing the plan (e.g. attend all sessions and do assigned homework). For a further discussion of these forms and examples see Chapter 6.

These forms can be utilized to ensure that clients know who the counselor represents, the limits of confidentiality, counselor beliefs or attitudes that may conflict with the client's objectives, and other information that might create a client-counselor conflict of interest. By providing such information to the client, counselors, agencies, and professional groups can promote consumer trust and confidence, reduce the chances of client/counselor conflict, promote honest communication, and help ensure ethical conduct on the part of the professionals.

PROBLEMS CREATED BY FAILURE TO INFORM

The courts, professional associations, and some insurance companies have stated that clients have a right to know what will take place in counseling. Failure to provide clients with pertinent information is not only unethical but also can jeopardize outcome. Clients have a right to know about the procedures to be used, their effectiveness and risks, and the qualifications of the provider or the professional to whom they are being referred. They also need to know that they have the right to question, object to, or withdraw from counseling or request a referral to another professional.

If information regarding treatment is not provided in advance, clients may develop unrealistic treatment expectations (i.e. counseling will result in employment), misinterpret the results of tests and interest inventories (because I scored X, I should be an engineer), trust themselves to incompetent or inadequately trained counselors, subject themselves to procedures they find offensive because the counselor "prescribed it," or engage in a new behavior such as being assertive with their boss without knowing the potential consequences.

The professional's duty to inform clients also extends to referrals to lay contacts or self-help programs. When referring clients to community resource people who have offered to share their expertise, alumni in related career fields, network support goups for minorities, "extern programs," and other programs staffed by lay personnel, clients have a right to know the qualifications of the provider, the obligations involved, if any, the potential benefits and risks, and their right to question or terminate help at any time.

These are but a few of the problems that can result from failure to inform clients of the nature and terms of treatment. For a further discussion, see Hare-Mustin, Marecek, Kaplan, & Liss-Levinson (1979).

Potential Corrective Measures

For career counselors to avoid these problems, they need to be aware that they exist and take definite preventive steps to ensure that clients have adequate information in advance of treatment to make a knowledgeable decision to participate.

As in the case of ethical problems created by client/counselor interest conflicts, the most expedient way to reduce the incidence of problems created by counselor failure to inform is for the NVGA, APGA, APA, and other associations to require the use of informed consent forms by their members and by career counseling agencies. The use of such forms will not prevent abuse by incompetent or malintentioned practitioners, but it will help limit abuses and protect the concerned professional. Examples of these forms can be found in Chapter 6.

PROBLEMS CREATED BY FAILURE TO OBTAIN CLIENT CONSENT

From a legal standpoint, informing clients is only the first step.

Before counselors can be sure that the clients' rights are protected, they need to obtain client consent. By obtaining verbal and, preferably, written consent from the client, the counselor receives formal approval to initiate treatment. By consenting, the client in effect says, "You have explained the procedures to my satisfaction and they are acceptable." It is not enough that clients understand what will occur in counseling, they must also agree to it (Everstein et al., 1980).

Failure to obtain client consent may result in charges such as the counselor misled the client by creating false expectations, failed to warn the client of possible negtive effects, or overcharged the client for services rendered. Although verbal or written permission to initiate counseling is an important part of client consent, it is also essential that the client is mentally competent, of legal age, fully informed in a manner that a lay person can understand, and is voluntarily entering into the agreement. If any of these conditions are not present, the counselor must question whether consent has been obtained (Everstein et al., 1980; Gambrill, 1977).

CONFIDENTIALITY OF CLIENT RECORDS MAINTAINED BY COMPUTER

Data, in the form of case notes and assessment results, are an integral part of the career counseling process. Recent advancements in computer technology have made it cost effective to store data electronically. Over the next ten to twenty years a gradual shift from paper storage to electronic record storage in career counseling will occur. The driving force behind this trend is the emergence of the microcomputer. The ease of use, low cost, and minimal maintenance requirements of the microcomputer has made available a high degree of computing power to small institutions and agencies.

Violations of confidentiality that have occurred with paper records also can occur with electronically stored records. Super (1973) states that computerized records have a greater potential for abuse than the traditional methods. The reason for this lies in the nature of the computer itself. In comparison with traditional paper records stored in filing cabinets, computer records can (1) include larger quantities of data cost-effectively stored for longer periods of time, (2) be accessed from a variety of locations via remote terminals, and

(3) be rapidly copied and easily transported on small floppy disks or over telephone lines to another computer. The end result is that far more confidential data than is necessary for the provision of services may be stored for an almost unlimited time. Without adequate safeguards, this data may be easily obtained by unauthorized individuals. Such a situation would clearly be unethical.

Potential Corrective Measures

While there is no universal solution to the above ethical dilemma, the following suggestions can help to minimize the problem: (1) limit confidential data stored in a computer to include only information that is directly relevant to providing services, (2) purge confidential data as soon as it is determined that the information is no longer of any value in providing services to the client, (3) if institutional policies permit, allow clients the option of not having confidential records maintained as part of receiving services, (4) require passwords on all computer accounts and files that include confidential data, knowledge of passwords needs to be strictly limited to appropriate individuals (appropriate individuals are identified in existing ethical standards), and passwords also need to be changed frequently to maximize security, (5) microcomputers need to be placed in work areas that can be secured to reduce unauthorized access, (6) floppy disks containing confidential data need to be placed in locked storage areas when not in use, (7) avoid storing any individually identifiable confidential data on a computer that can be publically accessed via remote terminals or computer networks, (8) when feasible, utilize specialized security techniques, e.g. making data hard to locate by scrambling the file directory, and (9) include on the client's consent for treatment form a description of the nature of confidential data that will be stored, the time period for maintaining the data, who will be allowed access to the data, and the situations that necessitate breaking of confidentiality.

COMPUTER APPLICATIONS AND COUNSELOR INTERVENTION

The use of computer applications in the career counseling and guidance process has necessitated a reformulation of the role of the counselor. Chapter 8 provides a description of the role of the counselor and the computer in providing services. A specific approach to counselor intervention is also described. The need for contact with a counselor becomes an ethical issue when clients make inappropriate use of a computer system as a partial result of inadequate counselor intervention.

The following situations illustrate potential ethical dilemmas when clients are not screened prior to using a computer system; individuals experiencing substantial emotional distress may receive invalid results because they are incapable of using the system in an appropriate manner. A similar situation can exist with clients who have learning disabilities or who lack reading and comprehension skills. When an introduction to the use of a computer system is not provided, computer anxiety and/or misconceptions about system operation may also invalidate a client's results. When a follow-up of client's use of a computer system is not provided, potential misconceptions and inappropriate use are not identified. The subsequent needs of the client may also not be discovered.

Potential Corrective Measures

First, screen all potential users of a computer system so that individuals experiencing substantial emotional stress or other difficulties can be identified and referred to a more appropriate resource. Second, provide an introduction to using a computer system that attempts to reduce computer anxiety and facilitate an understanding of the purpose and operation of the system. Third, provide a followup of system use that attempts to correct misconceptions that may exist as well as identify the subsequent needs of the client. Fourth, evaluate the extent to which clients understood the purpose and operation of the computer system by having individuals answer questions relating to their part of the resource. It may be possible to administer these questions as part of the computer system.

USE OF TESTS IN CAREER COUNSELING

An important part of the career counseling process involves helping clients explore their values, interests, abilities, and limitations. Test results can provide a valuable source of data needed in career decision making. The use of test also can lead to confusion and inappropriate decisions. Clients can misunderstand the constructs that the test is designed to measure, e.g. altruism, spatial relations, etc. Many clients can expect tests to provide the "answer" to solve their career choice dilemmas as opposed to expecting tests to provide information relevant to decision making. The inappropriate expectations of some clients are reflected in statements such as, "The test told me I should be an accountant."

Potential Corrective Measures

The negative effects mentioned above can be reduced if not eliminated when clients understand the role of testing in the decision-making process and the limitations inherent in most assessment instruments. (1) Clients need to understand the constructs being measured as well as how the construct relates to career choices, e.g. what are values and how do they relate to satisfaction with an occupation. (2) Clients need to understand that the responsibility for decision making rests with the client and not with "the test." Tests are designed to provide information and stimulate thinking and exploration, not provide answers. (3) Clients need to understand that tests are far from perfect measures of human behavior. The interpretation of any test needs to take into account the demonstrated reliability and validity of the instrument. Also, the interpretation of a test is influenced by the training and experience of the counselor providing the service. (4) Clients need to be informed of much of the above information through a consent for treatment form that spells out the limitations of the instrument being administered. (5) It also may be helpful to assess after the test interpretation is complete the extent to which the clients understand the role and limitations of assessment. This could take place via a structured interview or a written instrument administered by a counselor or a computer. (6) It is important to build on feedback mechanisms in the administration and interpretation of the test or to include appropriate safeguards. Examples of safeguards would include (a) checkpoints in which a counselor interviews a client or administers a paper-and-pencil instrument to assess the client's understanding of the testing process and (b) computer feedback mechanisms that would prevent clients from proceeding with the machine administration until they can demonstrate sufficient understanding. The latter would require software developers to become cognizant of the ethical problems created by machine administration and scoring and design software packages that reduce these risks.

SUMMARY AND CONCLUSIONS

This chapter has reviewed some of the ethical problems career counselors are likely to encounter, and it has suggested steps for minimizing potential dilemmas. Throughout the chapter, the point has been made that careful adherence to the concept of informed consent is an essential first step in preventing potential problems. It also has been suggested that a multidimensional approach to ethical problems is needed: (1) greater awareness on the part of career counselors to potential problems as well as the need for counselor intervention with computer systems, (2) greater emphasis by professional organizations on ethical considerations and greater effort on their part to get career counselors to use client rights forms and informed consent forms, etc., (3) the necessity of heightening consumer awareness regarding what constitutes ethical practice so they can help monitor the profession, and (4) the profession needs more sophisticated software packages and computer security mechanisms to reduce the chance of misinterpretation of data from machine administered tests and exercises and to protect client confidentiality.

BIBLIOGRAPHY

American Personnel and Guidance Association. *Ethical standards*. Washington, DC: American Personnel and Guidance Association, 1981.
American Psychological Association. Ethical principles of psychologists. *American Psychologist,* 1981, *36,* 633-638.
Bandura, A. *Principles of behavior modification*. New York: Holt, Rinehart and Winston, 1969.
Bergin, A.E. Psychotherapy and religious values. *Journal of Consulting and Clinical Psychology,* 1980, *48,* 95-105.
Ellis, A. Psychotherapy and atheistic values: A response to A.E. Bergin's psychotherapy and religious values. *Journal of Consulting and Clinical Psychology,* 1980, *48,* 635-639.
Everstine, L., Everstine, D.S., Heymann, G.M., True, R.H., Frey, D.H., Johnson, H.G., and Seiden, R.H. Privacy and confidentiality in psychotherapy.

American Psychologist, 1980, *35*, 828-840.

Gambrill, E.D. *Behavior modification: Handbook of assessment, intervention, and evaluation*. San Francisco: Jossey-Bass, 1977.

Hare-Mustin, R.T., Marecek, J., Kaplan, A.G., and Liss-Levinson, N. Rights of clients, responsibilities of therapists. *American Psychologist*, 1962, *34*, 3-16.

Kerr, P. Career counseling industry is accused of misrepresentation. *New York Times*, September 30, 1982, p. 21-22.

Krasner, L. Behavior control and social responsibility. *American Psychologist*, 1962, *17*, 199-204.

National Vocational Guidance Association. Guidelines for a quality career guidance program. *The Vocational Guidance Quarterly*, 1979, *28*, 99-100.

National Vocational Guidance Association. Vocational/career counseling competencies. *NVGA Newsletter*, 1982, *22*, 1-3.

Rosenthal, D. Changes in some moral values following therapy. *Journal of Consulting and Clinical Psychology*, 1955, *19*, 431-436.

Super, D.E. Computers in support of vocational development and counseling. In Borow, H. (Ed.), *Career guidance for a new age*. Boston: Houghton-Mifflin, Company, 1973.

Walls, G.B. Values and psychotherapy: A comment on "psychotherapy and religious values." *Journal of Consulting and Clinical Psychology*, 1980, *48*, 640-641.

NAME INDEX

A

Adams, G.A., 217, 227
Adams, J., 235, 243
Aiken, L.R., 72, 82
Alexander, J., 169
Alexander, L.D., 85
Alexik, M., 38
Alpin, J.C., 294, 298
Altschuld, J.W., 196
Amatea, E.S., 243
Amico, A.M., 153
Anastasi, A., 78
Anderson, J., 260
Anderson, S., 38
Antholz, M.B., 215
Appell, M., 255
Arcia, M., 35, 81
Arewa, O., 276
Arredondo-Dowd, P.M., 269
Aryes, M.E., 269
Ashcraft, L., 242
Aslanian, C.B., 139, 186
Astin, A.W., 291
Astin, H.S., 291, 234, 241
Atkinson, D.R., 240
Axelrod, V., 172, 196
Azrin, N.H., 108, 132, 134, 262

B

Babcock, R.J., 227
Babee, J.R., 108
Bandura, A., 328
Banks, J.A., 271, 279, 280
Banning, J.H., 165

Barak, A., 316
Bargo, M., 139
Barker, S.B., 213, 219, 223, 224, 228, 260
Barkhaus, R.S., 149
Barnett, R.C., 235
Bartol, K.M., 274
Barton, P.E., 191
Bartsch, K., 139, 227, 228
Bazin, J.R., 204
Beck, J., 269
Beckhard, R., 293
Benson, P.G., 297
Berentsen, M., 289
Bergin, A.E., 328
Berman, E., 328
Berne, R., 295, 296, 304
Besalel, V.A., 132, 134
Biggers, J., 61
Biklen, D., 253
Birk, J.M., 238
Birney, D., 134
Bloomquist, M.L., 152
Bogdam, R., 253
Bolles, R.N., 70, 90, 94, 97, 283
Bolyard, C., 296
Bonnell, Jr., R.O., 150
Borchard, D.C., 124
Borgen, F., 91
Borow, H., 214, 224
Boudin, H.M., 112
Bowlsbey, J.H., 150
Brammer, L., 53
Brandenberg, J.B., 241
Brewer, J., 6
Brewster, E., 90
Brim, O., 35

Broderick, C.A., 260
Brolin, D.E., 255, 257, 258, 259
Brooks, C.C., 272
Brooks, G., 204
Brunner, C.G., 112
Bryson, D.L., 150
Bucher, J.P., 277
Buck, J., 124
Buck, J.N., 283
Buehler, C., 31
Bunch, C., 228
Burack, E.H., 294, 295
Burck, H., 9, 13, 311, 313, 316
Byers, A.P., 148
Byrnes, E., 154

C

Cairo, P.C., 153
Campbell, D.F., 92
Campbell, N.J., 289
Campbell, R., 310
Cano, L., 238
Carkhuff, R., 138
Carlson, A., 260
Carney, C.G., 140, 220, 229, 316
Carter, D.E., 316
Carver, D.S., 217, 229
Carver, J.T., 258
Cascio, W.F., 85
Cassie, J.R.B., 147, 151, 155
Castro, R., 288
Chapman, E.N., 140
Chapman, W., 54, 60, 150
Ching, W., 269
Christensen, H.K., 301
Christensen, K.C., 103
Cloudman, D., 169
Clyde, J.S., 151, 154
Coates, T., 41
Cochran, D., 127, 136, 150
Cohen, S.L., 296, 298
Coleman, D.D., 203
Comas, R.E., 227
Cooper, J.F., 92, 99
Cordisco, J.H., 301
Cornfeld, J.L., 213, 226
Cotex, A., 289
Crabbs, M.A., 309
Crabbs, S.K., 309

Cramer, S.H., 80, 309
Crandall, R., 149
Cravey, B., 289
Crites, J.O., 12, 33, 35, 72, 228, 237, 269, 275, 287
Cronbach, L.J., 75
Cross, E.G., 243
Cross-Silverman, M., 153
Cummings, R., 150
Cunha, J., 215
Cutts, C., 81, 135

D

Daane, C., 128
Dalton, G., 300
Daniels, M.H., 124, 283
Danish, S., 54, 55, 63, 64
Darou, W.G., 269
Davidshofer, C., 136
Davis, J., 6
Davis, S.A., 253
Day, R.W., 227
Dean, S., 202
DeJong, G., 254
DeLoach, C., 253, 254
Devlin, T.C., 214
Dewey, C., 99
Diamond, E.E., 92
Dickson, J., 153
Dillard, J.M., 289
Dinklage, L., 95, 138
Dolliver, R.H., 91, 99, 100, 103
Domkowski, D., 185, 186
Draguns, J., 217
Drier, H., 172, 196, 310
Driscoll, P.F., 277
Drummond, R.J., 277
Dudley, E., 36
Dunphy, P.W., 57
Dyal, M.A., 215

E

Edwards, K., 30
Egner, J.R., 213
Ellis, A., 121, 328
Endicott, J., 316
Engelkes, J.R., 180
English, F., 311

Name Index

Epstein, C.F., 301
Erhart, J.F., 231
Erikson, E., 80, 213
Evans, J.R., 228
Everstein, D.S., 109, 327, 328
Ewart, C., 141

F

Fabel, M., 249
Fair, G.W., 255
Farley, J.E., 269, 271
Farren, C., 294
Faught, B., 203
Faux, V.A., 70, 101, 140
Ference, T.P., 301
Ferguson, M., 17
Ferrin, R.I., 191, 196
Figler, H.E., 95, 97, 98, 103, 140
Fitzgerald, L.F., 237
Flanagan, J.C., 316
Flores, T., 108, 134, 262
Fort, M.K., 301
Fredrickson, R., 184
Fretz, B.R., 274, 287
Frey, D.H., 327, 331
Friedman, L.M., 108

G

Gagne, R.M., 313
Galloway, J.L., 149
Gambill, T.R., 296
Gambrill, E.D., 111
Ganster, D.C., 213, 227
Garber, A.P., 274
Garcia, R.L., 267, 268, 270, 291
Gaymer, R., 101
Gelatt, H.B., 220
Gelso, C., 10, 103
Gershaw, N.J., 255
Gerster, D.K., 294, 298
Ghiselli, E., 91
Gillingham, W.H., 227
Gilmore, R.G., 214
Gimmestad, M.J., 212
Gingrich, D.D., 239
Ginsburg, L.R., 298
Ginzberg, E., 8, 31
Girrell, K.W., 139

Godin, S.W., 152
Goldman, L., 55, 63, 80, 90, 91, 92, 104, 185
Goldman, R.D., 236
Goldstein, A.P., 255
Gonsalves, J., 269
Goodkin, H.F., 253, 254
Goodson, W.D., 215, 216
Gordon, E.W., 257
Gordon, L.V., 82
Gordon, M., 271
Gorsuch, R.L., 281
Gottfredson, G.D., 29, 31, 187
Goulding, M.M., 109
Goulding, R.L., 109
Grabowski, B.T., 144, 146, 147
Grandy, T., 45
Green, C., 180
Greenhaus, J., 35
Greer, B.G., 253, 254
Gribbons, W., 35
Gummere, R., Jr., 97
Gunnings, T., 269
Gutteridge, T.G., 294, 295, 296, 297, 304
Gysbers, N., 310

H

Hackett, G., 227, 228
Hagberg, R., 228
Haimowitz, M.L., 108
Haimowitz, N.R., 108
Halasz-Salster, I., 208
Haldane, B., 94, 97
Haley, J., 121
Hall, D.T., 239, 295, 296, 300, 301, 304
Hall, F.S., 239, 294, 297, 300
Hall, O.T., 84
Haller, E.J., 317
Haney, T., 215, 219
Haney, W., 83
Hansen, J.C., 92
Hansen, L.S., 213, 215, 216, 218, 224, 229, 236
Hansen, R.N., 184
Hanson, M.C., 294, 216, 303, 305
Hare-Mustin, R.T., 112, 330
Harper, F.D., 269
Harren, V.A., 12, 37, 124, 224, 228, 279
Harrington, T.F., 98

Harris, J., 142, 145, 146, 150
Harris, M., 17
Harris-Bowlsbey, J., 223
Harrison, K.H., 213, 226
Hatch, R.N., 180
Hauselman, A., 30
Hayes, S., 269
Heald, J.E., 169
Healy, C.C., 138, 191, 208
Heath, K., 289
Helbing, J.C., 132
Heller, F., 138
Helms, S., 30
Henderson, G., 290
Henderson, R., 309
Henning, M., 243, 249
Hepper, M.J., 186, 205
Heppner, P.P., 213, 219
Herr, E.L., 69, 80
Hershenson, D.B., 150
Hess, H.R., 217, 227
Hesser, A., 303
Hesson, J.D., 277
Hewitt, B.N., 236
Heymann, G.M., 327, 331
Hicks, L.C., 260
Higginson, M.V., 249
Hilton, T.E., 38
Hinkle, J.E., 134
Hoffer, G.L., 153
Hoffman, S.D., 150
Holcomb, J.R., 213, 220
Holland, J.L., 12, 22, 26, 27, 28, 29, 30, 31, 77, 79, 90, 95, 98, 104, 180, 199
Hollingshead, A.B., 26, 285
Hollis, J., 58, 140
Hollis, L., 58, 140
Homme, L.E., 109
Hoppock, R., 176, 180, 183
Hosford, R.E., 165, 171
Howland, P.A., 215, 219
Hoyt, K., 191, 196, 198, 199, 200, 203, 310
Huddleston, M.R., 150
Hudson, J., 54, 55, 63, 64
Hughes, H., 30
Humes, C.W., 255
Hunt, R., 35
Hurst, J.C., 165

I

Inhelder, B., 313
Isaacson, L., 56, 65

J

Jackson, D.J., 213
Jackson, E., 185, 186
Jackson, R.L., 290
Jacobson, M.D., 142, 145, 146, 147
Jacobson, T.J., 169, 179, 186
Jakubowski, P., 108
James, E.M., 153
Janis, I., 125
Jardim, A., 243, 249
Jelinek, M., 301
Jenkins, A.H., 291
Johnson, H.G., 327, 331
Johnson, J., 132, 139
Johnson, J.H., 148, 152
Johnson, K.N., 148, 152
Johnson, N., 132
Johnson, R., 132, 135
Johnston, J.A., 184
Jones, G., 40
Jones, L.K., 99, 100
Jones, P.R., 296, 303
Jordaan, J.P., 213
Jordan, J.B., 255
Justin, B., 316

K

Kabrosky, K.R., 304
Kahnweiler, J.B., 239, 243
Kahnweiler, W.N., 234, 239, 241
Kane, G., 150
Kapes, J.T., 147
Kaplan, A.G., 108, 330
Kaplan, S.J., 134, 262
Kapurch, L., 305
Karelius-Schumacher, K.L., 241
Katz, M., 54, 60, 145, 150, 151, 154
Kaufman, H.G., 277, 289
Kaufman, M.A., 227
Kaufman, R., 311, 312
Kaye, B.L., 294, 296, 298, 300, 303
Keil, E.C., 108
Keller, K.E., 196

Kelly, G.S., 94
Kelly, J.J., 124
Kerr, B.A., 186
Kerr, P., 321
Kimmel, K., 172, 196
Kirk, A., 180, 183
Kirn, A., 102
Kirn, M., 102
Kirts, D.K., 211
Kisiel, M., 140
Klaurens, M.K., 215
Knapper, E.Q., 309
Knefelkamp, L., 127, 213, 227
Knezevich, S.J., 317
Knickerbocker, B., 136
Knosh, M.N., 241
Knowdell, R.L., 303
Koehn, S., 215
Kohlberg, L., 313
Koschier, M., 229
Kotter, J.P., 70, 101, 140
Krasner, L., 328
Krause, J.B., 213, 219
Kreinberg, N., 235, 236, 241
Kriger, S., 310
Krivatsy, S.E., 94
Kroll, A., 32, 95
Kruger, R., 159
Krumboltz, J., 12, 39, 64, 65

L

Lancaster, A.S., 295, 296, 304, 305
Lange, A.J., 108
Laramore, D., 215
Larson, C.H., 259, 260
Lee, D.J., 269
Lee, J., 38, 95
Leibowitz, Z.B., 294, 296, 305
Leiterman-Stock, P., 239
LeMay, M.L., 172
Lennon, T.C., 269
Leong, F.T., 274
Levinson, D., 213
Levinson, H., 301
Levitan, S.A., 253
Levy, R.L., 112
Lewis, J., 165
Lichtenberg, J.W., 140
Lindeman, R.H., 150

Lisansky, R.S., 223
Liss-Levinson, N., 330
Lister, C., 151
Lohnes, P., 35
London, M., 294, 305
Lonner, W., 271
Lonnquist, D.E., 253
Looft, W.R., 235
Loring, R.K., 249
Lounsbury, J.E., 227
Lovell, J.E., 213, 227
Lowentha, M., 35
Luschene, R.E., 281

M

Mackin, E.F., 196
Mackin, R.K., 213, 216, 218, 224, 229
Madison, S., 35, 81
Magoon, T.M., 94
Mangum, G.L., 196
Mann, L.K., 125
Maola, J.F., 150
Marecek, J., 330
Marinelli, R.P., 73
Martier, A., 294, 295, 296, 297, 300, 304
Martinez, L.M., 269
Mastie, M.M., 147
Mathys, N.J., 294, 295
Mayberry, M.E., 148, 149
Maze, M., 150
Mazzano, J., 213
McArthur, E.C., 70, 101, 140
McBee, G., 316
McClure, B.T., 235
McCoy, L.S., 13
McCoy, V.R., 140
McDaniels, C., 53, 60, 151, 153, 157, 303
McDavis, R.J., 269
McEver, C., 186
McGreevy, J.G., 260
McGregor, W.J., 199
McIlroy, J., 135
McNamara, J.R., 108
Mechel, N.T., 297
Meehl, P.E., 104
Melhus, G.E., 150, 151, 153
Menche, R., 136
Messing, J.K., 73
Meyer, H.H., 296, 298

Michelozzi, B.N., 140
Michels, E., 180
Miller, D.B., 296, 297, 298
Miller, G.P., 221
Miller, J., 277, 288, 310
Miller, J.M., 197, 202
Miller, J.V., 285
Miller, M., 54, 61, 63
Miller, P.M., 197, 202
Minor, C., 184
Mitchell, A., 40, 215
Mitchell, J.S., 249
Mithers, J., 244
Molinaro, D., 263
Montgomery, A.G., 109
Montgomery, D.J., 111
Moore, E., 310
Moore, K.M., 238
Moore, R., 144
Morgan, J.I., 102
Morgan, M.A., 294, 295, 296, 297, 300, 304
Morin, J.I., 102
Morin, W.J., 301
Morley, E., 38, 95
Morrill, W.H., 165
Morten, G., 290
Motta, W., 109
Murphy, P., 13
Myers, R.A., 150

N

Nafziger, D., 29
Nagy, D.R., 149
Nathan, P.E., 8
Nelson, L., 53
Nelson, R.E., 91
Neugarter, B., 35
Newman, F.L., 316
Nickles, E., 242
Nieves, L., 290
Noeth, R., 8, 215
Nordberg, O.S., 242
Norris, L., 150
Norris, W., 180
Novick, B., 183
Nugent, T.J., 254

O

Oetting, E.R., 165

Office of Education, 141
Ogawa, D., 29, 180
O'Hara, R., 36
Oliver, R., 301
Olson, S.K., 186, 244
O'Neil, J.M., 238
Osipow, S.H., 81, 229, 274, 316
Otto, H., 249
Overs, R.P., 62, 182

P

Palomars, V.H., 165
Parker, C.A., 165, 228
Parker, W.M., 269
Parish, P.A., 150, 151
Parrillo, V.N., 271
Parsons, F., 89, 101
Patrick, T.A., 150
Pattersson, C.H., 65, 93
Pedersen, P., 268, 271
Peevy, E.S., 153
Perry, W., 38
Peterson, G.W., 311, 313, 316
Peterson, M., 23, 208
Philips, S.D., 153
Phillip, R.A., 134
Piaget, J., 313
Pick, D.J., 147
Piel, E., 235
Pietrofesa, J.J., 236, 310
Pow, G., 112
Powell, C., 211
Powell, D.H., 277
Powers, R.J., 132
Prahl, E., 241
Prediger, D., 8, 69, 78, 79, 94, 215
Price, G.E., 150
Price, R.L., 300
Prince, J.S., 140
Prosen, S.S., 269
Putsell, T.E., 9
Pyle, K.R., 150

Q

Quick, T.L., 249

R

Ragsdale, R.G., 147, 150
Rayman, J.R., 153

Name Index

Reardon, R.C., 150, 169, 172, 184, 185, 186, 214, 215, 219, 226, 228, 260
Rector, A.P., 228
Regan, K., 219, 226, 228
Rice, D., 242
Richardson, J.M., 239
Ripley, T.M., 227, 229
Roach, D., 169
Robinson, M., 147, 150
Rogers, C.R., 93
Rose, J.D., 271
Rosenberg, H., 150
Rosenberg, M., 103
Rosenthal, D., 326
Roth, J.D., 8, 215
Rotter, J.B., 228
Royce, A.P., 270, 283
Rusalem, H., 56, 61
Ryan, C., 140, 150, 153
Ryan, T.A., 171
Ryan, T.E., 165
Ryan, T.G., 150

S

Samler, J., 56
Sampson, J.P., Jr., 149, 151, 156
Sanders, C., 208
Sandmeyer, L., 139
Savin, G., 150
Scheel, A.M., 243
Scherini, R., 183
Scherrei, R.A., 235, 238
Schien, E., 298, 300
Schlossberg, N.K., 169, 296, 305
Schmelter, H.B., 139, 186
Schneier, D.B., 87
Schneider, L.J., 10
Scholz, N.T., 140
Schrank, F.A., 218
Schroeder, W., 65
Schwartz, F.N., 250
Sechler, J., 172
Sedlacek, W.E., 103
Seiden, R.H., 327, 331
Seligman, L., 75, 241
Seling, M.J., 91
Seybolt, J.W., 295
Shannon, M.D., 150
Shatkin, L., 144, 145, 151

Shertzer, B., 124
Shoepke, J., 253
Shoon, S., 242
Shore, B., 309
Shostrum, E., 53
Siegel, C.L.F., 235
Silberman, C.E., 101
Silbey, V., 85
Simpkins, G.A., 269
Sinick, D., 53, 65
Skovholt, T.M., 102
Slepitza, R., 127, 213, 227
Smith, E., 149, 153, 180, 181, 184
Smith, E.J., 269, 274
Smith, J.D., 159
Smith, P.C., 286
Smith, P.M., 165
Smith, T., 215
Snipes, J.K., 151, 153
Snodgrass, G., 138
Solomon, C., 165
Sonnenfeld, J., 301
Space, L.B., 148
Spielberger, C.D., 281
Spivack, J.D., 223
Splete, H., 310
Sprafkin, R.P., 255
Srebalus, D.J., 73
Stahmann, R., 45
Stake, J.E., 237
Stein, W.M., 196
Stewart, N., 64, 236
Stone, W.O., 269, 272
Stoner, J.A.F., 301
Storey, W.D., 294, 295, 297, 303, 305
Stout, R.L., 148
Stover, R.G., 274
Strand, K.H., 150
Streutfert, D., 140, 179, 281, 282, 290
Sullivan, A.R., 255
Super, D.E., 12, 32, 33, 34, 35, 72, 82, 142, 216, 331
Swails, R.G., 217, 227
Sweet, D.H., 301
Szasz, T.X., 111

T

Taggart, R., 253
Taylor, H.R., 296, 303

Tennyson, W.W., 215
Themes-Hintos, P., 134
Thomas, A.H., 236
Thomas, A.M., 239
Thomas, L., 134
Thompson, A.S., 150
Thompson, P.H., 300
Thoresen, C., 41, 64, 65
Thornton, G.C., 297
Tiedeman, D., 12, 36, 145
Tittle, C.K., 92
Tofler, A., 17, 21
Tolbert, E.L., 182, 197, 198, 211
Touchton, J.G., 213, 226, 227, 229
Tracey, T.J., 103
Treichel, J., 208
Trimble, J., 269
True, R.M., 331
Tyler, L.E., 93, 96, 99

V

Vale, C.D., 148
van Aalst, F.D., 202
Varenhorst, B., 64, 220
Veres, H.C., 238
Vermillion, M.E., 150
Vetter, L., 235
Vontress, C.E., 269

W

Walker, J.W., 294, 295, 296, 297, 304
Walls, G.B., 328
Walsch, B.W., 274
Walz, G., 221, 295, 310
Webber, R.A., 301
Weinrach, S.G., 108
Weintraub, F.J., 253
Weisen, J.P., 290
Weissberg, M., 289

Weitz, H., 311
Welker, J.C., 203
Wells, C.F., 140
Wernick, W., 288
Wertheimer, L.C., 213, 226
Weselowski, M.D., 134
Westbrook, B.W., 35, 81
Westover, R., 132
White, P., 260
Whitney, D.R., 91
Wikler, N., 249
Wilkinson, L., 150
Wilkinson, M.W., 255
Williams, D.A., 84
Williams, R.D., 103
Wilson, E., 38, 95
Wilson, N., 5
Winefordner, D., 100, 140
Winer, J., 229
Wooley, D., 215
Wright, G.N., 252
Wright, R.B., Jr., 153

Y

Yalon, J., 125
Yamashita, D., 112
Yanico, B., 229
Yankelovich, D., 17
Yates, C., 132
Yorks, L., 301
Young, D., 242
Yu, C.Y., 269

Z

Zeigler, J., 35
Zeran, F.R., 180
Zunker, V.G., 69, 70, 76, 78, 140, 174, 179, 215, 234, 237, 238
Zytowski, D.G., 92

SUBJECT INDEX

A

Accountability and contracts, 110
Accountability in career development, 309
Accountability Model, 312
Achievement Tests, 8
  aptitude tests versus, 75
  California Achievement Tests, 76
  Stanford Achievement Test, 76
  uses of, 75
  Wide Range Achievement Test, 76
Acronyms of computer assisted programs, 145
ACT Interest Inventory, 78
  Map of College Majors, 78
  World of Work Map for Job Families, 78
African Americans, 269, 272
Alabama, University of, 272
Alumni networks, 204
American College Testing Program, 223
American Personnel and Guidance Association, 322
American Psychological Association, 322
Anglo-Americans, 272
Appalachia Educational Laboratory, 219, 223
Aptitudes
  assessment of, 71
  types of, 71
Armed Services Vocational Aptitude Test Battery (ASVATB), 75
Asian-Americans, 272
Assessment, 70
  assessment centers, 84, 85
  assessment of career decision making, 37
  assessment of career maturity, 80
  assessment of values, 82
  Career Maturity Inventory, 80
  criticism of, 70
  diagnostic, 70
  major types of, 71
  results, 70
  trait and factor approach in, 69
Attitudes, 9
Awareness of ethical conflict, 324

B

Behavioral Anchored Rating Scales (BARS), 86
Brigham Young University, 216

C

Career choice theories
  chart, 43
  comparison, 42
Career counseling
  use of tests, 92
  written self-interview, 10
Career days, 198
Career Decision-Making System
  career decision making, 94
  career decision-making process, 36
Career development
  academic experience, 214
  activities, 8, 9
  adults, 300
  benefits and risks, 300
  cognitive constructs, 94
  complexity, 11
  counselor activities, 310

definition of, 310
development theory, 37
disinterest in, 9
emphasis of, 8
evaluation, 303
history, 6, 7
in organizations, 302
ingredients in, 11, 12
life-stages, 6
model programs, 302
outcome criteria, 310, 311
prestige, lack of, 9, 10
problems, 296
program trends, 23
programs goals for disabled, 256
responsibilities, 296, 299
role of assessment, 95
stages of, 13, 32
tasks, 32
theory and practice, 3, 4, 12
trends, 306
Career development: A plan for all seasons, 301
The Career Development Bulletin, 304
Career Development for the Handicapped Project, 260
Career Development Inventory, 33
Career Development Program Model, 294
Career development specialist in organizations, 30
Career information
 aquiring, 58
 classification, 59
 client needs, 61
 evaluation, 181
 filing, 179
 layout, 179
 ordering, 179
 principles for use, 65
 purposes in use, 54, 55, 56, 57
 sources, 176
 suggesting for improving, 62
 types, 174
Career library indexing systems, 149
Career management, 298
Career Maturity Inventory, 33
Career Pattern Study, 33
Career Planning and Adult Development Newsletter, 301
Career planning courses

common program goals, 218
decisions and outcomes, 220
evaluation of, 228, 229
goals of, 218
summaries of, 224, 228
Career Planning and Decision Making for College, 219, 233
Career Planning Program, ACT, 222
Career Planning System Audit, 294
Career resource center
 considerations in development, 171
 equipment, 173
 establishment, 174
 evaluation, 184
 goals, 170
 location, 172
 materials, 173
 operation, 183
 personnel, 173
 staffing, 183, 115
Career selection, social learning theory of, 39
Career tasks, 13
Career — Thinking About Your Future, 218
Central Michigan University, 227
Client needs, 212
Client's rights, 114
College Board, 9
Community resources
 benefits of use, 192
 community benefits, 194
 consideration of, 195-196
 planning for problems in developing, 205
 school benefits, 193
 student benefits, 192
Competency development, 311
Competency evaluation
 assumptions, 311, 312
Complete Job-Search Handbook, The, 97
Comprehensive Employment Training Program Act (CETA), 275
Computer-assisted career guidance (CACG)
 advantages, 141
 career library indexing systems, 149
 cost effectiveness, 154
 counselor intenvention strategies, 151
 differences between systems, 145
 ethical considerations, 156

Subject Index

factors to consider in selection, 155
future trends, 157
human factor design, 152
implementation, 154
indirect access systems, 146
information systems, 142
placement systems, 148
rationale, 142
referrals to other resources, 153
research and evaluation data, 150
site management, 156
testing systems, 147
theoretical basis of systems, 152
use with various populations, 152
Contracts, procedural agreements, 115
Contractual arrangements, 108
  advantages, 110
  criteria for evaluation, 112
  defined, 108
  examples, 113
  need for, 109
  negotiation, 118
  procedures, 119
  reasons for, 109
  types of, 113
Costs of career development programs, 316, 317
Counseling-clinical dilemma, 8
Culture, 270
Curricular-Career Information Service, 225
Curriculum, Minnesota model, 218

D

Deciding, 220
Decision making, 57
Decisions and outcomes, 220, 221
Demassification, 21
Developmental approaches, 213
  need for, 213
Developmental self-concept theory, 31
Developmental stages, 13
Dictionary of Occupational Titles, 60, 62, 73, 176
  classification scheme of, 29
Differential Aptitude Tests (DAT), 73
  Career Planning Programs (CPP), 73
  career planning questionnaire, 73
Disabled
  barriers to employment, 253
  defined, 252
  intervention strategies, 257
  special needs, 252

E

Economic growth, 19
Employer panels, 198
Equal Employment Opportunity Commission (EEOC), 84
Ethical issues in career counseling, 321
  computer applications-confidentiality, 331
  conflict of interest — confidentiality, 326
  conflict of interest — third parties, 324
  conflict of interest — values, 326
  counselor intervention, 332
  failure to inform, 329
  failure to obtain client consent, 330
  potential corrective measures, 323, 327, 330, 332, 333, 334
  testing, 333
Ethical standards — APA & APGA, 322
Ethnic group, 268, 271
Ethnicity, 270
Ethnic Literacy Quotient, 273
Ethnic Minority group, 269, 271
Ethnocentrism, 269, 280
Ethnoentropy, 280
Ethnosyncretism, 280
Evaluation, in organizations, 303
Evaluation of career development programs, 309
  conceptualized, 12
Evaluation of computer-assisted career guidance systems
  cost effectiveness, 154
  counselor intervention strategies, 151, 156
  human factors design, 152
  implementation, 156
  referral to other resources, 153
  research and evaluation data, 150
  theoretical basis of systems, 152
  use with various populations, 152
Evaluation of job performance, 85
Everett Community College, 217
Experiential learning, 202
Exploring career decision making, 221

F

Family Rights and Privacy Act, 83
Females, 19
Flanagan Aptitude Classification Tests (FACT), 74
Florida State University, 219
Future trends, 18
Futuristic programs, 22

G

General Aptitude Test Battery (GATB), 72
  occupational ability patterns, 73
General Electric, 303
Goal setting, 109
Government, 20
Group career counseling
  assessment for assignment, 127
  curative factors, 125
  evaluation issues, 127
  opportunities, 125
  positive factors, 125
  process content continuum, 127
  types, 125
Guide for Career Development Inquiry, 294
Guided fantasy, 102

H

Handicapped
  defined, 252
Hispanic Americans, 269, 272
Holland's Hexagonal Model, 27
Human behavior, 14
  complexity, 12
Human values, 20

I

Immigration, 19
Individual differences, 215
Individualized rightss, 20
Informed consent, 115
  agreement, 116
Institutional needs, 217
Instructional packages, 220
Interest inventories, 76
  American College Testing Program Interest Inventory, 78
  Kuder Occupational Interest Survey (KOIS), 76, 77
  Strong-Campbell Interest Inventory, 76, 77
  Vocational Preference Inventory, 79

J

Job club, 132
  critique, 134
Job Finding Club, 262
Job seeking skills, 262

L

Labor force
  composition, 18
  women in, 19
Law School Aptitude Tests, 83
Lawrence Livermore National Laboratory, 303
Life/Career Development System, 221
Life-career rainbow model, 33
Life centered career education, 259
Lifelong Career Development Model, 258
Life Planning Workshop, 134
  critique, 136
  procedures, 135
Life stages, 13
Locus of control, 282

M

Maryland, University of, 226
Medical College Admissions Test, 83
  criticism of, 83
Michigan Model of Placement, The, 262
Microcomputers, 141
Microelectronics, 18
Minneapolis Public Schools, 218, 224
Multicultural career development issue, 273, 274
Multicultural competency strategies, 273
Multicultural intervention resources, 287, 288, 289, 290, 291
Multiethnic phases of development, 271, 280

N

National Council for Accreditation of Teacher Education, 272
National Vocational Guidance Association, 323, 328, 330
Native Americans, 269, 272
Negotiating a therapeutic contract, 117
NOICC/SOICC, 60, 61
North Carolina Occupational Information Coordinating Committee, 151
Northern Colorado, University of, 225

O

Occupational card sort, 99, 100
Occupational environments, 26
Occupational Outlook Handbook, 60, 62
Occupational types, 26
Occupations Finder, 29
Oregon, University of, 229
Organization development, 294

P

Paradigm of Multiethnic Phases of Development, 280
Peer influence, 16
Pennsylvania State University, 21
People today, 11-14
Performance Evaluation of Employees, 85
  Assessment Center, 84
  Behaviorally Anchored Rating Scale, 86
Personal Life and Career Planning Program, 223
Personality types, 27
Physical environs, 14
Placement, 201
Placement services for disabled persons, 262
Placement systems, 148
Post employment services for disabled persons, 263
Primary Mental Abilities Test, 75
Psychological environments, 14
Purdue University, 227

Q

Quick Job-Hunting Map, The, 97

R

Race, 271
Renewal stage, 13
Responsibilities for ethical conduct, 322
Rotary club, 198

S

Scholastic Aptitude Test (SAT), 83
Self-assessment
  advantages, 93
  cautions in use, 103
  cost effectiveness, 94
  history, 89
  self-motivation, 104
Self-awareness, 12
Self-concept, 12
  theory, 31
Self Directed Search, 28, 98
Self-rating scales, 103
Self-understanding, 12
Social Learning Theory, 39
Society, complexity of, 14
South Carolina Department of Education, 222
Southern Illinois University, 27
Special populations, 300
Stages of unemployment, 278
Standards for preparation — NVGA, 321
Success factor analysis, 97
Systems approach for career development, 293

T

Task approach skills, 40
Technological advances, 18
Telecommunications, 18
Test interpretation, problems, 92
Tests, 70
  reliablility of, 70
  validity of, 70
Therapeutic contract, 117
Transcultural, 271
Transethnicity, 280

Truth-in-Test Law, 83

U

Unemployment and career development, 276
 stages, 278
Unemployment needs and strategies, 279
University of Missouri-Columbia, 204

V

Virginia Polytechnic Institute and State University, 303
Vocational Decision-Making Checklist, 37
Vocational exploration group, 128
 critique, 132
 procedures, 129
 rationale, 128
Vocational identity scaless, 81
 Career Decision Scale, 81
 My Vocational Situation Test, 82
Vocational Interest Inventories, sex bias, 92
Vocational maturity, 32
Vocational Preference Inventory, 28

W

Washington State University, 228
Western College Placement Association, 199
Women
 counseling programs, 237
 emerging career patterns, 234
 high school, 235
 professional & business, 242
 programs, 236
 returning, 240
 science, 235
 traditional age, 238
Work Experience Program, 263
Work in America, 17
Work Values Inventory, 34
World views, 282, 283

Y

Young girls, 235
 counseling strategies, 237
 programs for, 236